Acclaim for
Telling the Next Generation

"Lutheranism has a rich educational heritage. Not only have Lutheran churches always been accompanied by Lutheran schools, those schools have featured a distinctive approach to education, one that stressed both the Word of God and the liberal arts, catechesis and academics, preparing young people for eternal life and for their God-given vocations in the church, the family, the workplace, and the culture as a whole. *Telling the Next Generation* recovers and preserves that heritage as it has been carried out in the Evangelical Lutheran Synod, doing so in a way that can inspire contemporary Lutheran schools as they carry out that same mission in our own times."

Dr. Gene Edward Veith, Jr., Provost
Patrick Henry College, Purceville, Virginia

"This anthology is notable both for its ambitious scope and for the discernment with which the editors have made each selection. The papers on church and state are indispensable reading for anyone seeking to understand the confessional Lutheran view concerning the relationship between the two kingdoms."

Mr. John David Ohlendorf, Attorney at Law
B.A., Bethany Lutheran College, 2007
J.D., Harvard University School of Law, 2010
St. Louis, Missouri

"This volume provides a powerful witness to the value of Christian education for children and for college students, and how past generations placed a high premium on that education. The section of the book on government aid to private education also presents readers with a challenge for the future. As the number of children in our schools declines and as financial support for education dwindles, will the next generation be as committed to Christian education as were past generations?"

Dr. Mark Braun, Professor of Theology
Wisconsin Lutheran College, Milwaukee, Wisconsin

"Knowledge of the past is the key to the future. As the members of the Evangelical Lutheran Synod plan their educational programs (seminary, college, elementary school) for the twenty-first century, they will benefit from reading *Telling the Next Generation*. This excellent work charts the course that served the Synod well in the past and which is the course that will also serve it well in the future—build all educational programs on Jesus Christ, the church's one foundation; and guide all programs by God's inspired and errorless Word."

Rev. Lyle W. Lange, Professor of Theology
Martin Luther College, New Ulm, Minnesota

"For nearly a century, the Evangelical Lutheran Synod has championed the conservative biblical philosophy on all levels of Christian education—from Lutheran grade schools to its high school, college, and seminary. This anthology methodically lays down the biblical principles of Christian education as taught by Scriptures and will serve future generations as a guiding beacon focused on the "one thing needful."

Mr. Victor L. Fenske, retired Christian high school teacher
Phoenix, Arizona

"What do twentieth-century Lutheran voices have to say to twenty-first-century ears about the sacred obligation to preserve God's timeless and indispensable truths over time? This masterfully compiled collection offers a harmonious chorus of such voices singing about ideas and issues relevant to the Lutheran task of telling the next generation about the permanent things of confessional purity. Thoughtfully organized, comprehensive in scope, compellingly written, this anthology offers a useful guide and much-needed encouragement for Lutherans seeking to understand their perennial duty regarding Christian education of the next generation."

Dr. Mark A. Kalthoff, Henry Salvatori Chair in History and Traditional Values, Professor of History
Hillsdale College, Hillsdale, Michigan

"I knew this book would be filled with history—interesting facts, anecdotal notes, highlights of key events and synodical milestones. I did not expect this book to also be uplifting and inspiring, but that too was in these pages. The writers represented in this anthology convey their impassioned desire to advance, support, and elevate Christian education. Their words leave little doubt that we are being called to join them in that effort. I was encouraged to find that words written decades ago have lost neither their relevance nor their appeal."

Mr. Allen M. Labitzky, Principal
King of Grace Lutheran School, Golden Valley, Minnesota

"As co-editor Ryan MacPherson states in his introduction, 'Historical study rightfully involves self-reflection. While inquiring about people from the past, we ask questions that penetrate into our own lives, here and now.' Such questions include the level of our own commitment to passing on the heritage we have been given to the next generation of Christians within the Evangelical Lutheran Synod as well as our understanding of that heritage and the importance of Christian education in home, school and church in retaining it. In dealing with these questions, this valuable anthology provides more than enough insight, guidance and encouragement to equip us to be faithful and successful in our task."

Mr. Allen Quist, member of the ELS Doctrine Committee and Professor of Political Science (retired), Bethany Lutheran College
St. Peter, Minnesota

"This remarkable anthology brings together in one volume the collective thoughts on Christian education of the Evangelical Lutheran Synod since its inception. By documenting the writings and events as well as the individuals who have contributed to this rich educational history Dr. MacPherson and his contributors have performed a wonderful service that will serve to inform the educational philosophy within the educational institutions of the Evangelical Lutheran Synod and its membership well into the future."

Mr. Ronald J. Younge, Vice President for Academic Affairs (Retired)
Bethany Lutheran College, Mankato, Minnesota

"*Telling the Next Generation* substantiates how richly the Word of Christ has dwelt within the Evangelical Lutheran Synod through Christian education—and the documentation lends credence to Luther's commendation that 'historians are the most useful of men, and the best of teachers. Nor can we ever accord too much praise, honor, or gratitude to them.' Everyone who wants to consider the value and not just count the cost of Christian education should read this book."

Rev. Joel A. Brondos, Headmaster
St. Paul's Lutheran School, Brookfield, Illinois

Telling the Next Generation:

The Evangelical Lutheran Synod's Vision for Christian Education, 1918–2011 and Beyond

Edited by

Ryan C. MacPherson

Paul G. Madson

Peter M. Anthony

*with the assistance of
Bethany Lutheran College
student interns*

Published by the Lutheran Synod Book Company for:

**Evangelical Lutheran Synod
Historical Society
www.els-history.org**

Mankato, Minnesota

Evangelical Lutheran Synod Historical Society
6 Browns Ct.
Mankato, MN 56001
www.els-history.org

Lutheran Synod Book Company
700 Luther Dr.
Mankato, MN 56001

Copyright © 2011 by the Evangelical Lutheran Synod Historical Society. All rights reserved.

Scripture passages are taken from:
 1. The Holy Bible, King James Version. 1611. Public Domain.
 2. The Holy Bible, New International Version®. Copyright © 1973, 1978, 1984 International Bible Society. Used by permission of Zondervan.
 3. The Holy Bible, GOD'S WORD®, © 1995 God's Word to the Nations. Used by permission of Baker Publishing Group.

ISBN-13: 978-0-931057-01-4

ISBN-10: 0-931057-01-9

Library of Congress Control Number: 2011906209

Library of Congress Subject Headings
Christian Education—Philosophy
Education—Philosophy
Lutheran Church—Education—History
Lutheran Church—Education—Philosophy
Lutheran Church—Education—United States
Lutheran Church—Evangelical Lutheran Synod
Lutheran Universities and Colleges

> Founded by members of the Evangelical Lutheran Synod in June 1996, the ELS Historical Society promotes interest in the historical and doctrinal heritage of Lutheranism, particularly of the Evangelical Lutheran Synod and its institutions; stimulates historical research; publishes historical studies; assists congregations in the preservation of local congregational history; preserves items of museum quality; and, provides assistance to the ELS Department of Archives and History.

Contents

A Note about the Sources 1

Contributors 3

Introduction

"We Will Tell the Next Generation,"
by Ryan C. MacPherson 5

Section 1: Education in the Christian Home

Introduction, by Ryan C. MacPherson 13

1.1 "The Relation of the Christian Home to the Christian School" (1927), by Carl Johan Quill 21

1.2 "The Right Use of the Catechism" (1929), by Joseph B. Unseth 30

1.3 "Lessons from History" (1921, 1958), by Gerhard Friedrich Bente 39

1.4 "Instruction in the Home" (1962), by Wilhelm Petersen 42

1.5 "The Task of Instruction" (1974), by Rodger Dale 45

1.6 "The Responsibility of Instruction" (1974), by Raymond M. Branstad 53

1.7 "The Priesthood of Parents" (1976), by Ardella Emery 60

1.8 "Education Philosophy: Who Should Teach Your Children?" (2008), by Ryan C. MacPherson 64

Section 2: Lutheran Day Schools

Introduction, by Norman A. Madson, Jr. 68

2.1 "The Norwegian Synod and the Christian Day School" (1928), by Norman A. Madson, Sr. 74

2.2 "The Christian Day School" (1930), by Christian A. Moldstad 86

2.3 "Concerning Christian Education" (1943), by Carl S. Meyer 95

2.4 "Christian Day Schools" (1951), by Theodore A. Aaberg 111

2.5 "Christian Day Schools" (1952), by Alfred Fremder 119

2.6 "On Starting and Maintaining a Christian Day School" (1966), by Theodore A. Aaberg 131

2.7 "The Effectiveness of Christian Schools in Mission Outreach" (1996), by Silas V. Born 139

2.8 "Lutheran Schools Flourishing in the Amazon Jungle," by Terry Schultz (2008) 153

2.9 Chart of Enrollment in ELS Christian Day Schools, 1928-2008 156

Section 3: Bethany Lutheran College and High School

Introduction, by Peter M. Anthony 157

3.1 "Bethany" (1928), by Ingebrigt J. Blåkkan 160

3.2 "Why Lutheran High Schools?" (1945), by Sigurd Christian Ylvisaker 164

3.3 "Do We Need Our Bethany Lutheran High School?" (1963), by Milton E. Tweit 174

3.4 "Letter to Pastors of the ELS" (1964), by the Board of Regents of Bethany Lutheran College 180

3.5. "No, Mrs. Troemel, It Is Not Good!" (1976), by John A. Moldstad, Sr. 185

3.6 "Address for the Bethany Lutheran College 50th Anniversary," by Paul Zimmerman 190

3.7 "Bethany Lutheran College and Mission Station" (1990), by Steven L. Reagles 199

3.8 "Philosophy and Objectives of the College" (2009) by the Board of Regents of Bethany Lutheran College 205

Section 4: Bethany Lutheran Theological Seminary

Introduction, by Paul G. Madson 208

4.1 "Proposal for a School Committee" (1919), by the Norwegian Synod in Convention 212

4.2 "Annual Address" (1919), by Bjug Harstad 214

4.3 "Seminary Opening Address" (1964), by Milton H. Otto .. 216

4.4 "Preparing Messengers of Peace" (1996),
by Juul B. Madson 221

4.5 "'Ask for the Old Paths': Sixtieth Anniversary Sermon on Jeremiah 6:16" (2006), by Gaylin R. Schmeling 252

Section 5: A Christian Liberal Arts Education

Introduction, by Erling T. Teigen 259

5.1 "Sermon Preached at the Fiftieth Anniversary of Bethany Lutheran College, and Thirtieth Anniversary of Bethany Lutheran Theological Seminary" (1977),
by Bjarne W. Teigen 264

5.2 "A Christian Liberal Arts Education" (1981),
by Norman S. Holte 274

5.3 "The Lutheran Liberal Arts College in the 21st Century" (2000), by Rolf Wegenke 292

5.4 "The Liberal Arts: Our Common Understanding" (2001), by the Bethany Lutheran College Faculty 313

5.5 "Luther, Lutherans, and Liberal Arts" (2005),
by Paul Lehninger 317

5.6 "Classical, Christian, Liberal Arts Education" (2006),
by Lutheran Schools of America 328

Section 6: Government Aid to Private Education

Introduction, by Paul Gunderson and Jeremy Costello 336

6.1 "At the Crossroads in Private Education" (1964),
by Bethany Lutheran College Staff Members 341

6.2 "Separation of Church and State with Special Reference to Governmental Aid to Education" (1967),
by Bjarne W. Teigen 349

6.3 "Aid to Private Education" (1967), by Milton H. Otto 359

6.4 "What Is Involved in the Private Education Struggle to Survive?" (1975), by Milton H. Otto 364

6.5 "Some Thoughts on Governmental Aid to Educational Institutions Which Are Church-Related" (1975), by Bjarne W. Teigen 372

Section 7: Academic Freedom and Christian Integrity

Introduction, by Andrew Shoop 386

7.1 "The Importance of a Spirit of Inquiry in Christian Higher Education" (1974), by Thomas A. Kuster 390

7.2 "Sermon for Dedication of the S. C. Ylvisaker Fine Arts Center" (1990), by George M. Orvick 415

7.3 "Bethany's Response to the Work 'The Prophesy' by Joel Hansen" (1995), by Marvin G. Meyer 424

7.4 "Religion and Censorship Make Art Show 'A Teachable Moment'" (1995), by Ryan C. MacPherson and Rachel (Olson) Hermanson 427

7.6 "How Would God Have Us Approach the Subject of Homosexuality?" (2007), by Donald Moldstad 433

7.5 "Position on Academic Freedom" (2007), by the Board of Regents of Bethany Lutheran College 438

Scripture Index 442

Lutheran Confessions Index 447

General Index 448

Order Form 460

A Note about the Sources

This anthology reproduces historic documents spanning nearly a century, authored by dozens of different persons, and representing several genres of writing. The editorial staff has sought to preserve the historic testimony of the authors with fidelity and precision. Even so, the editors have seen fit to make minor modifications to some of the documents. Any alterations made are intended to help readers re-connect with their historic roots, not—anachronistically—to bring the past "up to date" through present-centered editorializing.

First, obvious errors in spelling, punctuation, and grammar have been corrected without notice, and awkward or ambiguous phrases occasionally have been revised for clarity. In a few instances, factual errors have been corrected in editorial footnotes, which are preceded by *"Editors' note:"* to distinguish them from footnotes appearing in the original documents. Editorial footnotes also indicate any substantive alterations, such as when a document is reproduced in excerpts rather than in its entirety.

Second, all citations have been standardized. References to Holy Scripture and the Lutheran Confessions appear in parentheses within the main body of the text. Books of the Bible appear without abbreviation, whereas the confessional writings are abbreviated as follows:

- AC Augsburg Confession (1530)
- Ap Apology of the Augsburg Confession (1531)
- SC Small Catechism of Dr. Martin Luther (1529)
- LC Large Catechism of Dr. Martin Luther (1529)
- SA Smalcald Articles (1538)
- Ep The Epitome of the Formula of Concord (1577)
- SD The Solid Declaration of the Formula of Concord (1577)

Generally speaking, documents from the early to mid twentieth century quote from the Lutheran Confessions as printed in *Concordia Triglotta: The Symbolical Books of the Evangelical Lutheran Church*, trans. F. Bente (St. Louis: Concordia, 1921); whereas documents from the latter half of the century follow *The Book of Concord: The Confessions of the Evangelical Lutheran Church*, trans. Theodore G. Tappert (Philadelphia: Fortress Press, 1959). However, in some cases authors may have made their own translations from the underlying German or Latin texts.

Hymn verses are referenced by the following abbreviations:

ELH *Evangelical Lutheran Hymnary* (1996)
LHy *Lutheran Hymnary* (1913)
TLH *The Lutheran Hymnal* (1941)

Citations to other sources have been rendered according to the standard of today's historical profession, namely, Kate L. Turabian's *A Manual for Writers*. When the original document included a citation, it has simply been reformatted. When the original document alluded to, or even quoted from, a source without citing it, the editorial staff has attempted to locate that source and insert a proper citation, marking the footnote with "*Editors' note:*" in order to distinguish it from the text of the original document. The insertion of editorial footnotes and grouping of documents into sections have resulted in a renumbering of the footnotes that appeared in the original texts.

The photographs reproduced in this volume come chiefly from the Evangelical Lutheran Synod Archives, especially from the Walter A. Gullixson Collection. Bethany Lutheran College has provided a few faculty portraits and campus photographs of recent vintage. The portrait of Carl S. Meyer printed in the introduction to **Document 2.3** has been provided courtesy of Concordia Historical Institute, St. Louis, Missouri. This book's cover photograph (courtesy of the Walter A. Gullixson Collection) depicts Dalton Wolfrath student-teaching at Mt. Olive Lutheran Elementary School, Mankato, Minnesota, *ca.* 1960. Other illustrations, such as advertisements published in the *Lutheran Sentinel*, have been credited on the pages where they appear.

The editors and their publisher gratefully acknowledge the willingness of the authors, editors, publishers, photographers, and archivists who have granted permission for their respective works to be reprinted in this volume.

Contributors

The Board of Directors for the Evangelical Lutheran Synod Historical Society formally adopted this project at its February 25, 2006 meeting, appointing three members to serve as an editorial committee. The committee in turn collaborated with the Department of History at Bethany Lutheran College to enlist the services of several student interns who assisted in researching, writing, and illustrating this book. The students logged many hours in the Synod Archives, locating and scanning texts and images into electronic format. Students also wrote most of the biographical introductions appearing in this book, as well as two of the section introductions. Their participation demonstrates that the older generation in their midst has not merely said, "we will tell the next generation the praiseworthy deeds of the LORD" (Psalm 78:4), but also has taught the next generation how to do so. May God so bless these students that they, too, will pass down this tradition to "even the children yet to be born" (v. 6).

Editorial Committee

Ryan C. MacPherson, Ph.D., teaches American history at Bethany Lutheran College. For additional biographical information, please refer to **Document 1.8**.

Rev. Paul G. Madson serves as the Synod Archivist. A 1952 graduate of Bethany Lutheran Theological Seminary, he has pastored congregations in Iowa, Washington, Massachusetts, Minnesota, and South Dakota. Over the decades, he also has contributed frequently to the Lutheran Sentinel *as both a writer and an editor.*

Peter M. Anthony is a 1996 graduate of Bethany Lutheran College who has served as Sunday school instructor for Norseland Lutheran Church (Norseland, Minnesota). He has studied history at St. Olaf College and Renaissance English literature at Oxford University. Presently he is pursuing an M.S. in Agricultural Science at the University of Alaska in Fairbanks, where he lives with his wife Katy.

Student Interns

Abigail Bourman graduated from Bethany Lutheran College in 2010, having majored in history. With parents and siblings in the teaching ministry, Christian education is close to her heart. She now attends Marquette University, pursuing a Ph.D. in History.

Jeremy Costello *is a 2007 graduate of Bethany Lutheran College, where he majored in history. He attended Christian schools from kindergarten through college. Currently he lives in Des Moines, Iowa, while pursuing a J.D. at Drake University School of Law.*

Paul Gunderson *studied history and education at Bethany Lutheran College, completing a B.A. in Broad Field Social Studies in 2007. Presently, he is pursuing a J.D. at the University of North Dakota Law School in Grand Forks, where he lives with his wife Meredith.*

David Reagles *is currently pursuing a B.A. in History with a minor in Philosophy at Bethany Lutheran College. After his graduation (expected in 2011), he plans to pursue a Ph.D. in History, with an emphasis on intellectual movements in Western Civilization.*

Andrew Shoop *graduated from Bethany Lutheran College in 2009 with a B.A. in Broad Field Social Studies. He later studied Education at the University of Minnesota–Twin Cities and has taught ESL in China. He also has served as a youth group leader and Sunday school teacher.*

Contributing Writers

Norman A. Madson, Jr.*, is a retired ELS pastor. He and his wife Amanda live in North Mankato.*

Erling T. Teigen *teaches courses in Religious Studies and Philosophy at Bethany Lutheran College. He and his wife Linda live in Mankato.*

Additional Assistance Provided by:

Melvina Aaberg*, Research Assistant, Synod Archives*

Rev. George Orvick*, Curator Emeritus, Ottesen Museum*

Mary Jo Starkson*, Internship Coordinator, Bethany Lutheran College*

Cheryl Harstad*,* ***Eileen Heintz****, and* ***Betsy Hermanson****, Copy-editing*

Kyle Damiano*,* ***Philip Kaminsky****,* ***Stephen Sielaff****,* ***Annie Williams****, and* ***Josiah Willitz****, who completed service-learning projects for the ELS Historical Society as assigned for "History 460: Religion in American History" at Bethany Lutheran College, Spring 2010.*

(Authorship of biographical introductions is indicated by first and last initials enclosed in brackets at the end of the respective biographies appearing throughout this anthology.)

Introduction

"We Will Tell the Next Generation"

By Ryan C. MacPherson

We will tell the next generation the praiseworthy deeds of the LORD, His power, and the wonders He has done.

Psalm 78:4

The Evangelical Lutheran Synod (ELS) traces its heritage to a sermon delivered by the Rev. Johannes Wilhelm Christian Dietrichson on September 2, 1844 under two oak trees at Knut Aslaksen Juve's farm in Koshkonong, Wisconsin. Dietrichson was the first Norwegian pastor to come to the United States, and this was his second sermon in that new land. "Can God furnish a table in the wilderness?," he asked, quoting from Psalm 78:19.[1] The Psalmist was referring to the wayward children of Israel, who had forgotten how God had mercifully delivered their parents from

---

[1] J. Herbert Larson and Juul B. Madson, *Built on the Rock* (Mankato, MN: Evangelical Lutheran Synod Book Company, 1992), 4.

bondage in Egypt; they were now grumbling against Moses in the desert. Lest history repeat itself, the Psalmist exhorted parents to teach their children the things of God:

> I will utter hidden things, things from of old—
>   what we have heard and known,
>   what our fathers have told us.
> We will not hide them from their children;
>   we will tell the next generation
>   the praiseworthy deeds of the LORD,
>   His power, and the wonders He has done.
> He decreed statutes for Jacob
>   and established the law in Israel,
>   which He commanded our forefathers
>   to teach their children,
> so the next generation would know them,
>   even the children yet to be born,
>   and they in turn would tell their children.
> Then they would put their trust in God
>   and would not forget His deeds
>   but would keep His commands. (Psalm 78:2-7)

Pastors and also laypeople within the Evangelical Lutheran Synod have left a legacy for future generations, underscoring the importance of "telling the next generation" about the salvation that Christ has won, even "the children yet to be born." In addition to quoting from Psalm 78, they also frequently have referred to Deuteronomy 6:6-7, Proverbs 22:6, and Ephesians 6:4 (quoted at the end of this introduction).

This anthology transmits their legacy to yet another generation, with the hope that such historical recollection serves more than to satisfy mere antiquarian curiosity. The struggle of God's people to maintain their religious heritage has a long history. When entering the Promised Land, the Israelites erected monuments that were to be a testimony to future generations of God's good and gracious deeds. Joshua, for example, set up twelve stones at Gilgal and instructed the elders:

> In the future when your descendants ask their fathers, "What do these stones mean?" tell them, "Israel crossed the Jordan on dry ground." For the LORD your God dried up the Jordan before you until you had crossed over. The LORD your God did to the Jordan just what He had done to the Red Sea when He dried it up before us until we had crossed over. He did this so that all the peoples of the earth might know that the hand

of the LORD is powerful and so that you might always fear the LORD your God. (Joshua 4:21-24)

Initially, the plan worked. "The people served the LORD throughout the lifetime of Joshua and of the elders who outlived him and who had seen all the great things the LORD had done for Israel" (Judges 2:7). The elders were aided in teaching the next generation by several additional monuments erected throughout the Promised Land (Joshua 7:26, 8:29,32, 10:27, 22:26-27, 24:26-27). But then the lessons ceased:

> After that whole generation had been gathered to their fathers, another generation grew up, who knew neither the LORD nor what He had done for Israel. Then the Israelites did evil in the eyes of the LORD and served the Baals. They forsook the LORD, the God of their fathers, who had brought them out of Egypt. They followed and worshiped various gods of the peoples around them. They provoked the LORD to anger. (Judges 4:10-12)

What had changed? Parents had taught their children, but somewhere down the generations their children or grandchildren failed to "tell the next generation the praiseworthy deeds of the LORD" (Psalm 78:4). The same pattern may be observed not only in Canaan, but also in ancient Egypt, where one Pharaoh looked kindly upon Joseph and put him in charge of his kingdom (Genesis 41:42), but later "a new king, who did not know about Joseph, came to power in Egypt" and began to deal harshly with Joseph's descendents, enslaving them (Exodus 1:8). Much of human history has hinged upon the delicate task of one generation faithfully recounting the past to its children—or else failing to do so.

Never was this truth more clearly revealed than in the period of the Divided Kingdom, when both civic and religious leaders turned a deaf ear to God's prophets. Parents—rather than training their children in the knowledge of the Lord—tragically sacrificed them in the fire to the Canaanite god Molech (e.g., 2 Chronicles 33:6,10). In the seventh century B.C., young King Josiah, whose brothers and uncles had lost their lives in that pagan fire, learned that "Hilkiah the priest had found the Book of the Law of the Lord that had been given through Moses" (2 Chronicles 34:14). For a time, the Passover celebration was restored. The people again hearkened to God's Word. But this reformation was short-lived. Within decades, the leaders of Judah again "mocked God's messengers, despised His words, and scoffed at His prophets, until the wrath of the Lord was aroused against His people" (2 Chronicles 36:16).

Nevertheless, God remained faithful. He fulfilled His promise to the House of David. Though it appeared that the Lord had abandoned His people into Babylonian captivity, a voice of hope remained among the great prophets Jeremiah, Ezekiel, and Daniel. God brought His people back to the Promised Land, and His servant Ezra "devoted himself to the study and observance of the Law of the LORD, and to teaching its decrees and laws in Israel" (Ezra 7:10). Humbly, Ezra confessed to God, "You have punished us less than our sins have deserved, and have given us a remnant" that again could prosper in the Promised Land (Ezra 9:13). Under Ezra's leadership, the temple was rebuilt. It was a restoration of the temple first dedicated by King Solomon nearly five centuries earlier with this earnest prayer:

> Hear the supplication of Your servant and of Your people Israel when they pray toward this place. Hear from heaven, Your dwelling place, and when You hear, forgive. . . . When they sin against You—for there is no one who does not sin— and You become angry with them . . . if they turn back to You with all their heart and soul . . . then from heaven, Your dwelling place, hear their prayer and their plea, and uphold their cause. And forgive Your people, who have sinned against You; forgive all the offenses they have committed against You, and cause their conquerors to show them mercy. (1 Kings 8:30,46,48,49-50)

The second, post-exilic temple paled in comparison with the first temple from Solomon's day (Ezra 3:12). The ultimate temple, however, would be Jesus Christ himself, whose body was destroyed and then rebuilt in three days (John 2:18-22).

St. Matthew's Gospel emphasized the myriad ways that Jesus' conception, birth, life, death, and resurrection fulfilled Old Testament prophecies concerning the Messiah who would "save his people from their sins" (1:21). St. Luke's epic study of the early church, recorded in the Acts of the Apostles, demonstrated how Christ's apostles grounded their professions of faith in the history of God's Old Testament people and the biography of the resurrected Savior, Jesus Christ. They strove to keep the grand narrative of divine salvation always fresh in the minds of their listeners, lest God's lovingkindness would be forgotten and a new generation would grow up without hope (Acts 2:14-39, 7:2-53,

8:32-35, 13:16-41).

In the centuries that followed, each generation would face anew the challenges of preserving and transmitting this historic "faith which was once for all delivered to the saints" (Jude 3). By the sixteenth century, the message was nearly lost again, but Martin Luther and his fellow reformers sorted through layers of man-made dogma to discern, once more, the pure gospel of forgiveness by grace alone through faith alone in Christ alone, as revealed in Scripture alone. The Lutheran Confessions emphasized the reformation's continuity with the New Testament and the early church. Once more, God's message had been restored for God's people.

And yet, the church would ever remain but one generation from losing the purity of its confession. In 1917, swayed by the surge of nationalism that occasioned the First World War, Norwegian Americans from various church bodies merged into the Norwegian Lutheran Church in America. A small minority of pastors refused to join, concluding that the merger church had privileged ethnic unity over doctrinal integrity. The majority group included pastors of varying opinions on vital questions of salvation, willing to tolerate each other's peculiar doctrinal formulations. The minority resolved immediately to establish a new periodical, *Luthersk Tidende*, for rallying "pastors and members of congregations who desire to continue in the old doctrine and practice."[2]

The following year, eighteen "minority" pastors met at Lime Creek, Iowa, to form the Norwegian Synod of the American Evangelical Lutheran Church. Thus was born in June 1918 a church body today known as the Evangelical Lutheran Synod, rocked in the cradle of a periodical that now appears in the English language under the banner *Lutheran Sentinel*. During the 1920s and 1930s, articles emphasized the doctrinal heritage of this new synod and its theological continuity with both the sixteenth-century Lutheran Reformation and nineteenth-century American Lutheran orthodoxy. Together with those themes, an emphasis on Christian education also regularly appeared in the *Sentinel*—a principal source of the documents reproduced in this volume.

Other sources include synod convention essays, articles from *Lutheran Synod Quarterly* (a theological journal established for

---

[2] Theodore A. Aaberg, *A City Set on a Hill: A History of the Evangelical Lutheran Synod (Norwegian Synod), 1918-1968* (Mankato, MN: Evangelical Lutheran Synod Board of Publications, 1968), 76-77.

ELS pastors), and documents discovered in the Synod Archives. Together, these documents encapsulate the significance of Christian education in the minds and hearts of the people of the Evangelical Lutheran Synod. Like their theological forebears, they said, "We will tell the generation." But would the next generation care to hear of it?

In the broader landscape of contemporary theology, today's conservatives and liberals argue over whether to maintain traditional orthodoxy or become more culturally relevant, often with both sides in the debate missing the point: that to be orthodox means to profess those timeless truths which *always* remain relevant, because it is through sound doctrine that God Himself ministers to the human person. The writers in this anthology therefore returned repeatedly to those "ancient paths" (Jeremiah 6:16), but they did so precisely because they dwelt in the present—a time, like *all* times, when God's timeless truths are not merely relevant, but, in fact, indispensable.

No pretension to novelty will be found in these pages; if anything here has unique value, it is only because the Word of the LORD has become rare in our days (cf. 1 Samuel 3:1; Amos 8:11). Like God's prophets from of old, the pastors of the Evangelical Lutheran Synod have endeavored to keep God's Word before the people whom they serve. Their legacy may be demonstrated in the fact that not only they, but also some of the laypeople whom they have instructed, are contributors to this volume.

Much more, of course, could be said. The editors found it necessary to be selective in deciding which texts to include and which to leave for re-discovery at another time. Perhaps a future volume will explore the old synod's education philosophy from 1844—when that first sermon was preached under the oaks—to 1918—when the "Little Norwegian Synod" organized itself in resistance to the liberal trends of the merger movement. Meanwhile, the editors have focused on the period from 1918 to present, with the guiding principle of republishing those statements of our Lutheran fathers that spoke not only to their own time and circumstances, but also to ours and to the future yet to come.

The editors also wanted the material to be of immediate use to a broad audience, including mothers and fathers as well as pastors and professors. For that reason, some of the more "academic" treatments of Christian education have been omitted in order to make space for essays and sermons that speak the language of the laity. That is not to say that this volume has by any means been "dumbed down" to reach a mass audience. Rather, this collection samples a rich variety of literary genres, including poetry, press releases, policy statements, sermons, and devotional articles, and it provides analytical footnotes for those interested in learning even more.[3]

Editorial introductions supply readers with a context for exploring these texts. **Sections 1–4** guide readers through the philosophies of Christian education that have shaped the synod's homes, elementary schools, Bethany Lutheran High School and College, and Bethany Lutheran Theological Seminary. **Sections 5–7** focus more particularly on key issues in higher education: defining a distinctively Christian liberal arts tradition; contemplating the proper relation between church and state with respect to funding and accreditation; and resolving controversies that arise when academic freedom is misconstrued as an opponent to, rather than a servant of, Christian scholarship and teaching.

In future years, new controversies no doubt will arise, but the consensus of the documents reproduced here testifies that the old foundations will still hold firm. The church's formula for success in addressing the world's challenges remains as it always has been: "Go and make disciples of all nations, baptizing them in the name of the Father, and of the Son, and of the Holy Spirit, and teaching them to obey everything I have commanded you" (Matthew 28:19-20). May God guide those who tell the next generation the praiseworthy deeds of the LORD!

> Our lips shall tell them to our sons / And they again to theirs
> That generations yet unborn / May teach them to their heirs.
> (*ELH* 180:3)

---

[3] The following essays may be of particular interest for those desiring to research the ELS's approach to Christian education in relation to modern and postmodern philosophical movements: B. W. Teigen, "The Philosophic and Religious Foundations of Modern Education," *Lutheran Synod Quarterly* 6, no. 2 (Dec. 1965): 1-34; and, Edward L. Bryant, "For You and Your Children," *Synod Report* (2006), 40-80. Applying principles of natural law to public education, a member of the Synod's Doctrine Committee has prepared a penetrating analysis of curriculum reforms and textbook revisions, some of which also impact private schools and homeschool families: Allen Quist, *America's Schools: The Battleground for Freedom* (Chaska, MN: EdWatch, 2005). A detailed review of this book may be found in the Synod's quarterly, indicating a certain resonance with the themes found throughout this present volume: Ryan C. MacPherson, "Training Children As They Should Go?: Evaluating Government Education Standards That May Impact Lutheran Elementary Schools," review essay of *Fed Ed: The New Federal Curriculum* and *America's Schools: The Battleground for Freedom*, by Allen Quist, *Lutheran Synod Quarterly* 47, no. 1 (March 2007): 106–27.

These commandments that I give you today are to be upon your hearts. Impress them on your children. Talk about them when you sit at home and when you walk along the road, when you lie down and when you get up.

            Deuteronomy 6:6-7

Train a child in the way he should go, and when he is old he will not turn from it.

                Proverbs 22:6

Fathers, do not exasperate your children; instead, bring them up in the training and instruction of the Lord.

                Ephesians 6:4

SECTION 1:

Education in the Christian Home

Introduction

By Ryan C. MacPherson

Therefore let every head of a household remember that it is his duty, by God's injunction and command, to teach or have taught to his children the things they ought to know.

Martin Luther (LC V, 87)

The Lutheran Reformation of the sixteenth century had a focused theological agenda: *to restore the historic Christian proclamation of salvation by grace alone, through faith alone, in Christ alone, as founded upon Scripture alone.* What the Lutheran reformers accomplished, however, included not only theological reform, but also social reform. Specifically, Lutheran theologians renewed a biblical appreciation for marriage and parenthood in an age when the Papacy had presented celibacy as a holier vocation. In doing so, Lutherans also identified the family as the foundational institution for Christian education.[1]

To phrase it simply, the Lutheran Reformation was about going "back to the basics"—back to Scripture, back to salvation in Christ alone, and back to the vocations "commanded by God," such as "that a husband should labor to support his wife and children and bring them up in the fear of God, [and] that a wife should bear children and care for them" (AC XXVI, 10-11). But how could parents teach their children if not only parents, but also the pastors serving them, were ignorant of basic Bible truths? Recognizing the pathetic state of Christian education in his day, Martin Luther prepared his Small Catechism (1529) as a handbook by which parents could instruct their children in the chief parts of the faith. Each section is prefaced with this phrase: "in the plain form in which the head of the family shall teach them [e.g., the Ten Commandments, or the petitions of the Lord's Prayer] to his household" (SC, *passim*).

Similarly, Luther's Large Catechism (also prepared in 1529) began with a preface stating that "it is the duty of every head of a household to examine his children and servants at least once a week and ascertain what they have learned of it [the Catechism]" (LC Short Preface, 4). In the section concerning the Lord's Supper, Luther further added: "let every head of a household remember that it is his duty, by God's injunction and command, to teach or have taught to his children the things they ought to know" (LC V, 87). When children learned from teachers other than their parents, such instruction was to be regarded as under the auspices of parenthood. Luther identified the relationship between parents and teachers thus: "Where a father is not able by himself to bring up his child, he calls upon a schoolmaster to teach him." Hence, the command to "honor your father and mother" includes also a command to honor teachers and civil government, for "out of the authority of parents all other authority is derived and developed" (LC I, 141). Recognizing the importance of training children in the Christian faith, pastors not only taught the catechism personally to the youth, but also were exhorted to "take pains to urge governing

---

[1] Ewald M. Plass, *This Is Luther: A Character Study* (St. Louis: Concordia Publishing House, 1948), 243-73; Steven Ozment, *When Fathers Ruled: Family Life in Reformation Europe* (Cambridge: Harvard University Press, 1983); Christopher Boyd Brown, "Lutheranism and Music in the Home," chap. 6 in *Singing the Gospel: Lutheran Hymns and the Success of the Reformation* (Cambridge: Harvard University Press, 2005).

authorities and parents to rule wisely and *educate their children*" (SC Preface, 19, emphasis added).

The twentieth-century pastors, teachers, and parents of the Evangelical Lutheran Synod inherited this sixteenth-century consensus of Lutheran theology, subscribing to the Small and Large Catechisms as included in the *Book of Concord*. Pastor J. B. Unseth remarked, at the 400th anniversary of Luther's Small Catechism, that "it is as up to date in 1929 as it was in 1529 . . . and even today there is room for the use of the Catechism in the homes: indeed great need of it, for the benefit of all, both old and young" (**Document 1.2**). The essays in this section illustrate how ELS pastors continuously underscored the value of parents teaching God's Word within the home.

This section also demonstrates that the biblical commands for educating the youth in the home were not regarded as heavy yokes by which a demanding God burdened parents. Rather, Christian parents recognized that the commands positively protect blessings that are imbedded in a divinely established social order in which parents, as God's chosen agents, provide for their children's spiritual needs as well as their material needs. As noted throughout the Large Catechism, God attaches promises to His commands, such as the blessing of the Fourth Commandment: "that it may be well with you and you may live long on the earth" (Ephesians 6:3; LC I, 133). Similarly, in regard to the Sixth Commandment, Luther instructs thus: "Parents and magistrates have the duty of so supervising the youth that they will be brought up to a decency and respect for authority and, when they are grown, will be married honorably in the fear of God. Then God will add His blessing and grace so that men may have joy and happiness in their married life" (LC I, 218).

Viewed from this perspective, Christian education is not optional, but neither is it coercive. It is a fountain of God's blessings: "Blessed are the parents who in their homes together with their children diligently occupy themselves with the Catechism. . . . They will experience the blessing of the Lord" (**Document 1.2**). These blessings come from God, with parents serving merely as channels. Just as pastors, being called into the public ministry, serve as God's spokespersons within the congregation, so also fathers and mothers, having the vocation of parenthood, serve as "pastors" and "priests" within their homes (**Documents 1.3** and **1.7**).

Like the private ministry of parents within the home, the pastor's public ministry of Word and Sacrament also plays an indispensable role in training children in the Christian faith. Christian education properly belongs to both the home and the church, and for either party to surrender this task imperils children's souls. At the 1934 synod convention, Pastor P. T. Buszin identified the serious importance of this cooperative responsibility:

> Would it not, my friends, be an unfathomably gross breach of trust over against the Lord, who has given children to parents as a heritage and gift, and to the Church by their rebirth in baptism, to turn these beloved and honored little ones of God over—for a long or a short period of time—to caretakers of the species described in the Letter to the Ephesians (4:17-18), "walking in the vanity of their mind, having the understanding darkened, being alienated from the life of God through the ignorance that is in them, because of the blindness of their heart," or to have such a child trained for hours each day according to an educational program which of necessity and by design is without Christ, having no eternal hope, and without God in the world (cp. Ephesians 2:12), and then endeavoring merely by a slipshod admonition here and there in the home and by some short-time, makeshift arrangement in the Church, to counteract contrary, but well-planned and captivating, habituating influences?[2]

The documents in this section emphasize the irrevocable responsibility of parents to ensure, by their own efforts as well as through assistance obtained from their congregations, that their children receive a proper Christian upbringing. "Many homes, it seems, hold the church alone responsible [for nurturing children's souls]. ... It is true that the Lord has instituted the office of teaching in the church in order to assist parents in bringing up their children, but He has not thereby removed the responsibility from parents."[3]

Home devotions provide one means by which parents may exercise their responsibility in sharing the Gospel with their children. Mrs. Joslyn Moldstad, who now teaches at Jesus' Lambs at Peace Lutheran Preschool (North Mankato, Minnesota), wrote in the preface to her book of family devotions:

---

[2] P. T. Buszin, "Christian Education and the Parochial School," *Synod Report* (1934), 19-42, at 33.

[3] H. Ingebritson, "Parents are Responsible for Their Children," *Lutheran Sentinel*, 15 Aug. 1934, 261-62, at 261.

Our home is a place of refuge to which we come each evening to be with our family. Every day is bursting with its own frustrations, heartaches, and grief. To be a real refuge, our home must be a place where we run not only for rest and relaxation, but also to hear the word of God. Only through the Bible is there true peace for our souls, knowing our sin is forgiven through Jesus the Savior.[4]

Rather than regarding home devotions as supplements to a congregation's educational offerings, ELS pastors have seen things the other way around: home devotions play a fundamental role, later to be enhanced by "Sunday school, vacation Bible school, or perhaps a Christian day school" (**Document 1.4**). A writer for the *Lutheran Sentinel* summed it up thus in 1932:

> Commands of God in regard to religious instruction are addressed to parents—specifically to the father as the head of the family. Scripture, therefore, regards the home as the really appropriate agency for religious instruction. That, in comparison with all other agencies [church services, catechism class, Sunday school, vacation Bible school], may come nearest to reaching the Biblical standard. It then should be the aim of every Christian pastor to make the homes of his parishioners such agencies and the aim of every Christian parent to make his home such an agency.[5]

Home devotions at the "family altar" also lay the foundation for broader home-based education programs. "Homeschooling" has gained popularity in recent years, largely as a strategy for winning the so-called "culture wars" as to which values system the next generation of Americans will inherit—secular or religious, postmodern or traditional? Homeschooling in its most recent manifestations tends to be associated, religiously, with conservative Reformed and Roman Catholic subcultures and, politically, with the Religious Right. However, a distinctly Lutheran philosophy of homeschooling predates the current political struggles and transcends the contemporary preoccupation with moral reform. Lutherans focus not only on the Law that reveals our sins, but also the Gospel of forgiveness in Christ. Lutheran home education, as envisioned in the Large Catechism,

---

[4] Joslyn Wiechmann Moldstad, *At Home with Jesus: Devotions for Children* (Milwaukee: Northwestern Publishing House, 1992), vii.
[5] D[avid] L. Pfeifer, "Religious Education and the Christian Day School," *Lutheran Sentinel*, 22 June 1932, 193-96, at 195.

has an overarching goal: the preparation of young people to receive the Sacrament of Holy Communion (LC V, 87). And so it was, over fifty years ago, that *Lutheran Sentinel* readers learned that their "Christian homes should again become home-churches, homeschools, where the housefathers were both house-priests and house-teachers, performing the office of the ministry there just as the pastors did in the churches" (**Document 1.3**; cf. **Document 1.7**).

Expectations of the home's ability to train the youth ran high. "The real schools, where the real lessons of life are learned, are the Christian homes of America," proclaimed the *Lutheran Sentinel* in 1959. "There is no training to be had in school or college, or anywhere in the world which can take the place of discipline of the home. Every true Christian home is a university, fully equipped, amply endowed, and able to give the highest education which can be got in this world."[6]

But even as ELS pastors extolled the virtues of home education, they also tempered their idealism with realistic expectations. "If parents could do this at home, that would be the ideal thing. But under our conditions, this, in most cases, is just about impossible."[7] The Synod's Board for Education recognized, as early as the 1930s, that some parents are unable, others are unwilling, and still others, though able and willing, nonetheless struggle to find the time to educate their children properly[8] (cf. **Document 1.1**). As the documents in **Section 2: "Christian Day Schools"** illustrate, the Evangelical Lutheran Synod has found it necessary to establish parochial schools to fill these gaps. In the 1970s, the American family seemed woefully inadequate for Christian childrearing as fathers overcommitted themselves to work and community organizations, mothers increasingly took employment outside the home, parents divorced, and children

---

[6] "A Christian Home," *Grace Broadcaster*, rpt. *Lutheran Sentinel*, 8 Oct. 1959, 302.

[7] O. M. Gullerud, "Would You Not Do It?", *Lutheran Sentinel*, 25 May 1932, 169-71, at 169-70.

[8] "But it is my honest opinion that few parents would willingly take upon themselves this truly arduous task. For those of them who are capable of instructing their children in the truth of faith may lack the desire or the time to do so; while those who have both time and desire may be more fitly placed in the pupil's seat than in the teacher's chair." L.P.J., "Board of Christian Education," *Lutheran Sentinel*, 13 Apr. 1932, 122-23, at 122. The *Lutheran Sentinel* editor inserted the following between the two sentences just quoted: "This is an unfortunate statement of the author. All the foregoing can and should be undertaken by all Christian parents."

took their cues from a revolutionary youth culture, which itself was nurtured in the "vulgarity, cursing, violence, and explicit sex" that permeated mass media (**Document 1.5**). The need for Christian schools had become as vital as ever. Nevertheless, those schools were to serve not as replacements for, but rather as extensions of, the parental office, as well as of the congregation's mission and the pastor's public ministry. Indeed, one of the congregation's major tasks was to retrain mothers and fathers for Christian parenthood (**Documents 1.5** and **1.6**).

Thus, pastors hoped that Christian education in the ELS would involve the home, the church, and the school in mutual assistance to one another (**Document 1.1**). At times, tensions developed, particularly when the schools in question operated under the state rather than the church (**Documents 1.1** and **1.6**). But even parochial schools ran the risk of tempting parents to become complacent or neglectful. Pastors sought repeatedly to strike the proper balance. They did so with a recognition that the future of the family, the church, and the wider society depended upon it:

> For lasting influence and value to a child's life there is no substitute for the Christian home. The education which a child receives there, together with the help of its church, ranks first and foremost in all education. Nevertheless, whatever other instruction the young can receive by way of Christian elementary and higher education is invaluable. We believe that the more Christian-orientated education a person can receive, the better it is for that person, for his church, and for his country. So, when we speak of the purpose of instruction with a Christian setting, we have in mind not just that which is learned at mother's knee, but that which also follows the child out of the home, away from its local church, and into the world at large.[9]

While perusing the documents in this section, the reader will benefit from pondering not only their meaning to the generations of yesteryear, but also their implications for those yet to come. Historical study rightfully involves self-reflection: while inquiring about people from the past, we ask questions that penetrate into our own lives, here and now. It was while I was serving as the managing editor for this present volume that the editor of the

---

[9] Paul Madson, "The Purpose of Instruction," *Synod Report* (1974), 37-47, at 37.

synod's *Lutheran Sentinel* requested me to write a brief article on the philosophy of Christian education. My reply drew upon the historical understanding gained from the research for this book as well as my personal experiences and aspirations as a Christian husband and father. Republished at the conclusion of this section, the article summarizes what our Lutheran forefathers have taught and encourages that yet one more generation of fathers and mothers pass down that tradition to their children (**Document 1.8**).

DOCUMENT 1.1

The Relation of the Home to the Christian School (1927)

By Carl Johan Quill

Carl Johan Quill (1878–1940) instructed twenty congregations in the Christian faith during his thirty-three years in the ministry. He was born to Gudmund and Ingrid Quill on June 21, 1878, in Dodge County, Minnesota. At age twenty-six, Quill graduated from Luther College in Decorah, Iowa, completing his studies at Luther Theological Seminary three years later. Carl Quill married Bolid Braaten on June 30, 1907, only fourteen days after his ordination. In the first ten years of his work, he preached to fourteen congregations. Quill served ten churches at a mission field in Bowden, North Dakota, three congregations in Grove City, Minnesota, and Concordia Church in the Twin Cities. In 1923, Quill joined the newly organized Norwegian Synod. He served Our Savior's Lutheran Church in Albert Lea, Minnesota, for nine years. For the remaining seven years of his life and ministry, Quill served at the Western Koshkonong Church in Cottage Grove, Wisconsin. Pastor Quill died May 9, 1940, survived by his wife, brother, three daughters, and one son.[10] [DR]

Source: *Synod Report* (1927), 46-52.

---

[10] "Carl Johan Quill," *Lutheran Sentinel*, May 1940, 150, 155.

Two unspeakably important institutions loom before our mind's eye, loom high—the home and the Christian school.

These will never cease—nay rather increase—their cry and unconditional claim upon our attention, our most serious concern and consideration.

They tell our past, present, and future, tell what we *have been*, what we *are*, and what we may hope *to be*, as a church and as a people. Of this our church is not unmindful, but it is becoming ever more conscious.

In her sincere desire for a healthy Christian life and growth, steady progress and a future—sure and secure—our church, no doubt, must desire for her constituents a clear and ever more clear Lutheran consciousness of the significance of the Christian school and of the right attitude of the home *to it*. Hence the request for a paper on the subject to be read before the Synod in convention. The task assigned, as I take it, is to set forth, with all possible clearness and due emphasis, the relation of the home to the Christian school—the relation as it *should* be, rather than the relation as it *is*.

As the basis for my humble contribution, I have chosen the familiar words of Proverbs 22:6: "Train up a child in the way he should go, and when he is old, he will not depart from it."

In order to set forth most effectually the right relation or attitude of the home to the Christian school, it would be well, perhaps, to begin with a clear conception of the home—*the home* as it *should* be, the *real* home.

Much has been said; volumes and volumes have been written and read about the home.

The home has been called, and rightly so, the foundation of all society and order among men. The word "foundation" means "that upon which anything stands, or by which it is supported; the lowest and supporting layer of a structure, the groundwork."

The home the foundation! How important! Everything rests upon the foundation. Was the Lord, our God, concerned about its character when He laid the foundation for His church and His great redemptive work for man? Hear! "Behold I lay in Zion for a foundation a stone, a tried stone, a sure foundation" (Isaiah 16:28).

What was that foundation? "Other foundation can no man lay than that is laid, which is Christ Jesus" (1 Corinthians 3:11).

The home the foundation! How necessary that the home be of the highest type possible—the Christian home! And what do we mean by the Christian home? We mean the home that is *Christian*, not in name only, but in spirit and in truth—where Christ is all in all, the one supreme ruler, teacher, exemplar, whose word and will with each new day is dearer still, the center of peace and of joy, of sympathy and affection, where every Christian gift and grace is carefully cultivated, each member of the family seeking to display love such as was manifested by the Maker—patient, magnanimous, and sympathetic—the home, where the motto "for Jesus' sake" is the motto of the whole family—the home never too good to be left at the call of duty—the home of which we say with the poet:

> O happy home! Oh, home supremely blest,
> Where Thou, Lord Jesus Christ, art entertained
> As the most welcome and beloved guest,
> With true devotion and with love unfeigned;
> Where all hearts beat in unison with Thine,
> Where eyes grow brighter as they look on Thee,
> Where all are ready at the slightest sign
> To do Thy will, and do it heartily.[11]

That is the Christian home, the real home. Who would not wish to have a home like this? What Christian parents would not wish for their children, and children's children, a home like unto it? And we may all have it.

But a home like this is not built in a day, does not spring up overnight. It is the result of constant concern, of diligent, dutiful doing and sacrifice. Everything depends upon the home. There is the heartbeat of the nation. There is where the characters are molded. In almost all cases of a dissipated course of life, the *cause* may be traced to home-training, the roots found in a dark and sickening atmosphere of neglected childhood.

The home life has the strongest influence on the child. Nothing will leave such indelible impressions upon the child-soul as will the things seen and heard in the childhood home. What father and mother say and do, and how it is said and done, leaves its effect upon the child, more powerful and far-reaching than most parents realize. The home atmosphere and training will be reflected in the child's entire later life.

How necessary, then, that the child be given an early and thorough Christian training, that Christ be brought as early as

---

[11] *Editors' note*: Quill was reciting the opening verse of "*O selig Haus*," by C. J. Philipp Spitta, *ca.* 1833, as translated by Richard Massie, *Lyra Domestica* (1860), 81. For an alternative translation, which has enjoyed longer usage within the ELS, see *TLH* 626:1.

possible into the child's life and increasing consciousness.

The first requisite is knowledge. The child must be given to know Christ—not only to know a little of him, or *about* Him, as is the sad case with so many children called Christian—but to *know* him.

But knowledge implies instruction. Whose duty is it to give their child such instruction? First and above all, it is the parents' duty. And it is their first and most serious duty to their child. Nothing else can be compared with it in importance and eternal significance. "Train up the child in the way he should go and when he is old he will not depart from it" (Proverbs 22:6).

Originally, the religious instruction was given in the home. It was parental. The Jews were all supposed to teach their own children. The heads of each family were supposed to fear God and, fearing Him themselves, were to teach their households to fear Him also. Still some parents would be careless, and, from various causes, some children would be neglected. These were to be carefully instructed by others. At the feast of tabernacles, special attention was to be given to such as were ignorant of God. Hear what we read in Deuteronomy 31:10-13:

> And Moses commanded them saying, "at the end of every seven years, in the solemnity of the year of release, in the feast of tabernacles, when all Israel is come to appear before the Lord thy God in the place which He shall choose, thou shalt read this law before all Israel in their hearing. Gather the people together, men, and women, and children, and thy stranger that is within thy gates, that they may hear, and that they may learn, and fear the Lord your God, and observe to *do* all the words of this law; and that their children, which have not known anything, may hear, and learn to fear the Lord your God, as long as ye live in the land whither ye go over Jordan to possess it."

So carefully did the Lord provide against the leaven of ignorance that might in time leaven the whole lump of the nation. Originally, the religious instruction was parental. Over the course of time, it became necessary to give over at least some of the instruction to others.

Shall we be satisfied with the state of affairs in our day and age, as touching our children's opportunity to hear, learn, and know "*the one thing needful*" [Luke 10:42]? Nine months of the year and more—the best months—are taken by the public schools for secular instruction of our children, leaving little or no time—

and that during the hot summer months—for the religious instruction.

Under such a desperate state of affairs, it has become imperatively necessary for Christian homes to establish private schools, or Christian day schools.

What do we mean by the Christian school? Is it not clear to all? The word "Christian" speaks to the character of the school. It is a school where *Christ* is taught, where His Spirit rules, where His Word and precepts are the principal study, the first and the last in the instruction; where the heart and mind are brought to submit to His will revealed in His Word; where Christian children may daily move and develop in a Christian atmosphere. It should be clear that such a school is of the highest importance to the home. It should also be clear that the relation of the home to the Christian school should be the most earnest and intimate.

I. The Home

In the first place, the home *needs* the school. Most parents have not the time in our busy day and age to attend to the religious instruction of their children, their most sacred duty toward them, as is required of Christian fathers and mothers. Some parents lack the proper zeal and earnest. They may be willing and sincere, but for lack of due conception fail to realize the gravity of their duty and responsibility. Other parents wholly lack the necessary qualifications for teaching.

In the second place, the home entrusts the school with the care of its most precious treasures—the children—*entrusts* the school with the high trust to mold their character, to train and develop, to fit and equip them—mind and heart—for the battles and problems of life, and what is more, entrusts the school with the supreme trust to direct and train up their souls immortal for heaven and eternity. For these and many other weighty reasons, the relation of the home to the school should be most earnest and intimate, and Christian parents should welcome a thousand times the much needed assistance and service which the Christian school is most willing and anxious to render.

II. The Christian School

The Christian school *needs* the home. It exists *because of* the home. It is born out of the crying need of the home. Were it not for the home, it would not be, would not have been. It is *of* the home. The Christian school exists *for* the home. It was brought into being for the very purpose to assist and to serve the home in her endeavors and difficulties, to discharge her sacred duties, to solve her perplexing problems, and to increase in Christlike zeal, influence and beauty. The Christian school is *for* the home.

Since the Christian school exists *because of* the home, and exists *for* the home, it should be clear that it must also exist and continue to exist *by* the home. It is wholly dependent upon the home. It will be and do according to the interest and support given it *by* the home.

If the interest and support is half-hearted, the school, as a consequence, will be found in a weak, sickly, crippled state. How will the right relation of the home to the Christian school manifest itself?

In the first place, the home will manifest by word and deed that it realizes the pressing necessity of the Christian school, that such an institution should exist, must exist, and that the home is in desperate need of just such assistance as is offered by the Christian school.

This includes also the homes in which there are no children to be instructed. Every Christian home will belong to a Christian congregation, and every such home where the eyes are open to the crying need and care and special claim of the lambs in the fold and the express command of the Master concerning them—"Feed my Lambs" [John 21:15]—will manifest by word and deed that it is a matter which concerns even their home, and that they also are included. And hence they will show that the Christian school is an institution which should and must exist.

Until the home realizes the significance of the Christian school it will manifest hindrance instead of help, and the precious, priceless treasures of the home—the child-souls—will be denied the spiritual light and food and protection which they could have, should have, and which is rightfully theirs.

In the second place, the right relation of the home to the Christian school will manifest itself in action—in honest effort to establish such schools—born out of sincere, deep, and devout prayer for divine blessing upon the undertaking. And when established, the relationship will manifest itself in whole-hearted interest, support, and sacrifice, even unto suffering for the noble cause of Christ. Not only the homes that have children, but every home in the congregation, will be concerned and realize the responsibility resting upon them as Christians to their little

> *"Lord God, heavenly Father, in mercy You have established the Christian home among us: We beseech You so to rule and direct our hearts, that we may be good examples to children and those subject to us, and not offend them by word or deed, but faithfully teach them to love Your Church and hear Your blessed Word. Give them Your Spirit and grace, that this seed may bring forth good fruit, so that our home life may advance Your glory, honor and praise, our own improvement and welfare, and give offense to no one; through the same, Your beloved Son, Jesus Christ, our Lord, who lives and reigns with You and the Holy Spirit, one true God, now and forever. Amen."*
>
> Veit Dietrich, Collect for the First Sunday after Epiphany, in *ELH*, Collect #21, pp. 149-50.

brothers and sisters in the Lord. The interest and support will be general; a congregational cause and concern.

How will the interest and support be shown? By sending the children of the congregation to the school, by taking the school and its work to the Lord in prayer, and also by giving it financial support as God prospers.

I venture the question: "Is there any money better invested than the money given to the Lord's cause for the right instruction and guidance of child-souls?" Think it over.

But to begin a good work is *one* thing, and to keep it up is quite another. Patient continuance, steady perseverance will test the genuineness of interest and support. Hence—in the second place—real interest and support will be shown by the constant concern for the efficiency of the school and by efforts to acquire and maintain a high standard for the institution. The concern will be:

1. *The Teacher.* Nothing determines so much the standard of the school as does the teacher or teachers. Hence, the vital concern will be not only to secure and retain the most competent, qualified, and highly recommended instructors in the secular branches, but also, and especially, to exercise care and the best judgment

possible, that only such persons be placed in that high position as bear testimony to a thorough Christian character and are found competent and qualified for the position. For it is the inculcation of the eternal truths of Christianity and the power thereof exemplified in the teacher's life that is to be the great undercurrent in the whole instruction.

It will be realized that the teacher wields a tremendous influence over the young minds and souls, day after day, and week after week, and this repeated, perhaps, year after year.

Having secured a good and faithful teacher, the home will consider itself blessed with a great gift and will earnestly endeavor to carry on and cultivate a constant Christian cooperation with the school, ever bearing in mind the rights and authority, as well as the difficult and responsible position of the teacher—who is but human—bearing in mind, too, the fact that in school are children from many homes, specimens of many kinds of bringing up.

Surely the Christian home will be considerate and sympathetic with the teacher, who is given the difficult task to discipline diverse groups of children. The interest and support of the home will manifest itself in the concern about *how* the school is conducted. Hence—

2. *The System*. To acquire and maintain a high standard of efficiency, the school must be conducted according to a carefully prepared plan. There must be a system. "Order is heaven's first law."[12] Order in the schoolwork will give delight, beauty, and the best results. This the home will realize and hence will cheerfully cooperate and contribute its part that the work may be accomplished. When, therefore, the work is planned for the pupils from day to day, it is important that they are present to receive the full benefit. And the home will reveal its interest and support here in the regular attendance of the children.

3. *School Buildings*. The quarters where the school is conducted play an important part in the efficiency of the school. The school building needs considerable and constant attention. It is very often much neglected. For one thing, careful investigation will be made to ascertain whether the school receives sufficient light. Insufficient amount of light has caused and will continue to cause no insignificant amount of eye defect among the pupils. Then there is the question of heat. It certainly does not require the knowledge of a physician to understand that keeping a child at study in a cold room will subject the child to severe consequences

---

[12] Alexander Pope, "Essay on Man" (1733-1734), epistle IV, line 49.

and to much suffering during its later life. Negligence here, whether consciously or unconsciously committed, is dangerously close to cruelty.

Among many other things in this connection, which calls for consideration and concern where the right relation of the home to the Christian school exists, might be mentioned the matter of ventilation, sanitation, physical condition of the children, social environment, and the like.

Christian parents should jealously care for the physical health of their children, for surely it is one of life's greatest blessings. This everybody knows, if not before then surely after it is too late. *Mens sana in corpore sano.* "A sound mind in a sound body." This is a Christian mode of expression. "A sound mind in a sound body" is a blessing frequently held out and faithfully impressed on the hearts and minds in the Christian school.

Christian parents, friends! If we but stop a little in the ceaseless tearing toil and turmoil of life and turn to serious reflections on life's most precious, priceless possessions—our homes, our children, and our church—in the light of what we owe them, in the light of their eternal future, we shall find the Christian school to be a veritable God-send, the greatest and most blessed help in need.

May the Spirit of Christ prompt all Christian parents to acknowledge the significance of their parental call. May He prompt the *fathers* to dedicate as much as possible of their time to the home and the domestic sanctuary, to improve the time so dedicated to help lay the cornerstone of salvation with their children, to work patiently and ponder prayerfully for the spiritual up-building on the one foundation.

May He prompt the *mothers* to regard as the sweetest [blessing] of motherhood to pour out the sincere milk of the Gospel to their children, to banish the miserable and vain imagination that any other "can take the place of mother" in bringing them to Christ.

May He prompt the *parents* to see how spiritually poor most children leave the parental home, even the Christian home, to see and to welcome the extended helping hand of the Christian school.

May the time be not far distant for our Synod when the "day dawn" for all our homes and the "Day Star" of the Christian school arise [2 Peter 1:19] in the hearts of all Christian fathers and mothers!

DOCUMENT 1.2:

The Right Use of the Catechism (1929)

By Joseph B. Unseth

Joseph B. Unseth (1875–1966) *devoted his life to preaching the Word of God wherever it was needed. He was born in Vernon County, Wisconsin, on November 11, 1875 and was baptized into Christ on January 16, 1876. Unseth graduated from Luther College, Decorah, Iowa, with the class of 1897. From there he began his training in the Gospel at Luther Seminary in St. Paul, Minnesota. In 1900, Joseph Unseth received his first call to assist two pastors in North Dakota. After one year, on June 6, 1901, Unseth married Alice Bye. God blessed the Unseths with four daughters and three sons. Between 1913 and 1918, Pastor Unseth served eleven congregations. In 1923, after twenty-two years of marriage, Alice was called to her heavenly home. Six years later, Joseph Unseth married Ida Towley, on July 21, 1929. Pastor Unseth later received a call to Bagley, Minnesota, where he served four congregations. After fifty-one years in the active ministry, he had served twenty different churches.*  *Even after his retirement in 1951, Pastor Unseth continued to spread the gospel to the elderly at Kasota Valley Lutheran Home. Here, he preached Christ crucified at weekly services and ministered to the sick and dying from 1951 to 1956. Pastor Unseth died on January 16, 1966. Like God's faithful servant Job, he "saw his children and their children to the fourth generation" (Job 42:16): four daughters, two* *surviving sons, eleven grandchildren, and twenty great-grandchildren.*[13] [DR]

Source: *Synod Report* (1929), 47–53.

Luther wrote his Small Catechism that it should be rightly used by the old and the young. It was to be an *enchiridion*, a handbook, a constant guide for both old and young on the path of life. This book has also enjoyed an enormous circulation and has for four centuries been in universal use in home, school and church. Thirty-seven years after the publication of Luther's catechism, Mathesius wrote: "Praise God, it is said that in our times over one hundred thousand copies have been printed and used in great numbers in all kinds of languages in foreign lands and in all Latin and German schools."[14] And since then, down to the present day, millions and millions of hands have been stretched forth to receive Luther's catechetical classic. While during the last four centuries hundreds of catechisms have gone under, Luther's Enchiridion is still used in many countries as the best textbook of religious doctrine. It is the acknowledged pearl of childhood instruction, its merits being recognized not only by Lutherans, but by all men of all denominations.

In the Catechism we have simple affirmations of that which constitutes Christian belief and life, and this is its chief merit, which lifts it above the age which saw its birth and gives it a timeless quality. It is as one has remarked, "a booklet which a theologian never finishes learning, and a Christian never finishes living."[15] It is as up to date in 1929 as it was in 1529.

Luther wrote his Catechism chiefly for the Christian home, in order that the Christian homes should again become home-churches, where the housefathers were both house-priests and house-teachers. It was intended especially for the home, to be a home book to be used by parents for their own profit and as a

---

[13] "Rev. J. B. Unseth," *Lutheran Sentinel*, Feb. 1966, 45-46.

[14] *Editors' note*: F. Bente, "Historical Introductions to the Symbolical Books of the Evangelical Lutheran Church," in *Triglot Concordia: The Symbolical Books of the Evangelical Lutheran Church* (St. Louis: Concordia Publishing House, 1921), 1-266, at sec. 116. The contextual comments Unseth makes throughout this essay also closely follow Bente's presentation.

[15] *Editors' note*: Bente, "Historical Introductions," sec. 116, quoting from C. A. G. von Zezschwitz, *System der christlich-kirchlichen Katechetik*, 3 vols. (1862-1874).

textbook for the instruction of the young. At the head of each of the five chief parts of the Catechism stand these words: "As the head of the family should teach it in all simplicity to his household."

Even today there is room for the use of the Catechism in the homes: indeed great need of it, for the benefit and blessing of all, both old and young. It is true, we are living in a busy age; we have deviated quite far from the quiet, still mode of life of our fathers. But this has not served to make our homes better; on the contrary, we find homes even among the Christians that do not distinguish themselves from those of unbelievers. The day is begun and ended without prayer; never a prayer is said before or after meals. The members of the home come and go as they please, and it is difficult, yea, well nigh impossible to gather all together for the mediation of God's Word and for prayers. In many homes, the Word of God and prayer are wholly neglected, and the children as well as the parents starve and die spiritually. What is the real cause for the alarming situation which President Herbert Hoover pointed out when he told our country recently that "Life and property are relatively more unsafe in this land of ours than in any other civilized country in the world. No part of the country, rural or urban, is immune"[16]? Is it not godlessness, lack of faith and neglect of using the Word of God through which natural, corrupt man can be changed into a God-fearing lover of truth and righteousness? Speaking about the same matter, President Calvin Coolidge said: "The greatest need of America is religion, religion that centers in the home."[17] President Woodrow Wilson, shortly before his death, testified: "The one remedy for our evils is a widespread revival of the faith of our fathers, the faith which overcometh the world."[18]

It is still true what Luther said: If anything worthwhile is to be done against the devil and against crime and wickedness, we must begin with the children. We should strive more earnestly than ever to build Godly homes, where God's Word is heard. We must have home-instruction, family prayers, family worship. Not a day should pass by when the parents do not pray together with their children, together meditate upon a Word of God, together seek counsel, strength, and comfort from God. For such family

---

[16] *Editors' note*: Herbert Hoover, "Address to the Associated Press: Law Enforcement and Respect for the Law," 22 Apr. 1929, *www.presidency.ucsb.edu*.

[17] *Editors' note*: Calvin Coolidge, as quoted in George Walter Fiske, *The Christian Family* (n.p.: n.p., 1929), 17.

[18] *Editors' note*: The source has not been located.

devotion our Catechism is very suitable, often being called the "Little Bible" and the "Bible of the Laity,"[19] because it is a brief summary of the Christian doctrine. A brief scripture portion, a short lesson from the Catechism, a prayer, how little time such a family devotion requires! But what great blessings are involved in them! We must return to the practice of Luther, namely that we, together with our children, daily meditate upon and pray the Catechism. According to Luther it is the duty of every Christian to learn constantly, and he included himself in such study. In his preface to the Large Catechism we read:

> But for myself I say this: I am also a doctor and preacher, yea, as learned and experienced as all those may be who have such presumption and security; yet I do as a child who is being taught the Catechism, and every morning, and whenever I have time I read and say word for word the Ten Commandments, the Creed, the Lord's Prayer, the Psalms, etc. And I must still read and study daily, and yet I cannot master it as I wish, but must remain a child and pupil of the Catechism, and am glad so to remain. (LC Introduction, 7–8)

On April 18, 1530, Luther repeated this in a sermon as follows:

> Whoever is able to read, let him, in the morning, take a psalm or some other chapter in the Bible and study it for a while. For that is what I do. When I rise in the morning, I pray the Ten Commandments, the Creed, the Lord's Prayer, and also a Psalm with the children. I do so because I wish to remain familiar with it, and not have it overgrown with mildew, so that I know it.[20]

In another sermon of the same year, Luther warns:

> Beware lest you become presumptuous, as though, because you have heard it often, you knew enough of the Catechism. For this knowledge ever desires us to be its students. We shall never finish learning it, since it does not consist in speech, but in life. . . . For I also, D. Martinus, doctor and preacher, am

---

[19] *Editors' note*: "And because such matters concern also the laity and the salvation of their souls, we also confess the Small and Large Catechisms of Dr. Luther, as they are included in Luther's works, as the Bible of the laity, wherein everything is comprised which is treated at greater length in Holy Scripture, and is necessary for a Christian man to know for his salvation." Ep, Summary, 5.

[20] *Editors' note*: Bente, "Historical Introductions," sec. 102.

compelled day by day to pray and to recite the words of the Decalogue, the Creed, and the Lord's Prayer as children are wont to do. Be not ashamed to do likewise. You will experience excellent results.[21]

Elsewhere he says: "This Catechism is truly a Bible of the laity, wherein is contained the entire doctrine necessary to be known by every Christian for salvation."[22] How important to study it, to meditate on its contents!

Let us not forget that we and our children are and will remain poor sinners as long as we are here on earth. We will never attain perfect sanctification in this present life. Therefore, we must also be reminded of the Ten Commandments, in which God makes known His will and shows us what we lack and that we are all sinners. Nor let us forget that on account of the sins which still cling to us, the comfort of the gospel will not remain in our hearts. Therefore, we daily need to meditate upon the Creed which holds before our eyes and shows us the grace and mercy of God as revealed in Christ Jesus and offered us through the gospel. How slow we are to learn the great art of praying aright, that in the name of Jesus we may approach God and ask Him with all boldness and confidence as children ask their dear father for something [SC III, 2]. Therefore we must daily pray the Lord's Prayer, ever anew learn it. Likewise we daily need to be reminded of our baptism and the precious covenant of grace which God there established with us, and to diligently consider the blessed Sacrament of the Altar instituted for the nourishing of our spiritual life and in which Christ offers and seals unto us the gifts of grace procured by his suffering and death.

Attention must also be called to the "Table of Duties," better known as "*Hustavlen*" concerning which Daniel Kauzmann in his *Handbook* of 1569 says: "It is called '*Haustafel*' of the Christians because every Christian should daily view it and call to mind therefrom his calling, as from a table which portrays and presents to every one what pertains to him. It teaches all the people who may be in a house what each one ought to do or leave undone in his calling."[23] Truly, the Catechism is a precious gift of God to us,

---

21 *Editors' note*: Ibid., sec. 102.
22 *Editors' note*: Ibid., sec. 115; cf. Ep, Summary, 5.
23 *Editors' note*: Hustavlen and Haustafel literally mean "house-table" in Norwegian and German, respectively; in common Lutheran parlance, these terms refer to biblical principles of household order, or the "Table of Duties," as listed at the conclusion of Luther's Small Catechism. See Daniel Kauzmann, *Handbook:*

and how important that we diligently pray it and meditate upon it in our homes! This dear "Bible of the Laity" is indeed a main support for a happy and blessed Christian home and belongs in the home where it may be profitably used "for doctrine, for reproof, for correction, for instruction in righteousness; that the man of God may be perfect, thoroughly furnished unto all good works" [2 Timothy 3:16–17]. The Holy Scriptures—the Bible itself—should be read and studied daily, but when we go to the Catechism we are not leaving the Bible; for it contains nothing but God's Word, presenting, in a way easily understood, the fundamental truths of the way of salvation. Its use will help us to learn to know the Bible itself and to apply its lessons of instruction and comfort to our own lives.

Especially should parents whose children are attending school or are reading for confirmation occupy themselves with the Catechism and see to it that their dear ones are learning the Catechism well and not only learn it by heart, but also understand it; above all, that they may love it. The children are often timid and do not dare to direct a question to the teacher or pastor, and it may happen that they pass lightly over a lesson without understanding it. Here the parents can and should cooperate. They are the natural teachers of the children, ordained by God Himself. Incessantly, therefore, Luther urges the fathers and mothers not only to bring their children to church, where the Catechism was explained on Sunday afternoons, but themselves to teach the children. He was convinced that without their vigorous cooperation he could achieve but little. "The Christian home," he insisted, "must become church and school."[24] Every housefather is a priest in his own house, every housemother is a priestess; therefore see that you help us to perform the office of the ministry in your homes as we do in church. If you do, we shall have a propitious God, who will defend us from all evil. In the Psalms (78:5) it is written: "He appointed a law in Israel, which he commanded our fathers, that they should make them known to their children."

Luther blames the parents for the prevailing ignorance. "They are altogether careless." "Let the head of the household teach the servants, let the mother teach the maids, let both teach the

---

16 *Sermons on the Catechism* (1659), as quoted in Bente, "Historical Introductions," sec. 114.

24 *Editor's note*: The source has not been located.

> *"As I see it, a thoroughly Christian educational system is the chief of all conditions for our church body's health and development in this country. But the gross neglect thereof, in a non-Christian, irreligious, more or less worldly-minded training of our children and youth, I see the decay and destruction of our beloved church within a few generations."*
>
> President Herman Amberg Preus, Annual Address, Synod Report (1873), 18, translated by Paul Madson.

children! Beware lest you neglect your office!"[25] And he sums it up in his introduction to the Large Catechism: "Therefore it is the duty of every father of a family to question and examine his children and servants at least once a week and to ascertain what they know of it, or are learning, and, if they do not know it, to keep them faithfully at it" (LC Short Preface, 4).

Blessed are the parents who in their homes together with their children diligently occupy themselves with the Catechism, in the fear of God. They will experience the blessing of the Lord upon their own hearts; they will learn to understand the Holy Scriptures better, become more firmly grounded in the truth to salvation, increase in holiness, and become more rich in good works. And where the truths of the Catechism are inculcated upon the minds and the hearts of the children, these will increase in faith, be fortified against all false doctrines—which Satan scatters about to ensnare people—strengthened in their fight against sin and evil, and enabled to give a reason for the hope they entertain. Truly the Catechism belongs in the home as a book of instruction, comfort, and edification, as well as admonition and warning. "Let each his lesson learn with care, and all the household well shall fare" (SC Table of Duties, 15).

The training and education of the child belongs primarily in the home, to the parents. The God-ordained home is expected to care not only for the body, but also for the soul; for the whole education of the child. On judgment day, God will demand the children of their parents, and *they* will have to give account.

The other God-ordained educational agency is the church,

---

[25] *Editor's note*: The source has not been located.

whose commission is to save souls. "Go ye, therefore, and teach all nations, baptizing them in the name of the Father, and of the Son, and of the Holy Ghost; teaching them to observe all things whatsoever I have commanded you" (Matthew 28:19-20). An essential part of the church's work is to take care of its children, not only by baptism, but also by instructing and training them in the Word of God. In order to carry out its duties most economically and efficiently, the church establishes schools, parochial or Christian schools, which are maintained by it and conducted under its supervision. Because the church has the duty to teach those who are baptized to observe all things which Christ commanded—that is, the whole Word of God—therefore it becomes so necessary to establish Christian schools. Luther saw this need of Christian schools, and he devoted himself to the solution of the problems of establishing schools. In 1524 he sent forth, in the form of a booklet, a ringing appeal to the councilmen of all cities in Germany that they should establish and maintain Christian schools.[26]

When planning and writing his Small Catechism, Luther did not overlook the schools and the schoolteachers. His Catechism very soon became a textbook in the schools, and down to the present day no other book has become and remained a schoolbook for religious instruction to such an extent as Luther's Small Catechism. And rightly so, for even Bible History must be regarded as subordinate to it. The assertion of modern educators that instruction in Bible History must precede instruction in Luther's Catechism rests on the false assumption that Luther's Catechism teaches doctrines only. But the truth is that it contains all the essential facts of salvation as well, though in briefest form, as appears particularly from the Second Article [of the Apostles Creed], which enumerates historical facts only. Luther's Enchiridion presents both the facts of salvation and their divine interpretation. The picture for which the Small Catechism furnishes the frame is Christ, the historical Christ, as glorified by the Holy Spirit, particularly in the writings of the Apostle Paul. In the Lutheran Church, the Small Catechism therefore deserves to be and always to remain what it became from the first moment of its publication: the book of religious instruction for home, school,

---

[26] *Editors' note*: Martin Luther, "To the Councilmen of All Cities in Germany That They Establish and Maintain Christian Schools" (1524), *Luther's Works*, vol. 45, ed. Walther I. Brandt (Philadelphia: Fortress Press, 1962), 339-78.

and church; for parents, children, teachers and preachers, just as Luther had planned and desired.

Contrary to the view of some modern pedagogues, Luther stressed the need of *memorizing* the Catechism. He was satisfied with a minimum—the first three Chief Parts and the words of Institution, in the sections of Baptism and the Lord's Supper. He by no means overlooked the need of explanation and application, but as a foundation of thorough instruction he demanded that the teachers drill the Catechism text. As he says in his Introduction to the Small Catechism:

> Young and simple persons must be taught a definite text; otherwise, if you teach a certain form this year and another the next, you will simply confuse them, and your labor will be lost. Settle on a certain form and stick to it forever, then drill it word for word until they are able to know and recite it. (SC Preface, 7)

Self-evidently, it was not Luther's opinion that instruction or memorizing should end here. In the preface to the Small Catechism, he says:

> After you have thus taught them this Short Catechism, then take up the Large Catechism, and give them also a richer and fuller knowledge. Here explain at length every commandment, petition, and part with its various works, uses, benefits, dangers, and injuries as you find these abundantly stated in many books written about these matters. (SC Preface, 17)

Then, as Luther often repeats, Bible verses, hymns and Psalms were also to be memorized and explained.

Luther also laid great stress on the correct understanding. To him instruction did not mean mere mechanical memorizing, but conscious, personal, enduring, and applicable spiritual appropriation. He says: "After they [the children] have well learned the text, then teach them the sense also, so that they know what it means" (SC Preface, 14). Correct understanding was everything to Luther. Sermons in the churches and catechizations at home were all to serve this purpose.

DOCUMENT 1.3:

Lessons from History (1958)

By Gerhard Friedrich Bente

Gerhard Friedrich Bente (1858–1930) "was an alert, keen mind, and [was] characteriz[ed] as one of the acutest and profoundest thinkers of the second generation of the [Missouri] Synod." He is best known for his work with the Concordia Triglotta (1921), a parallel edition of the Lutheran Confessions in Latin, German, and English. Bente was born January 22, 1858, in Wimmer, Hanover, Germany, to Johann and Ann Marie Bente. Early in his life (1866), his family emigrated to Cleveland, Ohio. In 1872, at the age of fourteen, Bente entered Concordia College at Fort Wayne, Indiana. Following his graduation in 1878, he continued his education at Concordia Seminary in St. Louis. Bente accepted his first call on February 12, 1882 to Ontario, Canada. In addition to his pastoral duties, Bente also taught at the church's Christian day school. After working as a teacher, Bente remarked, "Considered from the right angle, a school teacher has a most delightful work." In 1884, Bente accepted calls to two congregations in Ontario. Bente preached at each congregation every Sunday. On July 12, 1885, Bente was betrothed to Josephine Haserot, with whom he had eight children. In addition to serving several congregations, Bente was the Missouri Synod's District President of British Columbia and a member of the Synodical Committee on calls. Bente also received the English theological professorship at Concordia Seminary and edited Lehre und Wehre, Lutheraner, and the Homiletisches Magazin. Bente died on December 15, 1930. His influence long was felt in the ELS with the Concordia Triglotta and his historical introduction to that work. [DR]

Source: "Historical Introduction to the Symbolical Books of the Evangelical Lutheran Church," *Concordia Triglotta: The Symbolical Books of the Evangelical*

Lutheran Church (St. Louis: Concordia Publishing House, 1921), 1-266, at 69-70; rpt., *Lutheran Sentinel*, 26 Jan. 1958, 29.

In order to bring the instruction of the young into vogue, Luther saw that church, school, and home must needs cooperate. The home especially must not fail in this. Accordingly, in his admonitions, he endeavored to interest the fathers and mothers in this work. He was convinced that without their vigorous cooperation he could achieve but little. In his *German Order of Worship*, 1526, we read: "For if the parents and guardians are unwilling to take such pains with the young, either personally or through others, Catechism [instruction] will never be established."[27]

In this he was confirmed by the experiences he had while on his tour of visitation. If the children were to memorize the Catechism and learn to understand it, they must be instructed and questioned individually, a task to which the Church was unequal, and for the accomplishment of which also the small number of schools was altogether inadequate. Parents, however, were able to reach the children individually. They had the time and opportunity, too, morning, noon, and evening, at the table, etc. Furthermore, they had the greatest interest in this matter, the children being their own flesh and blood. And they, in the first place, were commanded by God to provide for the proper training of their children.

The fathers and mothers, therefore, these natural and divinely appointed teachers of the children, Luther was at great pains to enlist for the urgent work of instructing the young. They should see that the children and servants not only attended the Catechism-sermons in church, but also memorized the text and learned to understand it. The Christian homes should again become home-churches, homeschools, where the housefathers were both house-priests and house-teachers, performing the office of the ministry there just as the pastors did in the churches.

With ever-increasing energy Luther, therefore, urged the parents to study the Catechism in order to be able to teach it to their children.

---

[27] *Editors' note*: Martin Luther, *The German Mass and Order of Service* (1526), in *Luther's Works*, vol. 53, ed. Jaroslav Pelikan (Philadelphia: Fortress Press, 1965), 51-90, at 65.

Concordia Triglotta

Die symbolischen Bücher der evangelisch-lutherischen Kirche,

deutsch-lateinisch-englisch,

als Denkmal der vierhundertjährigen Jubelfeier der Reformation, anno Domini 1917, herausgegeben auf Beschluß der evangelisch-lutherischen Synode von Missouri, Ohio und andern Staaten.

CONCORDIA TRIGLOTTA

Libri symbolici Ecclesiae Lutheranae

Germanice-Latine-Anglice,

monumenti instar in memoriam Anni Iubilaei MCMXVII quadringentesimi post inchoatam Ecclesiae reformationem communi consilio et mandato Synodi Missouriensis Lutheranae typis vulgata.

TRIGLOT CONCORDIA

The Symbolical Books of the Ev. Lutheran Church,

German-Latin-English,

Published as a Memorial of the Quadricentenary Jubilee of the Reformation anno Domini 1917 by resolution of the Evangelical Lutheran Synod of Missouri, Ohio, and Other States.

ST. LOUIS, MO.
CONCORDIA PUBLISHING HOUSE.
1921.

The Triglot Concordia *remains to this day a standard reference for Lutheran theologians.*

DOCUMENT 1.4:

Instruction in the Home (1962)

By Wilhelm Petersen

Wilhelm Walther Petersen (1928–) *was born on October 17, 1928 in Scarville, Iowa, to Rev. and Mrs. Justin A. Petersen. As a boy, he attended Scarville Christian Day School and later enrolled at Bethany Lutheran High School in Mankato, Minnesota. He graduated from Bethany Lutheran College in 1948 and continued his studies at Northwestern College in Watertown, Wisconsin. After college, he returned to Mankato and enrolled at Bethany Lutheran Theological Seminary. He was ordained by Rev. C. M. Gullerud on June 14, 1953 at Our Savior's Lutheran Church in Albert Lea. That same year, Petersen married Naomi Madson. In the following years, the couple was blessed with six children. In July 1954, Pastor Petersen was installed for his second calling: the Clearwater Lutheran Parish in Oklee, Minnesota, which included also the Nazareth, Little Oak, and Oak Park congregations. He had been serving these churches during the preceding year when they*  *withdrew from the Evangelical Lutheran Church to seek a more conservative affiliation. He later filled pastoral positions at Grace Lutheran Church in Madison, Wisconsin, and Mt. Olive Lutheran Church in Mankato. From 1976 to 1980, Petersen served as synod president, and in 1982, at age 52, Peterson accepted the call to serve as president of Bethany Lutheran Theological Seminary. Rev. and Mrs. Petersen currently reside in North Mankato, Minnesota. A collection of*

Petersen's sermons, *A Brief Legacy*, was published in 2004.[28] [PK]

Source: *Lutheran Sentinel*, July 26, 1962, 217-18.

P arents have no greater responsibility towards their children than to instruct them in the *one thing needful*.[29] To fathers St. Paul writes, "provoke not your children to wrath: but bring them up in the nurture and admonition of the Lord" (Ephesians 6:4). Stating it negatively, the same apostle says, "But if any provide not for his own, and specially for those of his own house, he hath denied the faith, and is worse than an infidel" (1 Timothy 5:8). Martin Luther once said that "parents cannot earn hell more easily than by neglecting to give their children a Christian training."[30]

Christian parents may be tempted to think that if they send their children to Sunday school, vacation Bible school, or perhaps a Christian day school that then they have done their duty in instructing their children. Surely, a Christian parent will want to make use of these agencies which the church offers to feed the lambs, but what God told Moses to tell the parents of his day applies to us today, too, "And these words which I command thee this day, shall be in thine heart: and thou shalt teach them diligently unto thy children, and shalt talk of them when thou sittest in thine house and when thou walkest by the way, and when thou liest down, and when thou risest up" (Deuteronomy 6:6-7). From this we see that the important matter of instruction is not to be a hit-and-miss affair, but a constant daily thing *in the home*. In this picture we see a family gathered around a table where the father, or one of the family, reads a section from the Bible or devotional book; we see a mother reading a Bible story to her little ones at bedtime; we see a parent answering the hundred and one queries of the youngsters. Fortunate the children that are brought up in this atmosphere! To be pitied, truly pitied, are the children who never hear God's name mentioned in the home, except perhaps in cursing.

---

[28] Wilhelm W. Petersen, *A Brief Legacy* (2004); see also Alexander Ring, ed., *In Jesus' Name: A Festschrift of Sermons in Honor of Wilhelm Petersen* (Bloomington: AuthorHouse, 2006).

[29] *Editors' note*: The allusion is to Luke 10:42, which is the source of the motto of Bethany Lutheran College.

[30] *Editor's note*: The source has not been located.

Mention must also be made that a very important part of instruction on the part of the parents is a Christian example, for that, after all, is the most effective teacher. Someone has said that "example is the school of mankind, and they will learn at none other."[31] Children are very sensitive and can easily discern the sincerity, or insincerity, of the parent. Parents can preach until they are blue in the face, but if this is not backed up with a proper example, much of the instruction will be in vain. But parents who train up their children in the way they should go, both by word and deed, have God's promise, "and when he is old he will not depart from it" (Proverbs 22:6). Only eternity will reveal the many souls that have entered the joy of heaven because of the Christian instruction they received in the home.

---

[31] *Editor's note*: The source has not been located.

DOCUMENT 1.5:

The Task of Instruction (1974)

By Rodger Dale

Rodger Dale (1942–) has served in the public ministry for over forty years. He was born April 29, 1942 to Melvin and Pearl Dale in Fertile, Minnesota, where he completed his elementary and secondary education. Upon graduating from high school, Dale attended the University of North Dakota and Bethany Lutheran College, each for one year, and then transferred to Mankato State University, where he earned his B.A. in 1963. Dale spent the next four years completing his education for the pastoral ministry at Bethany Lutheran Theological Seminary. From his ordination at Thornton, Iowa, in 1967 to his current congregation in Florida, Dale has preached God's Word and administered the Sacraments to six congregations in four states. During 2000-2005, Dale performed various duties including: a chaplain position with the Lutheran Institutional Ministry Association, service as a vacancy pastor for various congregations in the Twin Cities area, and also  one year as a teacher at St. Croix Lutheran High School in West St. Paul. In 2006, Dale transferred to the Wisconsin Evangelical Lutheran Synod, in which he currently serves as pastor at Open Bible Lutheran Church in Oxford, Florida. Pastor Dale and his wife Connie have been blessed with four children and eight grandchildren.[32] [DR]

Source: *Synod Report* (1974), 47-53.

---

[32] Telephone interview with Rodger Dale, 20 Feb. 2010.

"So the word of God spread. The number of disciples in Jerusalem increased rapidly, and a large number of priests became obedient to the faith" (Acts 6:7). This summary note illustrates the effect of the stubbornly courageous testimony of the very early Christians in Jerusalem during the days following Pentecost. Reading the first chapters of Acts you get the definite impression the Jerusalem Christians were all "wrapped up" in their faith. They had a passion for Christ. They studied and continued in the word of the Apostles. They worshiped God both in "church" and in *life*. They were courageous against powerful resistance, even to the point of gladly dying for their Savior. The total effect of this kind of living was a witness so powerful no one could silence or even intimidate them. "So the Word of God spread. The number of disciples in Jerusalem increased rapidly, and a large number of priests became obedient to the faith."

How many Christians do you know who are "wrapped up" in their Christianity? How many have a passion for Christ like that of the early Christians? How many have a deep understanding of their commitment to Christ and what it implies about daily living? Why doesn't the total witness of the church today have an effect like it did in Jerusalem? . . .[33]

I believe we are in a rut. And I believe a good part of our problem is that twentieth-century Christians don't comprehend the greatness of God, the greatness of Christ's redemption, and the greatness of our Christian faith. We have the words and doctrine, but not the fruits of committed witness and life. . . .

When a baby is born in the hospital, strict rules are observed to provide the best possible environment for the new baby. As a result, the mortality rate among babies in America, prior to permissive abortion, was remarkably low. This shows the value of optimum environment.

The same is true of a garden. You can ensure success by planting the best seed at the right time in the best soil. The Lord usually provides suitable weather. By providing these optimum conditions, you ensure success.

Wouldn't it be nice if we could do the same with our cultural environment? If we could order society just as we want so our

---

[33] *Editors' note*: Here and elsewhere in this document, ellipses indicate places where the editors have, in the interest of space, chosen to omit certain sections of Dale's presentation, especially some of his longer block quotations of contemporary books evaluating the influence of television upon American youth.

children could grow up in an optimum environment? If we could avoid the temptations of the world? But since the Garden of Eden, this has not been known. Since Adam and Eve obeyed Satan, this world has never been a paradise.

Though culture has never been optimum "soil" for Christianity since Adam's sin, it is plain that our culture grows even more adverse day by day. Senior citizens often express fears for the children today. They have observed the hurried demise of Christ in our culture. As one observer put it, "Christ has been relegated to the position of an historical footnote."[34]

A good measuring stick of the changes in our culture is to compare the way of life of the thirties generation with that of the sixties; or even the fifties with the sixties. This great change has made possible the discovery of the generation gap.

Our culture is in a state of radical change as a result of technology, affluence, mobility, and the declining influence of Christianity. Our lives are revolutionized by technology. Former generations used to spend most of their time with the daily task of living. Now most of those tasks are done by machine or purchased as services. Ours is an "easy come—easy go" culture where hard work, industry, and even honesty are no longer necessary virtues.

Affluence seems to make people more concerned about such important things as diet and hairstyle than their standing with almighty God. Instead of returning to give thanks to God, nine of the ten thoughtlessly go off to enjoy their blessings. Instead of giving thanks to God, affluent man thinks he is more independent than ever. Affluence has led to hardcore covetousness. The proper stewardship of affluence is a heavy stewardship for the Christian.

Not to be underestimated is the important effect of our mobility. Our mobility contributes to the change in culture because it almost prevents us from having roots in the past. We physically move away from the influence of our parents and community where we would be likely to continue in their morals and beliefs. The traditional is not only considered outmoded; it is despised by the progressive person in our culture. To be called "traditional" about morals and beliefs is to be dismissed as irrelevant.

Thus it is only natural in these changing times for our society to part with its traditional moral values, for fornication to become acceptable and with it now, homosexuality. Our society is so totally

---

[34] *Editors' note*: The source has not been located, though the sentiment was broadly shared among American evangelicals during this period in history.

preoccupied with sensuality we even find the sale of cow's milk increasing when sensuality is introduced into its advertising.

Bored, our rootless youth turn to drugs and new lifestyles, in search of the *real*, the Rock upon which to stand. Meanwhile, the Rock of Ages is a culturally neglected possibility. This is the most regrettable development; almost all that rested upon the Rock in our former culture is being swept away. And it is doubtful such movements as the "Jesus People" will recover the Rock for our culture. It is likely the next disoriented generation will drift even further from the only stable foundation for life, Jesus Christ.

Such culture is anything but an optimum environment for children and for our task of Christian instruction. But the task is not impossible. If we ever think it is, we should consider how Timothy could grow up in Greek-Roman culture, which was even more Christ-less. Or we should consider Joseph, who kept his bearings in Egypt, and Daniel in Babylon. Their Christian instruction had prepared them for the challenges of their culture.
. . .

To get to the point: while we accept the immense value of mass communications for society, we also regret that their potential is exploited for evil in pornographic books, pictures, and movies. Any newsstand provides a demonstration with numerous covers featuring nudity. All the movies but those rated G are likely to include vulgarity, cursing, violence, and explicit sex.

Popular songs, often an underestimated form of communication, have had a part in popularizing such things as the drug cult. But the constantly confused definition of love portrayed in popular songs has wider influence. It is predominately a self-gratification relationship. It is a "love" which does not recognize traditional morality. . . . There is no mention of marriage as a prerequisite.

But when all is considered, television probably has far and away the greatest impact on our society of any mass communication. TV is so pervasive. Dr. John D. Haney says, "By the time a youth graduates from high school today, he has viewed approximately 15,000 hours of television and taken in 500 motion pictures. During the same period he has spent 11,000 hours in school. . . . Television is their third parent and first teacher."[35]

The home is still the most important part of the child's environment. No one has more opportunity to influence children than parents. Notice I said *opportunity* to influence. This is

---

35 John D. Haney, n.t., *Instructor*, February 1971, n.p.

corroborated by no less authority than Scripture itself. Dr. Howard Hendricks, chairman of the Christian Education Department, Dallas Theological Seminary, in a recent book called *Heaven Help the Home* says: "Columbia University spent a quarter of a million dollars in research, only to corroborate the truth of Scripture. Conclusion: there is no second force in the life of a child compared with the impact of his home. The compelling crisis today is the training and equipping of parents to do the job."[36]

The American home, by far the most important school for Christianity, is in shambles. And of all the reasons, one of the foremost is that we think we are too busy to practice the basic principles of Christian living. Our lives are busy, but too often we confuse self-centeredness with legitimate tasks. To have a successful home we must serve each other, not ourselves.

Children in today's average American home suffer from what we might call "parental drain." Their parents "drain" themselves with their own activities so that little is left of them, emotionally, to give to their children. Parents need the little time they have at home to relax. Children are often made to feel like intruders upon their parent's badly needed relaxation. The obvious problem is that children are placed lower on the list of priorities than work and recreation. The results are tragic.

Parents, especially working mothers, ought to consider carefully whether they are "burning themselves out" for others and for unnecessary material benefits so that little is left for their most important possession of all, their children. The higher standard of living offers little satisfaction to a child who lacks the comfort of parental attention and guidance. The lack of understanding in teen years most surely results from lack of communication ten years earlier. This is not to say that a mother cannot work outside the home or that the father cannot be busy. We are saying that children should not be "sacrificed" on the list of priorities because of covetousness. Children should be given the highest priority next to God himself.

But by far the most critical problem in the average American home is the lack of family worship—real, creative worship. Religion is practiced as a sideline. Too often religion is compartmentalized into the Sunday morning slot. The rest of the week, God is just on call. Even in homes where there are daily devotions, they are usually not as creative and effective as they

---

[36] Howard Hendricks, *Heaven Help the Home* (n.p.: Victor Books, n.d.), 22.

Pastor Rodger Dale (left) sits with colleagues Paul Jecklin, Torald Teigen, Steven Quist, Erling Teigen, and James Lillo at a February 1969 pastoral conference.

should be.

The successful family in this culture must learn to know and worship God in their home, the arena of greatest influence. Children must learn in the home to know God's Word well enough to meet challenges to their faith. We emphasize the home because it is estimated that the average child is under the influence and instruction of the church only one percent of the time.[37] A Christian day school education raises the percentage considerably, but even so, a masterful job of education must be performed in the home to meet the challenges of today's culture.

Dr. Hendricks compares child-raising in today's environment to building a fire in the rain:

> Inculcating Christian standards is like building a fire in the rain. It requires willful determination, against all odds, to do what seems impossible. It calls for expertise—for know-how which understands the nature of the child and the nature of the hostile world. It demands a stubborn perseverance to keep fanning the flickering flame, to keep protecting the hot coals. A warm young life, glowing for Christ, is the most needed commodity in the damp, depressing chill of the marketplace

---

[37] Ibid., 21.

today.[38]

The church must recognize the plight of the American family home and cease to neglect the task of helping families perform their great task of instruction.

Furthermore, the church ought to consider its educational priorities. At the present time most programs are aimed at children. Teenagers, college students, adults, parents, and families are neglected. Lawrence O. Richards, professor at Wheaton Graduate School, has written a book called *A New Face for the Church*, in which he speculates about the future church. To a skeptical visitor at his future church who asks why there is not vacation Bible school and Sunday school, a character in the book replies:

> We care about children so much that we make sure they have a Christian home to grow up in. We go out and face adults; that's how much we care about kids. We don't sneak around and spend all our time with children because we're scared to death of grown-ups!"[39]

The home is the critical arena. It always will be. God meant it that way. Dr. Hendricks tells us about a famous pastor, Richard Baxter, who for three years preached with all the passion of his heart in his parish. Finally, one day, he threw himself on the floor and said to God, "O God, you must do something with these people or I'll die." Then:

> He said, "It was as if God spoke to me audibly, 'Baxter, you are working in the wrong place. You're expecting revival to come through the church. Try the home.'"
>
> Richard Baxter went out and called on home after home. He spent entire evenings in the homes helping parents set up family worship times with their children. He moved from one home to another. Finally the Spirit of God started to light fires all over that congregation until they swept through the church and made it the great church that it became—and made Baxter a man of godly distinction.[40]

---

[38] Ibid., 63.
[39] Lawrence O. Richards, *A New Face for the Church* (n.p.: Zondervan, n.d.), 270.
[40] Hendricks, *Heaven Help the Home*, 88.

The task of instruction in the light of modern conditions is a humbling one. Defections from the Christian faith, especially among the youth, force us to recognize our shortcomings. The haunting difference between the witness of the church in Jerusalem and today's church indicates a lack of understanding and commitment to the Christian faith. The church today needs more than superficial modifications in its education program. A path here and there will only treat symptoms. The church needs a revival.

Revival must begin with recognition of our failure as a church to appreciate and live the faith we hold. With sincere repentance we must seek from God the power and direction of His Holy Spirit. We must repent that we are so secular and unspiritual, so dull and so slow of heart to believe. We must surrender to Jesus Christ and renounce all that competes with Him. Then our lives will more fully be controlled by Him, our witness to the world will be powerful, and we will have the basis for communicating to our members, our children, and to the world a living Christianity, as opposed to the common variety known as "nominal Christianity."

DOCUMENT 1.6:

The Responsibility of Instruction (1974)

By Raymond M. Branstad

Raymond Marcellus Branstad (1916–2009) was born August 26, 1916 in Leland, Minnesota, but grew up in Lake Mills, Iowa. As a high school student Branstad worked for the local newspaper, but his pastor encouraged him to enter the ministry. He attended Bethany Lutheran College, earning an Associate of Arts degree. Branstad next attended Concordia Seminary in St. Louis, Missouri. He later earned a masters degree from the University of Minnesota and also pursued graduate work at the University of Wisconsin and Harvard University. Branstad was ordained in 1943 and served parishes in Duluth, Minnesota; Suttons Bay and Holton, Michigan; Eau Claire, Wisconsin; Minneapolis, Minnesota; Golden Valley, Minnesota; and finally Mayville, North Dakota, where he retired in 1995. He served as president of Bethany Lutheran College from 1970 to 1978. Raymond Branstad was blessed with a wife, one son, four daughters, twelve grandchildren, and five great-grandchildren. The following article assesses the delicate relationship between parents and the state when considering Christian education.[DR]

Source: *Synod Report* (1974), 54-61.

Christian education begins with the premise that responsibility for a child is basically that of its parents. The child, as a creation of God, belongs to God but is given to parents who have a God-given responsibility to train him up in the way he should go. Proverbs 22:6: "Train up a child in the way he should go and when he is old, he will not depart from it."

Because it is Scriptural, it is also Lutheran. Luther regarded the right training of children as a divine requirement. Parents are not free to do with their children as they please. They are entrusted with parental authority that they may train up their children for society and the church, and they are held to a strict account for the manner in which they discharge this duty. This thought is presented again and again in Luther's writing. He says:

> But this is again a sad evil that all live on as though God gave us children for our pleasure or amusement, and servants that we should employ them like a cow or ass, only for work, or as though all we had to do with our subjects were only to gratify our wantonness, without any concern on our part as to what they learn or how they live; and no one is willing to see that this is the command of the Supreme Majesty, who will most strictly call us into an account and punish us for it, nor that there is so great a need to be so intensely anxious about the young. For if we wish to have proper and excellent persons both for civil and ecclesiastical government, we must spare no diligence, time, or cost in teaching and educating our children, that they may serve God and the world; we must not think only how we may amass money and possessions for them. . . . Let everyone know, therefore, that above all things it is his duty (or otherwise he will lose the divine favor) to bring up his children in the fear and knowledge of God; and if they have talents, to have them instructed and trained in a liberal education, that men may be able to have their aid in government and in whatever is necessary. (LC I, 170-71)

Luther is not content with merely showing parents their duty. He urges them to its performance. The divine requirements are set forth; the evils resulting to society and the church through neglect of their children are clearly pointed out; their gratitude to God and their obligations to mankind are urged as motives; and the guilt and punishment they bring upon themselves and their children are fully portrayed. Hear what he writes in the Large Catechism:

> Think what deadly injury you are doing if you be negligent and fail to bring up your child to usefulness and piety, and how

you bring upon yourself all sin and wrath, meriting hell even in your dealings with your own children, even though you be otherwise ever so pious and holy. And because this is disregarded, God so fearfully punishes the world that there is no discipline, government, or peace, of which we all complain, but do not see that it is our fault, for as we train them we have spoiled and disobedient children and subjects. (LC I, 176–77)

Protestant Christians generally have held that the parent or guardian of a child has the right and duty to determine that child's education. It would seem that most Americans share this view. The impetus for the "ward of the state" concept, which we will discuss later, took a dramatic turn by World War II when Americans were shocked by the Nazi takeover of the youth. The tales of children informing on their parents and turning them in as enemies of the state caused Americans to shudder in horror.

The state acknowledges the right and duty to determine the child's education. In the 1920s a law was passed by the state of Oregon giving the state the ultimate right to determine the child's education, by requiring all children to attend the public schools of that state. But the law was struck down by the U.S. Supreme Court with the famous words:

> The child is not a mere creature of the state; those who nurture him and direct his destiny have the right, coupled with the high duty, to recognize and prepare him for additional obligations.[41]

While we may not dispute the prime responsibility of parents and home, and the principle remains a constant, the assumption of that responsibility and the extent to which the home can function as an education unit are variables.

It would seem logical that since America has the highest literacy rate of any nation of all time, the American home should be better able to assume responsibility for the education of its children and be able to provide more education in the home than at any time in history. Unfortunately, other factors prevent this ideal, and American home life has changed radically in the last few decades.

Already twenty years ago, the National Evangelical Association published a report, which it commissioned Dr. Frank E. Gaebelein to write, in which he stated:

---

[41] *Pierce v. Society of Sisters*, 268 U.S. 510, 535 (1925).

> It is not easy to evaluate sociological trends, least of all those of our own day. Yet few thoughtful observers can fail to recognize that something has been happening to the American home during the first half of this century. We are not just "viewing with alarm" when we speak of the decline of family life[;] we are discussing facts.
>
> That nothing short of a revolution in respect to the most basic unit of society has been taking place is apparent. Not that the American home is in danger of changing—it has changed, and we are faced with a *fait accompli* [an already accomplished fact] in that the home built upon spiritual and moral ideals, the center of life for parents and children, is no longer characteristic of America. The shift from country to city; a plethora of amusements from movies to radio and television; greatly increased leisure with insufficient inner resources to use it well; automobiles for almost everyone; alcoholic intemperance; divorce so prevalent that only two out of three marriages endure; men and women who, having been given a thoroughly secularized education, think they can do very well without God—all these are factors in the decline of the American home.[42]

Another factor, to which this report does not refer, is the economic one. World War II brought women out of the home and into the labor force as a war effort. Women never really went back to the house. Higher standards and higher costs of living have kept them out. As Gaebelein states, we are discussing facts, not dangers, when we speak of the decline of family life in America. Therefore we must do a great deal more than preach an ideal, we must face facts and deal with the problem as it is.

While the responsibility for the education of children rests primarily with parents in the home, it is quite another issue whether the home is capable of providing this education. In general, it must be said that the home never has had this capability. Cultures which have relied upon the home for the total education of children have been extremely slow to progress and have often failed to rise above a minimal level. In most cultures, parents have sought help outside the home to aid in the education of their children.

In the Christian context, the church shares the responsibility

---

[42] *Editors' note*: Frank E. Gaebelein, *Christian Education in Democracy: The Report of the N[ational] A[ssociation of] E[vangelicals for United Action] Committee* (New York: Oxford University Press, 1951), 237.

for the education of its children. What the parents cannot do alone, they have the right and duty to ask the church, the fellowship of believers, to do for them. So the church organizes, maintains, and supports schools of various types in accordance with need and popularity.

Again this is scriptural. Jesus commanded His disciples, not as parents, but as founders and leaders of the New Testament church: "Feed my lambs.... Feed my sheep" (John 21:15-17).

One cannot easily imagine the Christian who would argue that it is not the responsibility of the church, as well as parents, to provide spiritual training—religious education—for old and young. No one would argue that it is not the church's responsibility to provide more advanced training for pastors. This is one of the basic reasons for organizing larger church units, such as synods. But frequently there is an argument as to the church's responsibility for providing schools for what are called "secular" or "liberal arts" subjects. These are regarded as the responsibility of parents—or parents and the state.

This is not the problem of a state-church system. So it was not a problem for Luther and the Reformers. As we heard earlier, Luther believed in a "liberal education," i.e., not only what might be called strictly religious subjects, but also the languages, which he held in extremely high regard, "poets and orators whether they are heathen or Christian, Greek or Latin," arts and sciences, law and medicine.[43]

Naturally Luther placed the greatest importance on religious instruction, and he declared it to be the first duty of the parental relation. He writes: "See to it that you first of all have your children instructed in spiritual things, giving them first to God and afterwards to secular duties."[44]

At the same time, Luther recognized the difficulties, if not the impossibility, of adequate home training. Some parents are so lacking in piety, he believed, that like the ostrich they hardened themselves against their own offspring (Job 39:13-18). Others, by reason of their ignorance, are unqualified to raise children in a proper manner. And still others, who have the requisite piety and intelligence, are constantly burdened with cares and labors. As a matter of fact, Luther states that only such persons should marry

---

[43] Editors' note: Martin Luther, "To the Councilmen of All Cities in Germany, That They Establish Christian Schools" (1524), in *Luther's Works*, vol. 45, ed. Helmut T. Lehmann (Philadelphia: Fortress Press, 1962), 376.

[44] F. V. N. Painter, *Luther on Education* (St. Louis: Concordia Publishing House, 1965), 120.

as are competent to instruct their children in the elements of religion. "No one should become a father," he says, "unless he is able to instruct his children in the Ten Commandments and in the Gospel, so that he may bring up true Christians."[45] He was, however, realistic enough to recognize that such an ideal was beyond attainment. This he offered as another important reason for establishing schools to assist parents in their responsibility.

In the context of his times, Luther did not hesitate to appeal to the state rather than the church to establish and maintain schools for Christian education. His "Letter to the Mayors and Aldermen" of all the cities of Germany is a passionate appeal for "public" Christian education and led to what is often regarded as the first truly public educational system. . . .[46]

It would be a gross misunderstanding of Luther to insist that, because of his appeal to public officials, he indicated that he believed the liberal arts not to be the responsibility of the church. The fact is, he made no distinction between the sacred and secular in education. He did not compartmentalize education. . . .

Luther appealed to the government because the Lutheran church, newly separated from Roman Catholicism, was not in a financial position to establish the schools he proposed and, further, in the state-church system, he did not hesitate to ask the state to support Christian education. . . .

After the parents and the church, the state is an order authorized by God to promote the temporal welfare of the people.

That the state has a responsibility for its citizens is not challenged by the Christian. Scripture delineates their responsibility and authority from Romans chapter 13. Luther and the Lutheran Confessions expound this responsibility.

Included in this responsibility is a concern of government for the education of its citizens. Luther not only acknowledged such a responsibility, he placed it squarely on the shoulders of civic officials in his "Letter to the Aldermen and Mayors." He pointed out the necessity of education, not only for the maintenance of Christianity, but also for the civic government, and he concluded: "Therefore, dear sirs, take to heart this work, which God so urgently requires at your hands, which pertains to your office,

---

[45] Ibid., 119.

[46] *Editors' note*: Here and elsewhere in this document, ellipses indicate places where the editors have, in the interest of space, chosen to omit certain sections of Branstad's presentation, especially some of his longer block quotations from Luther, which are sufficiently referenced elsewhere in this volume.

which is necessary for the young, and which neither the world nor the spirit can do without."[47]

Surely in a democratic form of government such as ours, where the government is "of the people, by the people, and for the people," this responsibility is no less urgent.[48] In order for such a form of government to function, it must have an "enlightened electorate"—voters who not only can read, write, and count, but can make sound judgments by analyzing and evaluating what they see and hear.

Thus far there is no argument. The problem is the extent of this responsibility. For Luther, as we pointed out earlier, this was no problem. In the state-church system, an education which served the good of the state served the good of the church, for the rulers and citizens of the state were also members of the same church.

In our form of government, which guarantees the freedom of religion and forbids discrimination, the problem is a crucial and a sensitive one. How can the state assume its responsibilities without infringing upon the freedom of its constituents or discriminating against any of them? . . .

The responsibility of education must be shared by home, church, and state. In various areas they will overlap in responsibility. The prime responsibility rests with the parents. This is God-given. But parents may and must turn to the church and to the state to share this responsibility. . . .

---

[47] Painter, *Luther on Education*, 202.
[48] *Editors' note*: Abraham Lincoln, "Gettysburg Address" (1863).

DOCUMENT 1.7:

The Priesthood of Parents (1976)

By Ardella Emery

Ardella Emery *was a member of Bethany Lutheran Church in Luverne, Minnesota. The following essay is one of seven articles that Emery wrote for the Lutheran Sentinel during the mid 1970s. The expositions explain God's intention for the Christian family. She addresses the distinct vocations of husbands, wives, children, and parents. Mrs. Emery demonstrates how even those who are not in the public ministry are able to use their gifts for spreading the gospel of peace. She lived by example. Her work shows how lay people's actions may flow from a heart of faith rooted in that gospel.* [DR]

Source: *Lutheran Sentinel*, 24 June 1976, 186-88.

When I see myself in the mirror, as a wife and mother, it's hardly the picture I had in my mind of a priest. But I am, and my husband is also. Everyone who is a Christian is a priest. As parents, it is our responsibility to be priests to our children. We have been called and ordained by God to be priests right here, in our own home.

Martin Luther, during the Reformation, rediscovered a basic teaching of the Bible, which is the priesthood of all believers. "But you are a chosen people, a royal priesthood, a holy nation, a people belonging to God, that you may declare the praises of Him who called you out of darkness into His wonderful light" (1 Peter 2:9). This Bible verse gives each one of us, because we believe, a personal access to God. We are called to be priests to each other: to pray to God, and to present God to our children.

We present God to our children by setting an example, first of all, in our attitude, which must be one of love and devotion to God. "Hear, O Israel: The Lord our God is one Lord: And thou shalt love the Lord thy God with all thine heart and with all thy soul, and with all thy mind" (Deuteronomy 6:4-5). Just going to church every Sunday morning isn't enough. We need to have a living relationship with Jesus in our homes. If we don't, our children may grow up believing that religion is nothing more than dry rules and regulations without joy. The atmosphere in our home should be that of joy and peace and love, as described in the familiar passages of Galatians 5:22-23. The young people who rebel against God are often rebelling against dead religious formalism.

"And these words which I command thee this day, shall be in thine heart" (Deuteronomy 6:6). If we want our children to know God, we must first know Him ourselves, *"in our hearts."* We can know God by regularly studying His Word. Each person has the primary responsibility of feeding himself with God's Word. Begin by spending ten or fifteen minutes reading the Bible. The New International Version of the New Testament is written in the language of today and is easy to understand. A Bible study guide is of great help, too. A good place to begin is with the book of John. Read a few passages. Read them again and really think about them. Then pray. Pray for yourself, pray for the understanding of His Word, for your family, or for a friend. "I tell you the truth, My Father will give you whatever you ask in My name. Until now you have not asked for anything in My name. Ask and you will receive, and your joy will be complete" (John 16:23b-24). Through prayer, we establish a very personal relationship with Jesus, and when we show our children that we are giving our time to God, they learn that God is important to them.

Prayer in our daily lives cannot be overemphasized. No amount of church going can make up for a parent who does not pray regularly. And, when you ask something of God, look for an answer. An unanswered prayer is half a prayer. Try keeping a "Prayer Diary" and writing down each request you make of God—then note how and when God answers prayers. Prayer was of vital importance to many great men of God, such as Moses, Elijah, Daniel, and the apostles. The disciples asked Jesus to teach them how to pray. "One day, Jesus was preaching in a certain place. When he finished, one of his disciples said to Him, 'Lord, teach us to pray, just as John taught his disciples'" (Luke 11:1). They noted

> *"The setting for this short sketch is a little room just off from the living-room in a northern Minnesota farm home. There, every school day, the two children of the home, Luther and Lois [Vangen] by name, are busy in the pursuit of knowledge, not alone of the things that pertain to this life but, above all, to the eternal. The mother is the teacher.*
>
> *"When Luther was six years and three months old and Lois just five [1923], we began the study of the Norwegian language. We also devoted a short period each day to singing, and to reading, in unison, the five parts of the Catechism (not Luther's explanation) until memorized. . . . It has been a conglomeration of joy, peace, happiness, companionship, sacrifice, work, shortcomings. . . . Soli Deo Gloria."*
>
> Mrs. O. M. Vangen, "The Vangen School,"
in Jubilee Souvenir, 1853–1928
(Mankato, MN: Norwegian Synod, 1928), 22, 23.

that his power rose out of prayer.

Prayer has been an unending source of joy and comfort and peace in my personal life. Prayer has come to be relatively easy for me—when I am alone with the Lord. Offering a prayer, in the presence of my family is for me, to this day, very difficult. However, our children returned home from Bible Camp a few years ago and brought with them the idea that everyone at the table should have a turn at saying a prayer during family devotions. The moment came for me, and I knew I had to come up with something, since their reaction to my suggestion of a "silent prayer" was negative, and they didn't seem to think a prayer book was necessary either. . . . "Dear Lord, Thank you for the food we ate tonight. Thank you for my family. Watch over them tonight. Amen." Speaking the words aloud was a whole new experience for me. But God did hear. He did watch over us. This is what is important. He always hears us.

Parents are also to present God to their children by teaching.

We must take time for family worship. Worship is communion with God in which we receive his grace. Family worship makes God the center, instead of ourselves. Our family worship will vary according to the needs of the family, the ages of the children, and other circumstances. Some suggestions would be to read from a Bible story book or a devotion book; read the Bible; pray and teach the children to pray; learn a hymn; memorize some Bible verses. We have a simple family ritual where we join our hands in praying the Lord's Prayer together.

Our aim must be to cultivate a personal relationship with Jesus Christ through the power of the Holy Spirit; read John 14:16-20. We must relate to Jesus on a spiritual level, "God is spirit, and his worshipers must worship in spirit and in truth" (John 4:24). Jesus is Savior and we need His forgiveness, His love, and His acceptance, "This is love: not that we loved God, but that He loved us and sent His Son as an atoning sacrifice for our sins" (1 John 4:10).

As parents, we must present our children to God in prayer. Because we are priests, it is our primary responsibility to pray for our children and to ask the blessing of God upon them. If we do not pray for our children, we should not be surprised if they do not turn out well.

It is only with the help of God—which we must constantly seek through prayer—that we as parents can hope for success.

> Lord Jesus, forgive us if we have not used Your divine Word to instruct our children as we should have. And as we receive Your forgiveness, help us in our family to be kind and considerate, loving and forgiving to each other.
>
> With Your presence, bless our home and the homes and lives of those with whom we have enjoyed fellowship during our study of the Christian family. Help all of us to be prayerful people who come to You many times each day in prayer, sharing with You our needs, our joys, and our troubles. Also, help us to face the problems of everyday living as they come, and make us thankful for one another.
>
> Strengthen our faith and grant that we may strive more diligently to train our children according to Your Holy Word.
>
> This I pray in Jesus' name. Amen.

DOCUMENT 1.8:

Education Philosophy: Who Should Teach Your Children? (2008)

By Ryan C. MacPherson

Dr. Ryan C. MacPherson (1974–) teaches courses in American history, the history of science, and bioethics at Bethany Lutheran College in Mankato, Minnesota. He graduated with an A.A. in Liberal Arts from Bethany in 1995, followed by a B.A. in Integrative Studies at Arizona State University in 1997 and a Ph.D. in History and Philosophy of Science at the University of Notre Dame in 2003. Dr. MacPherson also has completed several courses at Bethany Lutheran Theological Seminary, where he has been enrolled part-time concurrent with his teaching duties at the college. As a husband, father, and former Sunday school superintendent, he has a strong passion for Christian education in both the home and the church. "Dr. Mac," as his students call him, is the founding president of The Hausvater Project, a nonprofit organization promoting a confessional Lutheran vision for family, church, and society (www.hausvater.org). His devotional writings have appeared frequently in the  Lutheran Sentinel *and other periodicals of the ELS and its sister church body, the Wisconsin Evangelical Lutheran Synod. Since 2004, he has served on the Board of Directors of the Evangelical Lutheran Synod Historical Society.*

Source: *Lutheran Sentinel*, Sept. 2008, 3.

Every child needs a Christian education.

Children are not born with knowledge of their Savior's love for them; rather, they receive this knowledge through the "baptism" and "teaching" referred to in the Great Commission (Matthew 28:19-20). Nor are children born with a "blank slate" ready to be filled with God's truth; rather, they are born with a sinful nature, predisposing their minds against God (Romans 8:7). Children, no less than adults, need to "be transformed by the renewing of [their] mind[s]" (Romans 12:2). The first source of their education is generally their parents.

Every parent is an educator.

Whether you feel qualified or not, if you are a parent, you are an educator. This is true not only because children are like sponges that soak up lessons from the people in their lives—especially from their parents—but also because God, who invented parenthood, wills that parents are educators (Ephesians 6:4). Education is not optional; it is integral to the parent-child relationship and begins already with the natural rhythms of feedings and diaper changes, progressing into the child's first steps and first words—and the first folding of one's hands for prayer.

Every Christian parent is a Christian educator.

"These commandments that I give you today," said God to his Old Testament people, "are to be upon your hearts. Impress them on your children. Talk about them when you sit at home and when you walk along the road, when you lie down and when you get up" (Deuteronomy 6:6-7). "Fathers, do not exasperate your children," spoke God to his New Testament people, "instead, bring them up in the training and instruction of the Lord" (Ephesians 6:4). Parents appropriately respond, "We will tell the next generation the praiseworthy deeds of the Lord" (Psalm 78:4).

A "Noah's Ark" theme in the nursery, family devotions at bedtime, table prayers at mealtime—these all are the beginnings of Christian education in the home. Nativity sets during Advent, a birthday cake for Baby Jesus at Christmas, family hymn sings, memory work, discipline informed by Law and Gospel—these home education experiences water the precious seeds that are planted in Holy Baptism. No wonder Martin Luther referred to fathers and mothers as the pastors and priests of their households, for that truly is what Christian parents are.

Every pastor is a Christian educator.

Pastors, too, are educators. It has been said that children belong to their parents by birth and to their congregation by baptism. Hence, the pastor of the congregation includes children in his ministry. Pastors provide Christian education to children through children's sermons, Sunday school classes, vacation Bible school, and youth confirmation class. The divine service also educates children, as they become familiar with God's Law and Gospel through the liturgy, hymns, Bible readings, and sermons, and as they crane their necks over adults' heads to witness a baptism that reminds them of their own.

All other educators either supplement or replace parents and pastors—so be careful about choosing which teachers will serve your children.

Teachers assist parents in the education of their children, as Dr. Luther wrote: "Where a father is unable by himself to bring up his child, he calls upon a schoolmaster to teach him" (LC I, 141). Teachers, both within the congregation and within secular society, can provide valuable assistance. But the responsibility remains with parents and pastors to ensure that such teachers truly are supplementing, rather than replacing, what the parents, pastor, and congregation have been teaching their children.

Children enrolled in public schools face special dangers because the curriculum often replaces the Christian education of the home and church with false doctrines concerning both God and man. The parents and pastors of children enrolled in public schools must stand ready to identify and counteract these harmful influences. For example, science lessons may teach that people have animals as ancestors, health lessons may teach that any sexual "lifestyle" is just as good as another, and social studies lessons may teach that all world religions are basically the same. Such teaching is not supplementing, but replacing, the Christian doctrines that God revealed in His Word: that He created Adam and Eve specially, that sexuality is a gift for marriage (which of course must be between one man and one woman), and that in Christ alone—not Muhammad, Buddha, or any other—do we find

God's gift of eternal life.

Parochial schools, in this regard, have a distinct advantage. When properly established, they faithfully assist parents and pastors in the Christian upbringing of children. However, the responsibility remains with parents and pastors to ensure that such schools are Christian in more than just name. God's Word must permeate the entire curriculum, so that His promise to Israel may be claimed as our own: "All your sons will be taught by the Lord, and great will be your children's peace" (Isaiah 54:13).

The Holy Spirit is your child's best educator.

When you homeschool your children—and all parents are homeschoolers to some degree—be sure that you are bringing them to what Luther called "the schoolhouse of the Holy Spirit," namely, God's Word.[49] If you enroll your children in a school, keep in mind that Christian schools uniquely employ God's Word as a light for your children's path (Psalm 119:105). Whatever doubts you may have about your own abilities, be confident in the promise God attaches to His command for parents: "Train a child in the way he should go, and when he is old he will not turn from it" (Proverbs 22:6).

---

[49] *Editors' note*: The allusion is to Luther's advice to "leave the job of teacher to the Holy Spirit," *Luther's Works, Vol. 1: Lectures on Genesis Chapters 1-5*, ed. Jaroslav Pelikan (St. Louis: Concordia Publishing House, 1958), 5.

SECTION 2:

Christian Day Schools

Introduction

By Norman A. Madson, Jr.

Where the Holy Scriptures do not rule, there I certainly do not advise any one to send his child. All must be ruined where the Word of God is not constantly exercised.

Martin Luther[1]

The Christian Day School is still the prince of all church schools. Dr. Walther has rightly called it the "Gem of the Lutheran Church." And it is a gem!

Theodore Aaberg[2]

---

[1]   As quoted in **Document 2.2**.

It was my good fortune to attend a Lutheran Christian day school for the first eight years of my formal education. It was also my good fortune to serve for nine years in a parish that had a Christian day school. That two-fold experience allows me to say "Amen" to the statement made above by Dr. C. F. W. Walther, a prominent American Lutheran of the nineteenth century, and repeated by Pastor Theodore A. Aaberg, a leader in our synod a century later: "The Christian day school is the gem of the Lutheran Church."

One year while serving in a parish that had a Christian day school, it came time to make preparations for observing an anniversary of the school. In doing so I was looking through old church bulletins for some historical information and ran across this:

> On January 1, 1960, our congregation [Western Koshkonong Lutheran Church, Cottage Grove, Wisconsin] will become the recipient of another wonderful gift. The Misses Clara and Alice Teisberg have informed the pastor that on that day, our congregation will be given possession of the late Alex Stephens farm north of Nora, which will be known as the Earle Teisberg Memorial Trust Farm. The income of which is to be used for our Christian day school, especially for transporting pupils. How thankful we should be for such good friends of our Christian day school. May their gift inspire us to ever greater heights in the matter of our stewardship. May God bless both the gift and the givers.[3]

Why do you suppose those two sisters singled out the Christian day school in their area as the part of a congregation's work to which they gave such a generous gift? No doubt it was because they had seen through the years what a blessing that particular Christian day school had been. And their gift was just another way for them to say, "Thank you, God, for Christian day schools!"

As the essays in this section point out, starting and maintaining Christian day schools has always been a high priority in our Evangelical Lutheran Synod. In a 1928 Synod Convention essay, marking the seventy-fifth anniversary of the Old Norwegian Synod and the tenth anniversary of the reorganized Norwegian

---

[2] As quoted in **Document 2.4**.
[3] Bulletin for Easter Sunday, 1959 (Cottage Grove, WI: Western Koshkonong Lutheran Church, 1959).

Synod, my father, Norman A. Madson, Sr. stated: "Not only have we proportionately more Christian day schools in our reorganized Synod than ever was to be found in the Synod of the past, but we can truthfully say that it has been given the chief place of prominence on the program of our church" (**Document 2.1**). Similarly, Rev. Aaberg in an essay delivered at the 1951 Synod Convention states: "If one were to look at the reports of our past Synod meetings, or to page through the old Church papers, he would rightly come to the conclusion that our Synod has been a strong champion of the Christian day school" (**Document 2.4**).

That the Christian day school is far and away the best means for the organized church to carry out the Lord's command to teach the young "all things whatsoever I have commanded you" (Matthew 28:20), is attested to by the fact that even in our foreign fields of labor today, like Peru and the Czech Republic, the starting and maintaining of such schools has become one of the primary objectives of our mission teams (**Documents 2.7** and **2.8**). Here in our homeland the importance of such an endeavor is shown by our Synod's recent establishment of "Lutheran Schools of America" (LSA), an arm of the church dedicated to establishing and maintaining Christian day schools. (See **Document 5.5** in **Section 5**: "A Christian Liberal Arts Education.")

Several of the essays included in this chapter also remind us that while there have been many different schools or agencies in use in our congregations—the Sunday school, the Saturday school, vacation Bible school in summertime, the release-time school during the school year, as well as the Christian day school (CDS)—there can be no argument as to which of all of those schools is the most effective in the Christian training of our children (**Documents 2.2, 2.3, 2.4,** and **2.5**). In answer to the question, "What kind of school will do the job best?," Rev. Theodore A. Aaberg, in his usual picturesque language, answers:

> If you have to haul ten tons of brick, and you are told to go out on the parking lot and take your pick of the vehicles there to do the job, and you go out and see a car, a pick-up, a station wagon and a large semi-truck, you will not hesitate to take the "semi" to haul the bricks. So it is with Christian education. When you see the job that is to be done, you look over the means of doing it, and you pick the best way there is to do the job. (**Document 2.4**)

And the best way, of course, is to use the Christian day school.

In an essay on Christian Education delivered at the 1966 Synod Convention, the Rev. Theodore A. Aaberg, who was instrumental in reopening the Christian day school at Scarville, Iowa, has given some wonderful advice in regard to starting and maintaining a Christian day school. His essay is deserving of a careful reading by pastors and congregations who are contemplating the opening of a Christian day school (**Document 2.6**).

"Children are an heritage of the LORD" (Psalm 127:3). And because they are the Lord's heritage, they are not to be brought up according to the whims and fancies of parents, but according to the will and command of the God who gave them. As Luther lamented:

> Everybody acts as if God gave us children for our pleasure and amusement . . . to treat them as we please, as if it were no concern of ours what they learn or how they live. No one is willing to see that this is the command of the divine Majesty, who will solemnly call us to account. . . . [He] has given and entrusted children to us with the command that we train and govern them according to His will. (LC I, 170)

And the Lord has some pretty specific directives regarding the religious training of children. He said to the mothers and fathers of ancient Israel, and those words are surely meant for mothers and fathers today: "And these words which I command thee this day, shall be in thine heart: and thou shall teach them diligently unto thy children, and shalt talk of them when thou sittest in thine house, and when thou walkest by the way, and when thou liest down, and when thou risest up" (Deuteronomy 6:6-7). In other words the religious training of our children is not to be a hit-and-miss affair. Nor should parents be satisfied with the least amount of religious instruction for their children. No, the directive is simple and clear—instruction in the Word of God is to be thorough and continuous!

The documents in **Section 1** identified the importance of parents providing Christian education to their children within the home; the documents in this section expand upon that theme as they consider the role of Christian elementary schools as an extension of the work that parents and pastors perform for the youth.

Chart 2.9 illustrates the long-term trend of the synod's Christian day school enrollment. It shows that the percentage of the synod's school-age children enrolled in CDSs fell below 10% in the 1960s, but then rose to nearly 50% by the century's end. In more recent years it has leveled off at about 40%. Although one might bemoan the fact that so few congregations in our synod have Christian day schools, we should rather praise and thank the Lord for the schools we do have. We should thank Him for the fathers, who like Manoah, the father of Samson in the Bible, prayed to the Lord: "O my Lord, let the man of God which Thou didst send, come again unto us, and teach us what we shall do unto the child that shall be born" (Judges 13:8). God bless the mothers who have the concern for their children that Hannah of old had for her miracle child, and who promised the Lord: "Therefore also I have lent him to the Lord; as long as he liveth he shall be lent to the Lord" (1 Samuel 1:28). It is because of mothers and fathers like these that we have as many Christian day schools as we have today.

We should thank God for the pastors and teachers among us who are vitally concerned about establishing and maintaining these schools, which the sainted H. M. Tjernagel[4] once described as being "the dearest and most beautiful plants in our Synod's garden."[5] How grateful we ought to be for teachers—and for pastors too—who have not been afraid to make some material sacrifices in order that a Christian day school might continue to operate within a congregation. Those servants of the Lord will one day be rewarded by hearing their Lord say to them: "Well done, thou good and faithful servant: thou hast been faithful over a few things, I will make thee ruler over many things: enter thou into the joy of thy lord" (Matthew 25:21).

But most of all, we ought to thank God for the instruction that is given our children in these nurseries of learning. We must constantly be reminded that we and our children are only pilgrims in this world. We do not have here an abiding city, but we seek one to come. And a question that we all must be vitally concerned about is this question: "When we and our children die, will we be

---

[4] **Helge Mathias Tjernagel (1871-1940)** served as the fourth president of the ELS (1930-1934), having joined the re-organized synod in 1923 as pastor of the Saude and Jericho congregations in northern Iowa. After his wife's death in 1924, he built a log cabin schoolhouse in her honor at the Saude congregation and began conducting classes. "H.M. Tjernagel," *Oak Leaves* 1, no. 1 (Spring 1997): 3; "Helge Mathias Tjernagel, 1871-1940," *Oak Leaves* 12, no. 1 (Spring 2008): 2-3.

[5] Theodore A. Aaberg, *A City Set on a Hill* (Mankato, MN: Evangelical Lutheran Synod, 1968), 95.

prepared to enter those heavenly mansions that our Savior has prepared for us?" The answer to that question can only be found in the Bible. In fact, the answer to all of life's vital questions can only be found in the Bible. And it is God's Word, the Bible, that is the heart and center of all instruction in our Christian day schools. It is that "Book of Books" that inspired a certain poet to pen the words:

> Thou truest friend man ever knew,
> Thy constancy I've tried;
> Where all were false,
> I found Thee true –
> My counselor and guide;
> The mines of earth no treasure give
> That could this volume buy,
> For in teaching me the way to live,
> It taught me how to die.[6]

And so while the children who are fortunate enough to be able to attend a Christian day school receive instruction also in those things that will help them to become good and useful citizens in this world, more importantly they are taught each day about their Savior, Jesus Christ, who has loved them with an everlasting love, and will take them at life's end to dwell with Him as citizens in the glorious home above.

The following essays, all of which emphasize the importance of *early* and *continuous* training for our children in the One Thing Needful, agree with Luther when he says: "When we are dead and gone, whence would come our successors if not from the schools. For the sake of the Church we must have and maintain schools."[7]

---

[6] George P. Morris, "My Mother's Bible," *Heart Throbs* (n.p.: Grosset & Dunlop, 1947), n.p.

[7] *Quotations and Illustrations for Sermons* (St. Louis: Concordia Publishing House, 1951), 102.

DOCUMENT 2.1:

The Norwegian Synod and the Christian Day School (1928)

By Norman A. Madson, Sr.

Dr. Norman A. Madson, Sr. (1886–1962) is best known for his faithful preaching during his forty-five years of ministry. Born on November 16, 1886 to Andrew and Mary Madson near Manitowoc, Wisconsin, Norman was the eleventh of fourteen children. Shortly after attending Luther College in Decorah, Iowa, he began training for the public ministry at Luther Seminary in St. Paul, Minnesota (1912-1915). Ten years later, Norman Madson joined the "Little Norwegian Synod" where he accepted a call to Our Savior's Lutheran Church near Princeton, Minnesota. After twenty-one faithful years of preaching God's Word and administering the Sacraments, Norman A. Madson became the Dean of Students for the newly established Bethany Lutheran Seminary in Mankato, Minnesota (1946). He remained at this position for the last fourteen years of his work in the church. Married to Elsie Haakenson, Pastor Madson had seven children.
He worked as the President of the Synod and also published two books: Evening Bells at Bethany (2 vols., 1948, 1952), and Preaching to Preachers (1952). In 1949, he received an honorary doctorate from Concordia Seminary in Springfield, Illinois. Dr. Madson died on December 10, 1962. He was the only man to have delivered a commencement address for each of the four seminaries in the

Evangelical Lutheran Synodical Conference.[8] The life of Dr. Norman A. Madson was one in service to God's church. He leaves us a lesson that he also left the first student body of Bethany Lutheran Seminary: "Viewed in the light of profit and loss on the world's sordid ledger, there is little which would attract us to the gospel ministry. But viewed in the light of eternity, what a glorious vista it reveals!"[9] [DR]

Source: *Synod Report* (1928), 75-82.

I. The Past

To observe the seventy-fifth anniversary of our Synod without giving due attention to the Christian day school would be like celebrating the Fourth of July, but forgetting the Declaration of Independence. For in spite of the fact that the Christian day school never came to occupy the place it deserved in the church of our fathers, yet it cannot be denied that the indoctrination of its youth has ever been one of the chief principles of the Norwegian Synod. When we today must deplore the fact that this blessed institution never was given the support which it deserved in the church of our fathers, we must not forget that there were extenuating circumstances. For these we must make due allowance, or else we are apt to sit in high judgment on men whose hearts were as filled with zeal for the cause of Christian schools for their children as is any heart among us today. Looking back over the history of our Synod, we do find certain obstacles in the way of a general interest in the establishing of these schools throughout the Synod. What were they? It is highly necessary that we have knowledge of these, lest we, on the one hand, misjudge the fathers, and lest we, on the other hand, imagine that we have a valid excuse for not doing more. We have in charity termed them *extenuating circumstances*, not daring to consider them excuses valid before God.

Our origin. First of all, we must bear in mind that our forefathers came from a land where they in youth had enjoyed instruction in the Lutheran faith in the common schools of their

---

[8] "Norman Madson," *Lutheran Synod Quarterly* 46, nos. 2-3 (2006): 205-206.

[9] Theodore A. Aaberg, *A City Set on a Hill* (Mankato, MN: Evangelical Lutheran Synod, 1968), 122.

country. While many of our forebears had received but very little schooling in the so-called "*omgangsskole* [itinerant teachers]" of the home country, what schooling they had enjoyed had placed the Bible, Luther's Small Catechism, the Bible History, and the Hymn Book as first requisites to a Christian child's training. And that was in *state-supported* schools. There had been no abridgment of this right on the part of the state, since the Lutheran church was the state church of Norway, even as it is to this very day. Schooling, in the minds of our immigrant forefathers, meant first of all instruction in the fundamentals of the Christian religion. As a consequence, they did not come to the land of their adoption with hearts and minds prepared to cope with the new order of things in a country where the tax-supported public schools could not, in the very nature of the case, give instruction in the Christian religion or in any other religion. That the founders of our Synod, for a time at least, labored under the delusion that the church might look to the state for aid in this work of Christian training we glean from the fact that, when a theological seminary was proposed, approaches were made to the University of Wisconsin to have it established in connection with that institution.

Not so among our brethren of the Missouri Synod. There we find that the congregational school was at once established and was considered a *sine qua non* [essential component] for the wholesome development of the church. But why this difference between immigrants, both of Lutheran stock? Because the Saxons in their homeland had suffered real persecution because of their faith. It was this persecution on the part of the decadent state church of Germany (nominally Lutheran, but virtually Reformed) which prompted C. F. W. Walther and his fellow Lutherans to emigrate to America. When they came, they were prepared to begin aright, since they did not entertain any false hope as to what might be expected from a state school. They had learned from sad experience that if their children were to be brought up in the nurture and admonition of the Lord [Ephesians 6:4], the congregation would have to provide for such training through its own private school. In the history of this outstanding denomination among Lutherans of today, we have exemplified the truth of that passage in Hebrews which says: "Now no chastening for the present seemeth to be joyous, but grievous; nevertheless afterward it yieldeth the peaceable fruit of righteousness unto them which are exercised thereby" (Hebrews 12:11). It was chiefly through their early association and affiliation with these conservative Lutherans that the fathers of our Synod learned to see the necessity of the Christian day school, yea, learned to see the signal blessings to which they had fallen heirs when God had led them to a land where church and state were separate. But though the Synod leaders had learned to see the necessity of congregational schools, they received anything but whole-hearted support from the rank and file of their followers, many of whom had not as yet been weaned from the erroneous view that somehow there could be a joining of interests. It was therefore an uphill fight which a Dietrichson, an H. A. Preus, an Ottesen, a Laur Larsen had to wage in the early years of our Synod in the interest of the congregational school.[10] But not being *"popularitetsjaegere* [crowd-pleasers]," these men were not dismayed by the odds against them. They fought a good fight also on this sector even unto the finishing of their course. And we bow our heads today in grateful acknowledgment of their Christian courage. May the very memory of them be blessed unto us.

Matter of language. In the second place, we find that the language question proved more or less of a hindrance. For when these faithful fathers of our Synod, through their contact with the Missourians, had learned to see the necessity and blessing of the congregational school, they could not quite reconcile themselves to anything but a school in their mother tongue. A congregational school meant, of course, a Norwegian school. But while the German, who by virtue of his national numerical strength, was invariably proud of the language spoken by millions throughout the world, the Norwegian, especially the uneducated, all too often felt ashamed of his mother tongue and therefore sought to drop it as soon as he had acquired a little smattering of English. Here, then, the pastors who sought to establish congregational schools met a real hindrance. We find intimations of this difficulty again and again in the half-century struggle for the maintenance of the institution.

Instead of being in a position to center their attention upon a Christian day school, therefore, which could do the full work of the

---

[10] *Editors' note:* **Johannes Wilhelm Christian Dietrichson (1815-1883)**, **Herman Amberg Preus (1825-1894)**, and **Jacob Aall Ottesen (1825-1904)** were three of the seven pastors who founded the Norwegian Synod in 1853. In 1859, **Peter Lauritz ("Laur") Larsen (1861-1902)** became a professor for Norwegian pastors-in-training at Concordia Seminary in St. Louis; two years later, the Norwegian Lutherans under his leadership started Luther College, now located in Decorah, Iowa. J. Herbert Larson and Juul B. Madson, *Built on the Rock* (Mankato, MN: Evangelical Lutheran Synod Book Company, 1992), 8-9, 12-13.

common school at the same time that it was a school in which the Christian religion was first of all inculcated and in which Christian discipline was exercised by teachers who accepted the Word of God as the only norm for faith and life, many precious years were frittered away in a discussion of the language question. Satan, the inveterate enemy of the Christian day school, saw to it that, wherever possible, interests were divided so that the prayers and pious plans of the faithful should not come to full fruition.

All sorts of compromises were concocted by some, whereby the establishing of the full-time Christian school might be made to appear as superfluous. Some sought to satisfy themselves with the securing of Norwegian-Lutheran teachers to conduct the common schools of their community. Others would have the public schools teach the common school branches for a part of the school term, and to have instruction in religion for the remainder of the term. And still others demanded that the state be petitioned for the right of having instruction in the Norwegian language made possible in the common schools. But in all instances the language question played into the detriment of the full-time congregational school.

But in spite of national origin, in spite of the language question which was constantly confronting them, in spite of the many compromises which were resorted to by the indifferent and halfhearted, the fathers of our Synod continued to plead the cause of the Christian day school until they finally got a hearing. It is not necessary here to enter upon any exhaustive review of their word and work. Suffice it to say that the cause of the Christian day school was kept before the people in the official church organ, in annual synodical reports, in papers read before synods and pastoral conferences, in circuit meetings, sermons, and in the private pastoral work. It is a source of true satisfaction to know that in the very first issue of the Synod's official organ (then called "*Maanedstidende* [*Monthly Times*]"), March 1855, there appears an article from the pen of the Rev. Dietrichson urging proper indoctrination of the children, and demanding the absolute separation of church and state also in the matter of schools. To quote briefly from this early statement:

> **TO EVERY CHRISTIAN CONGREGATION**
> Sustaining a parochial school in which
> Dr. Martin Luther's Catechism is used
> as textbook for the religious instruction
> of its young people
> > This Little Volume is Affectionately
> > DEDICATED
>
> Dedication page to Bjug A. Harstad, Is the Bible Reliable? Vital Questions Answered by Scientists, Christian Believers, and The Bible *(Parkland, WA: Published by the Author, 1929).*

In all too many quarters we notice also among us the spirit more and more permeating the congregations, that it must be considered sufficient when their children learn what is being taught in the public schools, and that it is a burdensome bond the pastor would place upon them when he demands that every member of his congregation shall contribute, and that the parents shall send their children, to the Christian school. But I nourish the fond hope that as Christian knowledge increases, the more [the Christian school's] necessity will be recognized and appreciated. But also here it is necessary that both pastor and congregation, trusting in God's sustaining grace, do not let themselves grow weary and faint-hearted, even though many burdens and hindrances oppose, but in meekness seek to convince the gainsayers and with Christian admonition and counsel cause them to understand what a vast responsibility they assume when they neglect to have their little ones made partakers of that which alone can make them happy here and blessed in the hereafter.[11]

This firm, yet thoroughly evangelical, statement from the pen of our sainted pioneering patriarch ought to be inscribed in letters of gold in the annals of our dear church.

That he is clear on the fundamental question of separation of church and state, we glean from his commentary on the resolution of the Pennsylvania Ministerium regarding the reading of the Bible in the public schools. We quote from the above-mentioned article in *Maanedstidende*: "When the committee proposes that only

---

[11] J. W. C. Dietrichson, n.t., *Maanedstidende*, March 1855, n.p.

such men shall be elected to the school boards as will see to it that Christian teachers are appointed and that the reading and explanation of the Bible be introduced, then I cannot agree thereto. For to read the Bible and expound religion in the public schools is contrary to the laws of the land, which demand that no religion shall be taught in these schools, lest anyone should be offended and, on religious grounds, be forced to keep their children out of school." Would to God that more of our present-day "Lutherans" had as clear a conception of this fundamental question.

Dietrichson closes his plea with these words: "May God's grace and blessing attend us, so that there may be awakened a serious concern among us for the Christian training of our youth; then the Lord will also grant us the spirit of wisdom to arrange everything in the best way, and will grant us the spirit of power, so that we shall not grow faint when we at times will meet with opposition where we expected to find support."

The first committee appointed by the Synod to consider ways and means for the establishment of congregational schools arrives at the conclusion that "all instruction must be given in the light of the Christian religion." This same committee expresses itself as follows regarding the influence of such schools:

> Especially will such a school wield so great an influence for the future that, as already stated, our congregations' continued existence, so far as human judgment goes, may well be said to depend more on this than on anything else. God grant that we may acknowledge this and act accordingly.[12]

In his annual report to the Synod in 1873, President H. A. Preus joins with those pastors of the Synod who have expressed it as their conviction that there is no hope of betterment and proper arrangement except through the establishment of Norwegian-English congregational schools. A set of theses prepared by President Preus this same year were printed and distributed. The following quotations from these theses will show where the sainted H. A. Preus stood in the matter of the Christian day school:

> The school is the forecourt to the church. . . .
>
> Parents cannot defend the committing of their children's instruction to unchristian teachers. . . .

---

[12] *Editors' note*: The source has not been located.

When the church or congregation, at the request of the parents, administers baptism to the little ones, it is not alone the sponsors, but the congregation as a whole which pledges itself, through the establishing and maintaining of schools in its midst, to see to it that all its children which through baptism have been grafted into Christ may remain with Christ. The school is the forecourt of the church; the church is the mother of the school. . . .

A congregation must, therefore, for the sake of Christ's command, for the sake of the children's salvation, and for the sake of its very existence and continuance, provide for the school. . . .

With fear and serious concern must we contemplate what the future holds in store for our children, our land and people. The only thing we have with which to construct a dam which shall shield us from the oncoming flood, threatening to carry away everything in its course, *is the Lord and His word*. With implicit trust in Him our hearts must be established. In the fear and love of Him we will as humble Christians and faithful citizens continue to testify and labor while it is day. . . .

In such a faith and committed to such a labor of love we earnestly strive by the aid of God to rear our children. . . .

Then shall neither that night of darkness, which threatens to enshroud the earth, nor the night of death, which most certainly awaits us all, terrify us or our children; we shall see light in God's light.[13]

In his annual report of 1875, President Preus says concerning the Christian day school:

But there is another thing [he has just spoken of the increasing worldliness of the church] which more than anything else causes me to fear that the spirit of the world shall gain the upper hand, even as we have evidence sufficient that it has already made its entrance. I refer to the little interest and the great neglect which shows itself in many quarters for Christian training and a Christian school system. I have again and again spoken about this matter, but though I shall have to suffer scoffing and scourging therefore, yet I will not cease so long as I am granted life to cry unto our church

---

[13] H. A. Preus, Annual Address, *Synod Report* (1873), 28, 29, 35.

body: 'Bring up your children in the nurture and admonition of the Lord' [Ephesians 6:4]. Perchance some, by this continued cry, could have their ears and eyes opened and grasp the importance of the matter. As I see it, a thoroughly Christian educational system is the chief of all conditions for our church body's health and development in this country. But in the gross neglect thereof, in a non-Christian, irreligious, more or less worldly-minded training of our children and youth, I see the decay and destruction of our beloved church within a few generations.[14]

Controversies and Unionism. In the latter half of the seventies and in the early eighties we see a general awakening in the Synod to the necessity of the Christian day school. A number of these institutions are established and are reported in a flourishing condition. On the same day, Sept. 3, 1877, Christian day schools were opened in the Decorah congregation and in Rev. Juul's congregation of Chicago, both institutions having a male and a female teacher in charge.[15] But due to the anti-Missourian controversy which arose in the eighties, the work so well begun was for a time disturbed.[16] However, the Christian day school, which had vindicated itself wherever it had been given a fair trial, continued to flourish, so that at the Synod's Jubilee celebration in 1903 it was given the most prominent place on the program of the church. Both President Koren in his annual report and Prof. Larsen in the opening sermon at that Jubilee celebration stress the absolute necessity of Christian day schools. And with renewed interest the Synod set about carrying into effect the most promising program to which it had ever been committed.

But again it encountered a hindrance which not only cooled the ardor of its love for the continuing of the schools it had already established, but which also caused a number of these institutions to be closed. Leaders arose who, while they with their mouths confessed that they were concerned about the feeding of the lambs, nevertheless by actions soon showed that they in their hearts carried a concern for something quite different. They sold their blessed birthright for a pottage of unionistic lentils. In every

---

[14] H. A. Preus, Annual Address, *Synod Report* (1875), 18.

[15] *Editors' note*: Pastor Ole Juul (d. November 1903) served Our Savior's Lutheran Church, Chicago.

[16] *Editors' note*: During the 1880s, a controversy broke out among members of the Norwegian and Missouri synods concerning the doctrine of election, from which emerged a party known as the anti-Missourians since they opposed C. F. W. Walther, the leading theologian of the Missouri Synod.

congregation of the Synod where these schools were to be found, but where the congregation entered the merger of Norwegian Lutherans based on the Madison, Wisconsin, "Agreement" of 1912, the schools were closed and remain closed to this day.[17]

II. The Present

In speaking of the present, let it be stated at once that in spite of what has again and again been said by our enemies concerning our right to call ourselves by the time-honored name, "The Norwegian Synod," we *are* historically justified in claiming it as our rightful heritage, and not least because of our attitude toward the Christian day school. Also here we have sought to remain true to our sainted fathers, not because we worship mere man, but because the fathers were in turn bound in the Word of God. And in this matter we have a divine injunction to "remember them which have had the rule over us, who have spoken unto us the Word of God: whose *faith* we should follow, considering the end of their conversation" [Hebrews 13:7]. It would ill become us to rear monuments to the memory of a Dietrichson, a Preus, an Ottesen, a Larsen with our lips, while we with our feet were trampling upon the dismembered corpse of their dearest child.

What of the present? In spite of all the ridicule which has been heaped upon us, in spite of the heartaches we have had to endure, in spite of the numbers which stand opposed to us in our struggle for the preservation of the faith once delivered unto the saints [Jude 3], we can rejoice in the fact that the last decade has been the most flourishing era in the history of this blessed institution among us. Not only have we proportionately more Christian day schools in our reorganized Synod than ever was to be found in the Synod of the past, but we can truthfully say that it has been given the chief place of prominence on the program of our church. And there is not to be found among us a single shepherd of souls who is not at heart committed to the cause. Also we have been chastised, but, by the grace of God, we have been made glad according to the days wherein He has afflicted us, and

---

[17] *Editors' note*: This 1912 agreement culminated in the 1917 merger of several Norwegian American church bodies into a pan-Norwegian Synod. Because both the preliminary agreement and the eventual merger involved doctrinal compromise for the sake of organizational unity, a minority of faithful pastors refused to participate, forming the "Little" Norwegian Synod in 1918, which today is known as the Evangelical Lutheran Synod.

> *"The great problem of all ages has been, and will continue to be, the bringing up, the training up of the children. As the children are, so will the future be. The church that is satisfied with makeshift expedients in the Christian education of her children has no other future prospect than failure, while the very portals of hell shall not prevail against the church that dutifully and faithfully and regularly leads her children to the fountain of life, Jesus Christ."*
>
> "Foreword," *Jubilee Souvenir, 1853–1928* (Mankato, MN: Norwegian Synod, 1928), 5.

the years wherein we have seen evil [Psalm 90:15].

What of the present? While we have nothing of which to boast, we are truly grateful to our kind heavenly Father, who, in spite of our all too little faith, has so signally blessed us. I, for one, would not exchange a single one of our humble day nurseries for the most pretentious institutionalized church of the Norwegian Lutheran Church in America.[18]

What of the present? Am I saying too much when I state that it is our greatest joy on the occasion of our Jubilee Synod Convention to hear in our midst songs of praise to the blessed Redeemer's name from the lips of children [Psalm 8:2] who in these very institutions have been taught that there is but one thing needful [Luke 10:42]? Could a more fitting *festskrift* [commemorative booklet] be presented than that which the Rev. Tjernagel today has placed in your hands, a work dedicated to our Christian day schools? Our *Jubilee Souvenir* speaks a language which needs no interpretation. It answers the question: "What of the present?"

III. The Future

But what of the future? Believing that it is God's will that all our children shall be taught of the Lord and that only then shall the peace of our children be great [Isaiah 54:13], we have no other

---

[18] *Editors' note*: The Norwegian Lutheran Church in America was the liberal merger church referred to in the preceding note.

program for the future than that which has governed us in the past. With renewed zeal in this endeavor we propose to carry on. Mindful of the faith of our true Synod fathers, it is our solemn resolve on this our seventy-fifth anniversary rather to be here rededicated to the cause for which they gave their last full measure of devotion. For just as certainly as we are bound in the Word of God in all matters of faith and life, just as certainly *must* we remain champions of the Christian day school.

We must, however, if the future is to be ours, never nourish the vain hope that the Christian day school will ever become popular in a world at enmity with God and in which all who will live godly lives in Christ Jesus shall suffer persecution. Our ideal is, and must ever remain, a Christian day school for every congregation of our Synod. To that ideal we have pledged ourselves as a church body. And in the attaining of that blessed consummation we must, even as a Moses of old, be ready rather to suffer affliction with the people of God than to enjoy the pleasures of sin for a season [Hebrews 11:24–26].

Courage and strength for the task will be found in Him alone whose strength is also today made perfect in weakness [2 Corinthians 12:9]. The question must ever be considered in the light of eternity. Let us not be over-much concerned about the world's vain standards. Patiently we will labor, fervently will we hope, that what a gracious God has committed to our trust shall not be lost to us because of our indifference and ingratitude, even though we shall have to bear the reproaches of Him who suffered outside the camp [Hebrews 13:12–13].

Preparing our little ones for the citizenship of heaven, we are rendering the land of our present sojourn the greatest service in giving it citizens who will be subject not only for wrath, but also for conscience sake [Philippians 3:20; Romans 13:5]. To this most momentous work of the future we go forth in the true fear and love of God, who has commanded us to pray and who has promised to hear us. This, then, shall be our earnest petition:

> Let Thy work appear unto Thy servants,
> And Thy glory unto their children.
> And let the beauty of the Lord our God be upon us:
> And establish Thou the work of our hands upon us;
> Yea, the work of our hands establish Thou it. [Psalm 90:15-17]

DOCUMENT 2.2:

The Christian Day School (1930)

By Christian A. Moldstad

Christian A. Moldstad (1882–1972) *served in the public ministry for thirty-eight years. He was born October 29, 1882 to Anders and Johanne Moldstad in DeForest, Wisconsin, where he spent his childhood years. He enrolled at Luther College, Decorah, Iowa, in 1899, earning his college degree in 1904. From the fall of 1905 to 1908 he attended Luther Theological Seminary in St. Paul, Minnesota. After receiving a Bachelor of Divinity degree, he was ordained at St. Mark's Lutheran Church in Chicago, Illinois, and that same year accepted a call to the Norwegian Lutheran Church in Boston, Massachusetts. Moldstad served the Boston congregation for twenty years, until in 1928 he accepted a call to Fairview Lutheran Church in Minneapolis, Minnesota. In 1937, Moldstad accepted a call to Bethany Lutheran College as a professor of foreign languages. He served at Bethany for nine years, retiring in 1946 and moving to Brewster, Massachusetts, where he and his wife opened a small inn called "The Manse."*[19]  *While at Bethany, Moldstad sat on several synod boards, was synodical president (1935–1937), and also served as editor for the* Lutheran Sentinel *(1938–1946). Even after his retirement, Moldstad remained active in ministry, holding church services for Brewster-area Lutherans in his own home.*[20] *At his seventy-fifth birthday celebration*

---

[19] David L. Pfeiffer, "'Retired' Pastor Honored," *Lutheran Sentinel*, Nov. 1957, 349-350.
[20] "In Memory of Christian Moldstad," *Lutheran Sentinel*, 13 Apr. 1972, 106–7.

(1957), he exhorted his guests "with much earnestness [concerning] the great importance and need of opposing religious liberalism and laxity and of holding fast to the Gospel."[21] On February 24, 1972, Christian A. Moldstad was called to his heavenly home. A son, Arden; two daughters, Hope Thompson Davis and June Moldstad; seven grandchildren; and five great-grandchildren survived him.[22] [JW]

Source: *Synod Report* (1930), 80-86.

The Christian day school has been discussed and written about at almost every Synod meeting of the old Norwegian Synod and of our present Synodical body. Never, as far as we know, has a voice been raised in our conventions protesting against the Christian day school. But, if you will search the Synodical reports, you will find that our Synod again and again has passed resolutions urging all our congregations to establish such schools, yes, even declared it a matter of life and death for our church.

One of the great arguments for union in 1917 was that it would help the cause of the Christian day school. At our Jubilee Synod in 1928 we had a special souvenir on the Christian day school. We seem to be agreed, then, that the Christian day school is necessary, but what troubles us is the carrying out of God's will and command.

What I have to offer on this subject will not, therefore, be anything new. But I shall endeavor to review, as it were, briefly the main arguments for the Christian day school, showing our duty, and urging all under God to do their duty in faith and trust to Him who has promised to give us all things in and through Jesus Christ.

The Christian day school is a school that takes care of the child's entire elementary education; a school where the Christian religion and the secular subjects, prescribed by the state, are taught side by side; where the entire plan, discipline and instruction, is based upon the Word of God. Such a school, when properly conducted, can and will be of real assistance to the Christian parents and the congregation in bringing up their children in the nurture and admonition of the Lord [Ephesians 6:4].

---

[21] Pfeiffer, "'Retired' Pastor Honored," 350.
[22] "In Memory of Christian Moldstad," 107.

Children are a gift from God. "Lo, children are a heritage of the Lord and his reward," says the Psalmist, "Happy is the man that has his quiver full of them" (127:3,5). God has given them to us that we should care for them according to His will and Word, so that they may be given back to Him. They are not ours to do with as we please. We have no right to starve them, neglect them bodily, or kill them. But just as we must care for their bodily welfare, so we must also, yes, first care for the soul. Here, too, we must do what God wants us to do. We are to bring them up in the nurture and admonition of the Lord. We are to care for them as God's children. How are we to do this? We must pray for our children, bring them to God in baptism, teach them to observe all things whatsoever God has commanded, and set them a good example.

God says: "Suffer little children to come unto me, and forbid them not: for of such is the kingdom of God" (Luke 18:16). "Go ye therefore, and make disciples of all the nations, baptizing them into the name of the Father, and of the Son, and of the Holy Ghost: teaching them to observe all things whatsoever I commanded you" (Matthew 28:19-20a).

"These words, which I command thee this day, shall be in thine heart: And thou shalt teach them diligently unto thy children, and shalt talk of them when thou sittest in thine house, and when thou walkest by the way, and when thou liest down, and when thou risest up" (Deuteronomy 6:6-7).

"Feed my lambs" (John 21:15). "Ye fathers, provoke not your children to wrath: but bring them up in the nurture and admonition of the Lord" (Ephesians 6:4).

God has promised to bless all those who seek to do His will, but He has also threatened to curse all those who disregard His commandments.

The commandments of God to parents and the church regarding the training of the children include the whole training of the child in body, mind, and soul. The child is to be brought up in such a manner as to be sound and useful for the state and community and not to be a burden or a parasite. But above all the child is to be prepared for eternity. "For what is a man profited, if he shall gain the whole world, and lose his own soul? Or what shall a man give in exchange for his soul?" (Matthew 16:26).

Can the parents alone, in our busy and complex civilization, train their children and attain the best results? We readily admit that if the parents have the time and the ability they are nearest to the child, understand the child best, and have the greatest influence over the child. But when we take the average home, we find that in most cases the child's training would be sorely neglected if left entirely to the parents without any outside assistance.

Can the public school help the Christian parents as they should be helped? We answer: No!

Because our Lord has commanded that our children should be brought up in the nurture and admonition of the Lord. This the public school is forbidden by law to do. In 2 Timothy 3:16-17 we read: "All Scripture is given by inspiration of God, and it is profitable for doctrine, for reproof, for correction, for instruction in righteousness: That the man of God may be perfect, thoroughly furnished unto all good works."

In Jeremiah 8:9 we read: "The wise men are ashamed, they are dismayed and taken: lo, they have rejected the word of the Lord, and what wisdom is in them?"

How then can the Christless public school give this most important element in education, which it does not have? Finally, we know from the Word of God that all things are hallowed and sanctified by the Word of God and prayer [1 Timothy 4:5]. This the public school lacks. Is it right then for the Christian parents to seek help for the training of their children in the godless public schools?

We do not propose to do away with the public schools. They are needed for the fifty percent or more of our citizens who are not Christians. A fundamental principle of our beloved country is the separation of church and state. We would not give up this principle. But as long as this law shall stand there can be no religious instruction in the public school. Therefore, if we believe what God declares and what our church has always maintained, that the most important thing in life is our Christian faith and Christian life, then we will and must provide for the Christian training of our children in body, mind, and soul.

The Christ-less school, be it ever so good, is not good enough for us Christians, because it leaves out the most important factor in the training of our children, namely the Word of God.

Martin Luther said: "Where the Holy Scriptures do not rule there I certainly do not advise anyone to send his child. All must be ruined where the Word of God is not constantly exercised, I have a great fear, that the schools are wide portals to hell, when they do not persistently and diligently use the Word of God and impress it upon the young."[23]

Nicholas Murray Butler of Columbia University has said:

> Religious training is a necessary factor in education, and must be given the time, the attention, and the serious continued treatment, which it deserves. That religious training is not at the present time given a place by the side of the study of science, literature, art or of human institutions, is well recognized.[24]

The Supreme Court of the State of Wisconsin declared many years ago in a case concerning the reading of the Bible in the public schools, that such practice was sectarian and contrary to the statutes of the state. The court furthermore stated:

> The priceless truths of the Bible are best taught to our youth in the church, the Sabbath and parochial schools, the social religious meetings, and, above all, in the home circle. There those truths may be explained and enforced, the spiritual welfare of the child guarded and protected, and his spiritual nature directed and cultivated in accordance with the dictates of the parental conscience.[25]

Most educators today admit that the Sunday school is entirely inadequate. And aside from the fact that the secular training in the public school is Christ-less and often anti-Christian, stressing out of all proportion the material and temporal side of life, is it reasonable that an hour in Sunday school once a week could begin to feed the lambs of Christ as He wants them fed [John 21:5]?

But some say we have a religious summer school for a month or two. Well and good, this does help to give the children some added historical knowledge of the Christian truths, and we would not belittle it. And still we must admit that it is forced feeding and can never take the place of the constant daily training that God has described.

---

[23] *Editors' note:* Martin Luther, *To the Christian Nobility of the German Nation concerning the Reform of the Christian Estate* (1520), in *Luther's Works*, vol. 44, ed. James Atkinson (Philadelphia: Fortress Press, 1966), 207.

[24] *Editors' note:* Nicholas Murray Butler, "Religious Instruction and Its Relation to Education," in *Principles of Religious Education: A Course of Lectures Delivered under the Auspices of the Sunday-School Commission of the Diocese of New York*, introd. Henry C. Potter (New York: Longmans, Green, and Company, 1901), 3-20, at 6.

[25] *Editors' note: State of Wisconsin ex rel. Weiss v. District Board of School District No. 8 of the City of Edgerton*, 76 Wis. 197, 44 N.W. 967 (1890).

The only real solution is the Christian day school. This can and does give and provide just what the Lord has prescribed. It is the best plan of all plans. To such a school the Christian parents can send their children, knowing that they are doing what God wants them to do. The only time that a Christian day school falls short of its God-given power and influence is when a teacher is unfaithful to his trust and a congregation is too stingy to provide what is necessary for the best interests of the school.

Now we admit that many have been able, by the grace and power of God, to bring their children to God without the Christian day school. But such parents devoted a great deal more time to instruct their children in the fundamentals of Christianity than most parents do today and they did not have the dangers to cope with in education that we have. We are living in a much more complex and diverting age than our forefathers did. Furthermore, the public school is not only a Christ-less school, but in many cases even an anti-Christian school, where soul-destroying doctrines contrary to the Bible are being taught.

Therefore, unless the Christian parent is able to give his child all his schooling at home, he is endangering the child's spiritual life by sending him to the public school.

Today more than ever the Christian day school is needed.

The great loss of newly confirmed is a sad commentary on the lack of daily Christian training. That religion is needed in education is heard on every hand from leading educators. The flood of crime and immorality is traced to the lack of religion in education.

Our goal must, therefore, be a Christian day school in every congregation of our Synod. We have agreed to this, at least on paper. How shall we reach this goal? By preaching and practicing the Word of God. We have been preaching for seventy-five years, but few have taken God's Word to heart and done what God has commanded. Would the storm of 1917 have destroyed the old Synod house, if the Synod had practiced what it preached with regard to the Christian day school? Let us beware lest we fall into the same lukewarm indifference and be satisfied because we have preached the necessity of the Christian day school and then do nothing more about it. Shall we not take God at His Word? Has He not promised to provide all things necessary for the carrying out of His will and the work in His kingdom? Why not begin at the beginning in our church work and lay the foundation that God wants? I fear that we have been so busy with the stray sheep that we have neglected the lambs that God has placed within the fold.

When we send missionaries to the foreign fields we begin by establishing schools for the children. In the same manner we carry on the work among the American Indians and the Negro in the south. Why not do the same when we send our missionaries to start new missions on the home mission fields? Are we not agreed that the training of our children is just as important as preaching to the adults? Why not start at the bottom and lay a foundation that will carry the superstructure?

Let our missionaries begin by starting a school. If necessary, leave out all other activities such as young people's societies, ladies' aids, men's societies, choirs, suppers and sales, until those things can be taken care of. First teach the children during the week and let all worship together on Sunday. Wherever this method has been tried, and it has been tried again and again, there the results have justified the procedure. The fruits may seem small and insignificant to begin with, but in the end you will win out.

"But where will the money come from?" is the cry that we always meet. I ask, where does the money come from to carry on any and all of the work in God's vineyard? Is it not God who provides by opening the hearts and the purses? Has he not asked us to prove him or try him? Malachi 3:10: "Bring ye all the tithes into the storehouse, that there may be meat in Mine house, and prove me now herewith, saith the Lord of hosts, if I will not open you the windows of heaven, and pour you out a blessing, that there shall not be room enough to receive it." Here we see that God has promised to bless our offerings so that there will be plenty if we give of His gifts as He has ordered. Would the expense for a missionary starting a new mission be much greater if he started a school at the beginning and did the teaching himself? Hundreds of Missouri Synod congregations have been started in that way. Could we spend our mission treasury in a more profitable manner?

In old established congregations it is often more difficult to overcome the life-long apathy and unmask the seeming impossibilities and objections. I am bold to state that it is not impossible for any well-established self-supporting congregation to have its own Christian day school, if the members really want it. Is anything impossible with God? If we really gave according as God hath prospered us, if we really dedicated ourselves and our money and goods to the service of the Lord, there is no doubt but that we would have all we need and more to carry on this work. But so many forget to place the kingdom of God first on their budget. Instead most people do not place it there at all or place it last and give only the leftovers. The love of Christ should constrain us and will constrain us to do everything to feed the lambs of God. But where there is no real love for God there is no concern for His little lambs either. In many congregations a school could be had for the money that the members spend for newspapers. The average person in the city spends ten dollars or more a year for newspapers. Is that more important than a Christian day school?

We shall briefly mention and answer some of the worn-out objections to the Christian day school: That it is unnecessary, inefficient, narrow, un-American, too expensive, and too far for many of the children. In the light of God's Word we have seen that it *is* necessary, if we are to do what God wants us to do. Where properly conducted, the results prove that the Christian school is more efficient than the public school. It is broader than the Christless school, because it develops Christian character and has the only true means of discipline, namely, the Word of God.

The Christian day school is most American; because the principle of separation of church and state intends that the church shall educate the children. And the record of our parochial school trained boys in the world war, together with the commendations received from superior officers who were not Lutherans, contradicts the statement that our schools cannot produce good Americans. Our schools are also the most economical of all schools, but even if they were not, what doth it profit a man, if he gain the whole world and lose his soul [Matthew 16:26]? That some children have too far to go can always be overcome in this age of transportation. Where there is a will, there is a way; and, where there is love of Christ and love for the children, there will be a way.

We must not expect to get all the members of a congregation with us from the start and make a big beginning. But let those who see the necessity and whose consciences are bound by the Word of God start by praying and giving and open a school, be it ever so small. The large schools of today all had a small beginning, and you never know till you try what the outcome will be. And what of it if your school never grew large, you would at least have done your duty—the growths and the increase rests with God. All the work in God's vineyard demands sacrifices. So also the work of carrying on a Christian day school. This is God's order of things. He wants us to make sacrifices because it is good for us. Why not be glad to make sacrifices because it is good for us. Why not be glad to make sacrifices if the Lord wills it and makes it possible for you to make them. Let no one delude himself into thinking that an old established school will run of itself without sacrifices. Oh, no!

The devil takes care of that. He hates the old established school fully as much, if not more, than the little beginner, and therefore, he is ever busy seeking to destroy it. I once heard an old pastor say that it was a continual fight to keep a school going even after fifty years.

Therefore, if we are certain that the conditions and problems of our age demand a Christian day school—if we as a congregation are to bring up our children in the nurture and admonition of the Lord and feed the lambs of Christ as He wants them fed—then let us go forth to battle in the name of the Lord God Almighty, merciful and good, knowing that with God all things are possible and that He will guide and keep and bless to the glory of His name and the salvation of our souls.

DOCUMENT 2.3:

Concerning Christian Education (1943)

By Carl S. Meyer

Carl S. Meyer (1907–1972) *is best known as the author and editor of many works on church history, including:* The Lutheran High School *(1945),* Moving Frontiers: Readings in the History of the Lutheran Church-Missouri Synod *(1964),* Log Cabin to Luther Tower: Concordia Seminary during One Hundred and Twenty-five Years toward a More Excellent Ministry, 1839-1964 *(1965), and* A History of Western Christianity *(1971). Prof. Meyer, originally from Wetaskiwin, Alberta, graduated from Concordia College in Fort Wayne, Indiana, and was a 1930 graduate of Concordia Seminary. After completing his course work at Concordia, he went on to get an M.F.A. degree from University of Chicago in 1931 and a D.Arts in 1954. Professor Meyer started his public ministry as hospital chaplain in Rochester, Minnesota, in 1931. He served there until 1934, when he accepted a position at Bethany Lutheran College, where he taught history and religion and served as registrar from 1934 until 1943. While at Bethany, Prof. Meyer instituted new methods of testing students to develop Bethany's counseling program into an "effective arm in student personnel work."*[26] *After his time at Bethany, he was called to be the principal of Luther Institute in Chicago, a Lutheran high school. The*

---

[26] B. W. Teigen, "In Memoriam: Carl S. Meyer," *Lutheran Sentinel*, Feb. 1973, 36-37.

school needed a "steady and competent leader" and after his time at Bethany Prof. Meyer was well-equipped for the job.[27] He received a Doctor of Divinity degree from Concordia Theological Seminary, Springfield, Illinois, in 1964. During his time at Concordia, Meyer was the director of the School for Graduate Studies, secretary of Concordia Historical Institute, and editor of Concordia Historical Institute Quarterly.[28] He was also made a Fellow of the Royal Historical Society of England in 1966.[29] He married Lucille Helen Pfeifer on July 20, 1935 and they had three children. Prof. Meyer was laid to rest in St. Louis, Missouri, in 1972.[30] [AW]

Source: *Synod Report* (1943), 47-56.

St. John the Divine, in addressing his first epistle to the Christians of Asia Minor as well as to us, says by inspiration of the Spirit of God (1 John 2: 12-14):

> I write unto you, little children, because your sins are forgiven you for His name's sake. I write unto you, fathers, because ye have known Him that is from the beginning. I write unto you, young men, because ye have overcome the wicked one.
>
> I write unto you, little children, because ye have known the Father. I have written unto you, fathers, because ye have known Him that is from the beginning. I have written unto you, young men, because ye are strong, and the Word of God abideth in you, and ye have overcome the wicked one.

He was an old man when he wrote these words, already beyond the three score years and ten spoken of by the psalmist [Psalm 90:10]. He is called the "Apostle of love," for he spoke much of love; he calls himself "the disciple whom Jesus loved"; and we often refer to him as "St. John the beloved." The characteristics of love and paternal affection are evident in the

---

[27] Ibid.
[28] Carl S. Meyer, ed., *Moving Frontiers: Readings in the History of the Lutheran Church-Missouri Synod* (St. Louis: Concordia Publishing House, 1964), n.p.
[29] Teigen, "In Memoriam," 36-37.
[30] Telephone interview with Laura Marrs (Concordia Historical Institute), 22 Feb. 2010.

words just read from his first letter. He addresses his readers as "little children," once using a word, which breathes love and affection, the second time using a word, which connotes his authority as a teacher and as apostle over them. He calls all his readers "children." He is their spiritual father, their father in Christ. He makes no reference to their chronological ages, for under this designation he includes both the parents and the children, those whom he later calls "fathers," and those whom he calls, "young men." Picture to yourself, if you will, the old man, now perhaps ninety or more years old, addressing these words to his beloved readers, the believers of Asia Minor and of all ages, regarding them with affection and love. What shall he write them and what specific message has he for each class of his readers?

I.

To all in common he writes the simple Gospel, the message of forgiveness of sins, and adds an exhortation to holiness in life.

The Apostle of love never tired of reminding his readers of the forgiveness of their sins. "The blood of Jesus Christ, His Son, cleanseth us from all sin," he writes (1 John 1:7). Again, "My little children, these things I write unto you, that ye sin not. And if any man sin, we have an advocate with the Father, Jesus Christ the righteous: and He is the propitiation for our sins: and not for ours only, but also for the sins of the whole world" (1 John 2:1-2). There is forgiveness of sins, forgiveness "for His name's sake," forgiveness for the sake of Christ Jesus. This message of the forgiveness of sins, total, complete forgiveness, forgiveness not because of any merit or worthiness in man, but for His name's sake, the sake of Him who suffered and died and rose again and by the perfect fulfillment of the law atoned for all sins, is the message which St. John would stress again.

"I write unto you, little children, because your sins are forgiven you for His name's sake. ... I write unto you, little children, because ye have known the Father." Speaking now with the voice of the teacher and the apostle of the Lord, he reminds them that, having the forgiveness of sins, they have come to faith in Christ Jesus. In this faith they know the Father, their Father and the Father of their Lord Jesus Christ. "Behold, what manner of love the Father hath bestowed upon us, that we should be called the sons of God," he cries out in evident wonder (1 John 3:1). And then he continues, "Beloved, now are we the sons of God."

Professor Carl S. Meyer, affectionately called "the Little Prussian" by his students, stands with President Sigurd Christian Ylvisaker.

As children of God, knowing God, they walk as children of God. How do they know that they know God? St. John answers (1 John 2:3-6):

> And hereby we do know that we know Him, if we keep His commandments. He that saith, I know Him, and keepeth not His commandments, is a liar, and the truth is not in him. But whoso keepeth His Word, in him verily is the love of God perfected: hereby know we that we are in Him. He that saith he abideth in Him ought himself also so to walk even as He walked.

Bringing men to a saving knowledge of God the Father through faith in the forgiveness of sins for Christ's sake, the work of the Spirit, and holiness of life are the primary aims of all true Christian preaching and teaching. The preaching of justification and of sanctification remains the primary objective of the church. Although St. John has written concerning these to all in common, it is not amiss to speak of these as also the primary aims of Christian education.

Dr. Edward W. A. Koehler has well expressed the relationship between these two objectives of Christian education in the following words:

> The child must first have become "wise unto salvation through faith which is in Christ Jesus" before he can be trained in righteousness and holiness of life [2 Timothy 3:15–17]. Because faith justifies him before God by accepting the saving merits of Christ, it also sanctifies him in his life by working in him a new mind and a new attitude toward God. The child now sees and judges the things of life from an entirely different viewpoint. Because he knows himself to be a child of God and an heir of heaven, his thought and desires are no longer earthward, but heavenward, not worldly, but spiritual. Because he is born again of the Spirit, he is also able to walk in the Spirit [Galatians 5:25]. Though we must therefore distinguish these two objectives of Christian education, they may not be separated. Faith in Christ is necessary if Christian training is to be possible and effectual.[31]

There you have the fundamental difference between a merely moral life and a truly Christian life, between a moral education

---

[31] Edward W. A. Koehler, *A Christian Pedagogy* (St. Louis: Concordia Publishing House, 1930), 117.

and a Christian education. The difference is not one merely in methods; it is a difference in goals. The point of departure, the starting-point, hence the whole road along which it travels, is different.

II.

As if he wanted to emphasize these facts for the training of children, St. John turns specifically to the parents among his readers and says to them: "I write unto you, fathers, because ye have known Him that is from the beginning. ... I have written unto you, fathers, because ye have known Him that is from the beginning." There is seemingly nothing new here. He had written to all: "I write unto you, little children, because ye have known the Father." The Father is He that is from the beginning. Why, then, should the Apostle repeat this thought, if not to impress parents that they might teach their children? He emphasizes the importance of knowing that God who gave His Son, who made us His sons, who is the Father of light in which we walk, that parents, as fathers and mothers, may so deal with their children. The fact that the Apostle speaks to the children and parents separately, after having addressed them all in common, makes this interpretation evident.

The apostle is speaking to Christian parents. They know God. They have the forgiveness of sins and walk in holiness of life. That knowledge, as children of God, they would impart to their children. That is the most precious thing which parents can give their children. We, as parents, worry and fret that our children have strong and healthy bodies, that they be well educated, that they be provided with this world's goods. But none of these things are of real importance compared to a knowledge of God.

This is the estimate, which God Himself makes. About twenty-five hundred years ago when another people was bent on conquest, having already destroyed the cruel Assyrian Empire and was about to destroy the kingdom of Judah, Jeremiah, speaking as the mouthpiece of God, reminded his people of fundamental values (Jeremiah 9:23-24):

> Thus saith the Lord, Let not the wise man glory in his wisdom, neither let the mighty man glory in his might, let not the rich man glory in his riches: but let him that glorieth glory in this, that he understandeth Me, that I am the Lord which exercise loving-kindness, judgment, and righteousness in the earth: for

in these things I delight, saith the Lord.

For our day these words of the prophet Jeremiah are not without significance. In the chaos and confusion of our times, augmented by a lack of true understanding and knowledge of God, men in high places are asking this nation to return to God and to religion. They speak of the necessity of rehabilitating the home, for in the home the very foundations of morals and religion must be taught. One investigator, for example, has attributed about ninety percent of disorders in conduct among children to poor training and discipline in the home. Another, writing on "The Challenge of Delinquency," shows how serious the breakdown in discipline in the schools has become. She says:

> War tensions have broken through the weakest links in our social fabric, creating little islands of anarchy, but what does it all mean? Youth, supposedly the seedbed of idealism, is not revolting for anything. The attack on discipline and traditional authority is negative, cynical, petulant. ... Normally, fundamental disciplines are the task of the parents. Now, with mothers being called into industry, and fathers occupied with war work or completely removed by military service, the home is not retaining its former influence. ... Accompanying this removal of authority, there is the fundamental moral upset of war itself. With hatred and violence, once decried from every hand, now a matter of national policy, the immature personality cannot keep its balance. The old virtues tarnish easily under such conditions, and with snipers and commandos the heroes of the day, what attraction is there in standing by and doing what the teacher says?[32]

The newspapers and popular magazines come to this theme again and again. Some articles tell us about shameful, horrifying conditions among the youth of our land. If a remedy is suggested the remedy is usually that of the home.

Modern educators and psychologists are rediscovering an old truth, the truth that Solomon expressed in these words (Proverbs 22:6): "Train up a child in the way he should go: and when he is old, he will not depart from it." These modern psychologists and educators will tell you that the pre-school years of the child are perhaps the most important of the child's life, especially for laying the framework of his personality and character. One man has said:

---

[32] Anne Crutcher, "The Challenge of Delinquency," *The Civic Leader*, 11 Jan. 1943, 1.

> Men have always felt that the first few years of home may make or break a child in his personal and social ways of behaving. There is now so much proof for this belief that it stands out as a major premise in all teaching. It is not too much to say that we will almost surely be in adult life the sort of person we have been trained to be almost before we have learned how to walk or to talk.[33]

Because of the rising tide of juvenile delinquency and the importance of the early years in the life of the child, Christian parents will be concerned that their children know Him that is from the beginning as they themselves know Him. Luther, in his day, said:

> That Christendom is now in such evil straits is all due to the fact that no one pays attention to the youth; and if things are to take a turn for the better, the beginning must certainly be made with the children.[34]

Luther, of course, stresses the responsibility of parents in the true education of children. We say "true education," because many parents do not know God and therefore cannot teach their children the true knowledge of God. Let us, as Christian parents, be more ready than ever before to provide our children with that education which is based on Christ, on the forgiveness of sin for His name's sake and love for one's fellowmen because of God's love towards us.

As the best institution or aid which parents can use for this purpose we point to the Christian school. By means of the Christian day school the church fulfills her responsibility, for the church, too, has the responsibility over against the children of the church of providing the knowledge of salvation and of pointing the way toward a God-pleasing life:

> The Lutheran elementary school is a church institution. It has been found to be the most efficient agency by means of which the local congregation may meet its obligation to teach and train children according to the solemn charge of Christ to His disciples of all times in the Great Commission: "Go ye,

---

[33] Coleman R. Griffith, *Psychology Applied to Teaching and Learning* (New York: Farrar & Rinehart, Inc., 1939), 523.

[34] Martin Luther, "Sermon on Luke 1:39-55," in *Luther on Education in the Christian Home and School*, edited by Paul E. Kretzmann (Burlington, Iowa: Lutheran Literary Board, 1940), 58.

therefore, and teach all nations (including the young) ... teaching them to observe all things whatsoever I have commanded you" (Matthew 28:19-20). It is an institution at the same time by means of which the called servant of the congregation or any of his official associates or assistants carry out the obligation of the congregation summarized by Christ in His word to Peter: "Feed My lambs!" (John 21:15). This agency of Christian training is therefore rightly called a parochial school, that is, a school of a parish and of a congregation. It is also owned and operated by the congregation as a corporate body, not by the parents, not by private persons, not by the state or the civic community, not by Synod.

The parents have their own particular obligation toward the children, regardless of what the congregation may or may not do by way of educating children. Their obligations parallel those of the congregation so far as religious and spiritual education is concerned, as will be seen from the command of Scripture: "Ye fathers, provoke not your children to wrath, but bring them up in the nurture and admonition of the Lord" (Ephesians 6:4). But parental obligations go farther in that they include the child's entire education, also for the common requirements of life. In the case of the Christian child or Christian parents, all education is Christian education.

Holy Scripture recognizes no dual education; neither does the Christian church nor the Christian parent. Hence, while the church as such has no command to teach anything but the Word, it undertakes a full educational program in its parochial school for these reasons: 1. The church has the example of the Old Testament church. 2. A Christian congregation bears a definite responsibility toward all the baptized children in its midst in keeping with Scriptural injunctions, e.g., Matthew 28:20. 3. The Word of God is taught not only during the so-called religious hour, but also in the form of practical application throughout the entire school day and the entire course. 4. In order to have the children present for continued observation, guidance, and training, the church school is made to substitute for the public school in general education. 5. Since education is never really non-religious, and since because of its moral objectives, it is as personal as religion itself, the Lutheran Church holds that the education of a Christian child should be wholly in the hands of his parents and the church of his faith.35

It is difficult to understand how those who have come to a knowledge of God, either as parents or members of a Christian congregation, can be indifferent toward fostering Christian schools. We think of the complaint of the sacred writer against those who show no growth in knowledge, comparing them to babies that still need milk when they ought to be eating strong meat (Hebrews 5:12-14). We think of that prayer which St. Paul uttered for his Ephesian Christians (Ephesians 3:17-19):

> That Christ may dwell in your hearts by faith; that ye, being rooted and grounded in love, may be able to comprehend with all the saints what is the breadth, and length, and depth, and height; and to know the love of Christ, which passeth knowledge, that ye might be filled with all the fullness of God.

III.

We think, too, of the description of the young Christian which St. John has given us of one who is victorious over the devil, strong, abiding in the Word of God.

In turning to the young men, the youth—and this includes both sexes in the younger years of life—St. John says: "I write unto you, young men, because ye have overcome the wicked one. . . . I have written unto you, young men, because ye are strong and the Word of God abideth in you, and ye have overcome the wicked one." They, too, have the forgiveness of sins and are the sons of God; they, too, know the Father.

They are strong, strong in faith and in the knowledge of God. In their strength they have overcome Satan, the wicked one, and his wicked ally, the world. "For whatsoever is born of God overcometh the world: and this is the victory that overcometh the world, even our faith. Who is he that overcometh the world, but he that believeth that Jesus is the Son of God?" (1 John 5:4-5). John the Beloved is emphatic in his distinction between those who love God and those who love the world. In the verses immediately following the words, "I have written unto you, young men, because ye are strong, and the word of God abideth in you, and ye have overcome the wicked one," he writes (1 John 2:15-16):

---

35 A. C. Stellhorn, foreword to *General Course of Study for Lutheran Elementary Schools* (St. Louis: Concordia Publishing House, 1943), iii-iv.

Love not the world, neither the things that are in the world. If any man love the world, the love of the Father is not in him. For all that is in the world, the lust of the flesh, and the lust of the eyes, and the pride of life, is not of the Father, but is of the world.

Christian boys and girls, Christian young men and women, will find themselves in conflict with the world. They must be strong, able to overcome. They will be the stronger because of a Christian education. They go from strength to strength and from victory to victory, because the word of God abideth in them. Their faith, their strength, and their victories come from God. They are not sufficient in themselves. They have followed the words of St. Paul (Ephesians 6:10-17):

Finally, my brethren, be strong in the Lord, and in the power of His might. Put on the whole armour of God, that ye may be able to stand against the wiles of the devil. For we wrestle not against flesh and blood, but against principalities, against powers, against the rulers of the darkness of this world, against spiritual wickedness in high places. Wherefore take unto you the whole armour of God, that ye may be able to withstand in the evil day, and having done all, to stand. Stand therefore having your loins girt about with truth, and having on the breastplate of righteousness: and your feet shod with the preparation of the gospel of peace: above all, taking the shield of faith, wherewith ye shall be able to quench all the fiery darts of the wicked. And take the helmet of salvation, and the sword of the Spirit, which is the Word of God.

Strong in the power of God's might, equipped with truth, righteousness, faith, salvation, and the Word of God, they are prepared to stand and to win the victory.

Also, in the warfare against the devil and his cohorts must youth fight the great battles? It is one of the tragedies of war that young men—entering the vigor of maturity, alert, eager, and strong—are cut down. It is a grim fight, which the youth of our land face against the hordes of Nazi Germany and pagan Japan. The two, five, seven, or ten million young men that go out against them must be physically fit, properly equipped, imbued with the highest ideals of patriotism to make the supreme sacrifice, if necessary, for their country. But there is another warfare, grimmer in its aspects and more momentous in its outcomes, demanding spiritual fitness, proper spiritual equipment, God-inspired ideals, and that is the warfare against the wicked one and the wicked world. It is one of the glories of this warfare that young men and young women, strong, abiding in the Word of God, overcome the wicked foe.

Prepared adequately to meet this foe with weapons from God's own arsenal they stand boldly, strengthened with might by His Spirit in the inner man. That Word which makes them free, that Word which enlightens them and gives them wisdom and understanding, that Word which is their spiritual food, *that Word* abides in them. They recognize it as the Word of very God. To them it is the most precious truth, superseding the speculations of the philosophers, the theories of the scientists, and the hypotheses of the sociologists.

St. John, in his second letter (2 John 8-9), points out the necessity of abiding in God's Word, when he says:

> Look to yourselves, that we lose not those things, which we have wrought, but that we receive a full reward. Whosoever transgresseth, and abideth not in the doctrine of Christ, hath not God. He that abideth in the doctrine of Christ, he hath both the Father and the Son.

If anyone were to question the need of Christian education, we could point to that passage alone. If anyone were to ask what the outcomes of Christian education are, we could point to that passage and say that by a sound Christian education our youth will the better abide in the doctrines of Christ and thereby have both the Father and the Son, the Savior. The Word of God abides in our Christian youth and they are strong, able to overcome the wicked one.

The secular schools cannot do that. They cannot prepare for the battle against the world and the devil. They cannot strengthen the inner man. They cannot teach the doctrines of Christ. These are the outcomes of a Christian education and of a Christian education alone.

> Ye therefore, beloved, seeing ye know these things before, beware lest ye also, being led away with the error of the wicked, fall from your own steadfastness. But grow in grace, and in the knowledge of our Lord and Saviour Jesus Christ. To Him be glory both now and for ever. Amen. (2 Peter 3:17-18)

We feel sorry for those of the coming generation who cannot attend Christian elementary and secondary schools. We expect to

Student teacher John Boehme instructs pupils at Mt. Olive Lutheran Elementary School in Mankato, Minnesota, about a half mile from the Bethany campus, ca. 1960.

see growing immorality, a still greater disregard of God's Word, tribulations for the children of God; yea, perhaps even bloody persecutions. The rosy dreams of the social planners do not impress us. They look for a near-millennial society in which abundance and freedom will be the watchwords. Their hopes of a mundane paradise may deceive even Christians. When these dreams and hopes do not materialize and instead perilous times appear, they may be in great danger of falling away. We must face the coming of the last days realistically, as St. Paul did, preparing this coming generation according to the manner in which Timothy was prepared. To him St. Paul wrote (2 Timothy 3:12-17):

> Yea, and all that will live godly in Christ Jesus shall suffer persecution. But evil men and seducers shall wax worse and worse, deceiving, and being deceived. But continue thou in the things which thou hast learned and hast been assured of, knowing of whom thou has learned them; and that from a child thou hast known the holy scriptures, which are able to make thee wise, unto salvation through faith which is in Christ Jesus. All scripture is given by inspiration of God, and is profitable for doctrine, for reproof, for correction, for

instruction in righteousness: that the man of God may be perfect, thoroughly furnished unto all good works.

Trained as was Timothy, our Christian youth will not be so easily deceived, nor will they be vacillating, but will be strengthened, established, settled, strong, abiding in the Word of God, overcoming the wicked one, withstanding in the evil day, and having done all, to stand.

IV.

These, we sincerely trust, are the outcomes of a Christian education. This education is begun in the home, fostered by diligent Bible study and regular attendance in God's house, and is the chief aim of Christian elementary and secondary schools.

We are not trying to distinguish between the need of Christian training in the elementary grades and in the secondary grades. To us it seems that it should be a Christian education, whether in the first, the seventh, or the fourteenth year. The command to parents to train their children in Christ's nurture is not nullified when the child reaches the age of six or sixteen. The command to the church to pasture Christ's lambs is not abrogated when the lamb reaches the age of ten or fourteen. It is not too much to say, I believe, that the entire education of the child through the age of adolescence should be a Christ-centered education.

The common goal of Christian elementary education and Christian secondary education is one reason for asking that we think of Christian education in terms of this common goal. The aims of both are alike. The desired outcomes are alike. We cannot foster an artificial rivalry, as if Christian elementary education excludes Christian education on the secondary level. It cannot be either the parish school or the high school under church auspices. To do that would be denying, as said, the common goal, the common aims, the common outcomes of these agencies.

The nature of the child likewise excludes the desirability of thinking of different kinds of education on various levels. The growth process of the child is a continued one, proceeding, it is true, according to a varied tempo, yet not one, which is divided into easily perceived periods. The boy of two years ago is not a fully matured man today. He may be on the road to manhood, but he hasn't arrived yet. And while we distinguish between adolescence and childhood or between adolescence and adulthood, we recognize that childhood and adolescence alike belong to the years in which the developing and maturing child is preparing for adulthood. Since this is true, we believe that the educational process should be a continuous one, continuous in the sense that throughout it is to be founded on the infallible Word of the infallible God.

The nature of the schools, too, argues for the continuous nature of the underlying guiding principles of the schools. Let me quote briefly what Hollis I. Caswell, Professor of Education at Teachers College, Columbia University, has to say on this point. He writes:

> Now agreement is increasing that the elementary school and the high school should not be considered institutions, which differ in function. They both should be concerned principally with the general education of the citizen, and their programs should center around the same broad objectives and should recognize that education is a continuous process.[36]

He, of course, is speaking of the common school system of our country. He is thinking of the education of future citizens of the terrestrial city. We are thinking of the education of citizens of the city of God. We have the same broad objectives in Christian elementary and Christian secondary education.

A growing number of educators is recognizing the importance of the junior college years as belonging to these years of general education. We would include these years under "secondary education." The particular type of organization for the schools and the desirable administrative divisions do not interest us now. We are merely concerned with pointing out the unity in the educational philosophy—if you wish to use that term—of Christian elementary and secondary education.

Nor are we concerned now particularly with the so-called part-time agencies of Christian education, the Sunday school, the Saturday school, summer schools or vacation Bible schools. Their aims are laudable; their outcomes are desirable. Their very designation, however (part-time agencies), tells us at once that they cannot fulfill the functions demanded of Christian educational institutions as efficiently as can the full-time agencies, Christian elementary and secondary schools.

It will not make one strong to engage in physical exercise only

---

[36] Hollis L. Caswell, *Education in the Elementary School* (Cincinnati: American Book Company, 1942), 28.

once a week or for two or three weeks a year. We cannot say that the Word of God abides in one who returns to it only now and then at more or less regular intervals. If we think again of the words of John the Divine, "I have written unto you, young men, because ye are strong, and the Word of God abideth in you, and ye have overcome the wicked one," we still say that this ideal of Christian youth can best be attained in our Christian elementary and secondary schools. Their sins forgiven, knowing God and walking in the holiness of God, steadfast, strong, these are the products of Christian schools.

We pray for our children in the words of Jane E. Leeson:

> Let Thy holy Word instruct them;
> Fill their minds with heavenly light;
> Let Thy powerful grace constrain them
> To approve whate'er is right;
> Let them feel Thy yoke is easy,
> Let them prove Thy burden light. (*TLH* 627:4)

DOCUMENT 2.4:

Christian Day Schools (1951)

By Theodore A. Aaberg

Theodore A. Aaberg (1925–1980) *was born January 29, 1925 to Rev. Theodore and Alette Aaberg in Wildrose, North Dakota. He attended Bethany Lutheran College and soon thereafter attended Concordia Seminary in St. Louis. For the next three years, Aaberg served a vicarage in Iowa. He performed duties as a vacancy pastor for two churches and as a Christian day school teacher. After transferring to the ELS Theological Seminary in 1948, he received a call to the Scarville-Center parish in Iowa where he served from 1949 to 1968. Meanwhile, he was also president of the ELS from 1962 to 1963. Having been blessed with a wife in 1951 and the birth of five children, Aaberg advocated for the Christian day school. He believed that "the Christian day school plays a vital role in building up the faith of the child and in maintaining a spiritually strong, enlightened, and active membership in the congregation."*[37] *He reopened the Scarville grade school and served on the ELS youth board during his nineteen years at the Scarville church. Theodore Aaberg died January 8, 1980, at Immanuel St. Joseph's Hospital in Mankato, Minnesota.*[38] *Aaberg's message of education and preservation for the foundations of the past are witnessed through his* A City Set on a Hill, *a historical account of the "Little Norwegian Synod," that is, the ELS.* [DR]

---

[37] Theodore A. Aaberg, *A City Set on a Hill* (Mankato, MN: Evangelical Lutheran Synod, 1968), 94.
[38] "Theodore Aaberg," *Lutheran Synod Quarterly* 46, nos. 2-3 (2006): 227-228.

Source: *Synod Report* (1951), 35-40. Rpt. in 2 pts., *Oak Leaves* 10, no. 2 (Summer 2006): 6-7, and no. 3 (Fall 2006): 5–7.

In Deuteronomy 6:6-7 we read: "And these words, which I command thee this day, shall be in thine heart: And thou shalt teach them diligently unto thy children, and shalt talk of them when thou sittest in thine house, and when thou walkest by the way, and when thou liest down, and when thou risest up." And in Ephesians 6:4: "And ye fathers, provoke not your children to wrath, but bring them up in the nurture and admonition of the Lord." In these words God tells parents, and especially the fathers, that He wants them to teach their children His Word. Parents are not at *liberty* to decide whether or not they will teach their children the truths of Scripture, for God simply tells them that they *are to do it*. He will require an accounting from them on the Last Day. It is not enough that parents provide food, shelter, clothing and other earthly necessities for their children; they must also provide the "One Thing Needful" for them; they must teach them of Christ.

The congregation also has a duty towards the children in its midst. Jesus told Peter not only to feed his sheep, but also to feed His lambs. The congregation is to provide for the instruction of both young and old. Children will get much out of a sermon, especially if the pastor makes his sermons clear and plain. But the children also need the special instruction which the congregation offers in its various schools.

Teaching children is a real job, a difficult one. For one thing, most fathers are busy during the day, often away from home, so occupied with making a living for the family that they do not have much time to teach their children. Then, too, parents do not always find it easy to teach others. It is one thing to know something yourself but quite another matter to impart that knowledge to someone else.

For this reason, the congregation conducts various schools—in order to help the parents in carrying out their God-given duty of educating their children. Before going on to a discussion of the different types of schools, and especially of the Christian day school, we should first say a little more about teaching in the home.

While Christian parents ought, as a rule, to make use of the help which the Church offers them in teaching their children, they should not feel that they can place the whole responsibility of teaching their children in the lap of the church, as though now they are free from that worry, since they send their children to such and such a school. The home will ever remain the most important school for the children. There they will learn the most, both by word and example. Christian parents do not need to be recognized teachers in order to instruct their children. Let the parents be diligent about family devotions every day, let Bible stories be read to the children from an early age, and above all let the parents lead a truly God-pleasing life. Let them live their Christianity, and there will be some real teaching done in the home. If the parents do not have a Christian home, do not live God-pleasing lives, then there will still be teaching done there, but it will be the wrong kind of teaching. Parents need not expect a school of the congregation to train their child in Christianity and be successful, if they tear down everything the school builds up by their godless living in the home.

In what way does the congregation help the parents to teach their children? Many different schools or agencies are in use in the churches. There is the Sunday school, the Saturday school, the summer school, the release time school, and the Christian day school. Perhaps there are still others, but these are the ones in most common use. What about these schools?

We should first of all bear in mind that Christ has never told the Christians that they must conduct such and such a school in their midst. There is no divine institution for any particular type of school in a congregation. They are all strictly something that the congregations, in Christian liberty, have established. God has commanded that parents teach their children. The church is to instruct its members in His Word. He lays down no rules as to the type of school in which this teaching is to be done.

What type of school, then, should a church establish in its midst in order to teach the children? While God has not given any instructions as to which school to have, e.g. a Sunday school or Christian day school, He does expect the Christian to use the head which He has given him. There should be one question uppermost in the minds and hearts of the congregation, and that is: "How can we best train the children?" "What is the best type of school?" "What kind of school will do the job the best?" If you have to haul ten tons of brick, and you are told to go out on the parking lot and take your pick of the vehicles there to do the job, and you go out and see a car, a pick-up, a station wagon and a large semi-truck,

> *"This verse means to me that by God's love I am saved and that I didn't do anything to deserve or receive this but that by God's grace I am saved and should want to live a holy life. I should also want to spread the news to others. I should not boast or brag that I am better than anyone else. But that all are equal and sinful. Therefore we should be very thankful to God."*
>
> A Sunday school student's summary of John 3:16, as printed in the Lutheran Sentinel, 13 Feb. 1964, 41.

you will not hesitate to pick the "semi" to haul the bricks. So it is with Christian education. When you see the job that is to be done, you look over the means of doing it, and you pick the best way there is to do the job. Let us then briefly discuss the different agencies which Churches use to educate the children and see which is best.

The Sunday school is an excellent missionary agency; it is a wonderful school to have in order to get unchurched children to the Savior. And the children, in turn, can be a great help in getting their unchurched parents to the Lord; but as a school in which to teach children the Word of God, it has its weak points. For one thing there is the matter of time. One hour a week, nine months of the year, makes about thirty-six hours of instruction. Then subtract about one third to half of this time to allow for opening devotions and other affairs, and there isn't much time left for actual instruction in God's Word. And what about the teachers? Many of them are not only consecrated workers, but also able teachers. But then again, there no doubt are many who are very consecrated, but yet do not have great ability in teaching. If the Sunday school is all the instruction that a child gets from the church, then he is living pretty much on crusts of bread. The odds are too much against the Sunday school to make it a thorough agency for bringing up children in the nurture and admonition of the Lord.

The Saturday school, where the children, instead of coming to Sunday school, assemble on Saturday morning for three hours of instruction is a much better agency than the Sunday school, as far as thoroughness in teaching is concerned, since there is three times as much time for instruction.

The summer school, or vacation Bible school, as it is more commonly called now, is an excellent agency for reaching the unchurched, and also for teaching children of the congregation. Congregations would do well to conduct such a school every summer, especially with the view of reaching the unchurched children. But that too has serious limitations. Time is short, and it lasts only two or three weeks. This is not the best agency the church has to offer.

What about the Christian day school? It is without a doubt the best school which a congregation can have for the thorough teaching of the children. To find out *why* it is the best school, one needs to consider what the Christian day school is, how it operates, what it does for the child.

Many people will describe the Christian day school as being the same as the public school, except that the Church operates and pays for it, and that it teaches one hour of religion every day. It is true that most Christian day schools devote the first hour of every school day to the study of God's Word. And this is no small matter. Just this one hour a day amounts to about 180 hours of instruction during the school year, which is about *five times* as much as one gets in Sunday school, or *four times* as much as one gets in a three-week Summer school. This allows for a thorough study of the Bible, catechism, explanation, hymn book, and church history. One hundred and eighty hours a year—think of what that means to a child who goes to a Christian day school for eight years!

But much more can be said for the Christian day school than its one hour of instruction each day. There are the opening and closing devotions which play no small part in the education of the child.

And what about the other subjects which are taught in the Christian day school—history, science, health, geography, etc.? Is that done in the same way as in the public school? By no means! All of these subjects are taught in the light of God's Word. In *geography* the child not only learns the names of continents and oceans, he not only studies the different nations and how they live, but he also learns that God has created these lands and oceans, that He is the one who has made provision in His creation so that people the world over can keep alive. In *history* the child not only learns about the nations and how they have carried on in the past years, but he also discovers that God has His hand in the affairs of the nations. That He directs the rise and fall of the nations and other affairs for His own purposes. In *science* the child not only learns about the plants and animals and other things belonging to science, but he also learns that it is God who has created these things, and they see the wisdom and power of God in the marvelous ways in which all of creation is constructed and in its ways of operating. In *health* the child not only learns the proper rules for caring for his body, but he also learns the proper motive for such care, namely that his body is a temple of God, and that God wants him to care for it properly.

Consider also that in the Christian day school the pupils are, for the most part, of the same congregation. There is Christian fellowship. They study, work, and play together with fellow believers. This builds up a close relationship between the pupils which lasts long after they have finished school and are adult members in the congregation.

The discipline which prevails in such a school is also very valuable. School discipline is not based on vague and general moral lines, but on what God has written in the Ten Commandments. If children are to be disciplined for, let us say, cursing and swearing, they are not told by the teacher that they shouldn't say such things because it is not nice, and nice boys or girls don't say such things, etc.; but they are told that they should not do it because God has said in the Second Commandment: "Thou shalt not take the name of the Lord thy God in vain."

These are things which make the Christian day school a great school, and if you will truly consider them you will agree that the Christian day school is still the prince of all Church schools. Dr. Walther has rightly called it the "Gem of the Lutheran Church." And it is a gem! If one were to look at the reports of our past Synod meetings, or to page through the old church papers, he would rightly come to the conclusion that our Synod has been a strong champion of the Christian day school. But we have nothing of which to boast on this score. It is true that we have spoken much on behalf of the Christian day school, and some fine, stirring speeches have been made on the Synod floor and elsewhere on the virtues and importance of such schools. The Christian Day School Fund of Synod has always had sufficient funds on hand for its work. But there are some seventy congregations in the Synod and only eleven schools. What kind of record is this? In these eleven schools there are some two hundred pupils, and if one should count the number of school children in these congregations with schools, he would find no doubt that less than half of them go to the Christian day school.

What is the cause of this? Much of the blame can be laid squarely on the shoulders of the pastors. It is the pastor who must take the lead in establishing such schools, and all too often we have been negligent about presenting this important matter to the people. No doubt, many more of our congregations would have schools today if their pastors had only had the energy, the courage, the willingness to "stick their necks out" and plead the cause of this blessed institution. God bless that pastor in our Synod who in trying to begin a school was approached by members who urged him to forget the school, so that the congregation could provide him with a larger living quarters and a bigger salary, but who went right ahead and got the school going! We need more of that spirit.

The pastors are not the only ones to blame for the shortage of schools in our congregations. The members themselves—parents and others—must also shoulder some of the guilt. Too many times we have failed to give our support to the establishment of a Christian day school, because it costs money to run it. Others may have opposed the opening of these schools because of some foolish notion that they are not American, not patriotic, or because they valued their standing in the community and desired to keep in the good graces of outsiders more than they valued the Christian training which can be given the children of the congregation in the Christian day school. Parents may have failed to cooperate with a school because they lived a little distance from it, and it meant driving a few miles every day, and it wasn't too handy. The day may come when they drive many miles, spend much money, and go through sleepless nights, trying to care for their wayward child who could have been led close to the Savior in the Christian day school.

We soon celebrate our centennial. We have many plans for celebrating. If we would do nothing else for the centennial than this, that every pastor go home and do everything in his power to start a school in his congregation, present the cause, contact families with children, the other members too, bring it to a vote, even teach it for a while if necessary, so that everyone of us could honestly say that he has done everything in his power—then that would be a real centennial celebration! And the power, the influence of the many schools that would be started would be felt for years to come, yes, even for eternity. Walther not only called the Christian day school the "gem of the Lutheran Church," but also added: "For on it depends, humanly speaking, the future of the Lutheran Church."

Let all of us pastors, delegates, and others, go home to our congregations and plead the cause of the Christian day school. If we have never approached the people with the idea that we start a school, let us do it now. If we have spoken on the matter but have not been able to get one started, then let us go home and try again. If we already have a school in our midst, let us go home and go to work and make it a better school, get more children enrolled, and more interest worked up for the school.

If there are congregations which do not have the necessary financial means to get such a school in operation, the Christian Day School Board of the Synod stands ready to consider every request that may come for help financially or otherwise. *There is a large balance in the Day School Fund, over $5,000.00.* If congregations are not able to secure a teacher from our school or the schools of sister synods, or are unable to finance their salary, let the pastor seriously consider teaching the school himself for a year in order to get it going. If he doesn't have the strength for such labor, let him ask God for that, and if God wants him to teach in addition to his pastoral duties, He will see that he gets the strength.

Let us build for the future, build wisely and strongly. There is nothing which would make Satan feel "bluer" on our centennial celebration than to hear that we had started a great number of new Christian day schools. May God grant us the wisdom, strength, and courage to forge ahead in the field of Christian day schools!

DOCUMENT 2.5:

Christian Day Schools (1952)

By Alfred Fremder

Dr. Alfred Fremder (1920–2006) is best known for the musical contributions he provided to the church. Dr. Fremder was born March 14, 1920, to Emil and Emma Fremder, in Sioux City, Iowa. He attended Concordia Seminary in St. Louis, graduating with the class of 1942. Just one day after his graduation, he married Ernestine Duever, with whom he had two sons. Soon after the ceremony, the couple moved to Mankato, Minnesota, where Fremder spent the next eleven years as the Bethany Lutheran College choir director. While there he raised the standards of discipline for the students. Dr. Fremder sought to achieve "a dedicated well-trained choir who would proclaim in song the powerful and saving message of Scripture to many congregations."[39] However, his work with the BLC choir was not his only contribution. He compiled Rite III in the Evangelical Lutheran Hymnary and he arranged an eight-part setting to the familiar prayer of Thomas Kingo, "On My Heart Imprint Thine Image," which the Bethany Lutheran College Choir performs every year.[40] Dr. Fremder received his masters degree from the University of Minnesota in 1955 and obtained his Ph.D. from North Texas State University in 1970. In 1979, he became the associate professor of practical theology at Concordia Seminary in

---

[39] Dennis Marzolf, *With Hearts and Lips Forever We Shall in God Rejoice!* (Mankato, MN: Bethany Lutheran College, 2002), 63.
[40] [Mark DeGarmeaux], "Sing a New Song: Divine Service, Rite Three" (n.d.), http://www.blc.edu/comm/gargy/gargy1/ELH.Rite3.html.

St. Louis until his retirement in 1991. Dr. Fremder died on April 19, 2006. [DR]

Source: *Synod Report* (1952), 34–41.

> *Behold, to obey is better than sacrifice, and to hearken than the fat of rams.*
>
> 1 Samuel 15:22b

There is a sad picture which came to my attention recently—a girl who was contemplating marriage with a Roman Catholic boy and had determined to have her marriage blessed by a priest. Undoubtedly a marriage contract was involved, a contract which promises to rear children in the Roman faith, a contract which promises to do worse to these children than snatch bread from their hungry mouths, to do worse to these children than to throw them to hungry beasts, to deprive them of the water of life.

The parents, members of a Christian church, feel badly about the situation, as well they might and well we might if such a thing would happen to us. They have double reason to beseech God, for although this could happen to any child, they were parents who did not see the value of a Christian day school training. They grieve at the lack of opportunity for future youngsters to be fed the bread of life, but they denied their own this constant attendance upon the Word of Life which a Christian school could have given. They need to pray to God that the doom of future souls be averted. O how foolish not to give the "one thing needful" [Luke 10:42] in the greatest abundance possible!

Too many such incidents are taking place every day. We need to hearken unto the voice of God! "My son, give me thine heart, and let thine eyes observe my ways" (Proverbs 23:26). "Cease from thine own wisdom. Wilt thou set thine eyes upon that which is not?" (Proverbs 23:4b,5a). "Buy the truth, and sell it not; also wisdom, and instruction, and understanding" (Proverbs 23:23). "Take fast hold of instruction; let her not go: keep her; for she is thy life" (Proverbs 4:13). "These words which I command thee this day shall be in thine heart; and thou shalt teach them diligently unto thy children" (Deuteronomy 6:6-7). We need to hearken unto the voice of our God, humbly, heartily, prayerfully, for He encourages us in that path, the only path, when He says; "To this man will I look, even to him that is poor and of a contrite spirit and trembleth at My Word" (Isaiah 66:2).

Objection No. 1

But do we need so much religion? Isn't God satisfied just that we believe in Christ? Must we spend so much money and time developing Christian day schools? Isn't our Sunday school giving us the true Gospel? Why can't release time education be enough?

In emergencies many ways can be found to teach the Word. We shall not dispute that.

There is a tremendous task confronting the Christian of any day and that is to bring the Gospel to every creature, to bring sinners to the Lord. Christ tells His disciples: "I have given you an example, that ye should do as I have done to you" (John 13:15). His example was that lowly task of washing his disciples' feet, an admonition to them and us that we serve others. Christ's ministry was a bounteous one. He laid on Himself the iniquity of us all, true. More than that, He considered it His duty to spread His health-giving Word. He more than once pointed that out for His disciples' benefit. When He, the Lord of all, could say this: "The Spirit of the Lord is upon Me because He hath anointed Me to preach the gospel to the poor; He hath sent Me to heal the brokenhearted, to preach deliverance to the captives, and recovering of sight to the blind, to set at liberty them that are bruised" [Luke 4:18]—when He could say and do this, then we can follow Him, and we must be prepared for this task, intensively prepared.

To apply medicine to physical sicknesses needs some training, some skill. To instruct, comfort and help others in need of spiritual medicine needs some training, some God-given skill. You need all the training you can get to fight God's fight in this world surrounded by His foes. Don't any of you say that we have pastors and teachers for that work. God has called each of us to work for Him, regardless of our earthly occupation. Not to be able to talk of your God to a stranger is a sterile Christianity; not to be able to comfort a sick brother with the healing message of His grace is a sickly Christianity; not to be able to warn a fellow Christian that his life may lead him to lose the grace of God is poor help for the Kingdom of God.

The engineer who plans the building of a mammoth bridge did not acquire his skill by wishing or avoiding. He had to dive into the countless books and courses that would ultimately lead him to such a mighty work. He was once a boy whose endless delight may have been the throwing of a ball or the climbing of a tree or the skipping of some stones. Now he has been trained. He can build the world's highest and longest bridge. We need many mighty builders for God's Kingdom. They must be trained, immersed in God's will and ever learning. Since our Christian day schools for a specific time of life can immerse better than any other plan, can constantly train better than any other plan, can spend more time with the tools needed to be and live as Christians than any other plan, then our path is clear. Paul told Timothy: "Meditate upon these things; give thyself *wholly* to them; that thy profiting may appear to all" (1 Timothy 4:15). For the profit of many, that they may be saved, we need to hearken to the voice of our God!

Our future leaders—pastors, teachers, laymen—must be soaking up this Word of God throughout life, if we wish them to be and if they are to be God-pleasingly successful. The future leader of Israel, Joshua, after Moses' death, was reminded of this by the Lord:

> This book of the law shall not depart out of thy mouth; but thou shalt meditate therein day and night, that thou mayest observe to do according to all that is written therein: for *then thou shalt make thy way prosperous, and then thou shalt have good success.* Have not I commanded thee? Be strong and of a good courage; be not afraid, neither be thou dismayed: for the Lord thy God is with thee whithersoever thou goest. (Joshua 1:8-9)

For God to go with them and to be with them at all times they need to absorb this Word in rich abundance, not just later on, but now, as children!

Objection No. 2

True, more work is done with the Word of God in a Christian day school than by other means; yet, my child has to be trained well in some other field and needs to enter a school which has the best equipment possible, so that he or she isn't held back in necessary training.

It has still to be proved that a Christian day school has nullified a child's chance for success in any occupation!

Plush carpets, expensive manuscript paper, the greatest and most learned teachers, lace-trimmed shirts, a gilt-edged bank account have never made a great composer yet, and never will! Nero found that out! Franz Schubert—a limited education musically, little or no money—wrote some of his finest works on the backs of coffee house menus. Carl Maria von Weber wrote some of his finest music when half-dead. Our own Johann Sebastian Bach had to learn by stealth in the moonlight. Geniuses are not stifled by having less than the best.

Besides, our Christian day school children are not generally denied any opportunity other school children receive. As evidence, ask their record when they face the competition of children schooled elsewhere. Suppose, however, that they would lose a great deal of knowledge by staying in a Christian day school. Parents, you who love Christ and are eternally grateful that He has saved you from hell for heaven and eternal bliss; parents, you who love your children more than earthly life itself and wish them to have every advantage; Christian, selfless parents, I ask you before God, do you want a child of yours to be wealthy, to be admired, to be famous, to be revered, to want nothing in this life for seventy years or so and even to be honored centuries later, and perhaps burn in hell for all eternity? Or do you want a child of yours, no matter how humble the earthly occupation, to share heaven with you for all eternity?

The objection continues: "But he doesn't have to make that choice. It doesn't have to be 'either'—'or.' I'll bring him to church and Sunday school and teach him at home and, in addition, I'll let him go to the school where he may have the greater material advantage and convenience."

This Christianity is not such an easy thing to maintain and cultivate as some people imagine. There is a devil! Because I accept the revelation of the Word of God, therefore I believe that

Adela May (Halverson) Faugstad, who completed an Associate Degree in 1959, served Mt. Olive Lutheran Elementary School as a student teacher while enrolled in Bethany's three-year synod-certification program.

there is a devil who is a very real and personal being. Moreover, I believe that the devil is interested in me and in *my* children, that is, in my destruction and my children's destruction. He goes about as a roaring lion seeking whom he may devour. He is my adversary and my children's adversary, and I must arm myself and I must help my children arm themselves with the armor of God to stand against the wiles of the devil. He works unceasingly to destroy the Christian church, to destroy me, to destroy my children, to destroy everything and everyone. He is supported by my sinful flesh, by my children's sinful flesh, and he is aided and abetted by worldly allurements and considerations. I must face the devil constantly. My children must face him constantly. We must face him with more than pop-guns and firecrackers.

Be assured of this: you can triumph over the devil but you cannot fight him with human weapons. "With might of ours can naught be done. Soon were our loss effected."[41] There is only one

---

[41]   *Editors' note*: Martin Luther, "A Mighty Fortress Is Our God," *ELH* 250:2.

effective weapon against Satan—"*It is written.*"[42] The sword of the spirit, the armor of God, the Word of Life—that is the God-given spiritual weapon against a deadly, spiritual foe. We must arm our children to the teeth.

We cannot leave the pointing out of truth, the disclosure of spiritual weapons, to a future pasture some forty or fifty years from now and be content with a vague, general piety which will at least keep the traditional Christmas tree and Easter parade from dying out. My children—and yours—will have to face a relentless, horrible, real foe, not a dummy scarecrow. It will not be a mock battle. Cream puffs and custard pies will not suffice. Deadly weapons are needed to conquer a deadly foe. If you think that perhaps Satan will not bother your children—; the devil dares to tempt the sinless Christ, and we can be certain that it is Christ's dearest children—yes, the "little ones which believe in Him" [Mark 9:42] together with the strongest of Christian adults whom he most seeks to destroy!

"Seek ye first the kingdom of God, and his righteousness; and all these things shall be added unto you" (Matthew 6:33). Seek ye first the kingdom of God and his righteousness for your children and they shall not want. Your children can never get too much spiritual food. Feed them to the full while God gives the strength, life, and grace to do so. More parents need the selflessness of a Moses who pleaded with God; "Oh, this people have sinned a great sin, and have made them gods of gold. Yet now, if Thou wilt forgive their sin—; and if not, blot me, I pray thee, out of Thy book which Thou hast written." That was true unselfishness. Commendable as it was, let us not forget God's answer: "Whosoever hath sinned against me, him will I blot out of my book" (Exodus 32:31-33).

A parent cannot say on judgment day: "Please, God, send me to hell in place of my children." Christ died to save them. No other atonement can be made. Our work is now! We must give our children the rich feasts now and not scatter crumbs before them. Before our privilege to do this passes from us through time or force, let us hearken unto the voice of our God! Sacrifice material things, if you must! Yea, let your children sacrifice material benefits, for eternal life is worth more than a sideways glance or a puny gesture.

---

[42] *Editors' note*: This frequently recurring biblical phrase serves as the motto of the Evangelical Lutheran Synod. See, for example, Luke 4:8,10.

Objection No. 3

My children have made many friends in other schools. They will be unhappy, if they cannot keep close contact with these friends.

O shallow thought! How many have not cursed the day they thought it! If there is anyone in this world who makes Christ's image fade for you or causes you to love other things more than Christ, or causes you to think less of your Savior, or causes you to choose the tents of wickedness—which tents may be very respectable outwardly, but are void of Him—then lose that friend! At least, do not pay him homage to the exclusion of Christ.

There is a "friend of sinners" [Luke 7:34] to be valued above all. He says: "Greater love hath no man than this, that a man lay down his life for his friends. Ye are my friends, if ye do whatsoever I command you" (John 15:13-14). *If ye do whatsoever I command you.* He says: *"Learn of Me!"* Our children need to be well acquainted with this *friend*. With Him they stand! Without Him they shall fall!

All human friends who contribute to the learning about this friend are friends indeed. Friendship with those who love the Lord needs to be cultivated. God wants His children to talk about Him to one another. In Malachi we read: "Then they that feared the Lord spake often one to another: and the Lord hearkened, and heard it, and a book of remembrances was written before Him for them that feared the Lord, and that thought upon His name" (Malachi 3:16).

As for those who do not love the Lord Jesus, the greatest service to them will be our friendship with Jesus. That friendship with Jesus will be noted, make no mistake about that! After Peter—who had been imprisoned with John—testified to the rulers of the Jews that Jesus alone saves, these outsiders were forced to admit that Peter and John "had been with Jesus" (Acts 4:13b). We need to help our children make fast friends with the Lord. "Draw nigh to God, and He will draw nigh to you" (James 4:8). Cause your children to draw nigh to God, and He will draw nigh to them.

Objection No. 4

You talk as if only Christian day school products turn out well. I know of some who have left the church and some who even have criminal records. You are making a claim that isn't so!

The Bible tells all parents to teach their children diligently, to bring them up in the nurture and admonition of the Lord, to beseech God for their well-being [Ephesians 6:4]. The Bible does not tell parents to believe for their children. God's Holy Spirit, not the Christian day school, brings men to faith. In the Christian day school our children are constantly given the Word of God through which this Holy Spirit works faith. We can't believe for them, nor are we required to do that. We can only see to it that they are taught and pray God's blessing upon them. God promises me and all parents: "Train up a child in the way he should go: and when he is old, he will not depart from it" (Proverbs 22:6). That is a blessed assurance!

When a pianist practices six or eight hours a day for years and then makes a glaring mistake in performance, you would be a fool to say that practice does not pay and that you will never practice to play the piano. If you were wise, you would say that more practice is needed. With the teaching of the Word of God, when a person forsakes God, it is not because of too much religion or because the learning of religion cannot help him. Don't forget to reckon with the devil, the world, and, above all, that sinful flesh! Parents need to do their work just as a pastor does his. They need to say: "We have planted our children's Christian teachers, and we have watered these plants. God giveth the increase. In His hands rests the success for which we pray. Trust Him to fulfill His promise that His Word shall not return to Him void. More than that we cannot do."

A Christian parent knows that it is impossible to force a child to be a Christian. What a Christian needs to say is this:

"I want my child to have every opportunity to be a Christian. I want my child to know exactly what true Christianity is. I do not want my child to be confused concerning the issues of Christianity. God supplies the faith. I must teach the knowledge.

"When my child is confronted by a severe temptation, I want him to know that God can make him strong enough to resist that temptation and that prayer and the Word of God will help him overcome it.

"If others are making false and superstitious uses of the Word of God, I want him to know in advance that you cannot use the Bible as you would a lottery wheel. I want him to know in advance that when you flip the pages of a Bible and place your finger at random on a passage, you will not always find your thought to live by for the day. Otherwise he might run into the kind of situation one poor duffer suffered as he paged for his thought to live by one day. The passage which first confronted him was this: 'And Judas went out and hanged himself' [Matthew 27:5]. Being terrified at the prospect, he tried again and came up with this: 'Go and do thou likewise' [Luke 10:37]. Trembling like a leaf he tried once more (for, after all, the third time is the charm) and crawled back into bed after he read: 'That thou doest, do quickly' [John 13:27]. His day was shot! I want my child to know what to live by from the entire Bible and to seek daily that important knowledge for his growth in the faith.

"I do not want my child to be confused, when taking a Scriptural stand on some issue of the day, by some modern Ahab who will sneer at him: 'Art thou he that troubleth Israel?' I want him to know that Elijah replied: 'I have not troubled Israel, but thou, and thy father's house, in that ye have forsaken the commandments of the Lord' (1 Kings 18:17). I want him to know that Jesus warned the apostles that they would be called troublemakers (John 16:2). If he should be a leader of the church, I want my child to know that it is wrong to cry: 'Peace, peace, when there is no peace' (Jeremiah 6:14).

"When someone approaches him to send his boys to an organization which tends to confuse the minds with the talk of many similar religions—the main difference being of personal opinion—I want my child to know that the choice of a religion is a matter of life or death, and I want him to be able to say: 'Man, I cannot risk my child's eternal safety by letting him absorb a philosophy which makes un-momentous the choice between Baal and God. My conscience would not allow it. Even if the church says it is alright, a plague take your synodical resolutions. My child's soul is at stake! I'll teach him to tie knots, I'll camp out with him, but cause him to be confused?—Never. He'll have enough confusion to battle later on when I'm gone. I must strengthen, and not weaken him.'[43]

"When my child becomes discouraged with life and its problems and the problems of the church, I want him to know that there was once a man, a prophet of the Lord, who was also discouraged, not knowing that there were 7,000 who had not

---

43   *Editors' note*: The author has in mind the Boy Scouts. See Paul R. Zager, "The Christian and Scouting: How Compatible?," *Lutheran Synod Quarterly* 41, no. 4 (Dec. 2001): 330–52.

bowed the knee to Baal, when he thought he alone was faithful [1 Kings 19:18]. When my child is distressed over the huge number of the opposition forces and wonders where to turn next, I want him to know in advance, before someone else has to push the sixth chapter of the Second Book of Kings under his nose, that the Word of God is all-sufficient, no matter who or how many the foe. I want him to be able to say with all courage and confidence with Elisha: 'Fear not: for they that be with us are more than they that be with them' (2 Kings 6:16), and I want him to know how the Lord opened the eyes of Elisha's servant and how he then saw the mountain full of horses and chariots of fire round about Elisha (v. 17).

"If my child should ever have the privilege of pushing forward in the work of the church and of passing through the doors of opportunity to continue and to expand God's work here on earth, I want him to know that he can say: 'The Lord has given us this opportunity to serve Him better. Let not the lack of money hold us back. The Lord's work it is. He'll see to it that we can carry on for Him. Christ did not first say, 'Preach the Gospel to every creature' [Mark 16:15] and then add 'if you have enough money.'

"In all probability my child later on will have to suffer the loss of parents through death. When that time comes, I do not want him to go around gibbering like a spiritual idiot: 'My father (or mother) should not have died at this time. If that's what the God of the Bible does, I just won't go to church anymore.' I want him to know that he can say with all confidence: 'God's own time is the best. In Him we live, and move, and have our being as long as we live. And in Him we die, at His good time, when He wills.'[44]

"When my child is on his deathbed and the devil comes to him tempting him, 'Are you sure? Will you truly rise from the dead? Will God give *you* salvation?' I want him to know that he can say with all confidence: 'Christ died for all!' (2 Corinthians 5:15a) and 'I know whom I have believed, and am persuaded that He is able to keep that which I have committed unto Him against that Day' (2 Timothy 1:12). 'Oh, that my words were now written! Oh, that they were printed in a book! That they were graven with an iron pen and lead in the rock forever! For I know that my redeemer liveth, and that He shall stand at the latter day upon the earth: and though after my skin worms destroy this body, yet in my flesh shall I see God: Whom I shall see for myself, and mine eyes shall behold, and not another' (Job 19:23-27a). Listen to me,

---

44   J. S. Bach, Cantata No. 106.

devil: 'I am persuaded, that neither death, nor life, nor angels, nor principalities, nor powers, nor things present, nor things to come, nor height, nor depth, nor any other creature, shall be able to separate me (us) from the love of God, which is in Christ Jesus, my (our) Lord' (Romans 8:38-39)."

If there be some in the world today who consider this brand of thinking too straitlaced, too naive, too literal, too simpleminded, let them so consider it. *We* need to hearken unto the voice of the Lord our God, so that the Lord will continue to rejoice over us for good, as he rejoiced over our fathers (Deuteronomy 30:9–10).

DOCUMENT 2.6:

On Starting and Maintaining a Christian Day School (1966)

By Theodore A. Aaberg

*(A biography of Theodore A. Aaberg may be found at **Document 2.4**.)*
Source: *Synod Report* (1966), 58–62.

The Christian day schools of our Synod have a fine history. To be sure, they have not been as imposing as many of the schools of German Lutheran congregations, which often have been like large farms staked out on the rich valley floor, while ours have been like little farmsteads scratched out on the rough hillsides. Yet for all of that, remembering the many handicaps under which our schools have had to fight both for birth and preservation, we must say that these schools have stood in our midst these many years as notable testimonies to the grace of God. The full histories of these schools—the dedication and service of Christian teachers, pastors, parents, students, and friends—is known only to the Lord. And while some of our schools have long since closed their doors, their record is still being written in the hearts and lives of former students and their offspring through the Word which was daily sown so long ago, and the final entry in each school's record will not be made until the Last Day. Only then is school really dismissed. Only then is a school really closed.

As one looks to the future of Christian day school education in our Synod, there appears to be a new stirring of interest, and for this we should be most grateful. At the same time there are many problems, which continue to confront the operation of our schools. This brief paper is offered in the hope and prayer that it may contribute somewhat to a renewed conviction and zeal for the opening of new schools in our midst, and for the preservation of those now in existence. May we all have that high regard for the Christian day school expressed by Dr. Walther when he called it "the gem of the Lutheran Church."[45]

Matters Which Are Basic Both to Starting and Maintaining a Christian Day School

When a contractor sets to work to erect a building, he does not begin by taking a few bricks and a batch of cement in hand. There is a lot of groundwork to be done before he sets the first brick in place. So with the opening of a Christian day school, as well as its continued operation, there is a certain groundwork on which the school must be built.

The first piece of groundwork, basic both to starting and maintaining a school, is that there be a firm conviction regarding the Word of God as a Means of Grace. Jesus' petition to His heavenly Father on the eve of His crucifixion, "Sanctify them through Thy truth: Thy word is truth" (John 17:17), teaches us that God sanctifies His people through His Word. Luther's explanation of the Third Article therefore cannot be a dry confession to be recited and then forgotten, but must burn in our hearts and minds so that we can never forget it:

> I believe that I can not by my own reason or strength believe in Jesus Christ my Lord or come to Him, but the Holy Ghost has called me by the Gospel, enlightened me with His gifts, sanctified and kept in the true faith, even as He calls, gathers, enlightens and sanctifies the whole Christian Church on earth, and keeps it with Jesus Christ in the one true faith. (SC II)

There must be no patronizing attitude on our part toward the Word of God, but a determined possessiveness as we realize the truth of Moses' words regarding the Word of God: "For it is not a vain thing for you; because it is your life" (Deuteronomy 32:47).

In this connection we would warn against making the

---

[45] *Editors' note*: The source has not been located.

foundation of the Christian day school too narrow. We do this, for example, if we stress the teaching of evolution in the public school as the reason for establishing a day school in the congregation. Now when evolution is taught, be it atheistic or theistic, false doctrine is being taught, and thus the teaching of evolution in the public schools is a reason, and a very good reason for establishing a school. But it is only one part of the whole picture. Even if the teachers in a certain public school did not teach evolution, the congregation in that place ought to have a day school. And why? Because the Word of God can be taught in such a school, and the Word is a means of grace, with the power for the regeneration and sanctification of the individual. We must see the broad sweep of the benefit of Scripture as given by Paul to Timothy: "All scripture is given by inspiration of God, and is profitable for doctrine, for reproof, for correction, for instruction in righteousness: That the man of God may be perfect, thoroughly furnished unto all good works" (2 Timothy 3:16-17). It is that our children might receive all of these benefits of the Word in abundant measure that we establish our schools, not merely that they might be protected from this or that false teaching.

A second piece of groundwork that is basic both to starting and maintaining a day school in the congregation has to do with the Lord's Great Commission. As little as we can ignore the Lord's command to baptize all nations, so little can we disregard the command which immediately follows: "teaching them to observe all things whatsoever I have commanded you" (Matthew 28:20). The Christian day school, as an institution, is a matter of Christian liberty, but Christian education most assuredly is not, for the Lord of the Church says: "Teaching them. . . ." Nor are we to determine the degree or extent of that education. Jesus has already done that for us when He said: "Teaching them to observe all things whatsoever I have commanded you." We are not suggesting that when a congregation provides a day school for its children that it can then say: "Now we are doing all that Jesus has commanded us to do in this matter." God forbid! But by the same token we feel we have a right to ask congregations, pastors, and parents who give the impression of being one-hundred per cent satisfied with lesser forms for instruction, such as the Sunday School: "Have you not read your assignment from Jesus to teach them all things?"

That brings us to the third piece of groundwork, namely that there must be a firm conviction that the day school offers the best means available to the church for the carrying out of his God-given task of teaching the Word to the young. A school is a heavy burden, financially and otherwise, on both pastor and people, and even more so on the teacher, and only the conviction that it offers the best way of fulfilling the Savior's command makes it bearable, and then, of course, a joy and a delight. Even when pastor and people have such convictions they may still not be able to establish a school, but without those convictions a real attempt to get a school started, or to keep it going, will hardly be made.

Some Suggestions on Starting a School

A diligent, persistent effort must be made to impress upon parents and other members of the congregation the importance of teaching the Word to the young, and the unique character of the Christian day school, which enables it to accomplish this task. This effort must be made on many fronts—in sermons, topics at meetings of various church organizations, etc. One must be willing to go to a lot of effort and trouble to inform and to persuade people on these matters. Our goal should be that people will not merely say: "Shall we start a school?" but "We must start a school."

This will not be accomplished overnight, but will very likely require a long, faithful process of instruction. We must be patient in our efforts to establish a school. We must be willing to plant, and if necessary, to leave both the watering and the reaping to others many years hence. Nor must we seek to dictate the exact harvest. Perhaps it may be the establishment of a school in the parish, and, if not, perhaps the supplying of young people from the congregation for teaching in other parishes, or of getting certain parents concerned who may later be instrumental in establishing a school elsewhere. Even if the effort to start a school results only in the congregation working that much harder to make more effective use of their other educational agencies, at least some good has been accomplished.

All efforts to establish a school must be evangelical and "above board." We must work in an orderly fashion through regular congregation channels, and not seek to go ahead on our own authority.

While one must be patient and willing to talk, one must also have the courage to start. There is a time to strike, a time for action. Conditions will never be entirely ideal for starting a school, and therefore we must have the courage to commend the matter to the Lord, and then like Peter to venture over the side of the boat and start walking [Matthew 14:22–33]. A beginning must be

Denny Radichel teaches a geography lesson to Mt. Olive elementary students while completing his Christian day school certificate program at Bethany Lutheran College, ca. 1960.

made.

    Not all Christians have the same quickness or imagination in spiritual matters, and as in so many other projects of the Church, once a beginning is actually made so that the school becomes a reality, others may see the benefit and perhaps become some of the school's staunchest supporters. Once a school is started, many of the fears will disappear, and the project will flourish.

    One should by all means seek to have the entire congregation sponsor and support the school. This is proper in itself because of the Savior's word: "Feed my lambs," and it is surely best for both congregation and school in the long run. A private association within the congregation should be formed only as a last resort to the establishment of a school, and even then diligent efforts should continue to have the entire congregation sponsor and support the school.

Close attention should be paid to the local situation. The overall condition of the congregation must be considered its size, the number of children, their ages, building programs, congregation indebtedness, etc. Certain times are more favorable than others in the life of a congregation for the establishment of a day school, and we should strike at the best time. Certain parents are more concerned with the spiritual training of their children than others, and if we have such parents we have a good nucleus for a beginning. The community situation must also come in for scrutiny. There are many changes taking place in our communities these years, with many local institutions being closed down or absorbed in reorganizations, and in this state of flux there often is not quite the opposition to the establishment of a day school as in earlier years in many areas. During building programs, one can try to include facilities that could be used later for a school. One cannot ignore the matter of federal aid to education, nor the various proposals in the several states for aid in one form or another, if not for the school itself, at least to the pupil. If certain privileges are granted, and if they are of such a nature that they do not jeopardize the Christian character or the future of the school, so that they might be accepted with a good conscience, such aid might play a role in a decision to open a school.

One must look to the brethren, the Synod, for help in starting a school. This may be in the form of financial subsidy for a season, but even more important is the moral support and encouragement. The example of other schools, the articles and reports in the *Sentinel*, the *Christian Day School Bulletin*, the Christian day school promotion at the convention, the efforts of Bethany to recruit and train teachers—all of this plays a vital role in the opening of a school. The support and encouragement of the brethren can be of great help in the struggle to establish a school. Thus pastors who may not have been able to establish a school in their own parish may still be able to do much to help someone else start one elsewhere.

Some Suggestions for Maintaining a School

It would be folly to suppose that once a school has been established, it will run on its own power. Old problems simply give way to new ones, and the school thus requires the continued, fervent labors of its supporters.

The spiritual reasons underlying the opening of the school must continually be stressed during its operation so that monotony, weariness, and dissatisfaction do not set in. As the Gospel itself has an eternal freshness about it, so these Gospel schools must have a like freshness about them. "Thy people shall be willing in the day of Thy power, in the beauties of holiness from the womb of the morning: Thou hast the dew of Thy youth" (Psalm 110:3).

By way of practical suggestions on keeping our schools going, we would say that it is quite important that a congregation continue to seek to improve its school from year to year. To pay the teacher a low salary is not a bargain for the congregation, and for spiritual reasons alone we should continue to seek greater remuneration for these consecrated workers in the church. We must be willing to spend money to keep our schools up to date in the matter of textbooks and equipment. The physical property, including the general appearance of classroom and school grounds, deserves our continued attention and care.

The welfare of the school demands that we co-operate with the state. While we are not to budge one inch when it comes to our rights and liberties, neither are we to look for trouble, or imagine evil where none exists. We are to co-operate with the county superintendent, the county nurse, the fire marshal, and others in such things as reports, teacher certification, fire regulations, and the like. We are subject unto them in certain things, and we are to obey them (Romans 13:1). Let us not moan too loudly over state standards. To be sure, they at times are a problem, but they are also a challenge, keeping us on our toes, and may thus also serve for good, under the blessing of God.

Pastors must play a key role in the school if it is to continue and to flourish. We must be willing to be bothered with the school's problems. We must tend to things, give attention to detail, and lend a helping hand wherever and whenever possible.

The Synod must also help, and that in many ways, but perhaps chiefly by a simple consensus regarding the value of such schools. Individual schools ought to be able to feel that they are part of a system a synod system of schools. The Synod ought to be just as concerned with the recruitment and training of teachers for our schools as of pastors for our pulpits. One cannot maintain a school without a teacher. In this connection we believe that President Joseph Petersen's recommendation that our Synod seek to work out a training program for our teachers with Dr. Martin

Luther College of New Ulm, ought to receive our wholehearted support.[46] Not only would this arrangement enable our future teachers to continue their education in a Christian school, but whenever we might have a surplus of teachers they could more readily serve in the schools of our sister synod, and in those years when we need more teachers than are available from our own midst, we might prevail on them for assistance.

In conclusion we would say that we live in a day when it is easy to write the Christian day school off as a lost cause, and to lay the blame on the problems which confront us, saying that they are too great to overcome. However, we must remember that there were problems also in an earlier day when our schools flourished. Most important of all, if the problems of today are greater, we have only to lay the greater demands upon God in prayer, remembering Jesus' own words: "If ye then, being evil, know how to give good gifts unto your children, how much more shall your Father which is in heaven give good things to them that ask Him?" (Matthew 7:11). And it is there that we would leave this matter both of starting and maintaining day schools: at the throne of grace.

---

[46] Joseph Petersen, in *Synod Report* (1966), 15.

DOCUMENT 2.7:

The Effectiveness of Christian Schools in Mission Outreach (1996)

By Silas V. Born

Silas V. Born (1938–) was born in Minneapolis, Minnesota, on October 26, 1938.[47] He attended Trinity Lutheran School in Waconia, Minnesota, followed by Dr. Martin Luther High School in New Ulm, Minnesota. Remaining in New Ulm for college, he completed a B.S. in Education from Dr. Martin Luther College in 1963. Born was first assigned to teach upper grades at St. John's Lutheran School in Sparta, Wisconsin, where he served from 1959 to 1969 and again from 1970 to 1971. In 1970, Born also received his Master of Science degree from the University of Wisconsin, Milwaukee, specializing in curriculum and supervision. In 1971 Born started a school at Holy Cross Lutheran Church in Madison, Wisconsin, where he served as both principal and teacher until 1992. In that year he was called to Škola Martina Luthera in Plzen, Czech Republic, where he started School for Nationals, serving as both teacher and principal until 1997.
While in the Czech Republic, he published the Škola Luthera Letter, a biweekly, bilingual newsletter on education; he also designed bilingual curriculum materials for mathematics, science and religion.[48] In 1998, Born returned to the United States as professor of education at Bethany

---

[47] Ray Diepenbrock, "Mr. Silas Born," *Lutheran Sentinel*, Aug. 1985, 12-13.
[48] Silas Born, *Curriculum Vitae*, 2007.

Lutheran College in Mankato, Minnesota. *From 1998 to 2002, he served as the Director of the Student Success Center. Since 1998, Born has served as the ELS director of Christian Education. From 1997 to 2004, he served as editor of the* ELS Educator, *a biannual periodical for teachers in the synod. He is married to Mary (Ibisch) Born with whom he has two sons, John and Peter.* [AB]

Source: Paper delivered at the Peru Mission Conference of the ELS, Lima, Peru, Jan. 1996.

Because we are dealing with the souls of men, women and children in our mission work in Pilsen, [Czech Republic], I thought it might be good if some of our people could speak to you today. In fact, a number of the students had asked if they could go with me when I told them about my trip to Lima, Peru, for the missionaries' conference. I told them I was sorry, but they couldn't go along, they would have to stay behind and work hard at their lessons. Therefore, during this hour, I would like to bring you some thoughts from various sources regarding the use of Christian day schools in mission outreach.

By the time Petr Keller had found me on Monday morning, he had already recorded several children's and adult's answers. Now with his clipboard and pencil in hand he rushed up to me and asked, "Is it better to love someone or to be loved by someone?" Since Petr had arrived just at the beginning of fifth and sixth grade religion class, his question could serve as an opening for our morning devotion, for it was a question that opened the door for a discussion of the greatest love known to mankind—God's love for each of us in sending Jesus to be our Savior. Yes, Petr's question could be the springboard to all the Bible story topics we would concentrate on this year. But more importantly, the answer to his question could be integrated with the whole purpose for our church and school in Pilsen. I was pleased that he had come with his question. Hopefully, he and his classmates would see that the ultimate answer to his question could only be found in the Bible.

Petr's question on love was only one of many self-designed surveys for the teachers and students at Martin Luther School in Pilsen. On another occasion, he had taken a survey on the pros and cons of nuclear energy and the building of the nuclear reactor at Temelín in the Czech Republic.

Recently, he came during snack time and asked me, "Do you

believe?" When I asked him to clarify his question even though I knew what he meant, he said, "Do you believe in Jesus?" But before I could answer, he told me he knew my answer and began to put a mark on his tally sheet.

"Why do you think you know my answer?" I asked.

"I think all the Americans believe," he said, "but I don't think all the Czech children believe." When I asked why he was taking the survey, he said, "Pastor Matthew Luttman talked in chapel about how the children come to believe in Jesus through hearing God's Word, but I don't think most of the children believe. I think they only listen, but don't really believe." As I sneaked a glance at his clipboard, I asked him what he had found so far. He answered, "Most children say they believe."

"Isn't that wonderful?" I responded.

"Hmm, I don't know ... ," he mumbled hesitantly. But before I could pursue his hesitant reaction, the bell signaled the end of the morning snack period and we had to rush off to separate classrooms. Fortunately, this would not be the end of our discussion, for our paths would cross many times again that day.

Petr is an interesting sixth grade boy who was born with a heart defect and his appearance is that of a much younger child. Because of his condition, he has been given an extra set of textbooks to use at home, so he doesn't have to carry a heavy load of books to and from school each day. Unfortunately, he also suffers some of the problems resulting from a "broken home" and the remarriage of his mother. Petr has on occasion indicated that he doesn't believe in Jesus as his Savior, but he does listen to God's Word and has many questions. Petr usually comes to church alone when his class is scheduled to sing on Sundays. Occasionally, he will show up on Sundays when he isn't scheduled to sing.

Petr's surveys are certainly thought provoking and provide me with an opportunity to apply God's Word in our discussion of what people's answers might mean. Sometimes his surveys provide a springboard for my classes' morning devotions.

But Petr isn't the only one who has taken surveys. Two years ago, Miss Eisberg's first graders were working at their desks and talking about various things when one of her students asked the class, "Who believes in Jesus?"

Without hesitating all of the students raised their hands except for one little girl who spoke up, "B h neexistovat." (God doesn't exist.)

To which another girl responded, "I'll pray for you; God loves you." Last year that prayer was answered, for the little girl who had said God didn't exist, now came and asked to be baptized because she believed in Jesus as her living and redeeming Savior!

We may be surprised to hear of children taking these surveys. For the children, these are not peculiar activities. For some unknown reason, they don't mind asking questions—even questions about spiritual things. Furthermore, they don't mind answering these questions. It is rather refreshing to find children who have not become inhibited by the thought, "I wonder what is the most appropriate or teacher-acceptable response?" That is not to say that many of the children's questions or answers at our school may occasionally reflect the thinking of their parents. But young children, as you well know, are often very candid in their responses. It is quite easy to determine which comments from a younger child are simply the expressions of parents, grandparents or the child.

Polls or surveys are not a new phenomenon. Jesus' disciples were even taking them on one occasion to determine who was the greatest in the kingdom of heaven. The evangelists Matthew, Mark and Luke record this incident for us. We read the following from the book of Matthew: "At that time the disciples came to Jesus and asked, 'Who is greatest in the kingdom of heaven?' He called a little child and had him stand among them. Then He said to them, 'I can guarantee this truth: Unless you change and become like little children, you will never enter the kingdom of heaven. Whoever becomes like this little child is the greatest in the kingdom of heaven. And whoever welcomes a child like this in my name welcomes me'" (Matthew 18:2-5).

On another occasion Jesus had to rebuke His disciples because it was their opinion that children were a bother to Jesus. Again, the evangelists Matthew, Mark and Luke record Jesus' desire to have children brought to Him. From Mark's account we read—"Some people brought little children to Jesus to have Him hold them. But the disciples told the people not do that. When Jesus saw this, He became irritated. He told them, 'Don't stop children from coming to me! Children like these are part of the kingdom of God. I can guarantee this truth: Whoever doesn't receive the kingdom of God as a little child receives it will never enter it.' Jesus put his arms around the children and blessed them by placing His hands on them" (Mark 10:13-16).

Finally, the words of Jesus' great commission to disciple all nations have always been understood to include children:

All authority in heaven and on earth has been given to me. So wherever you go, make disciples of all nations: Baptize them in the name of the Father, and of the Son, and of the Holy Spirit. Teach them to do everything I have commanded you. And remember that I am always with you until the end of time. (Matthew 28:19-20)

The emphasis on educating children in the truths of God's Word is also found in the Old Testament as God reminds us in Deuteronomy 4:9: "However, be careful, and watch yourselves closely so that you don't forget the things which you have seen with your own eyes. Don't let them fade from your memory as long as you live. Teach them to your children and grandchildren." And again we read from Deuteronomy 11:18: "Take these words of mine to heart and keep them in mind. . . . Teach them to your children, and talk about them when you're at home or away, when you lie down or get up." In Proverbs 22:6 God gives us the following advice: "Train a child in the way he should go, and even when he is old he will not turn away from it." The words from these two Old Testament passages appear to give a specific directive to parents. But what if parents are unbelievers? Then whose responsibility is it to teach the children the truths of God's Word? Is that not why Jesus included them in His great commission?

Sometimes our teachers have wondered how much spiritual understanding the little children in kindergarten and first grade acquire after being in our school for just a few months. An incident over two and one-half years ago has helped to provide some insight into that concern. It was at the baptism of Nikola, the first Czech child to be baptized at our mission, that most of her kindergarten classmates sang and observed her baptism. When Pastor James Krikava asked Nikola the questions that you and I have repeatedly heard at baptisms, "Do you believe in God the Father, Almighty Maker . . . ?" all of the children answered in unison, "Ano!" (Yes). "Do you believe in Jesus Christ . . . ?" Again, all of the children answered, "Ano!" (Yes). Regarding each question, the assembly, heard a clear and unrehearsed "Ano!" (Yes). It was clear these children had learned about the love of Jesus in their classroom and the Holy Spirit had created faith in their hearts. Furthermore, they were not afraid to confess their faith—even in the presence of their unbelieving parents. Yes, out of the mouths of babes [Psalm 8:2], for these children could just as well have repeated the words spoken by Peter and John, "We cannot stop talking about what we've seen and heard" (Acts 4:20).

Škola Martina Luthera in Plzen, Czech Republic, conducts classes inside this historic building, first constructed in 1897 and purchased by Thoughts of Faith from the City of Plzen in 1993. A legal encumbrance ensures that this facility will continue to be used for non-commercial, educational purposes. For more information, visit www.sml.cz.

Each year the children from kindergarten and the primary grades present a fall and a spring program for their parents, grandparents and anyone interested in coming. Recently, the children from grades two and three presented their fall program. Almost the entire program was devoted to religious music. A brief comment after the program from one of our American visitors will suffice to make my point. He simply said, "Those children sang right from the heart!" What was significant was that the parents and grandparents heard their children sing from their hearts the message of God's love.

As one Christian parent remarked later, "My child has been singing those songs at home all the time. I think I almost know them!"

Yes, music is a great vehicle for teaching children and adults. Just as Luther's Reformation sang its way into the hearts of the people, so our mission field message of salvation through Christ Jesus can be proclaimed through the medium of music. Each school year we choose a theme on which our teachers and students can focus their attention. The theme is illustrated on the bulletin boards in the school, so not only the students and teachers remain focused, but also so that visitors and other outside groups that use our building can learn a simple basic scriptural truth. The theme also becomes the core for the many classroom devotions and Wednesday morning chapel talks. Furthermore, it becomes the basis for a "theme song" for the school year which the children sing in chapel each Wednesday. . . .

But what about the parents and grandparents who are avowed atheists? What is their reaction to the child's faith or confession of faith in the home? This is a difficult question to answer, but a story related by one of our parents after an eight week information class may give us some insight into a family situation where the children become believers before the parents.

One of our fathers told this story when we were discussing the importance of the Christian day school at the final session of an eight week information course. He said that he had come home from work one evening. When the whole family was seated around the table eating, his daughter Martina, who was a sixth grader at Martin Luther School at the time, left the table and returned with a little green Advent wreath that her sister So a had made in kindergarten that day. In her other hand she was carrying a book. She handed both of them to the father and asked him to read from the book. When he looked at the book, he noticed it was a Bible. He said he got upset with his daughter and told her he was hungry and tired and wasn't interested in any of this Bible stuff. But each night Martina came with the Bible and little Advent wreath asking her father to read even though her request was continually rejected. He was surprised at her persistence. He said she never had been this persistent about anything before. He needed to find out what was in this book that she wanted him to read. So he began reading the Bible to his family. After Christmas he enrolled in Pastor Krikava's adult instruction class and after eight weeks he and his two daughters were baptized into the Christian faith. Eventually, the mother also attended an instruction class and was baptized. These parents said that they would not have come to hear about the Savior if their children had not been enrolled in the mission school.

In another family, it was the daughter who helped to bring her mother to the church. Lenka who is nineteen years old is presently a senior at Minnesota Valley Lutheran High School in Minnesota. The first year our school was permitted by the Czech ministry of education to enroll Czech nationals, Lenka became a freshman in our high school which was primarily designed to fulfill the secondary education requirements of our missionaries' children. During that year, she began confirmation instruction with Pastor Krikava. After completing her catechetical studies, she was baptized and received into membership in the Lutheran church. She continued to study with our American high school students through her sophomore and junior years. While she was completing her junior year, she also assisted Mrs. Born for the last half hour of kindergarten each day. This experience brought her to the realization that she could serve the church and her own people by becoming a Christian day school teacher. It was also during her junior year that her mother began taking instruction in the Christian faith and was eventually baptized and received into membership in the Lutheran church. Since all but one of our juniors were returning to the United States to complete their high school senior year, and since Lenka had been offered a place to live by a generous American family if she wished to attend a Lutheran high school, she was encouraged to take advantage of this opportunity. After this year she plans to continue with her college studies for becoming a Christian day school teacher.[49]

Not all parents are willing to learn more about the new-found faith of their child. Sometimes it is the grandparent who takes the active role in bringing the child to church regularly. Even though the grandfather in one family is an active Roman Catholic, he brought his grandson Ji í (George), who was in our Christian day school, to be baptized in the Lutheran church and continues to bring him to the Lutheran church regularly on Sundays.

Some parents obviously feel they are losing control of the situation when their child knows something or believes something the parents haven't learned to accept. During home visits, some parents make this quite clear with such remarks as, "I don't think my child knows enough yet or really understands everything." Meanwhile the child is sitting in the same room and makes a simple confession of faith and asks to be baptized. What the parent is probably saying is, "I'm not ready. I don't understand why my child believes. I don't want to show my ignorance." Other

---

[49] *Editors' note*: The author was referring to Lenka Steffelova, who graduated from Minnesota Valley Lutheran High School in 1996. She enrolled thereafter at Wisconsin Lutheran College in Milwaukee where she earned her teaching degree in 2001. She has been teaching in the Wauwatosa School District (suburban Milwaukee) ever since. In 2001 Lenka married Steve Wendland, the son and grandson of Lutheran missionaries who have been serving in Africa for the last forty years. Lenka and Steve now have three children and still live in the Milwaukee area. Email from Lenka Wendland, 20 March 2011.

parents are very frank and admit they don't know anything and indicate that they don't want to know. At the same time, we must remember that we probably wouldn't even be talking to this family if it wasn't for the fact that the child was in our Christian day school. Home visits are a very important part of mission work. The visits serve to build trust and respect between the home, the school, and the church in addition to allaying fears, answering questions, and, most importantly, sharing the Gospel. Because the child is in school, we have many opportunities to communicate with the parents. We have what sometimes has been referred to as a "captive audience." It is an "audience" that must be visited frequently through personal evangelism calls.

Interestingly, several of our school families have used a similar argument for expanding the mission school into a *gymnasium* (high school department for the Czech students). They have suggested that if the children and parents are exposed to the influence of God's Word through the Christian day school from the time the child is five years old until age eighteen, the entire family will have become loyal and devoted members of the congregation during that time. Obviously parents recognize the influence of God's Word on their children. As one mother who is a judge remarked at a recent open house, "I've seen the change in my children since they have begun attending Martin Luther School."

There is an interesting phenomenon among many of the Czech people. They have a great interest in the mission school and want their children to attend Škola Martina Luthera. Many of them want their children to learn English from native English speakers. When they are informed that first and foremost our school is an extension of our Lutheran mission, and that their children will learn about Jesus Christ, the Savior of mankind, from the Bible, they respond, "That's fine. We have no problem with that." But when we explain that Jesus is also their Savior and we welcome their participation in learning from God's Word, they answer with the words, "I'm too old." We have tried to understand what the age factor has to do with our invitation. Not only our youngest missionaries, but also old people like myself have gotten the same response. On one occasion, I "pressed" for clarification by telling the "aged" thirty-eight year old gentleman that since I was much older than he, and since Christ Jesus obviously didn't feel I was "over-the-hill" yet, he certainly wasn't too old to learn about his Savior. He turned to me and with a somber voice replied, "You don't understand what the communists did to us."

Whereupon he began to tell how the communists had destroyed the church in a subtle but insidious way. When he finished, I was enlightened but saddened. And worst of all I wasn't sure whether the "too old" for Christianity idea was a remnant of past fears or simply an "adult attitude" problem.

We have since taken a different approach which sounds something like this, "We realize that you will want to know what your child is going to be learning at Martin Luther School since the purpose, philosophy, and some of the subject matter is different from the schools you attended as a child. Therefore we are asking you to attend an information course that meets for an hour one evening per week for the next eight weeks." The topics covered in these meetings are as follows:

1. Children are a precious gift with basic needs
2. Teaching subjects from the Christian point of view
3. The origin of all things—creation vs. evolution
4. Who is Jesus and why do we teach about Him?
5. Baptism—what, why, how, when, benefits
6. Home and school relationships

Let me share some thoughts from the handout that is given the parents regarding the area of spiritual needs:

> Has your child ever done something wrong or disobeyed you in any way? Has your child ever asked you if it is right or wrong to do something? Did you know that your child's question indicated a spiritual need of the child? Your child wasn't asking if there was a law in Pilsen regarding such behavior, but simply whether it was right or wrong. All human beings have a sense of right or wrong. Generally, if we do something wrong, we immediately recognize it. It is because of this that people are law-abiding citizens. When your child did something wrong, what did you do? You probably showed your child in some way that it was wrong. Maybe you even got angry with the child's behavior. Your child was probably sorry for the wrong he/she committed. This also demonstrates a spiritual need in your child. This is a need for forgiveness—it is the need to be assured that the wrong the child has committed has been taken away.
>
> At Martin Luther School it is our philosophy that all people have important spiritual needs. All men have a natural

sense of right and wrong. When people do wrong things, they need to be reminded that they have wronged someone. We call this wrong-doing sin. The person who does something wrong is called a sinner. All sinners need forgiveness. The wonderful thing that your child will learn at Martin Luther School is that this forgiveness is free because God sent his son Jesus Christ to take all our sins away.

When the Apostle Paul, after whom our chapel has been named, visited Athens, Greece, during his travels, he talked to a group of people and said, 'I perceive that you are a very religious people.' These words may seem strange since Paul was talking to people who were heathens. What Paul was talking about was that these people had a spiritual need which they were attempting to meet. But they could not meet their spiritual need without Christ. Only the true God can fulfill our spiritual needs. We will discuss this in greater detail in a future meeting. In conclusion, we want to assure you that Martin Luther School has been established to meet all the needs of your child. (Information Course I)

Some topics generate more discussion among the parents than others. The topic relating to evolution vs. creation receives considerable reaction since the information they have learned under communism has been untrue or the scientific discoveries refuting evolution made by people connected with the church, such as Gregor Mendel, have been withheld or banned in the past.

The information course becomes the stepping-stone to an in-depth course of instruction in Christianity for the adult. Sometimes parents enroll in the in-depth instruction course prior to taking the information course. Adults not connected with the school simply take the in-depth course of instruction.

When parents enroll their children in the Christian day school, it is important that parents understand that their children will be learning about Christianity. Since most parents have been schooled by atheistic parents and teachers within an atheistic society controlled by atheistic communism, the parents and, in some cases also the grandparents, have no knowledge of Christianity, so a program for sharing information must be developed to inform parents of the purpose and philosophy of the school. In some cases, the fear of something new becomes an impediment. In other cases, a distrust for an established organization, whether it be the church or school, becomes an impediment. After 40 years of communism, there is so much that is new, it is difficult for them to discern fact from fiction. Many of them know the communists lied to them.—What about the new establishment?—What about the church?—With the demise of communism, many adults are faced with a large ideological void.

This was brought to my attention after a kindergarten program last spring when two fathers told me how thankful they were for the mission school, for our school's teachings were providing something for their children to believe. They said communism had left them spiritually bankrupt. There was nothing left for them to believe. Unfortunately, now they felt they were too old to accept the simple truths of Holy Scripture, but they recognized its importance for their children.

We can be comforted by the fact that creating faith in the hearts of these two fathers is the work of the Holy Spirit and not dependent upon our frail efforts. Since they are willing to read to their children the materials we send home, and they are willing to welcome us into their homes, and they occasionally come and hear the message proclaimed in our church, we can be confident that the Holy Spirit's miraculous work of creating faith will be accomplished, for we have God's promise recorded for us in Isaiah 55:11: "My word, which comes from my mouth, is like the rain and snow. It will not come back to me without results, but it will accomplish whatever I want and achieve whatever I send it to do."

It *is* important that parents are informed regarding the things their children are learning in the Christian day school. Being uninformed can be the greatest threat to cooperation. It is quite natural for parents to say, "If I know what my child is learning, I can feel comfortable that my child isn't learning something that I don't know."

Not only must we inform parents of what their children are learning, but we must be careful to respect their cultural heritage when doing mission work. In some situations we must help them understand the true origin of their cultural heritage. An example would be their celebration of various festivals, such as, All Saints Day on November 1 or Saint Mikoláš Eve on December 5. Has the visit to the cemetery become a cultural ritual without any meaning or understanding? Does the visit from "Saint Mikoláš, some devils, and some angels" have any Christian historical significance or is it simply a fun activity? Another example would be the singing of their national Christmas carol "Narodil se Kristus Pán," which is so rich in the true meaning of Christmas. How did this wonderful carol become the Czech national Christmas anthem, which is sung at the conclusion of all gatherings at Christmas time? In many ways these issues might be handled more easily with the children than with the adults since the original historical roots of some customs have been lost over the years, and the adults have only a secularized understanding to pass along to their children. . . .

This process of informing parents must not stop after the informational course. It must be a continuous process that starts when parents first inquire about enrolling their children in the school. It must follow a plan by which parents are given materials that their children will eventually use in school, namely, a Bible, Bible story lessons, a memory book, Luther's Small Catechism, a Bible study course, the church and school newsletter, devotional materials as well as any other religious materials. When these materials are distributed, parents should be asked to cooperate in using them in the home. For instance, when our parents are first given a Bible, they are told that their child will come home from school having learned various Bible stories. Would they please help their child review the Bible story by reading that part from the Bible that relates to the story?

This fall with the publication of Luther's Small Catechism in the Czech language, parents are encouraged to study and help their children who are studying the catechism in religion class with Pastor Steven Sparley. In the visits to the fifth, sixth, seventh and eighth grade students' homes, discussions can have an easy "opener" as the "new book at school" is identified—a copy of Luther's Small Catechism is displayed; the "new book" is briefly reviewed as to contents, importance and use; and given to the parents asking them to help their children in learning the lessons. Depending upon the "reception" one is given, it might also be the time to "enroll" parents in the new adult instruction class that is being organized.

Our biweekly bilingual newsletter called the Luther Letter also contains Bible stories taught by the teachers in school. At the end of the Bible story, we ask the parents to read the selection from the Bible with their children, so they can learn more than what is contained in the brief account in the newsletter. Sometimes the newsletter also contains Sunday sermons and Wednesday morning chapel talks and prayers. Other issues carry a series of articles on some specific topic, such as creation vs. evolution, selections from Luther's Small and Large Catechisms, or historical and cultural events. Future church and school activities are a regular feature of the newsletter as well as follow-up articles to recent baptisms and confirmations.

Do parents always cooperate by reading the materials that are sent home? We have never taken a survey of our readership, but on occasion parents will inform us that their child had failed to bring home the latest issue of the *Luther Letter*. Other times individuals have pointed out typing or translation mistakes they have noticed. Several times individuals have stopped by to pick up an issue they have missed which contained one part of a continuing series. Some of our people read it because it is in both Czech and English and provides a means through which they can practice and improve their English language skills. Also, several of our Czech staff members take three or four copies to give to relatives and friends. Copies are also distributed at our Thursday evening English conversation club for adults.

What will happen to the young catechumens who will publicly confirm their faith in their Savior? Will there be a "spiritual safety net" for them after they leave Martin Luther School? There is great concern among our mission staff for the future of our Czech confirmands whose parents are not Christians at the present time, knowing that even in a Christian home there can be a failure of parents in providing the necessary spiritual support and guidance for the children after confirmation. What will it be in a home where the parents are avowed atheists? . . .

There is a danger with such concerns for the "spiritual safety" of our students in that they may cause us to attempt to set spiritual goals for our school parents' conversion. Our focus may become a "numbers game" instead of simply saving souls. It seems that we who have grown up in the church are often very impatient with those who have been reared in unbelief. Our Czech brothers and sisters in Christ have told us many times, "You must be patient with us! It is difficult to undo in one or two years what the communists have done to us in forty years!" Yet, at the same time, we must persevere in our calling. We must use all the gifts and avenues our Lord has given us to preach and teach the good news of salvation through Christ Jesus, for indeed the fields are white unto harvest and the time of the harvest lasts but a season.

DOCUMENT 2.8:

Lutheran Schools Flourishing in the Amazon Jungle (2008)

By Terry Schultz

Dr. Terry Schultz (1954–) was born May 3, 1954, in La Crosse, Wisconsin. Schultz was raised in West Chicago, Illinois, where he attended the local public school. His passion for music developed throughout his high school years, which prompted him to enroll at Eastern Illinois University, where he earned a Bachelor of Music in 1976. A second passion, teaching, led Schultz to continue his education at this institution, where he received a Masters of Science in Education in 1978. God used these talents in the spreading of His Gospel message. Schultz entered Bethany Lutheran Theological Seminary and earned his Masters of Divinity in 1996. After a vicarage at Mt. Olive Lutheran Church in St. Paul, Minnesota, Schultz was called by God to spread the Gospel in South America. For nearly fifteen years Missionary Schultz served various Peruvian tribes in the Amazon Jungle as well as groups in the Andes Mountains.[50] His monthly emails to the United States, known as "Jungle Journals," testified to the grace of God in working through Terry and his wife Mary to communicate Christ's love to "every language, tribe, people, and nation" (Revelation 5:9). In February 2011, Missionary Schulz, who had recently begun serving the Wisconsin Synod in the Dominican Republic, defended his doctoral dissertation to complete a D.Min. in Missions and

---

50 Terry Schultz, email interview, 2 May 2009.

Evangelism at Trinity Evangelical Divinity School in Deerfield, Illinois.[DR]
Source: *Lutheran Sentinel*, Oct. 2008, 7.

The first time the missionary and his group of men appeared outside the jungle village of Nueva Barranquita, many of the adult villagers were convinced (due to their centuries-old tribal stories) that the intruders had but one objective: to steal the children and enslave the young men! Not a single villager knew that the message we brought could do the very opposite: save the children and adults from eternal slavery and torment in hell!

Today, in the village where the mothers swooped up their children and ran in panic at the sight of us, where the men quietly gathered to meet us with machetes at their sides, we now operate a vibrant Lutheran grade school. Numerous souls have been saved!

Such is the true, oft-repeated history of our work among the Shawi tribe of the Peruvian Upper Amazon. (The tribe used to be called "the Chayahuitas," a Spanish form of their indigenous name. The natives now prefer the name "Shawi.")

When the Shawi children first spotted the white missionary at the edge of the village, they thought he was a walking ghost, a phantom. It took nearly a dozen evangelism trips before a child mustered the courage to quietly creep up behind me and carefully poke my arm to see whether it was solid or made of some ghost substance that he could push his finger right through.

Today, the school's religion classes include a Bible-based understanding of the spirit world. Among the children and parents where we operate our schools, there is much less fear of the evil spirits (real and imagined) that populate their jungle and their legends.

The Holy Spirit has indeed been working through the Law and Gospel lessons presented at our two jungle schools, in Nueva Barranquita and Louis Terry. Eternal souls continue to be added, and daily spiritual life has dramatically improved. Of course, reading, writing and mathematics are also taught in our schools, just like in the United States. The outside world is encroaching on the Amazon tribes at an incredible rate. The natives need to be able to interact with "non-natives" in order to avoid exploitation of themselves and their resources. However, our school's primary focus will always be that precious new names be written in the Book of Life!

We are now blessed with local native pastors (trained at our Tarapoto Bible Institute) who teach the religion classes at the two grade schools. Bible student Eloy is moving to remote Nuevo Oriente in 2009 to establish and teach at a third Lutheran grade school. Our three religion instructors will have a tremendous new resource at their disposal next month: a Spanish/Shawi translation of a simplified version of Luther's Catechism. This unique instructional book, a blessing of our Lutheran heritage, will be distributed to every child and home in the three villages. It also will be distributed in the other dozen villages our native evangelism team now serves, where occasionally they encounter a native who can read.

We often speak of Lutheran grade schools as being an effective outreach tool. Perhaps nowhere is this more obvious than with our Amazon schools. Native adults often have trouble leaving the old tribal ways and turning to faith and trust in Jesus. After school every day in Nueva Barranquita and Louis Terry, dozens of very small missionaries leave for home where they can tell Mom and Dad about the love of their Savior, who died and rose for them. What a critical and exciting time to be operating Lutheran grade schools in the Amazon!

CHART 2.9:

Christian Day School Enrollment in the Evangelical Lutheran Synod

Source: Data compiled from "Parochial Report," in *Synod Report* (1928-2008).

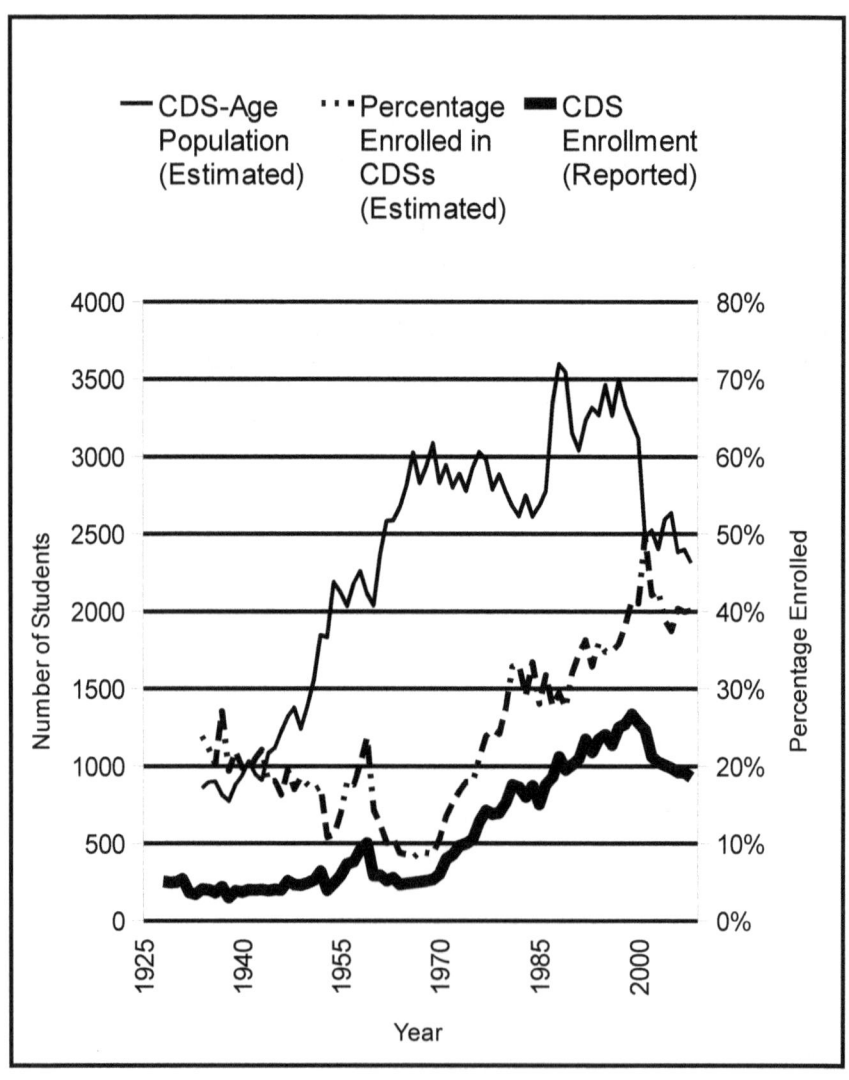

SECTION 3:

Bethany Lutheran College and High School

Introduction

By Peter M. Anthony

Martha, Martha, you are worried and troubled about many things. But one thing is needed, and Mary has chosen that good part, which will not be taken away from her.

Luke 10:41-42

For many of her alumni, Bethany Lutheran College has provided the defining experience of a Christian education. For this alumnus in particular, that defining experience rested on a faith in God held by both faculty and fellow students. This trust in God does not stand idle, but draws and compels to action (**Document 3.1**).

At Bethany, we have seen this motivation to action throughout her history. It motivated the well-known words "I move we take over the school," by which a small group of predominantly rural Christians took on the challenge of operating their own high school and college.[1] We see the compelling fear of God in the zeal of the letters that follow from S. C. Ylvisaker, Milton E. Tweit, and the Board of Regents, exhorting the parents and congregations of the ELS to send their sons and daughters to Bethany (**Documents 3.2, 3.3,** and **3.4**). We see it in the audience gathered to hear Paul Zimmerman's address on the occasion of Bethany's fiftieth anniversary (**Document 3.6**).

In the selections that follow, we also glimpse Bethany's response to changes in attitude toward education since 1927. In his essay "Why Lutheran High Schools?," S. C. Ylvisaker pointed to a time in the not so distant past when adulthood began after elementary school, and the responsibilities for the Christian education of children could rightly be considered to cease with confirmation. Ylvisaker noted that in his day, Christian education ought to extend beyond confirmation and into the high school years (**Document 3.2**). Today, parental responsibilities are often considered to extend well beyond high school. Parents are less willing to see their children depart from home as teenagers, and many Lutheran boarding high schools, including Bethany, have closed their doors. Bethany's transition from a high school (1927–1969) and junior college (1927–2001) to a baccalaureate-granting institution (2001–) is in part explained by this cultural shift in the age of adulthood.

At the same time, there is perhaps greater concern among parents over whether their children will leave their roof for a school that teaches what John A. Moldstad, Sr. termed "a real set of values" (**Document 3.5**). The search for real values has provided Bethany with ever-increasing opportunities to provide Christian education in ways not in the forefront of her founders' minds. While the early essays in this section articulate the role of Bethany in the continuing education of Christian youth, Steven L. Reagles's 1990 article points to the growing proportion of the studentry which does not come to Bethany with faith in Christ. Here, our college has a profound opportunity to offer the core of

---

[1] Pastor George A. Gullixson made this motion at the 1927 synod convention. Founded in 1911 as a Christian ladies' college, the school had been devastated by financial troubles following the Great War. Under the auspices of the Evangelical Lutheran Synod, Bethany would survive the Great Depression and prosper into the twenty-first century. See Erling Teigen, "'I Move We Take Over the School': A History of Bethany Lutheran College," *Oak Leaves* 6, no. 2 (Nov. 2002): 1-5.

her college seal, the "one thing needful" (**Document 3.6**). The importance Bethany places on this opportunity is reflected by the Board of Regents in a continuing commitment to maintain the very first "Objective of the College": "To grow in grace and in the knowledge of the Lord and Savior Jesus Christ by means of the Gospel" (**Document 3.8**).

Christian education points us to the objective truths of Christ's atoning sacrifice for our sin. However, our experience of that education may rightly be called subjective, for, as S. C. Ylvisaker wrote, "education takes hold of the whole of man, his mind, his will, his emotions, his heart" (**Document 3.2**). A Bethany education is so often a superlative Christian education, because it not only takes hold of the whole of man, but provides him with "joy above measure, that fills all my needs" (**Document 3.4**).

DOCUMENT 3.1:

Bethany (1928)

By Ingebrigt J. Blåkkan

Ingebrigt Johnson Blåkkan (1862–1944) *was born on November 15, 1862 in Halse, Nordmøre, Norway, to John and Marie Blåkkan. As a teen he attended Trondhjem Borgenskole and other schools in Orkedalen and Halse, followed by the Trondhjem school for non-commissioned officers in his early twenties.*[2] *After immigrating to the United States in 1884 he attended Luther College in Decorah, Iowa, and Luther Seminary in Robbinsville, Minnesota. He began his pastoral ministry in 1895 in Eureka, California. In 1899, Blåkkan married Clara Wiger, with whom he had one son, Luther. Between 1898 and 1930, Blåkkan served congregations in Everett, Washington; Rockford, Washington; Coeur d'Alene, Idaho; Spokane, Washington; and Holton, Michigan. Blåkkan was also one of the founding members of the Norwegian Synod of America in 1918.*[3] *He retired from the ministry in 1930 and in 1933 moved to Los Angeles, California, where he remained until his death on October 17, 1945.*[4] *Besides his long career as a pastor, Blåkkan's legacy lives on within the many poems that he wrote for and about the Norwegian Synod. At the 1946 synod convention, President Norman A. Madson, Sr. remarked*

---

[2] *Who's Who Among Pastors,* trans. Rasmus Malmin, O.M. Norlie, and O.A. Tingelstad (Minneapolis, MN: Augsburg, 1928), 63.
[3] *Synod Report* (1918), 87.
[4] "Departed," *Lutheran Sentinel,* 12 Nov. 1945, 320.

that Rev. Blåkken "will ever be remembered among us as our poet pastor."[5] [AB]

Source: *Synod Report* (1928): 83-86; rpt., *Oak Leaves* 4, no. 3 (Fall 2000): 6–7.

The fear of God is the beginning
Of all the wisdom worth the name.
True fear of God is always winning
Our victories in Him who came
And won for all in Heav'n a place,
Now offered to each one through grace.

Such fear of God is not a feeling
Of terror in the heart of man,
But filial, yearning and appealing
To God in His good grace to stand.
Thus God gives courage, strength and cheer
In life and death naught else to fear.

The love to God, all love excelling—
Save His great love to sinners lost,
Which is a fountain ever welling
In deserts drear, of priceless cost.
Each languished soul who drank thereof
Has found the true, eternal love.

The world with all its gold and glory
Has naught but husks to feed our soul.
And sad but true is the old story
Of dearest friends that oft grow cold.
But through all change of loss or gain,
A constant friend will God remain.

In Him then trustingly abiding,
We place our hope, our life, our all.
We leave each step unto His guiding
And gladly hear our Master's call.
Be it through cross in valleys deep,
Or sunny heights, He will us keep.

---

5   *Synod Report* (1946), 16.

Thus fear and love and trust combining,
To honor God in study here,
Shall, in a world of darkness, shining
Proclaim to people far and near
The value of each costly gem,
Worn as our students' diadem.

Within these portals generations,
If so it please our gracious Lord,
Shall come to train for different stations
In church and state, by deed and word.
May ev'ry one who comes here find
What most they need for heart and mind!

To you, our honored tutors, greeting
In His great name whose cause you serve.
Whatever problems you are meeting
From this true course you will not swerve:
To teach, to guide our students here
In heav'nly wisdom God to fear.

To you, as teachers, we have given
Our greatest treasures in your care,
Immortal spirits who in heaven
Salvation's bliss with us shall share.
To mold them for such destiny,
Your honored calling here will be.

Nor are we in our aim forgetting
The knowledge needful for this life.
Nay, rather better we are fitting
Them for their mundane toil and strife.
The highest type of man we see,
Where knowledge vies with piety.

With joy today our salutation
We to our students will extend.
Whatever work, or cause, or station
To which you later may attend,
You know, that here, your faithfulness
Will largely shape your life's success.

In you, dear students, we are placing
Our fondest hopes for future days.
The problems that you will be facing
Your fathers met and solved by grace.
If you'll be true as they have been,
Ev'n through defeat you then shall win.

No privilege, we know, is greater,
Than to attend a Christian school.
No training for you can be better
Than under God's own guiding rule.
His glories of a life to come
Illumine ev'n our earthly home.

To ev'ry synod congregation
And fellow Christians here today:
Receive our kind solicitation
For Bethany to work and pray,
That she may live and thrive and grow
And countless blessings from her flow.

A ring of men and women praying,
O let us form 'round Bethany!
Nor hesitating or delaying
Her from encumbrances to free.
It is, we know, God's gracious will
With generous hearts such schools to build.

Then she shall stand a beacon, shedding
More lights upon the paths of man.
Then she shall grow, diffusing, spreading
More knowledge over sea and land,
Till distant peoples yearningly
Shall look for light from Bethany.

O Jesus, Thou who often wended
Thy way of yore to Bethany
And there Thy mission-work attended
For dead and living lovingly,
Come help us make our Bethany
A humble place, O Lord, for Thee!

DOCUMENT 3.2:

Why Lutheran High Schools? (1945)

By Sigurd Christian Ylvisaker

Sigurd Christian Ylvisaker (1884–1959) "*was a gifted and consistent preacher of the Gospel.*"[6] *He was born June 15, 1884 to Johannes and Kristi Ylvisaker in Madison, Wisconsin, and spent his early years in Robbinsdale, Minnesota, where he was homeschooled by local seminary students. At age fifteen, Ylvisaker enrolled at Luther College, Decorah, Iowa. After his graduation from Luther College in 1903, Ylvisaker studied Latin and Hebrew at the University of Minnesota for one year. In 1904 he attended Luther Seminary, graduating* summa cum laude *in 1907.*[7] *He next traveled to Leipzig, Germany, where he studied Semitic languages and philosophy. It took only three years for him to achieve his Ph.D. at the University of Leipzig. Dr. Ylvisaker then accepted a call to First Evangelical Congregation in Minot, North Dakota.*[8] *After his first call, Ylvisaker spent seven years serving a parish in Madison, Wisconsin. He taught Greek and Hebrew at Luther College and at Concordia, St. Paul. Even though Ylvisaker determined never to marry, saying, "Therefore it is best that I remain a bachelor," God had other plans. He met Norma Norem of Milwaukee, Wisconsin, and married her after one year of courtship. Together they had five children. Ylvisaker came to Bethany Lutheran College in Mankato, Minnesota, in 1930, where he led the school as president for twenty years. He ended his presidency due to health problems, and retired two years later saying, "I leave my cherished work at Bethany with but one prayer . . . that [God] will bless*

---

[6] Juul B. Madson, Erling T. Teigen, and Norman S. Holte, *Sigurd Christian Ylvisaker, 1884–1959: A Commemorative Volume at the Centennial of His Birth*, ed. Peter T. Harstad (Mankato, MN: Lutheran Synod Book Co., 1984), vii.
[7] Ibid, 8.
[8] Ibid, 185.

us all in His own rich way by preserving us in faithful loyalty to His Word and unswerving faith in His promises."⁹ Dr. Ylvisaker died April 26, 1959 in Bryan, Texas. [DR]

Source: Chap. 1 in *The Lutheran High* School, ed. Carl S. Meyer (St. Louis: Lutheran Education Association, 1945), 11-16; rpt., *Bethany Lutheran College Bulletin* 15, no. 3 (1945) and *Lutheran Sentinel,* Nov. 4, 1968, 398-99, 417-22.

Christian education is the education of a Christian. As soon as this is accepted as the only proper definition of the much-discussed term, the problem really ceases to be a problem, whether we think in terms of elementary or higher education.

Teaching may confine itself to the training of the hands, of the feet, of the eyes, of the intellect. We can conceive of the teaching of typewriting, of painting, of the playing of the violin or other musical instruments as a teaching that is concerned merely with the technique of learning certain skills. A man may learn to farm, to swim, to build a house, to become an architect, a lawyer, a physician, to employ scientific methods in a laboratory, etc., and still remain, so far as his studies go, in the field of mere technical skills.

We admit freely that it is very difficult for a child to be trained even in the technical skills without, at the same time, being influenced to a greater or less degree by his teacher or by his surroundings while being taught. Few teachers can possibly remain so neutral in their attitude but that they in some way or another will influence the character of those whom they teach. Children are naturally more easily influenced in this way than those who are more mature.

And yet we must distinguish between the mere teaching of certain skills and that which may properly be called education. Education takes hold of the whole of man, his mind, his will, his emotions, his heart, and then also, that which these control, the body. It is the whole person of a man that is involved in what we call education. In other words, where teaching sets out to build character or determine a person's view of life, we at once find ourselves in the field of education, properly understood.

---

9   Ibid, 52.

President Ylvisaker was pastor, teacher, scholar, and administrator in one man—as well as husband and father.

The Purposes of Christian Education

When we are made to realize that the person to be educated in this case is my child, and that this child of mine again is God's child, committed to my care and keeping, the greatness of the cause and of the responsibility is seen in its proper light. And then only.

Then the bidding of God is clear and spoken with the authority of God Himself: "Ye fathers, provoke not your children to wrath: but bring them up in the nurture and admonition of the Lord" (Ephesians 6:4). Then the promise is clear and sure: "Train up a child in the way he should go: and when he is old, he will not depart from it" (Proverbs 22:6). Then the Church, too, has a clear road to travel: "Feed my lambs" (John 21:15). Thus Christian education is there by divine command and by divine promise. The manner in which this command is to he carried out will have to be left to the circumstances in each case.

Before us as parents and as a church rises the great and

responsible work of educating our children and training them as the children of God that they are. We may call this character training if we thereby understand all that this properly includes: the building up of true Christian faith, by which the whole person grows and in Christian trust, knowledge, virtue, view of life, Christian thinking and judgment, sympathetic understanding of his fellowmen and readiness to serve them, zeal for the truth and for the Church, "that the man of God may be perfect, thoroughly furnished unto all good works" (2 Timothy 3:17).

Does this make the situation too complex? We have learned to thank God for the simple message of the Gospel that we are saved by grace through faith, and that this faith is a God-given trust in the saving merits of Christ which may be grasped by an infant child, by the trembling old, by the dying sinner, by the learned and unlearned alike. Let us never forget that this is essentially a very simple thing. However, we know, too, that this faith may be destroyed by a mere gust of false teaching, and that this may be accomplished the more easily if that faith is not well founded and grounded in the Word. We know, too, that faith has a work to do, an unlimited mission to perform, and the more mature faith is, the more deeply it is rooted, the stronger it has become, the better informed it is both in the affairs of God and of men, so much more able it will be to reach out a hand to help others on a road through life that is none too easy. When God said, "Ye fathers, ... bring them up in the nurture and admonition of the Lord," it was not for the purpose that the child might serve selfish ends, but as if God in the same moment pointed to the fields ripe unto the harvest and to the mission of that child in the field when the time came. That harvest field appears in Scripture under the picture of a field which must be planted, where the toiler must know the good seed from the bad and be on guard at all times against the enemy who sows tares among the wheat; it appears as a field which must be tilled and worked from day to day, watered and fed, that the seed may grow to full maturity; as a vineyard which must be pruned and cut, but with sound knowledge and judgment; as a field of battle where the tillers of the soil have become warriors who must know how to use their weapons with strength and skill; as a sea, which all of a sudden may rise up in fury and overturn and destroy the ship of the church unless those who are in it know how to find Christ in the ship, the ruler of wind and wave; as a flock of sheep which easily stray and would be lost if the shepherds were not there, taught by God, to lead the sheep where the green pastures are, where the still waters flow, and where the sheepfold will guard them against the wolves by night.

As we thus study the purpose for which our children are to be trained and educated, we stagger the more at our responsibility of providing them with the proper kind of training. They are themselves to be saved from a wicked world into the heaven God has prepared for them. On the way they are to be as those sent by very God to save others from an untoward generation, to serve as a light in a dark world, as salt in an unsavory and decayed world, as living examples of what faith and Christian living mean, as those who by word and deed direct men away from hell to heaven. They are those who are called by God Himself to be a "chosen generation, a royal priesthood, an holy nation, a peculiar people: that ye should shew forth the praises of Him who hath called you out of darkness into his marvelous light" (1 Peter 2:9).

The education of such children of God is my responsibility as a parent, our responsibility as a church. And they are our children as long as they can rightly be considered children, i.e., while they live as dependents of ours under our roof and in our care. They are our children as long as this term applies to them, i.e., until they have reached that maturity which enables them to establish their own household and assume the responsibilities of life for themselves. There was a time when children were expected to assume these responsibilities very soon after confirmation or graduation from the elementary school, and in many cases the parents actually shifted their responsibility to the children themselves at that point. Thus parents and church were satisfied to provide for the training of the children until the age of confirmation. This will help us to understand why our people have been so reluctant to face the fact that their duty in the matter of a Christian education for their children continues on into the high school and even junior college age. This change may have come more or less unnoticeable to many, but it is there as a fact to be faced and no longer a question to be debated.

The Nature of the Adolescent

As circumstances are today, the post-confirmation years are definitely to be considered as a period of character development, of preparation for life, of continued planting and tilling. It is not time of maturity of knowledge, of judgment, of a view of life, or of readiness to undertake a special calling in life. These years constitute a difficult age, not only because of the peculiar

> *"Let us set the goal high: useful and noble lives, strong Christian characters, respected and sturdy citizens in church and state."*
>
> This vision statement by S. C. Ylvisaker appears on the back cover of *Sigurd Christian Ylvisaker (1884-1959)*, a commemorative volume distributed each year by Bethany Lutheran College to the recipients of the Ylvisaker Scholarship, which covers 100% of tuition costs.

adjustments that become necessary during adolescence, but because the child now has, through closer contact with the world about him, begun to rethink and re-evaluate what he has learned and thought and believed. It is an age of questioning, of introspection, of emotional stress, and all the rest of the symptoms that characterize youth of that certain age. But for all of this, it is the age when youth craves sympathetic understanding, patience, and wise counsel more than ever, and a time when he will respond readily to good counsel as well as bad.

A wise father and a wise church will recognize both the difficulty and the importance of this post-confirmation training age. Parents who are vitally concerned about their responsibility as parents cannot afford to neglect this period in the training of their child, much less shift their responsibility without further ado to the child himself or to teachers whom others may choose for him. Nor can a church afford to disregard the opportunities it has to assist the parents and cooperate with them at this particular stage in the development of a child.

Circumstances will have to dictate as to whether this help should be brought through formal schooling or in some other way. We must not despise the manner of the pioneers in this regard. They were largely dependent on the home and on the church services for what education their children could obtain during this period. But what homes! Homes where the Word of God was a household possession and a guide in all things; where piety and prayer walked hand in hand; where the Fourth Commandment taught respect toward parents, elders, superiors, and the government alike. Out from such homes went men and women of high Christian culture, of sound judgment and wisdom, and even of a sort of learning that could pass many a difficult test, though not of the modern adding-machine type. And these succeeded in building a strong nation and a strong church.

We must admit that circumstances today are quite different,

for we live in an age when nothing has suffered so much as the home. There are, thank God, homes which are truly Christian, where children still enjoy all the privileges and advantages which the Christian home may own of Christian companionship, culture and refinement, respect for the elders, home study of the Word of God as the sacred key to all other learning and knowledge. There we do not have to worry too much about formal instruction in order to produce sturdy citizens and consecrated members of the church. And yet, the day has come when the whole nation, as it were, is "going to school." Formal schooling has become a demand of modern society and of the government itself. It is no longer a matter of choice as to whether children should be educated in the home or in school. They must attend school until they have arrived at the age specified by the government. Thus the question of formal schooling is one which the church and Christian parents must consider seriously.

Must we now introduce a long and detailed argument to show that the public schools, elementary or high school, are no place for our children, as if we must find fault with them in order to win favor for the schools of the church? Is it necessary to show the ill fruits of the attempts of the public schools at educating the youth of our country, decrying its never-ending efforts at new experiments in education, warning against its present renewed aim of introducing the teaching of religion (a new paganism!), the deplorable situation with regard to morals among teachers and students alike, the gradual breaking down of standards of scholarship, of study habits, and the like? Others might make a strong argument in favor of the public school system by pointing to the need of these schools for the sake of an intelligent citizenry, to real accomplishments of these schools and to the high standards which many of them have actually set. We cannot argue that the state has no right to set up a system of schools as a bulwark of democracy and as a place where the arts and sciences may be developed for the advancement of learning and the general progress of a nation.

It is no negative argument we wish to present. It is understood that the responsibility of the Christian as a citizen of the state places upon him the obligation to support the public school system as a means of preserving the American way of living.

Nevertheless, the one consideration which we as Christians must at all times keep before us is this: to what school must I send my child for the kind of training that can properly be called education or character training during the years when this must remain the essential thing? Into whose care do I dare to commit my child? What do I owe to God, to whom the child properly belongs, in order that I may face Him on that great day, assured that I have done what I could to fulfill my sacred obligation? What do I owe my child as the one great heritage he has a right to expect of me as his parent and servant of Christ? The answer must be: where character building is involved, where it is a matter of educating that child as a child of God and a member of the Christian church, that school must be a Christian school. It is only in such a school he can be educated in the full sense of the word and trained as one whose real home is heaven and whose great mission is to reflect the light which is of heaven.

The Character of the School

And just what is a Christian school? It is, as we have said, a school which is there to educate Christians. In other words, its primary purpose is to serve Christian young people, i.e., those who by baptism and further instruction in the Christian faith are members of the household of God.

A Christian school is, in the next place, one where all instruction is based on and presented in conformity with the Word of God. This is not as simple a thing as it may appear to be, particularly on the high school and college level. This presupposes that Scripture truth regarding such fundamental concepts as God, man, sin, justification, sanctification, heaven, should always be there in the foreground as of the greatest significance to teacher and pupil alike. It presupposes that all other truths are viewed and taught on the basis of these and in conformity with the revelation of God. Christian instruction will direct the student to a sincere love of the Gospel and of that which proclaims this Gospel. "Search the scriptures; for in them ye think ye have eternal life: and they are they which testify of Me," Christ says (John 5:39). This study and instruction will lead on into every other field of knowledge, give the proper directive, furnish the right incentive, and serve as a continual guide in the face of every erroneous course. Christian instruction will so permeate every teaching in the arts, sciences, or professional courses, that Christ Himself will reign supreme in the heart of the pupil, ever more glorious, more gracious, more mighty, more loving and beloved.

Again, a Christian school is one which furnishes a true goal and aim in life. One of the most deplorable faults of modern education is to be found in this very thing that it in the end is so futile. It has helped to produce a money-mad, pleasure-seeking, selfish generation, jealous of personal power and influence—or again, a generation which is left to wonder what it is all about, going along aimlessly drifting, to land wherever wind and wave take them—or still again, a generation which may be eager to serve, but so often not knowing how, when, or whom to serve. Contrasted with all of this, Christian education from start to finish leaves no one in doubt as to his purpose in life, and furnishes from day to day the one safe guide into every new day and every new opportunity for service. Above it all shines the bright Day-star of hope and of our final goal.

Because of these lofty aims with their specifically Christian background and content, only devoted Christian teachers can qualify as instructors in Christian schools. Such a teacher must in his own heart believe these truths; in his own life he must live them. His whole being must be so permeated by them that he in his own person has become that light of which Christ speaks (Matthew 5:14). A Christian school is, then, one in which only Christian teachers are invited to teach. Let no one apologize for this, as if these would represent a backward trend in education or a backward scholarship, backward methods and aims. As a Christian who has been chosen to direct young fellow Christians on the difficult and responsible way of life, he may well be expected to devote himself the more eagerly and seriously to his preparation, and with humility and consecration serve as in a holy cause. Because he in the Word has the only sure foundation of truth, he may lead with a sure tread those who are entrusted to him to the lofty heights in any field of learning, pointing the young at every turn to new glories in the realms of nature, of the mind, or of the spirit. His work will in truth be the glory of God and the edification of these children of God. Where others so easily make the teaching profession a stepping-stone to higher ambitions, the Christian teacher is satisfied to know that he in this calling has found a service as important as any and one for which only God Himself can properly equip and prepare him.

In the years that are gone and even today the Christian elementary school has been a challenge to the faith of parents and of the whole church; it has tested the love of Christians; it has been an object lesson to teach the proper sense of values in the church. Today the Lutheran high school movement rises to voice a similar challenge and to offer a like test. In principle there is no difference between the two. We may add that this same challenge and test continues on into the years of the junior college or beyond as a period when the foundation is still being laid for the education of those who may still be regarded as children in the home. And as the obligation of parents and of the church continues on to this point in the development of the child, so the promises of God also continue on. Let no one say that we dream idle dreams or put on parents or on the church a greater burden than they can bear when they are confronted with the challenge of Lutheran secondary schools. Let no one say that it cannot be done when the call comes to erect such Christian high schools and junior colleges for the Christian education of the youth of the church. Has the arm of the Lord been shortened that He cannot do it [Numbers 11:23]? Must He rise up once more and rebuke us as those who are of little faith [Matthew 8:26]? When our children ask for bread, shall we be as those who give stones for bread [Matthew 7:9]? When they deserve the best at our hands, shall we prefer for them what is admittedly a poor substitute? Shall we calmly let the enemy continue to sow his tares among the wheat while we sleep [Matthew 13:24–30]?

If it is faith we need, may God grant us faith in great measure. If we need to learn obedience, then may God grant obedience to His sacred bidding. If it is the opening of our eyes to the plight of our youth and the need of our church, then may God mercifully open our eyes and let us see our mission also here. And may the same gracious God grant us as parents and as a church the Christian conviction and courage to do as He so clearly commands, and the faith to receive at His bounteous hand the blessing He so lovingly has promised.

DOCUMENT 3.3:

Do We Need Our Bethany Lutheran High School? (1963)

By Milton E. Tweit

Milton Elmo Tweit (1908–2005) was born December 4, 1908, in Glenwood, Minnesota, to Bernt and Mabel Tweit. He attended the elementary schools of Pope County, Minnesota, for his early education. Tweit then attended Concordia Lutheran Academy in St. Paul, Minnesota, graduating in 1930. For his theological studies, Tweit went to Concordia Seminary in St. Louis, Missouri. He was ordained into the public ministry in 1936. The following year, Tweit married Delphine Sonstegard, with whom he had six children. He served the Norwegian Grove and Norseland, Minnesota, parish from 1937 to 1958. He then answered a call to two congregations, Saude and Jerico, in Lawler, Iowa, from 1958 to 1971. In 1962, two years after the death of his first wife, Tweit married Dagny Dale Hoyord, the widow of a pastor. During 1971 to 1974, Tweit served two congregations in Luverne, Minnesota, and for the last seven years of his ministry, from 1974  to 1981, Tweit served two congregations in Waterville, Iowa. Besides his extensive experience as the shepherd of a congregation, Tweit was president of the ELS from 1957 to 1962. He also was a member of the Board of Regents of Bethany Lutheran College and Seminary for thirty-two years, and it was in this capacity that he wrote the following essay. Other positions he held include: Chairman of the Home Missions Offering Committee, Board for Stewardship, and Synod Review Committee. Tweit died on June 22, 2005, leaving six children, seventeen grandchildren, thirty-six great-grandchildren, one step grandchild, and two step great-grandchildren.¹⁰ [DR]

Source: *Lutheran Sentinel*, 1963, 232-35.

A generation or so ago, our Synod bought the buildings of our present Bethany and established a Christian school with a Junior College and a High School Department. For twenty-five years the enrollment of our high school department continued to grow so that in the 1940s it was quite flourishing. Since about 1950 the enrollment has gone steadily downward until today it is so low that we are in danger of having to close this department of our school. The problem is not that our teachers have left, or that the buildings have been condemned, or that the school is not doing its job properly. The problem is that we do not have enough students, and this at a time when all over our country there is a shortage of room and teachers to take care of the young people of high school age! In the midst of an abundance of young people of high school age we have so few that we are faced with the question of whether we can keep going. Let us face it, something is wrong or has gone wrong.

Our people of previous generations prayed, worked, and sacrificed in order to establish our high school department. Many Christian parents sent their children to Bethany to get their high school education at our Christian high school. It is true some of these students were preparing themselves for the work of the ministry and for teaching in Christian day schools, but by far the majority were preparing for a life of Christian living in whatever profession they later chose to follow. What is happening or what has happened in our present generation of church members and Christian parents? What has happened anyway, that there should be fewer boys and girls in attendance at our high school now when the membership in our Synod has grown so that we might rightly expect that there should be more attending?

Some of our members are fortunate enough to live in areas where there are Christian high schools where they are sending their children. However, the majority are not so fortunate. Where, then, are the children and why the small enrollment? Have there

---

10 "Rev. Milton Elmo Tweit," obituary, *Mankato Free Press*, 23 June 2005, n.p.; email from Paul Tweit, 9 May 2011.

been changes for the better in the world about us and especially in the cities and communities where our parishes are located? Have our children improved so much that there is no longer need for a thorough Christian training during the years of growth and development which many, even among non-Christians, call the most formative and crucial years in growing up? Is the Word of God needed less in the training of the young people today than it was a generation or two ago? If anything, it is needed more and not less. The confusion, the tension, the fear troubling the world has hardly ever been more disturbing or frightening than today. Anxiety mounts on every side. People are seeking answers and trying to allay their fears with tranquilizer pills, aids for positive living and thinking, beatnik colonies, and the like. Yet the anxiety only grows because none of these give the right answer.

But apart from all this, there is a very basic reason for the need of the Word of God in the Christian training of the young at all times. Lest we forget, our children are all "shaped in iniquity and conceived in sin" (Psalm 51:5). Very strikingly and almost shockingly, the Word of God declares: "The imagination of man's heart is evil from his youth" (Genesis 8:21). Yea: "The heart is deceitful above all things and desperately wicked" (Jeremiah 17:9). Any education which does not take this into account and reach and change the heart is completely missing the mark. Now only God knows our hearts and how to change them. Only He is able to change them, and only He can keep our hearts with Christ Jesus after they have been changed. The means to do all this, the power for this marvelous work, is found in Holy Scripture. It is clearly stated that we are "born again, not of corruptible seed, but incorruptible, by the Word of God, which liveth and abideth forever" (1 Peter 1:23). And furthermore we learn that we are "kept by the power of God through faith unto salvation ready to be revealed in the last time" (1 Peter 1:5). When the question is asked: "Wherewithal shall a young man cleanse his way?" the Lord answers: "By taking heed thereto according to My Word" (Psalm 119:9). This is surely the only right answer to the whole question. If there is any place where the "Word is to be a lamp unto our feet and a light unto our path" (Psalm 119:105), it certainly is in the training of young people. Let us not suppose that it is a good thing to give our children over to an educational system which leaves out the Word of God, the one thing needful [Luke 10:42].

The soul-searching question therefore arises: Do we really and fully believe that the life-giving Word of God is a necessity in the education of our children? Are we persuaded that we must have Christian teachers who implicitly believe the Holy Scriptures to teach our children? Teachers who use the Word of God as the basis and source for all their instruction and who therefore reach the heart of our children so that they grow in grace and in the knowledge of our Lord and Savior, Jesus Christ? Our Lord commands: "Train up a child in the way he shall go," and adds the promise "and when he is old he will not depart from it" (Proverbs 22:6). Do we get the full meaning of this simple assignment? Do we understand that such training is possible only where the Gospel is found so that Jesus is the beginning, middle, and end of all instruction?

Many Christian parents choose to send their children to public high schools instead of to a Christian high school. Now there is no quarrel with the public high schools as such. We are fully convinced that it is not the duty of the government to do the work of the Christian home and the Christian Church, namely, to provide religious and spiritual training for our Christian children. We are not claiming, either, that Christian young people cease being Christian as soon as they step into the classroom of a public school. But we do insist that such a school is not able to do what Christ asks when he commands: "Train up a child in the way he shall go." This can only be done in a Christian school where the Word of God is the foundation of all training and instruction. If we agree that such Christian training is the most important, yea, the very heart of the training needed by all Christians, then we will think carefully before we make use of the school where it is not the center. Under those circumstances where the children are not in a Christian high school we are compelled to try to add the one thing needful in the spare time which our young people have. Is it ever good to make the most important matter of life a spare time activity?

There is a story told of a chicken farmer who had quite a problem with one of his roosters. Every morning at exactly 2 a.m. he would begin to crow with all his might, disturbing not only the chickens but the whole neighborhood as well. No one was able to figure out why the rooster would crow in the middle of the night instead of at sunrise. But finally the mystery was solved. There was a train that went by a two o'clock in the morning and its headlight shone right into the chicken house. The poor rooster mistook the headlight for the sunlight. He was not a very discriminating rooster.

Unfortunately, people have been taught, even by religious leaders, to make the same mistake in the matter of religious training. They fail to see the vital difference between "headlight" (filling the mind with all kinds of earthly knowledge) and "sunlight" (Sonlight—filling the mind and heart with Jesus who alone is "the way, the truth, and the life" [John 14:6]).

It is good to see that other Lutherans, though not in doctrinal agreement with us, are beginning to be concerned about this same matter. Recently there appeared in the *Standard*, a magazine or organ of the American Lutheran Church, an article entitled: "Is the Christian High School a Relic, a Luxury or an Urgent Need?" It is a thought-provoking article. We think the closing words of that article which we here quote are to the point:

> Certainly we have no quarrel with the public schools, even though they cannot take care of the church's interests in education. We have no objection to the great principle of separation of church and state. It is valid and necessary. But if we Lutherans claim that the Word of God is infinitely more important than all of man's accumulated learning, we are guilty of a strange inconsistency. We profess that in the Word alone is the power for salvation and Christian living. And yet with a spirit of abandon we give our young people in their most formative years to an educational system in which it is prohibited by law to teach the very Word of God.[11]

Lutheran high schools? They're neither a relic nor a luxury. They are an urgent need for our day.

Fellow redeemed: The question is not how shall your boy or girl receive an education and training which prepares them for a job of some kind enabling them to make a living and a good one. This is indeed the chief aim of the unbeliever. Nay, the question is this: How shall your boy or girl get an education and training which prepares them for this life and the life to come? This is the only kind of training which agrees with the instruction of our Savior when He states most emphatically: "Seek ye first the kingdom of God, and His righteousness; and all these things shall be added unto you" (Matthew 6:33).

Yes, we need our Bethany High School. Our children need it. Our Christian parents need it. Our Synod needs it. Let us pray for it. Let us support it. Let us bring our sons and daughters.

---

[11] *Editors' note*: The source has not been located.

Bethany Lutheran College
MANKATO, MINN.

Junior College   School of Music
High School   Commercial College

For

Men and Women

Expenses as low as possible.

Write for catalogue.

ADDRESS

Bethany Lutheran College
Mankato, Minn.

This advertisement appeared in the November 16, 1929 issue of the Lutheran Sentinel, just three weeks after "Black Thursday," October 24, 1929, when the New York stock market crashed. Every generation faces the question of whether Christian education is worth the cost. Pastors, during the Great Depression and at other times, have sought to remind students and their parents that a great cost also is involved in refusing the opportunity for Christian education.

DOCUMENT 3.4:

Letter to the Pastors of the ELS (1964)

By the Board of Regents of Bethany Lutheran College

Source: ELS Archives, S420A 1964.

Board of Regents
To the pastors of the ELS—
Dear Brethren:

> One thing needful! This one treasure
> Teach me, Savior, to esteem;
> Other things may promise pleasure,
> But are never what they seem;
> They prove to be burdens that vex us and chafe us,
> And true lasting happiness never vouchsafe us;
> This one precious treasure, that all else exceeds,
> Gives joy above measure and fills all my needs. (*LHy* 227:1)[12]

Surely, brethren, we have no other business at any time in our busy lives than to proclaim the "one thing needful." If there is anything we and our fellow sinners need above all it is the

---

[12] *Editors' note*: The motto of Bethany Lutheran College, "One Thing Needful," comes from Luke 10:42. A hymn based on this text, which the Regents quote in the beginning of their letter, has been sung regularly at Bethany commencement exercises.

message of a full and free (unconditioned) forgiveness for all our sins through the merits and work of Jesus Christ. May this message give you peace and joy in abundance, and may you with renewed vigor and zeal proclaim it to your people.

We who have been elected to the Board of Regents by you and your people earnestly desire to make Bethany a good school where Christ is the center of all teaching and activities. "One thing needful" is not just another slogan with us. We believe it to be a matter of life and death for our young people of high school and junior college age, for all of us as a synod, for our children yet to be born, yea, for the generations to follow.

We do not propose to come into your congregations to instruct Christian parents and Christian children about the need for attending Christian schools. This God requires of you, who are the shepherds of the sheep and lambs of Christ. We do want to visit with you about this matter by means of the written word and seek to stress the great urgency of having our children in attendance at Bethany. We want to encourage you in doing this vital work among your people.

We don't have to tell you to go in spirit to the manger in Bethlehem to look into the face of God's "unspeakable gift," or to take your place at the foot of the cross and look earnestly upon the crucified Savior. We are sure you always do this very thing even as the hymn writers have so well said. See *Lutheran Hymnary*, 309, 1 & 5, and 185, v. 4.[13] At that manger and beneath that cross let it sink deeply into our hearts and minds that here is the only Savior who has commanded: "Go ye therefore, and teach all nations, baptizing them in the name of the Father, and of the Son, and of the Holy Ghost: *Teaching them to observe all things whatsoever I have commanded you*[14]: and, lo, I am with you alway, even unto the end of the world. Amen" [Matthew 28:19–20]. How have we and how are we carrying out the command to teach everything He has commanded us?

How else can we really and fully do it to the best of our ability than through Christian training by Christian parents at home; through Christian training by Christian pastors and teachers in the

---

[13] *Editors' note*: The verses referenced begin as follows: "O sinner, for a little space, Lift up thine eyes discerning . . ."; "Now mark, O man, and ponder well / Sin's awful condemnation . . ."; and, "That God hath laid His anger by, He by His gift hath shown us; He gives His Son for us to die, In Him He now doth own us. . . ."

[14] *Editors' note*: The Regents' letter underscored the phrase here reproduced in italics.

church; through Christian training by Christian teachers in Christian schools?

Is it really acceptable with our Lord if we do this: have our Christian parents train the children at home and have Christian pastors and teachers train them for a couple of hours once or twice a week, and then send them for training and instruction to unchristian schools and most of the time under unchristian teachers, who train them all day long five days a week with no proper reference to Christ or use of His saving Word? Do you perchance object to calling public schools unchristian? We then ask: can you call them Christian? <u>Somehow we and our people have gotten the false idea that teachers and school can be neutral and have no effect upon the character, thinking, and conduct of the students they train and instruct.</u>[15] Even secular educators recognize that this is impossible. The last *Bethany Bulletin* makes that very clear.[16] It should make us stop and think when we are faced with the thought of having our children trained without having Christ at the center of it all.

It may be argued that, while we know that the public school and its teachers certainly <u>do teach false doctrines</u> and have a completely wrong philosophy of education, yet it is better that we have our children at home so that the parents can counteract all that is false and give their children counsel and love. This seems to have a lot of merit. And yet there are several questions that arise and demand answer in this connection also. *How many of the parents who do not send their children to Christian schools actually have time or take time to find out what their children are being taught and give them such help and counsel? Would it be 10%, do you think? Before you brush aside such a low percentage as utterly foolish, remember how hard it is to get parents to take enough interest <u>in their children to help them with Sunday school and confirmation lessons.</u>*[17] Again we might ask: when we deliberately send our children to such schools where admittedly false teachings are taught, can we really counteract it fully? Another question: does the fact that false doctrine is taught in public schools make it less dangerous <u>than when it is taught by Boy Scout leaders, lodges, the A[merican] L[utheran] C[hurch], or

---

15   *Editors' note*: President B. W. Teigen underlined this statement on his personal copy of this letter, as preserved in the Synod Archives.
16   *Editors' note*: The source has not been located.
17   *Editors' note*: Teigen drew a line in the margin along side the sentences that are here reproduced in italics, and underlined the final phrase as indicated.

the Missouri Synod?[18] Christ commands: "Beware of false prophets" [Matthew 7:15]. To us that has always been a general injunction.

Simply and clearly Jesus tells us: "Seek ye first the kingdom of God and His righteousness" [Matthew 6:33]. This must be true of all that we and all children of God are doing. Certainly it must be applied also to the education of our children and will be the deciding factor in choosing the school they shall attend.

We hope you all have a copy of *Luther's Letter to the Mayors and Aldermen of all the Cities of Germany on behalf of Christian Schools*.[19] From it we quote the following:

> I should prefer, it is true, that our youth be ignorant and dumb rather than that the universities and convents should remain as the only source of instruction open to them (namely, the young). *For it is my earnest intention, prayer, and desire that these schools of Satan either be destroyed or changed into Christian schools.*[20] But since God has so richly favored us, and given us a great number of persons who are competent thoroughly to instruct and train our young people, it is truly needful that we should not disregard His grace and let Him knock in vain. He stands at the door; happy are we if we open to Him. He calls us; happy is the man who answers Him. *If we disregard His call, so that He passes us by, who will bring Him back?*[21]
>
> My dear countrymen, but while the market is at your door; gather the harvest while the sun shines and the weather is fair: use the grace and Word of God while they are near. For know this, that the Word and grace of God are like a passing shower, which does not return where it has once been. The divine favor rested upon the Jews, but it has departed! Paul brought the Gospel into Greece; but now they have the Turks. Rome and Italy once enjoyed its blessings; but now they have

---

[18] *Editors' note*: Teigen underlined this statement. The ELS had formally severed its ties of doctrinal fellowship with the Missouri Synod in 1963, a year before this letter was written. Much of the controversy stemmed from Missouri's practice of prayer fellowship with the more liberal American Lutheran Church.

[19] *Editors' note*: The Regents quote, although from a different translation, the passage found in Martin Luther, "To the Councilmen of All Cities in Germany That They Establish and Maintain Christian Schools" (1524), *Luther's Works*, vol. 45, ed. Walther I. Brandt (Philadelphia: Fortress Press, 1962), 339-78, at 352.

[20] *Editors' note*: Teigen marked an X in the margin next to the statement that here is reproduced in italics.

[21] *Editors' note*: Teigen marked an X in beneath the statement that here is reproduced in italics.

the Pope. And the German people (we would add "and ourselves") should not think that they will always have it. Therefore seize it and hold fast, whoever can; idle hands will have an evil year.[22]

After you have read Luther's letter, the last *Bethany Bulletin*, and this letter with its plea, we urge you to discuss these matters with all your societies, with the parents and the young people individually. *Deo volente* [Lord willing], the future welfare of our people, God's work among us, lies with our young people and how well they have been indoctrinated. We have been entrusted by our Lord to teach and train them. How well are we doing the job? Are we truly faithful stewards? Can we justify using substitutes, not nearly as good, for the much better means—our Christian school? Help fill our Bethany to overflowing with students. Next to your own sermonizing and teaching, you can do no more useful and blessed work.

May you find joy, peace, and happiness in the Savior, and may you always possess this joy as you go about "seeking first the kingdom of God and His righteousness" [Matthew 6:33].

With fraternal love and greetings,
THE BOARD OF REGENTS

---

[22] *Editors' note*: The two parenthetical comments were inserted by the Regents.

DOCUMENT 3.5:

No, Mrs. Troemel, It Is Not Good! (1976)

By John A. Moldstad, Sr.

John Moldstad, Sr. (1926–) *has been known to many as one who would sacrifice his time for the benefit of others and the church. He was born June 5, 1926 to Rev. John and Ethelyn Moldstad in Chicago, Illinois, and was baptized June 20.*[23] *After graduating from Bethel Christian Day School in 1939, he spent two years at Luther Institute in Chicago before attending Bethany Lutheran High School, in Mankato, to finish off his high school. After spending two years at Bethany Lutheran College, he finished his B.A. degree at Northwestern College, Watertown, Wisconsin, in 1947. He then enrolled at Bethany Lutheran Theological Seminary, graduating in 1950.*[24] *On August 5, 1951 he was married to Gudrun E. Madson. This same year, Moldstad was installed as pastor at Immanuel Lutheran Church, Lengby, Minnesota. He served there for five years before being installed as pastor at Thorton, Iowa. Bethany Lutheran College then gave*  *Moldstad a call to be the Dean of Men in 1965.*[25] *He stayed at Bethany until 1978, when he was installed in East Grand Forks, Minnesota, where he remained until called to Vero Beach, Florida, in 1985. His wife passed away in 1987 at the age of sixty-three. John and Gudrun were*

---

23 "Vitae: John Moldstad," *Lutheran Sentinel*, 12 Dec. 1951, 364.
24 Ibid., 364.
25 Interview with Donald Moldstad, 16 Feb. 2010.

blessed with four children: John, Donald, Lois, and James (who passed away one day after birth). A year after the death of his first wife, Moldstad married June Besterveldt. Following his time at Vero Beach, Moldstad served in Cottage Grove, Minnesota, from 1991 to 1996 and part time in Audubon, Minnesota, from 1996 to 2001.[26] Moldstad retired following his time in Audubon, but continued his long-term service on the Bethany Lutheran College Board of Regents. He and his wife now live in McFarland, Wisconsin.[27] [KD]

Source: *Lutheran Sentinel*, 9 Sept. 1976, 263-65.

She was eighty-one, going on seventy. We had expected someone certainly much older looking! For we were interviewing the first graduate of Bethany Ladies College in 1913! In fact, she was the entire graduating class of that year.

Mrs. Marie Muench Troemel of Sioux Falls, South Dakota, proved to be most interesting as she reminisced about that first year of Bethany's existence. "The furnace wasn't working yet, so each room had a temporary kerosene stove. Wasn't much good for heat, but I remember it worked well for making fudge on top of it. It was against the rules, but we put tape around the door so the smell wouldn't go out into the hallway," she winked.

"During the week we couldn't go downtown without signing out for which stores we would stop at and when we would return. On Sundays we all marched down the hill to church in groups of six—each group with a chaperone," she recalled wistfully.

"We all had to wear our blue uniforms during the week. White on Sunday!" She smiled. "But I wouldn't trade that year at Bethany for anything. It was so very important in shaping my life. We were taught right from wrong and that some things were proper and some weren't." She went on, "Today's young people don't seem to know what is right and what isn't. They call it 'doing their own thing,' but it is not good."

No, Mrs. Troemel, it is not good!

Sad to say, even many colleges which call themselves Christian no longer teach a real set of values, a moral system from Mt. Sinai, a right from wrong. Society hears so little reference to sin anymore, so little old-time preaching about repentance, that

---

[26] *ELS Directory: Pastors and Congregations* (Mankato, MN: Evangelical Lutheran Synod, 1998), 98.

[27] Interview with Donald Moldstad, 16 Feb. 2010.

Paul Moldstad, brother of John Moldstad, Sr., stands second from the right in the back row of this Bethany class picture, taken in the late 1940s. David Ylvisaker, son of S. C. Ylvisaker, stands in the back center.

one wonders whether we have become a "sinless society."

The blue uniforms and chaperones have joined the kerosene stoves in Bethany's attic lore. But we hastened to assure our first graduate that we still teach a value system at Bethany based on the Holy Scripture. Hairdos, clothing styles, bedtime hours may change from decade to decade, but some things never change.

That which God has called right and called wrong will always be so—even if society or the Gallup Poll declares otherwise.

Many people feel that the threat of secular education is the teaching of evolution. "We can take care of that at home and through our church" is the attitude we hear so often.

But to this writer, there is a far greater threat to the spiritual life of the student from secular instruction: *a wrong set of values.* He may still hold to the Adam and Eve story, but may be taken in by the value system of the public school system.

At Bethany Lutheran College we still set forth before our students an education for this life, which endeavors to aid the students to keep their lives in proper perspective. "For here we have no continuing city, but we seek one to come" (Hebrews 13:14).

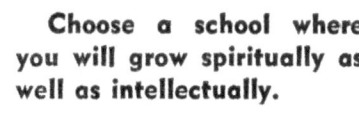

This advertisement appeared in the May 12, 1960 issue of the Lutheran Sentinel. *It shows students lining up for chapel and tells of the uniquely Christ-centered education that Bethany offers. In the early twenty-first century, chapel services have continued to take place at 10 a.m. each weekday morning, with Wednesday evening Vespers and Bible study opportunities also being provided.*

DOCUMENT 3.6:

Address for the Fiftieth Anniversary Reunion of Bethany Lutheran College (1977)

By Paul Zimmerman

Dr. Paul A. Zimmerman (1918–) *was born to Mr. and Mrs. Albert C. Zimmerman on June 25, 1918 in Danville, Illinois. He graduated from Trinity Lutheran School in Danville and was confirmed in 1932 by Rev. Albert C. Bernthal. He graduated from Concordia College in Fort Wayne, Indiana, in June 1939 and from Concordia Theological Seminary in St. Louis, Missouri, two years later. In September of 1942, he received a call to teach religion and the sciences at Bethany Lutheran College in Mankato, Minnesota. In 1943, he returned to Concordia Seminary and received his Masters of Divinity in May 1944.[28] As recognition of special work in the field of systematic theology, he was also given a Bachelor of Divinity. He went on to receive a Ph.D. in chemistry from the University of Illinois. Between 1944 and 1953, Zimmerman continued to serve Bethany as professor of science and theology. From 1949 to 1953, he also served as the principal of the high school on Bethany's campus. In 1953, he left Bethany to teach at Concordia Teacher's College in Seward, Nebraska.[29] In 1954 he became president of the school and during his tenure the school became accredited and enrollment almost doubled. In 1961, he moved to Ann Arbor, Michigan, to become the first president of Concordia Lutheran Junior College. In 1973, he became the seventh president of Concordia*

---

[28] "Vita," *Lutheran Sentinel*, 27 Oct. 1944, 318-19.
[29] "Around the Synod," *Lutheran Sentinel*, 27 June 1953, 190.

Teachers College in River Forest, Illinois.[30] Zimmerman has also held many offices in educational associations including the Presidency of the Nebraska Association of Church Colleges in 1957. On June 11, 1944, Zimmerman married Genevieve E. Bahls with whom he had two children, Karmin and Thomas. [AB]

Source: Delivered in Mankato, MN, July 23, 1977, transcribed by David Ylvisaker from an audio recording, and polished for publication by the editors of this volume. The transcription manuscript is filed in the Synod Archives.

There are certain times in history, which are very rare, when something special happens—times that very few people are privileged to participate in, or an event, something which may not be repeated, or anything like it, for a long time. I have a feeling that we are participating in such an event tonight. Who among us, including the most optimistic, would have thought when a fiftieth anniversary celebration for Bethany Lutheran College was planned, that the loyal sons and daughters would come to fill a banquet hall so large that we would have to move into a state university or that some 700 of us would be here and perhaps another 300 or 400 others participating in one way or another? That says something tremendous about this school. Why have we come here tonight, from all over the country, from varying occupations, and from widely varying age groups? What is the magnet that draws us? We have come, you know, to pay tribute to an institution that has molded our lives, whether we be former faculty members or students.

Bethany! Remember where that name comes from? It was the little hamlet in Palestine where Jesus' friends lived, Mary and Martha and their brother Lazarus. It was there that the Lord Jesus told Martha about "the one thing needful," which indeed is the motto of this college [Luke 10:42]. Those that have come to this college, those that have taught here, and those that have supported it have made it a Bethany, the place where the Lord Jesus dwells, where we have met Him in Word and Sacrament, and found "the one thing needful."

---

[30] Service of Installation for Paul Zimmerman at Concordia Teachers College, River Forest, IL, 2 Dec. 1973.

Professor Zimmerman instructs Bethany students in geometry.

We have come to honor a church body, the Evangelical Lutheran Synod, affectionately called "the little Norwegian Synod," which for fifty years has sustained and supported this college, so that not only its sons and daughters, but Lutherans and non-Lutherans from a wide variety of situations could enjoy the privileges of being students here.

We've come tonight to recall with fondness the men and women who have come here, served here, and gone to school here. Tonight you and I can relive a bit the days of our youth and hear the echoes of lessons that down through the years have been a benediction on our lives.

Above all, we have come across these generations and over the years to thank our gracious God, who has made Bethany what it has been, what it is today, and, pray God, it will be in the future. Our gracious God has touched our lives in a special way through this school.

Tonight I'm sure in the minds of each and everyone sitting here there is a recollection of how you and I first came here. Perhaps you came as freshmen in the high school or as freshmen in college. Well, I came as a vicar in 1942. Johnny Ylvisaker, the president's son sat next to me in the seminary in St. Louis. His dad told him he was coming down to see if he could find a few vicars to help fill the faculty positions back here. Specifically he was looking for a science man to teach chemistry and physics. John knew I'd done a little reading in psychology and he told his dad, "Hey, there's a good man to go out and talk to." When I came to Bethany, I had taken eleven hours of chemistry, but during the time that I served here, by the grace of God and the indulgence of the Board, that work added up to a Ph.D.

When I came, they also asked me to teach college physics; I'd had high school physics. That shows you the spirit of the faculty in those days. And I still recall, somewhat shamefacedly, there was one fellow in the class that seemed to somehow always be catching up. I was always one chapter ahead. I was afraid that one day there was going to come a time when he was going to ask me a question I couldn't answer. And then he got in trouble and they dismissed him from school. Somehow I enjoyed that physics class a lot more then.

Dr. Ylvisaker told me when he talked to me about coming to Bethany that that year we were going to introduce that physics course, and that he had just purchased material for a new laboratory. When I arrived that summer I discovered that they had purchased the materials from a small high school that had shut down its laboratory—quite a bit of very good material. The only trouble was that it was packed in chicken feathers. I scratched for the next month!

I should say, too, that after I had vicared, I returned to Bethany in 1944 and brought with me my bride. This was my first call. My son and my daughter were born during the time we were here. They were great years. We thank God for them.

But what did we find when we came here to Bethany? Well, we found that the roots of this institution went back beyond the time of June 20, 1927, when the Norwegian Synod formally took over the college. It goes back beyond the year 1911, the year when Bethany started as a Lutheran Academy for Girls. It goes back beyond that. It goes back to the sturdy theology of the pioneer American Norwegian Lutheran theologians. Dr. Ulrik Vilhelm Koren in the year 1890, one of the pioneers of the Norwegian Synod, wrote an article called "What the Norwegian Synod Has Wanted and Still Wants," and I'm sure must still want today. In that article Koren, one of the great theologians of the Synod, wrote, "There are two main pillars of Lutheran proofs. The first principle is the proof that the Holy Scripture is the only sure and perfect rule of our faith and life." He spoke in that article words that are contemporary and have meaning in our current controversies in the Lutheran Church today about the inerrant scripture. Then he added that the second great truth is that Jesus

Mrs. Harms, Mrs. Ingebritson, and Mrs. Effie Nerison served Bethany students in the cafeteria during the late 1950s.

Christ is the way to salvation for all believing souls, in other words, that a man is justified and saved for Christ's sake by faith alone without the deeds of the law. There are three "solas" of the Lutheran reformation—*Sola Scriptura*, scripture alone—*Sola Gratia*, grace alone—and *Sola Fide*, faith alone. At the conclusion of that essay Koren said, "Our heart's desire is to preserve the old doctrine in which our fathers found their peace. We have learned to see that this doctrine and this alone is founded on God's Word."[31] That is what was in the hearts of the fathers of this synod when fifty years ago they assumed their responsibility for the operation of Bethany Lutheran College. And it is still their purpose and unwavering aim today. That's what we found.

We found also a modern progressive philosophy of education. Dr. S. C. Ylvisaker was president when I came and the greater part of what I learned about the philosophy of education and still practice today I learned from that man in private conferences,

---

[31] Ulrik Vilhelm Koren, "What the Norwegian Synod Has Wanted and Still Wants," in *Faith of Our Fathers* (Mankato, MN: Lutheran Synod Book Company, 1953), 47–112, at 112.

faculty meetings, and division meetings. I have the highest respect for the leadership he provided. I remember what a scholar he was when he used to stand up in front of a pastoral conference with just his New Testament in hand and deliver a learned exegetical paper. I remember how he helped launch the four-year junior college, a concept that was way ahead of its time. I remember many other things that he said and did, but I will let him speak tonight from an old copy of the *Bethany Scroll* that goes back to September 1942. Dr. Ylvisaker was quoted from a chapel talk in that September '42 issue of the *Scroll*. He said, "If you have helped but one soul to see Christ in His majesty, His love, His graciousness, then you have accomplished a mission that will stand throughout all eternity." That was his philosophy. That's what he taught his students and faculty alike.

Another great man who has gone on to the reward of grace was Norman Madson. We still have his *Evening Bells at Bethany* at home and we read it every once in awhile at our family devotion.[32] He was the first dean of the theological seminary that started in 1946. And there were other Norwegian giants like George Lillegard and C. U. Faye. Then there were those great and devout souls like Pete and Ma Oslund who cleaned the halls and cooked our food and many, many others like them.

And we have found now—that since the time that I was called away, you have found noble successors—men and women who have walked in those footsteps. To my right, B. W. Teigen. B stands for "Bjarne," but it also stands for "builder" because when I was here, there was just that central block of buildings. And you see what is there now: the dormitory, the library, the gymnasium. By his efforts and those of faithful members of Faculty and Board and Synod that supported him, those buildings have arisen. Marvelous people like the Andersons who sit to my left[33]; wonderful people like Norman Holte and Rudy Honsey and others that I don't know because they have come since that time but in

---

32   *Editors' note*: Norman A. Madson, *Evening Bells at Bethany* (Mankato, MN: Lutheran Synod Book Company, 1948). The older tradition of "Evening Bells at Bethany" has adapted to the twenty-first century, bringing an evening devotion to students, parents, and alumni via BLC-TV broadcasts and video webstreaming at *www.blc.edu/worship*.

33   *Editors' note*: Professors Sophia T. Anderson and Ella B. Anderson, sisters, both retired in 1970, after thirty-six and twenty-five years, respectively, of service to Bethany Lutheran College. In their honor, the the Board of Regents named the women's dormitory Anderson Hall. See J. Herbert Larson and Juul B. Madson, *Built on the Rock* (Mankato, MN: Evangelical Lutheran Synod Book Company, 1992), 213.

that same spirit. President Ray Branstad—his work now in the launching of the Development Program, the seminary building, the present faculty that in 1974 received North Central Accreditation. And that is no small feat for a small college with struggling finances. You know they used to say in the days when I was here—I came shortly after the Great Depression—they used to say that Bethany College was located on a "bluff" and run on the same principle. All through the years with those financial struggles, Bethany has held up because the Lord has made it work. It is a first-class school and has been for a long time—North Central has now recognized it.

What about the future? We can spend a lot of time tonight talking about the difficulties of private higher education. I'm sure you know it, and I know it, too. Escalating costs—costs of tuition going up and up. You've probably heard the story of the mother who went to the art store and demanded to see a very fine frame. She said, "I have a very expensive picture that I want framed." Finally the man brought out one that was covered with gold and was very ornate. She said, "That's about right." He said, "What's the worth of the picture?" She said, "$15,000.00." He said, "That's a lot of money for a picture." She said "It sure is." He said "Have you got it with you?" She said, "Yes I have." He said, "I'll put it in the frame right now." She said, "O.K. Here's my son's college diploma." That's what it costs these days, and it's going to cost a lot more.

We are in competition with state universities with their state support. Bethany College doesn't have that kind of support. We have the problem of government interference to the point that regulations are imposed upon private colleges often in inequitable ways. Regulations drawn up originally for the great schools have been imposed upon small colleges, where they work great hardship and sometimes make no sense. Not too long ago the president of a private college had a board of control meeting and he said to his board: "I bring you good news and bad news. The good news is we have complied with all the governmental regulations. The bad news is we are bankrupt." And there's a lot of real meaning to that.

But the importance of private Christian education remains. One of the greatest tragedies that could happen to America would be that the private college would disappear because of the financial problems we face and the resources that sometimes seem so small. Far greater would be the tragedy if Christian schools were to vanish from the face of America. But I have the confidence that they will not because God needs them for His people, because His people need them, because His "people are willing" as the Psalmist says "in the day of Thy power" [Psalm 110:3]. And you are living testimony of that tonight by your presence, by your coming across the miles and years to be here.

A couple weeks ago in River Forest I happened to meet an alumna of this institution, a mother who is taking some courses in our graduate school there. She recalled for me the days when I was dean of students and wasn't always the most flexible. And we talked about some of the rules we had then and I said "Well I suppose the rules have probably changed back at Bethany as they have at other places." She said, "I hope they haven't changed too much. My son is going there this fall and I hope he finds the same kind of Bethany it's always been—a Christian school that takes its Christianity seriously—not only a Christian school but a Lutheran school, one which has been so faithful to the Lutheran Confessions not only in their word, but also in their spirit." Also with the seminary. This small but faithful, efficient seminary is providing for the Synod its own pastors. It too is bearing fantastic blessings.

The word I have tonight for this private Lutheran College is that I am confident we can give you God's promise that, as the past has been a blessing and a success, so will be the future. The church body is there to support it. I talked to John Moldstad. He told me about the last Synod meeting when they were launching the project of a seminary building. And then he challenged them and I admire him for that. He said, "I want every one of the delegates here and I want the pastors here—pastors and lay delegates—to pledge. What I want is a thousand dollars from each one of you." Now only John Moldstad could think of that. But I tell you that it was a thrill that they got that average from the lay delegates, and not too far behind were the pastors. The pledge over a three year period on that occasion was for $135,000. Just that sample shows you that the hearts of a little Norwegian synod still beat strongly.

Or the Alumni: not only Norwegians but us Germans and others. I take it as a great compliment (as a matter of fact, President J. A. O. Preus told me it was) to speak at the fiftieth anniversary of a Norwegian school. I talked to one of the Norwegians here about it, who said, "We figured we had you for ten years to sort of straighten you out." But the alumni stretch across many, many lines. For we have this common conviction that here indeed can be found "the one thing needful" [Luke 10:42]. Above all, being faithful to that, we know that the Lord will bless; that He who is almighty has saved through His Son. He who has sustained the martyrs in the years when their blood was shed, who has stood by His people in His church in all generations, will stand by this school. It will survive and it will prosper.

It's a great privilege to be with you tonight to speak these words, to try to express a faith that I know is in your hearts, that which if you were here at this rostrum you'd want to say. One of the greatest days of my life is to be honored thus. My good wife, too, when she heard that we were coming back to Bethany for this occasion, said "If I have to hitchhike, I'll be there." We didn't hitchhike. We came by North Central! On the back of your program is the Bethany song:

> High amid the trees you stand,
> Bethany, O guide of youth.
> Pointing up with kindly hand,
> Filling hearts and minds with truth.
>
> When we leave your sheltered side,
> May we all your hopes fulfill.
> May your lessons e'er abide,
> May your hand point upward still.
> To Bethany we sing.

It is a great song and a great spirit! It is a great college! A great gathering of alumni! Our Lord Jesus once spoke to Martha at Bethany. She was worried because Mary was sitting at His feet and wasn't helping her prepare the dinner. He said, "One thing is needful." You remember that is the school motto. Jesus said, "Mary has chosen that good part and it will not be taken away from her" [Luke 10:42]. Neither will that good part which we have chosen be taken away from us nor this school of our Lord and Savior. God bless you. Keep Bethany in your heart.

DOCUMENT 3.7:

Bethany Lutheran College and Mission Station (1990)

By Steven L. Reagles

Dr. Steven L. Reagles (1947–) was born in LaCrosse, Wisconsin, on August 3, 1947. He attended First Lutheran School, where he graduated and was confirmed in 1961. He graduated from Luther High School in Onalaska, Wisconsin, in 1965 before attending the University of Wisconsin–LaCrosse for two years with a major in English. From 1967 to 1975, Reagles served in the military where he also received his commercial pilot license. In 1974, he graduated from the University of Wisconsin–LaCrosse with a Bachelor of Arts degree in English. After graduation he studied classical and Koine Greek as well as Hebrew at Bethany Lutheran College in Mankato, Minnesota. From 1979 to 1980 he served as a vicar at St. John's Evangelical Lutheran Church in Redwood Falls, Minnesota. During the next year, he served as a vicar at St. John's Evangelical Lutheran Church in Lannon, Wisconsin. In 1981, he graduated from  Wisconsin Lutheran Seminary in Mequon, Wisconsin, with a Master of Divinity degree.[34] From 1981 to 1983, Reagles served as the pastor at Our Savior Evangelical Lutheran Church in Jacksonville, Florida. In 1983, he returned to Bethany where he served as an assistant professor in addition to acting as the Dean of Students until 1988. In 1988, he became a full professor of religious studies and communication. From

---

34   Steven Reagles, *Curriculum Vitae*, 2007.

1984 to 1986, he pursued graduate work in rhetoric and composition at Iowa State University and Purdue University before graduating from Mankato State University with a Master of Arts degree in Speech Communication. In 2001, he also received his Ph.D. in English with rhetoric and composition from Indiana University of Pennsylvania. In 1976, Reagles married Patty Swing, with whom he has six children. He and his wife have also been blessed with ten grandchildren. His current research examines the relationship between technology and its use in worship as an effective communication tool.[35] [AB]

Source: *Lutheran Sentinel,* May 1990, 10-11.

Ever since Christ's Great Commission, the church has identified as vital to its mission the task of sending missionaries into all the world, to preach the saving message of the Gospel. The church was created to operate in a "go mode." Paul and his missionary companions spent long years on the "go," traveling throughout the Mediterranean world as evangelists and "church planters." But they also spent years in a "stop mode," or "mission station mode," witnessing to the truths of Scripture in a set locale. Rather than going out to the people, Paul drew the people to a "stop" station.

In Ephesus, Paul set up a school where, as Luke reports, "He had discussions daily in the lecture hall of Tyrannus. This went on for two years so that all the Jews and Greeks who lived in the province of Asia heard the Word of God" (Acts 19:9,10). Later, in Rome, while he was waiting to go on trial Luke writes that, "For two whole years Paul stayed there in his own rented house and welcomed all who came to see him. Boldly and without hindrance he preached the kingdom of God and taught about the Lord Jesus Christ" (Acts 28:30–31).

"Two whole years" to share the Gospel with those who *come* to you may not fit the typical picture of outreach mission work. Nevertheless, every established congregation understands this kind of evangelism. And at Bethany Lutheran College "two whole years" and "those who come" to hear have special meaning. While a Christian liberal arts college is not the exact equivalent of Paul's fixed location work in Ephesus and Rome, at Bethany tremendous opportunities arise for teaching about the kingdom of Christ to

---

[35] Steven Reagles, interview by Abigail Bourman, 30 Apr. 2010.

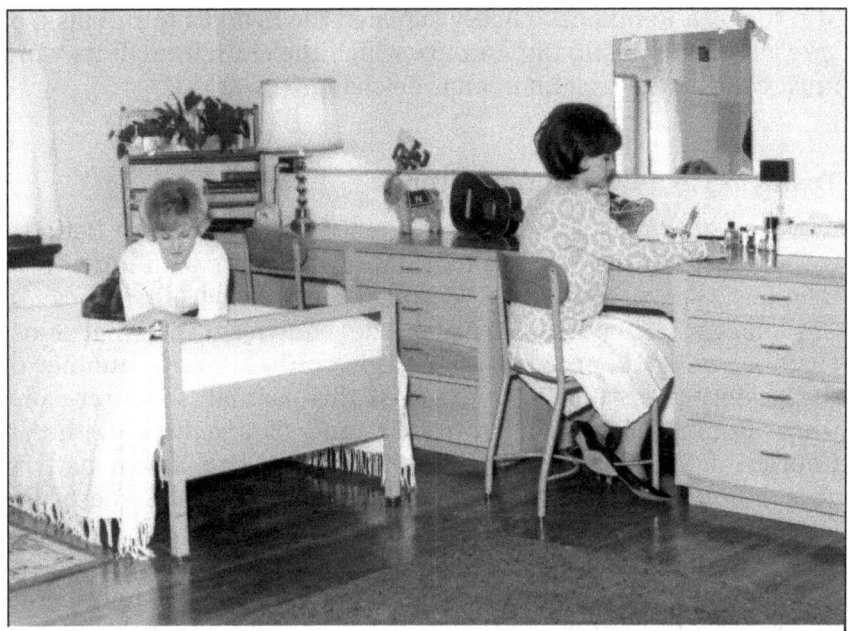

Dormitory life has always played a significant role in the Bethany experience. As two or more students learn to share a common living space, they also share each other's joys and griefs and have the opportunity to mentor one another spiritually. Though hairstyles and room decor may have changed since this photograph was taken in the 1960s, dorm life remains an important part of the freshmen experience.

students from home and abroad, who come to study for two years.

Those Who Come

Years ago the typical student who enrolled at Bethany tended to be the ELS's "own," its sons and daughters and the sons and daughters of those in its fellowship. Within the last twenty-five years, recruitment trends have brought more students from outside the circle of fellowship. In 1964, of the 81 freshmen enrolled at Bethany, 66% came from the Evangelical Lutheran Synod (ELS) or Wisconsin Evangelical Lutheran Synod (WELS). In 1989, 181 freshmen enrolled, of whom only 32% were of ELS/WELS background.

What these statistics do is call the entire Bethany staff to ever more faithful witnessing to those who come as students. Robert Preus's classic devotion before the Thirty-fifth Annual Convention of the Evangelical Lutheran Synod on June 3, 1953, titled "Our

Mission as a Remnant," clearly signaled the Synod's future task, of "preaching and testifying," a duty which the church in all its work must continually reclaim in an ever-changing world.[36]

Testifying in a Classroom Setting

One of the places where mission work takes place at Bethany is the classroom, or "lecture hall." Many students with little or no religious background are enrolled in "Basic Doctrines of Christianity," a course which is the equivalent of what most pastors would call an adult instruction course. A large number of the seventy-five students in the class this past fall semester came from Roman Catholic, Protestant and Evangelical Lutheran Church of America (ELCA) backgrounds. A half dozen had no church connection. Three students were Buddhists. Some of the students came from ELS/WELS congregations.

During the first period of class, students were asked to fill out a "Religious Inventory Survey," so that the instructor might better understand the nature of the audience and its understanding of biblical truth. The results of the survey reveal the clear need for "preaching and testifying" and clarifying Scripture. One question on the survey reads as follows: "All religions teach that there is some sort of 'heaven.' How do you believe that a person gets to heaven?" While many students answered in a biblical way, a number of answers revealed a serious misunderstanding of the basic meaning of salvation by grace, through faith in the atoning work of Christ alone. Some answers show a total ignorance of biblical truth. The following are samples of actual responses to the above question:

> "When a person dies I believe everybody goes to heaven." (Christian, didn't know Synod)

> "I believe a person should repent and ask God to fill them with the Holy Spirit and do according to His Word. They will get into heaven." (Pentecostal)

> "Our God is all-forgiving, so yes, I do believe that all people go to heaven." (ELCA)

> "People who obey God's rules (the Ten Commandments, etc.), attend church on a regular basis . . ." (Catholic)

---

[36] *Synod Report* (1953), 85.

"I'm just blank on who is picked and why?" (LCMS)

"I am not sure that I believe in heaven. It doesn't seem realistic to me." (I'm a Roman Catholic, but I'm starting to fade)

"I really don't know the answer to that and really no one else does." (Baptist)

"I don't believe anything, when the time comes we'll all find out." (No church background)

"I believe that all people go to heaven after they die." (Buddhist)

"I am not sure, but I would like to have an understanding of heaven and hell, if they exist." (I have never attended church)

The responses to that one question, "How do you believe that a person gets to heaven?" alone demonstrates the need for clear mission "witness" at Bethany Lutheran College. Each year a steady stream of students comes to Bethany for a liberal arts education. By God's grace, many of these same students leave with more: a clear understanding of the Gospel of Jesus Christ. While Bethany's mission will continue to be defined as "Educational" rather than "Home Mission" or "Foreign Mission," the changing nature of the student body will demand a faithful witness akin to the kind Paul practiced at the mission stations of Rome and Ephesus. That was what the Synodical fathers had in mind decades ago when they founded a "Stop" station in Mankato, Minnesota, and called it Bethany Lutheran College.

(*Lutheran Sentinel Editor's Note*: Three students from the freshman class received adult instruction in the Christian faith at Mt. Olive Lutheran Church, two of them then also being baptized.)

BETHANY LUTHERAN COLLEGE

Mankato, Minn.

Your own High School and Junior College will welcome you most heartily if you are seeking an education which will strengthen your Christian faith while you prepare yourself for your life's work, whether it be in the ministry, in schools, in the home, or in the business world.

Together with these courses Bethany offers you a thorough course in music.

The Present Faculty

President, Sigurd C. Ylvisaker
Registrar, Alvin J. Natvig
Dean of Men, Oliver B. Harstad
Director Musical Department, Walter E. Buszin
Prof. E. J. Onstad, Business Manager
Clara M. Hagen, B.S.
Ruth Seidel, A.B.
Olga Lillegard, Dean of Women
Amanada Jacobsen, Commercial Teacher

Now is the time to send for a catalog.

Appearing in the July 23, 1940 issue of the Lutheran Sentinel, *this advertisement reflected the college's commitment to preparing young men and women for Christian vocations in the home, in the church, and in society. One's vocation, as Dr. Ryan MacPherson explains to Bethany students in the early twenty-first century, is "how your station in life serves as a channel of God's blessings to the people around you."*

DOCUMENT 3.8:

Philosophy and Objectives of the College (2009)

By the Board of Regents of Bethany Lutheran College

*The **Board of Regents of Bethany Lutheran College**, in consultation with the Faculty and Administration, has established and periodically revised the philosophy and objectives of the college. The version shown below appeared in the 2009 academic catalog. It differs from prior versions chiefly in two respects. First, it omits a sentence in the second paragraph, as indicated below. Second, it refers to the Bachelor of Arts degree, which the institution began conferring in 2001. During the years that followed, numerous courses and several new majors were added to the curriculum. To ensure that the expanded curriculum would advance the objectives stated below, the Faculty Assembly adopted during the 2004-2005 school year a "Form for New Course Proposals" that requires departments proposing a new course to indicate the course's "relation to Bethany's distinctive mission: Which of the 'Objectives of the College' would this course promote, and how?" In February 2011, the Regents approved minor stylistic changes to the college's list of objectives in order to conform to the Higher Learning Commission's recommendations for re-accreditation; for example, "to practice critical thinking" was revised to read: "to demonstrate critical thinking." For history's sake, the 2009 phrasing is retained here.* [RM]

Source: Bethany Lutheran College, *Academic Catalog, 2009-2011* (Mankato, MN: Bethany Lutheran College, 2009), 6-7.

Philosophy of the College

Bethany Lutheran College is a Christian liberal arts college. The college and the Evangelical Lutheran Synod are committed to the Holy Scriptures, the inspired and inerrant Word of God, as the sole authority for faith and life. The Lutheran Confessions are accepted as the correct understanding of the teachings of the Holy Scriptures. This commitment is summarized by the Reformation principles: Grace Alone, Faith Alone, and Scripture Alone.

Specifically, the college confesses that through faith in Jesus Christ the individual receives the forgiveness of sins and eternal life. Such faith is produced in human hearts by the Holy Spirit through the Word and Sacraments.[37]

The Christian faith governs the entire educational process at Bethany. Christian education implies a unique perspective on the past, present, and future. It assumes a specific view of people and their relationships both to God and to others. The college is committed to the position that these relationships are to be understood in the light of the knowledge that Jesus Christ is the Savior and the Lord of the universe.

Objectives of the College

In order to carry out the philosophy of the college, Bethany has the following specific objectives for the students:

1. To grow in grace and in the knowledge of the Lord and Savior Jesus Christ by means of the Gospel.

2. To practice independent critical thinking so that they are not shaken from the eternal foundations on which their moral and spiritual growth is based.

3. To become responsible citizens, aware of social realities, through the study of American and world cultural heritage as well as contemporary social, economic, and political issues.

4. To develop an appreciation for art, music, and literature so that as educated young people they will lead more full and satisfying

---

[37] *Editors' note*: Earlier versions of this statement included at this place the following sentence: "The Bible is not regarded as a mere source book of religious precepts for legalistic or moralistic application, but rather as a living book in which the Gospel of Jesus Christ is the power of God for salvation." See, for example, *Academic Catalog, 1993-1995*, 10.

lives.

5. To encourage an attitude of Christian stewardship with regard to their talents and abilities that they be used for the glory of God and the welfare of mankind.

6. To increase their ability to use written and oral English effectively.

7. To secure a foundation in mathematics and the sciences for a better understanding of the world.

8. To develop, through curricular and extracurricular experiences, positive attitudes toward physical and mental health.

9. To acquire the necessary skills for achieving a satisfactory vocational adjustment.[38]

To fulfill these objectives, Bethany provides:

1. Religion courses, daily chapel services, and other opportunities for the exercise of the Christian faith.

2. A Common General Education Core for all students; and,

3. A growing number of majors culminating in a Bachelor of Arts degree.

---

[38] *Editors' note*: The 2011 revision reads: "To demonstrate competency in a major field of study to serve productively as a member of a family, workplace, church, and community."

SECTION 4:

Bethany Lutheran Theological Seminary

Introduction

By Paul G. Madson

In order that we may obtain this faith, the ministry of teaching the Gospel and administering the Sacraments was instituted. For through the Word and the Sacraments, as through instruments, the Holy Spirit is given, and the Holy Spirit produces faith, where and when it pleaes God, in those who hear the Gospel.

AC V, 1–2

Pastors, in their own way, are educators also. In their vocation as ministers of Christ they are not only to "make disciples" but also to "teach" (Matthew 28:19). The Lutheran Church has always made Christian education a high priority, not only as it pertains to the education of children and of young people, but also as it pertains to those who wish to prepare for the Christian ministry. The latter are required to pursue further studies in their post-college years if they are to serve in the capacity of a pastor. Continued study in Biblical doctrine is, of course, paramount, and along with this is included the study of the Biblical languages (Greek and Hebrew). Also helpful to the Lutheran pastor is some knowledge of Latin and German. The Lutheran pastor should become familiar with his Church's formal confession of faith, the Book of Concord, to which he will be asked to subscribe. He should have an appreciative knowledge of church history and of the church fathers. All of this requires a seminary.

For many years after its reorganization in 1918, the Evangelical Lutheran Synod had entertained the hope of one day having its own seminary. The Synod was appreciative of sister church bodies in the Synodical Conference for making their seminaries available to its students, but it was felt that the ELS had a unique heritage worth preserving and could make its own contribution to Lutheranism and Christendom in general. There was the added concern that "dangerous unionistic tendencies," even in some areas of confessional Lutheranism, made it "increasingly imperative that we train our future pastors in our seminary."[1]

Eventually, at the Synod's 1931 convention, a committee was appointed to plan for a discussion of the matter at the General Pastoral Conference. However, it was not until the convention of 1942 that any progress was made, when the Board of Regents of Bethany Lutheran College was authorized "to make the necessary adjustment at our Bethany College, to the end that our seminary students may be given their last year's training in our own school. If possible, this work is to be begun this fall."[2] Though it was not possible to open a seminary that year, the wheels for action had begun turning. Plans would now proceed with a sense of greater urgency.

In 1946 the Evangelical Lutheran Synod fulfilled a long-sought need for training its own pastors when it opened a seminary on the campus of Bethany Lutheran College in Mankato, Minnesota. No longer would the ELS have to use the seminaries of sister synods. The task of getting this blessed venture off the ground was given to my father, the Rev. Norman A. Madson, who was called to be the first Dean of the Seminary. From its

---

[1] *Synod Report* (1944), 51.
[2] *Synod Report* (1942), 58.

beginning to the present day, the seminary has been signally blessed with faithful leadership and faculty, who are solely dedicated to preparing "Messengers of Peace."

Dean Madson, himself a gifted preacher, "inculcated in his students his own deep interest in and love for preaching."[3] He was assisted by several college professors in teaching the seminary courses. All went well with this new endeavor, and the dean's report at the end of the first year ended with these words: "It is to the ineffable grace of our merciful Father that we commend our infant 'school of the prophets.' With the sainted Dr. Walther we also pray: 'God preserve unto us a pious ministry!'"[4]

Two new professors were soon added to the seminary staff: the Rev. George O. Lillegard (Old Testament studies) and Prof. Christopher U. Faye (librarian). Dr. S. C. Ylvisaker, who had been president at its inception, continued to teach in the seminary until his retirement in 1952. Upon the retirement of Dean Madson in 1959, Bethany College President B. W. Teigen served as acting dean of the seminary until 1968. The Rev. Milton Otto served as seminary dean from 1968 to 1981. Others who in succeeding years served as president of the seminary were the Rev. Raymond Branstad, the Rev. Theodore Aaberg, the Rev. Glenn Reichwald (acting president), and the Rev. Wilhelm Petersen. Since 1997, the Rev. Gaylin Schmeling has been its president.

Each fall the seminary sponsors a popular series of lectures known as the "Reformation Lectures," a tradition dating to 1965. It also publishes a professional periodical for the clergy, *The Lutheran Synod Quarterly* (1961–), the successor of *Clergy Bulletin* (1941-1960). In the summer of 2006 a special anniversary issue of the quarterly, edited by President Schmeling, commemorated the seminary's sixtieth anniversary.[5]

The documents in this section begin when the re-organized Norwegian Synod was still in its infancy and our founding fathers sought to provide for Christian education at all levels, from elementary school through theological seminary **(Document 4.1)**. To be sure, Christian day schools received the greatest attention in the early years **(Document 4.2; cf. Section 3**: "Christian Day Schools"). However, the importance of training the next generation of pastors remained a priority that could not be

---

[3] Gaylin Schmeling, "Sixty Years at Bethany Lutheran Theological Seminary," *Lutheran Synod Quarterly* 46, nos. 2 and 3 (2006): 134-203, at 147.
[4] *Synod Report* (1947), 52–53.
[5] *Lutheran Synod Quarterly* 46, nos. 2 and 3 (2006).

ignored, particularly not after the bitter lessons of the 1917 Merger. Decade after decade, sermons would underscore the vital role of a seminary in instilling sound, biblical doctrine in the clergy it trained (**Documents 4.3, 4.4**, and **4.5**).

DOCUMENT 4.1:

Proposal for a School Committee (1919)

By the Norwegian Synod in Convention

*The **Norwegian Synod of the American Evangelical Lutheran Church**, later renamed the Evangelical Lutheran Synod (ELS), was formally established by a re-organizing convention held in June 1918 at Lime Creek, Iowa. This convention was necessitated by the dissolution of the Old Norwegian Synod and the merger of the majority of its membership into a liberal church body in June 1917. A minority of pastors from the old synod recognized that the merger compromised their heritage of biblical doctrine. Within a day of the merger, the remnant theologians formed a temporary association at the Aberdeen Hotel in St. Paul, Minnesota, and the following year they convened with like-minded pastors to establish the "Little Norwegian Synod." To safeguard the Gospel for future generations, the new synod resolved at its 1919 convention, held in Albert Lea, Minnesota, to establish a permanent committee that would provide for the educational needs of Christian children as well as of young men having the potential to serve as pastors.*[6]

Source: *Synod Report* (1919), 32–33, translated by Paul Madson.

---

[6] Theodore A. Aaberg, *A City Set on a Hill* (Mankato, MN: Evangelical Lutheran Synod, 1968), 44-81, 91; J. Herbert Larson and Juul B. Madson, *Built on the Rock* (Mankato, MN: Evangelical Lutheran Synod Book Company, 1992), 54-69.

The founding pastors of the re-organized Norwegian Synod, convened in June 1918 at Lime Creek, Iowa. Back row: *Christian Anderson, Holden Olsen;* middle row: *L. S. Guttebo, A. J. Torgerson, T. J. Thoen, Rev. Steger (a Lutheran Church–Missouri Synod observer), Bjug Harstad;* front row: *C. N. Petersen, H. Ingebritson, J. A. Moldstad, L. P. Jensen, G. P. Nesseth;* not pictured: *Emil Hansen, G. O. Lillegard.*

1. We recommend that a standing school committee of three members be elected.

2. That a church school fund be established where needy congregations can get support for a church school, which takes care of a child's whole instruction, and that this fund be managed by the school committee.

3. That the Synod seek to establish a professorship at the Missouri Synod's college[7] in St. Paul, Minn., which can take young men from our synod who will prepare for theological study or other high aspiration.

4. That the school committee be authorized to carry this out.

---

[7] *Editors' note*: Concordia College, St. Paul, now part of the ten-member, nationwide Concordia University system, was established in 1893 to train pastors for the Lutheran Church–Missouri Synod.

DOCUMENT 4.2:

Annual Address (1919)

By Bjug Harstad

Bjug Harstad (1848–1933) was born December 17, 1848 at Valle, Sætersdalen, Norway, to Aanong Tellefson and Torbjørg (Kittelsen) Harstad. In 1861, Bjug emigrated with his family to America, where he attended Luther College (1865–1871) in Decorah, Iowa, followed by Concordia Seminary (1871–1874) in St. Louis. He served as pastor in Mayville, North Dakota; Parkland, Washington; San Francisco, California; Los Angeles, California; and Farmington, Minnesota. Pastor Harstad also was temporary professor at Luther Seminary (1889–1890) the founder of Pacific Academy, now Pacific Lutheran University (1890). He later served as the first president of the reorganized Norwegian Synod (1918–1921). He married Guro Svendsen Omli (Omlid) in 1877; the couple had eleven children. Pastor Harstad died June 20, 1933. In 1983, his son Adolph M. Harstad—at the time eighty years old—had the joyous privilege of visiting Valle, Norway, for the dedication of a monument in honor of Bjug Harstad and other Norwegian emigrants from that region.[8]   [RM]

Source: Synod Report (1919), 16-17, translated by Paul Madson.

---

[8] "Bjug Harstad—One Who Had the Courage of His Convictions," *Lutheran Sentinel*, Sept. 1984, 4–5; "Unveiling of the Bjug Harstad Monument," *Lutheran Sentinel*, Sept. 1983, 13; "Bjug Harstad," *Oak Leaves* 8, no. 1 (Spring 2004): 7.

But I cannot, without sinning, neglect a sober reminder as to how it stands with us regarding our children's instruction in the fear of God. Are we bringing them up in the nurture and admonition of the Lord as the Lord commands us parents to do? Are we bringing our children up in the fear of God when we, eight to ten months out of the year, send them to teachers who are not to teach them that Christ is God's Son, because that is forbidden as sectarian teaching? Or is the best we can do for them to let them attend a Sunday School, from where they go home or out into the street while Christians are gathered in the church to hear God's Word, to pray, and to sing. Many think they have done well when they later on allow them one or two months of religious school in the middle of summer. Can reasonable people think that this is a proper treatment of Christian children, who just as much as other children need a vacation in the warmest time of the year?

Do we really believe that our children do not need more of God's Word and strength to live in difficult times than what the previously mentioned schools, after confirmation instruction, can give them? Then one must think that it is so easy for them to understand the distinction between Law and Gospel, to understand and detest the dreadful harm of inherited and actual sin, together with grasping and receiving faith in the Triune God's essence, His will, and His great deeds for the whole world. Or, I wonder, can we stand on the day of accounting, if we do not teach them the truth? It is my prayer and admonition that we ponder well this matter at this meeting and wherever we can.

For those who can use some help we offer the following points as a guide for deliberation, with this word of Luther as a motto:

> What else are we elders to live for than that we should care for, teach, and educate the young?

> And what would it help, however, if we had everything and did everything, so that we even were perfectly holy, if we neglect that for which we exist most of all, namely to care for our youth?[9]

---

[9] *Editors' note*: F. V. N. Painter, *Luther on Education* (St. Louis: Concordia Publishing House, 1965), 131.

DOCUMENT 4.3:

Seminary Opening Address (1964)

By M. H. Otto

Prof. Milton Henry Otto (1914–1982) *graduated from Concordia Seminary in St. Louis, Missouri, in 1940, having served his vicarage in Princeton, Minnesota. He briefly taught at Eau Claire, Wisconsin, until he was called to the parish of English Lutheran Church in Cottonwood, Minnesota. Following this, he served as pastor in the Saude-Jerico parish in Lawler, Iowa, where he also served as president of the ELS from 1954 to 1957. That year, he was called to teach at the campus of Bethany Lutheran College and Seminary, where he taught church history, dogmatics, homiletics, and practical theology. In 1969 he was named dean of the seminary. Upon his retirement in 1980, Otto remained at the seminary as a librarian and would assist students in their sermon writing.*[10]  *He also encouraged continued education within the church, often speaking to congregational groups regarding the public ministry.*[11]   [JC]

Source: *Lutheran Synod Quarterly* 5, no. 2 (1964): 2-5.

---

[10] "Dean Emeritus Milton Otto Dies," *Lutheran Sentinel*, Sept. 1982, 12.
[11] J. Herbert Larson and Juul B. Madson, *Built on the Rock* (Mankato, MN: Evangelical Lutheran Synod Book Company, 1992), 233.

We are this morning pausing for a few moments to mark the opening of our Seminary's nineteenth school year. While this may not be a very impressive record as far as anniversaries go, it is something that involves us all. Some of us will be attending or working in this institution, and all of us belong to congregations that are served by pastors and which, sooner or later, will be calling other pastors, who have been trained at this or some other seminary.

It then behooves us all to know something about the characteristics and requirements of this office, especially when the Scripture makes it incumbent upon every lay Christian carefully to judge the doctrine he hears proclaimed from his pulpit, as when it, for example, says, "Beloved, believe not every spirit, but try the spirits whether they are of God: because many false prophets are gone out into the world" (1 John 4:1). How is a Christian congregation to know if its pastor is faithful in the performance of the duties of the office to which it has called him, if its members are not acquainted with the demands of this office?

To aid us in appreciating what our interests and responsibilities in this respect are, let us on the basis of our text—God's Holy Spirit assisting us—answer this question: *What should a theological seminary seek to accomplish?*

For one thing, it should seek to *train students that will have the approval of God*.

It is not the purpose of a theological seminary to train men to be popular with their fellow-men, to be good "mixers," or to take the lead in every civic and community project. Rather, that they should have God's approval. Any needful and honest vocation is pleasing to God, but the work of a pastor is particularly so, for as Paul tells Timothy, "If a man desire the office of a bishop, he desireth a good work" (1 Timothy 3:1). It is through this office of the ministry that God, "Who will have all men to be saved, and to come unto the knowledge of the truth" (1 Timothy 2:4), draws men to Himself and to the grace He has prepared for them in Christ Jesus. Luther refers to the pastor's office as the highest office in the church, with that of a Christian teacher running a close second. Surely, filling this office, which has as its one aim the leading of souls to Christ, has the full blessing and approval of God. Our text says, "Study to shew thyself approved unto God."

A seminary should seek to have its students enjoy the approval of God insofar as their intellectual and spiritual growth and development is concerned, too. This involves giving attention to doctrine. The inspired apostle tells Timothy and everyone who aspires to be a pastor, "Take heed unto thyself and unto the doctrine; continue in them: In doing this thou shalt both save thyself, and them that hear thee" (1 Timothy 4:16). Just because one is studying to be a pastor does not mean there is a different way to heaven for him than for others, as if his work would entitle him to special consideration by God when it comes to his salvation. He must give heed to what the Bible teaches just like anyone else. And those who hear the pastor preach must give just as much heed to the doctrine as does the pastor. "Study"—literally, "do your best"—"to shew thyself approved unto God, a workman that needeth not to be ashamed."

What a tragedy it is when a seminary forsakes the sure Word of Scripture for a theology that is highly speculative and, in the end, certain of nothing. All too many so-called seminary and church leaders in this country today are proclaiming a theology or an emphasis in theology imported from Europe, though it is already *passé* and outmoded over there. One contemporary writer put it this way, "Unless they (namely, American theologians) stand in the mainstream of evangelical Christianity, committed to the God of Moses, Isaiah, and Paul, they are forever resurrecting the ghosts of recently buried European speculation."[12] The Apostle Paul makes it very clear on what a pastor's theology should be based when giving this clear-cut instruction to another pastor, Titus, saying that a pastor should "hold fast the faithful Word as he hath been taught, that he may be able by sound doctrine both to exhort to convince the gainsayers" (Titus 1:9). "Study" (do your best) "to shew thyself approved, a workman that needeth not to be ashamed." Hence, a theological seminary must, above all else, train students that will have the approval of God, by directing and holding them to the pure, impregnable, and eternally abiding Word of God. If they have been thus trained, they will not have to be ashamed for what they themselves believe, nor for their holding out that same gospel hope to others.

Along this same line, but more pointedly, a theological seminary should seek to train its students rightly to divide the Word of Truth. "Study" (do your best), "to shew thyself approved unto God, a workman that needeth not to be ashamed, rightly dividing the word of truth." These last words have always been taken to mean that a pastor must know how properly to distinguish between Law and Gospel. This, incidentally, has such

---

[12] "Theological Default in American Seminaries," *Christianity Today*, 11 Sept. 1964, 29.

an important place in theology that whole books have been written on this subject.

But what does it mean to distinguish between Law and Gospel? It means that a pastor must rebuke sin—that, when it concerns leading people to become aware of their sins, he must preach the Law to them in all its thundering severity. Any other course of action is apt to cause a sinner to become carnally secure or wholly indifferent to the status of his soul and thus lead to his damnation.

In the same way, a pastor is to apply the Gospel where there is repentance, where people sorrow over their sins and look for relief for their heavy-laden hearts. Any other course of action could lead to the sinner's despairing of any hope for him and thus also could cost him his soul's salvation. But to become proficient in making this distinction between Law and Gospel calls for conscientious study and application. "Rightly dividing the word of truth" is one of the most important aptitudes a seminary has to instill and develop in a student who is preparing himself for the ministerial office, because the salvation of souls will be at stake.

These words, instructing a would-be pastor to study that he may rightly divide the word of truth, spell out the obligation in general to use the particular Word of God that applies in a given situation. A good example of such misuse and distortion of Scripture is the oft-quoted verse, "Where there is no vision, the people perish" (Proverbs 29:18). This has no reference to vision in a political or sociological sense, as it almost always is implied, but to there being no vision of God's grace, no preaching of the Gospel—there people will perish. A theological seminary is thus to train men not to strain a word beyond its proper meaning and application.

It is not out of order to remind ourselves that a theological seminary worthy of the name should not only strive for, but also succeed in giving unequivocal definitions to various scriptural concepts and terms, such as the very common expressions "sin," "grace," "righteousness," "justification," and the like. A writer of the Reformed persuasion makes this observation in a current periodical when speaking of the failure of the delegates to the Lutheran World Federation convention at Helsinki, a year ago, to come to an agreement on an acceptable definition of "justification":

> If the church of Christ cannot issue a statement telling its contemporaries how to be justified through faith and what it

means to be so justified, and if it cannot declare that "sin" is the kind of reality from which a man can be "justified" through "grace," then something is woefully wrong and the trumpet no longer sends out a certain sound.[13]

God forbid that it should ever come to pass that our Seminary is unable to give articulate expression to the doctrines revealed in Holy Writ; rather, it is our prayer that every young man trained in this institution will be enabled to preach and teach with such conviction and clarity that all who hear them will be led to confess, "I know whom I have believed and am persuaded that He is able to keep that which I have committed unto Him against that day" (2 Timothy 1:12).

"Study (do your best) to shew yourself approved unto God, a workman that needeth not to be ashamed, rightly dividing the word of truth." May God make our Seminary such a blessing to its students! May every last one of us insist on that kind of minister for what we call our home-churches, because, in the end, our eternal salvation depends on it. We ask this in the name of the Chief Shepherd, Jesus, to whom His undershepherds are to lead us [1 Peter 2:24–25]. Amen.

---

[13] *Christianity Today*, 25 Sept. 1964, 44.

DOCUMENT 4.4:

Preparing Messengers of Peace (1996)

By Juul B. Madson

Juul Benjamin Madson (1920–2008) is best known for his contributions to Bethany Lutheran Theological Seminary, where he served as professor of New Testament exegesis. Born to the Rev. Norman and Elsie Madson on November 17, 1920 in Bode, Iowa, he was baptized by his father at St. Olaf Lutheran Church in Bode, Iowa.[14] He was confirmed at Our Savior's Lutheran Church in Princeton, Minnesota, in 1934.[15] He enrolled at Bethany Lutheran High School in 1934 and at Bethany Lutheran College in 1938.[16] He also attended Northwestern College in Watertown, Wisconsin, where he earned his B.A. Degree in 1942. At Wisconsin Lutheran Seminary at Thiensville, Wisconsin, he received his diploma in 1945.[17] From 1946 to 1970, he served as pastor at five Lutheran parishes: Norwegian Lutheran of Somber and Northwood, Iowa; Lakewood Lutheran of Tacoma, Washington; First American Lutheran of Mayville and Sheyenne, North Dakota; English Lutheran Church of Cottonwood, Minnesota; and Zion Lutheran Church of Tracy, Minnesota.[18] He served as

---

14   "Juul Madson (1920-2008)," *Lutheran Sentinel*, March-Apr. 2008, 13.
15   "Vita," *Lutheran Sentinel*, 28 Jan. 1946, 29.
16   "Juul Madson (1920-2008)," 13.
17   "Vita," 29.
18   Ibid., 30.

president of the Evangelical Lutheran Synod from 1966 to 1970.[19] *From 1970 to 1992, he served as professor at Bethany Lutheran Theological Seminary and also taught for the Mequon Program at Bethany Lutheran College. Among other accomplishments, he served as Bethany's college chaplain and he was a member of the Catechism Review Committee. He married Clarice Huso in 1946, and they were blessed with nine children. Pastor Madson died on April 3, 2008.*[20] [SS]

Source: Synod Report (1996): 53–77.

> Peace to soothe our bitter woes
> God in Christ on us bestows;
> Jesus bought our peace with God
> With His holy precious blood;
> Peace in Him for sinners found
> Is the Gospel's joyful sound. (*LHy* 49:1)

The Apostle Paul, renowned New Testament messenger of the Lord Jesus Christ, is merely echoing the words of his Old Testament counterpart Isaiah when, in writing to the Christians at Rome, he exults in the glory of the public ministry, saying, "How beautiful are the feet of those who preach the Gospel of peace, who bring glad tidings of good things!" (Romans 10:15; cp. Isaiah 52:7). And just before quoting the prophet's words, Paul asked an important question: "How shall they preach unless they are sent?" (v. 14). To which we append another question, which may well be seen as but a subdivision of the previous one: "How shall they be sent unless they are prepared?"

This year the members of the Evangelical Lutheran Synod are celebrating fifty years of involvement in the preparation of messengers of the Gospel of peace in our own Bethany Lutheran Theological Seminary. Those fifty years have seen one hundred fifty-four graduates emerge into the public ministry of the Evangelical Lutheran Synod. According to the information available to this essayist, of that total number of Gospel messengers produced by this seminary, sixteen have died, ten have retired within the synod, thirty-eight no longer remain in our synod, and ninety-one continue in the public ministry within the Synod. In another assessment of these figures, it appears that the

---

[19] "Juul Madson (1920-2008)," 13.
[20] Ibid.

Evangelical Lutheran Synod has retained about seventy percent of its seminary's graduates.[21]

The number of graduates over this span of time is certainly not very large, nor has it even sufficed to fill our own needs, for in the growth and expansion that our Synod has experienced over the years, we have from time to time had to undergo ministerial transfusion from other sources—in more recent times mostly from our brethren of the Wisconsin Evangelical Lutheran Synod, but also from clergymen of other Lutheran bodies who for confessional reasons have sought fellowship in the ELS. The transfusions from the Wisconsin Synod can, in one sense, simply be said to constitute a tradeoff: in the last three decades our Bethany Lutheran College, at the request and with the support of our sister synod, performed an educational preparatory function for many second-career men who sought entrance into both the seminary and, eventually, the ministry of the latter synod.[22]

Old Testament Messengers

From earliest times the Lord has provided spiritual leadership for his people. The program for training such leaders in Old Testament days has not been set forth in detail, nor did it apparently always follow the same pattern. Even after the fall into sin, God spoke directly to people whom he selected as spiritual leaders. In the book of Genesis, chapters 6-9, it is recorded that God spoke directly to Noah, and in the New Testament writings Peter refers to Noah as a "preacher [herald] of righteousness" (1 Peter 2:5). Of Abraham it is written in Genesis 12:8: "There [between Bethel and Ai] he built an altar to the Lord and *called on the name of the Lord.*"[23] In his exposition of the book of Genesis, Luther expounds on this italicized phrase thus: "[Abraham] erects an altar on this mountain ... in order to perform his duty as bishop; that is, he instructs his church concerning the will of God, admonishes them to lead a holy life, strengthens them in their

---

[21] *Editors' note*: An appendix listing the seminary graduates from 1947 through 1996 was originally published with this essay and referenced here. An updated listing, extending to the present year, may be found online at *www.blts.edu/students/index.htm*.

[22] This program was understandably called the Mequon Program in our circles, while in Wisconsin Synod circles it was known as the Bethany Program. (Many of the students compromised by calling it the Meq-Beth Program.)

[23] *Qarah B'shem Yaweh* in Hebrew.

faith, fortifies their hope of future blessing, and prays with them. *The Hebrew verb includes all these things.*"[24]

We have likewise seen from the Scriptures that God directly called Moses to serve as leader of His Old Testament church, the Israelites, yet not until this candidate had undergone considerable training in distant Midian.[25] In addition, Moses was given a brief crash program in connection with his being commissioned to bring a strong message from the Lord to an unrepentant Pharaoh: "Let my people go!" It is not insignificant that this Moses became the prophet according to the pattern of which our God would, in His good time, raise up the true prophetic antitype, namely, the Lord Jesus Christ, the ultimate Shepherd and Bishop of our souls (Deuteronomy 18:15; 1 Peter 2:25). And let us not forget Moses' likely training at the hands of his mother before he was turned over to the control of Pharaoh's household.

The Old Testament also records that the prophet Samuel received training at the hands of Eli, who had greater success with this son of Elkanah and Hannah than with his own sons (1 Samuel 2); and that Elisha was trained for the prophetic office under the great prophet Elijah, a double-portion of whose spirit he sought when he was about to bid farewell to his famous mentor (2 Kings 2). Any thorough concordance of Holy Scripture will have many entries under the word "prophet"—in both Testaments. Most of these references are to the prophets of God, of whom Jeremiah records the Lord as saying: "Since the day that your fathers came out of the land of Egypt until this day, I have sent to you all my servants the prophets" (Jeremiah 7:25). Nor are the words of these prophets to be forgotten even in the New Testament era, for Peter reminds the readers of his second epistle that they "should remember the words spoken beforehand by the holy prophets" as well as "the commandment of the Lord and Savior spoken by [the] Apostles" (2 Peter 3:2).

But there were other prophets also—undesirable prophets—of whom the same Jeremiah records: "Thus says the Lord of hosts, 'Do not listen to the words of the prophets who are prophesying to you. They are leading you into futility; they speak a vision of their own imagination, not from the mouth of the Lord'" (Jeremiah 23:16). And through the divinely appointed prophet Micah, the

---

[24] Martin Luther, *Luther's Works*, vol. 2 (St. Louis: Concordia Publishing House, 1960), 286, emphasis added.
[25] The Holy Record also shows that Moses inadvisedly elected himself to a leadership role before he was sufficiently prepared for it.

Lord again speaks in the same vein when He refers to "the prophets that make my people err" (Micah 3:5). In the original Greek version of the New Testament, there is even a combined word for the expression "false prophet," namely, the word which is transliterated directly into the English language as *pseudoprophet*.[26]

New Testament Messengers

It is this word which the Savior employs when through the Evangelist Matthew he records several serious New Testament warnings such as these: "Beware of false prophets, which come to you in sheep's clothing, but inwardly they are ravenous wolves" (Matthew 7:15); and again, "Many false prophets shall arise and shall deceive many" (Matthew 24:11). The Evangelist St. John was aware of the same reality and therefore wrote: "Many false prophets have gone out into the world" (1 John 4:1). The Apostle Peter was likewise aware of this grievous condition when he reported: "There were false prophets also among the people, even as there will be false teachers among you" (2 Peter 2:1).

Because the Church of God is desirous of producing true prophets of God, it will of necessity have concern for the preparation and training of only those candidates for the office of the public ministry of whom it can be said that they are men after God's own heart. In the early days of the New Testament our Lord and Savior Himself selected twelve of His disciples, or learners, whom He then named apostles (cf. Luke 6:13). He personally instructed these twelve during the three years of His visible ministry upon this earth and placed them in the vanguard when He gave command to His church to "go into all the world and preach the Gospel to every creature" (Mark 16:15). The Apostle Paul—who had been originally trained at the feet of Gamaliel (Acts 22:3), one of the leading Jewish rabbis of his time, and "had advanced in Judaism beyond many of [his] own contemporaries" (Galatians 1:14)—was later called by God into His service through a special revelation and a subsequent period of training that apparently included a three-year preparatory stint in Arabia (Galatians 1:17–18).

When we inquire about the formal manner in which the early New Testament church trained its pastors and missionaries, we

---

[26] Greek: *pseudoprophetai*.

find little information either in sacred or profane sources. Apparently the Apostle Paul, as well as the other apostles, trained his co-laborers and successors by personal instruction. The epistles of Paul, therefore—especially his pastoral epistles—are no small help in determining the preparation, as well as the role, of a minister of the Gospel even today. Later in the early Christian church, catechetical schools that had been established primarily for instruction in Christian doctrine preparatory to membership in the church took on the added assignment of preparing men for the holy ministry, but information on the conduct of these schools is very meager.

The Middle Ages

During the Middle Ages a decline in the standards for this preparation became quite apparent; it is reported that the training became so deficient "that bishops found it a burdensome task to preach a short sermon, and many priests had difficulty in reading the Scripture lessons for the Sunday."[27] In the thirteenth century, a significant change occurred when the schools for theological training were joined to the universities. When the Renaissance followed in the fourteenth to sixteenth centuries, it also left its imprint on the theological training in the church. Of positive influence from this movement was the restoration of the study of the languages in which the Bible was written. Of negative influence was the dominating influence of Scholasticism, in which the attempt was made to comprehend and prove the transcendental (that which is beyond the experience of the senses), not simply from the divinely inspired Scriptures, but from reason.[28]

---

[27] Louis J. Sieck, in *Lutheran Cyclopedia* (St. Louis: Concordia Publishing House, 1955), 683.

[28] In dogmatics Scholasticism tried to comprehend, harmonize and prove doctrines rationally.

Professor Juul Madson taught New Testament Studies at Bethany Lutheran Theological Seminary from 1970 to 1994. He also served as chaplain and professor of religious studies at the Bethany College.

The Reformation Era

When the Reformation began to take hold in the sixteenth century, the training of pastors again became a very lively concern. Luther discovered in his visitation of congregations in electoral Saxony and Meissen in 1528 and 1529 that many priests in the church of his day were exceedingly poorly trained for their task. In the preface to his Small Catechism he writes:

> The deplorable conditions which I recently encountered when I was a visitor constrained me to prepare this brief and simple catechism or statement of Christian teaching. Good God, what wretchedness I beheld! The common people, especially those who live in the country, have no knowledge whatever of Christian teaching, *and unfortunately, many pastors are quite incompetent and unfitted for teaching.* (SC Preface)

As at least a partial remedy for this deplorable condition, several of the leaders of the Reformation became the core of the faculty at the University of Wittenberg, most notably Dr. Martin Luther and Philip Melanchthon. By the time of Luther's death, most of the men ordained into the ministry were quite highly educated, and the standards for ordination had become much more exacting. Furthermore, the foundation for the later division of the theological curriculum into the four departments of the curriculum that even today constitute the educational program at our own seminary had now been laid.[29]

Within a century, however, even the religious training at the universities had become primarily intellectual and philosophical, without sufficient concern for the spiritual. Reaction within the church soon led to the development of Pietism with its great emphasis on personal religious experience. In the nineteenth century, Rationalism[30] had become the monster that controlled the theological faculties in the universities, and the effect of this development on the kind of ministers produced for the church can quite easily be imagined. Scientific and liberal thinking came to dominate especially Protestant theology in Europe, and the waves produced by this storm soon lapped also at distant shores. It was

---

[29] For further consideration of this aspect of the seminary program, see below.

[30] In the religious context Rationalism may be defined as "reliance on reason as the basis for the establishment of religious truth."

not uncommon that under such conditions the schools themselves were undermining the very faith of the church whose future ministers they were now educating.

Interestingly enough, the rise of seminaries, at least as distinct and separate entities, seems to be greatly attributable to the spiritual deterioration of the European universities, especially the theological departments of the same. The establishment of separate theological seminaries seems to have come about largely to counteract the undesirable effects of university training and also to supplement its spiritual deficiencies.

In America

In the early days of the Christian church in America, all denominations at first depended on the European schools for their supply of pastors and teachers. But as the various churches in this country became indigenous—native and self-sufficient—there arose for each of them greater need, as well as desire, for establishing their own educational institutions for the training of their clergy. The early schools in America were church schools—at every level. Well-known institutions of higher learning, such as Harvard, William and Mary, Yale, and Princeton, were also established for the purpose of preparing students for the ministry.

Concerning this development Dr. Louis J. Sieck, at one time president of Concordia Seminary in St. Louis, wrote in 1954:

> Today we are familiar with the distinction between college and seminary. In the early days, the American college of liberal arts was a distinctively religious institution, and the education offered was centered in equipping men for the ministry. The Bible was taught in the original languages, and all students were obligated to acquaint themselves with its doctrines and precepts. Then followed special chairs of divinity in these schools. The first was the Hollis Professorship of Divinity at Harvard (1721). [S]chools exclusively intended for ministerial training ... were established at Harvard and Yale in 1819 and 1822 respectively. During this period other schools exclusively devoted to the training of ministers appeared. Some of these were church controlled, some were independent. The first separate seminary was established by the Dutch Reformed Church at Flatbush, Long Island, New York, in 1774.[31]

---

[31] Lous J. Sieck, *Lutheran Cyclopedia*, 685.

Many of the American seminaries that now began to proliferate accepted students without college preparation, a condition that continues to exist in some denominations of the Christian church.

The first American seminary with Lutheran moorings, though at its founding not an official institution of any church, is reportedly the somewhat private seminary established in 1815 (incorporated a year later) by representatives of the estate of Rev. John Hartwick and located at Hartwick, New York.[32] The first *official* Lutheran theological seminary in the United States directly related to a church body was opened at Gettysburg, Pennsylvania, in 1826 by the General Synod of the Evangelical Lutheran Church in the United States of America, and it continues to this day, now under the auspices of the Evangelical Lutheran Church in America.

Far more important to our synodical history and development was the establishment of Concordia Seminary, St. Louis, Missouri, by the Evangelical Lutheran Synod of Missouri, Ohio, and Other States. Its early home was a log cabin near Altenburg in Perry County, Missouri, and it was founded as a classical college and school of theology in 1839 by emigrants of Saxony, Germany. The members of its first faculty were young graduates of German universities, namely, candidates of theology C. F. W. Walther, J. F. Buenger, O. Fuerbringer, and Theo. Brohm. After the organization of the Missouri Synod in 1847, ownership and control of this institution was assumed by that synod. This seminary's first president—until his death in 1887—was the aforementioned Walther: pastor, professor, editor, and defender *extraordinaire* of the faith.

Dependent Efforts—Twice Experienced

This school was to have a profound effect on the Norwegian Synod chiefly for two reasons. When the early version of the "Norwegian Synod" (officially The Norwegian Evangelical Lutheran Church in America) came into existence in 1853 and found itself for some time without its own theological training school, a specially commissioned search team later in that decade found Concordia Seminary in St. Louis to be the ministerial training school of its choice especially because of the close

---

[32] Ibid.

doctrinal and spiritual bond between the two synods.[33] One of the results of this close alliance was that first Prof. Laur Larsen and, later, Prof. F. A. Schmidt, of the Norwegian Synod were attached to this seminary in order to serve especially the Norwegian students in attendance.[34] Although the synod founded Luther College in Decorah, Iowa, in 1861 as its pre-theological institution of higher learning, it did not boast a seminary of its own until Luther Seminary was established in Madison, Wisconsin, in 1876.[35]

Again, early in the twentieth century, when a conscience-bound minority was unwilling to enter into the fateful merger of 1917, this later version of the "Norwegian Synod" found itself without a preparatory school for its pastors. The previously manifested willingness of the Missouri Synod to open the doors of its schools to the struggling but faithful Norwegians once more was in evidence, permitting this "plucked chicken"[36] to begin the slow and often difficult task of growing feathers again. Besides Concordia Seminary at St. Louis, its sister seminary at Springfield, Illinois (later relocated at Fort Wayne, Indiana), also received for study some of the young men of the Norwegian Synod who aspired to the office of the public ministry.

When relationships in the Synodical Conference grew increasingly tense in the 1940s because of serious doctrinal

---

[33] The members of the search team were Pastors J. A. Ottesen and Nils Brandt, who in 1857 made their visit to the seminaries at St. Louis, Columbus, and Buffalo, after which they published a lengthy report in *Maanedstidende,* the monthly periodical of the church body.

For an expression of the theological rapport between the Norwegian Synod and the Missouri Synod, and also the former's use of the latter's seminary, see Carl S. Meyer, *Pioneers Find Friends* (Decorah, IA: Luther College Press, 1963).

[34] In 1875 the Missouri Synod had moved its so-called "practical" seminary to Springfield, Illinois. At that time the Norwegian Synod placed Pastor Ole Asperheim as its professor on the Springfield faculty, where he served but one year. (See following footnote.)

[35] This institution began as a "practical" seminary, with Ole Asperheim and F. A. Schmidt comprising the faculty. Two years later, in 1878, a theoretical department was added. That autumn nine students were registered in the theoretical department and fifteen in the practical. Professor Asperheim now resigned under pressure from his colleague because of the former's criticism of the Missouri Synod. See *Striving for Ministry,* ed. Quanbeck, Fevold and Frost (Augsburg Publishing House, 1977), 21ff. It is somewhat ironic that in a few short years that same colleague would himself become a bitter enemy of the leader of the Missouri Synod, C. F. W. Walther, in the election controversy of the eighties.

[36] In Norwegian, *en rybbet høne,* as the reorganized synod was scornfully referred to by one of the merger folk.

disagreements which had developed among the synods of that federation, Wisconsin Lutheran Seminary at Thiensville, Wisconsin (now incorporated into Mequon), became a haven for three of the Norwegian young men (including your essayist) in the years just before the Norwegian Synod finally established its own seminary, even as the Wisconsin Synod's Northwestern College at Watertown, Wisconsin, became a senior college preparatory school for several additional Norwegian Synod students (including the current presidents of our synod and our seminary).[37] (One other Norwegian Synod student, the sainted Dr. Neelak Tjernagel, had some years earlier attended and graduated from Wisconsin Lutheran Seminary.)

The members of the synod had been deeply appreciative of the gracious assistance of both the Missouri Synod and the Wisconsin Synod in providing educational training for its prospective pastors and teachers during these early difficult years. Nevertheless, this beleaguered remnant from a large church merger had since its reorganization dreamed of a day when it might again have its own synodical schools to assist it in its God-given task. It had to wait only ten years before it became the grateful and proud owner and operator of Bethany Lutheran College and High School in Mankato, Minnesota. But it had to wait almost two more decades before it could realize its other educational dream, that of possessing its own theological seminary for the training of its pastors.

Move toward Independence

Despite the excellent training that had been afforded by the Synodical Conference seminaries named above, there had been a persistent desire among "synod folk" to establish their own seminary with its own special flavor, under the control and administration of their synod. As the inter-synodical problems in the years that followed revealed, again, the folly of putting one's trust in men, even such as had at one time been a source of great strength to them in an earlier time of anguish, the desire of not being left in a position of extreme dependency on such friends gained much ground. For thirteen years the people's hope of establishing their own seminary had just lain there smoldering. But in 1931, the synod in convention took its first significant step

---

[37] *Editors' note*: At the time, George Orvick served as the synod president, and Wilhelm Petersen as the seminary president.

in fanning the smoldering fire. In response to an urgent petition from some of its pre-theological students, the delegates at that convention resolved to authorize President H. M. Tjernagel to appoint a committee of three to study this matter and to present its findings to the General Pastoral Conference for discussion.[38]

Notwithstanding this action by the convention, not even a tentative plan materialized for another eleven years. But in 1942, at the urging of Synod President Henry Ingebritson, the convention authorized the Board of Regents of Bethany Lutheran College to take action to provide that the synod's ministerial candidates have "their last year of training in our own school" and to begin the program that very fall, if possible.[39] When the Board reported a year later that it had been unable to put the desired initial program in motion that quickly, but also that it was convinced that the synod's goal of having its own seminary could best be obtained "by establishing at once a complete theological seminary," the convention upgraded the earlier plan by authorizing that the Board of Regents "establish our own [full] theological seminary as soon as possible."[40]

Because World War II was in progress, the Board of Regents now had to answer also to an earthly authority, this time the U.S. Selective Service Administration, which had strict guidelines concerning the establishment of new seminaries in wartime, particularly in respect to granting seminary students exemption from the military draft.[41] An eventual change in ruling by the SSA finally brought governmental approval for the proposed seminary. The official letter from Selective Service Headquarters in Washington stated: "Bethany Lutheran College comes within the definition of a theological or divinity school." It further stated that when "an institution fulfills the requirements of the Selective Training and Service Act as a recognized theological or divinity school and continues to do so, changes in the curriculum or the addition of graduate courses will not change the status of the

---

[38] *Synod Report* (1931), 131. Could it have been that the memorial service at the convention in honor of the noted theologian of the Missouri Synod, Dr. Franz Pieper, whose death had been reported only days before the convention, helped to prompt the delegates to this action? Cf. also *Beretning af Den Norske Synode [Synod Report]* (1931) for three personal testimonies (in English) delivered by clergymen of the Synod who had studied under the venerable Doctor Pieper.
[39] *Synod Report* (1942), 58.
[40] *Synod Report* (1943), 70.
[41] The U. S. government granted *bona fide* seminary students a 4-D classification exempting them from military service.

school."[42] The intervening end to the armed conflict in which our country was engaged did not significantly change the course of synodical action, and the 1946 convention finally resolved "in the name of the Triune God [to establish] a full Theological Seminary course at Bethany Lutheran College, this course to begin in the fall of 1946."[43]

Bethany Lutheran Theological Seminary

That very September, the long desired seminary became reality when four students, whose number was to swell to five at semester time,[44] showed up on the campus of Bethany Lutheran College to begin class work under the first and only convention-elected dean of the seminary, Norman A. Madson, and five additional instructors who were merely on loan on a part-time basis from the college faculty.[45] In the early years following his own graduation from the seminary of the pre-merger Norwegian Synod, N. A. Madson had briefly been an instructor at Luther College in Decorah, Iowa, a missionary on the Iron Range in Minnesota, and a chaplain in World War I, before serving as a parish pastor in Iowa and Minnesota from the end of the war until 1946. It was in July of 1925 that he had followed several other clergymen in leaving the "merger church," the Norwegian Lutheran Church in America, for the newly reorganized remnant of the old Norwegian Synod.

This new school of the prophets at Mankato was, at its inception and for some time thereafter, closely tied to the college. President S. C. Ylvisaker explained the reason for this association in his report to the 1946 convention: "From the organizational point of view, it will be necessary to consider that as long as the Selective Service Act is in force, the theological seminary will have to remain a part of our Bethany establishment."[46] At least partly because of this new institution's close association with the college, the president of that institution served also as the titular, or

---

[42] *Synod Report* (1946), 62.
[43] Ibid., 65.
[44] Robert Preus transferred from Luther Seminary, St. Paul, MN for the second semester.
[45] Pres. S. C. Ylvisaker, Professors A. Fremder, M. Galstad, B. W. Teigen, and P. A. Zimmermann.
[46] *Synod Report* (1946), 64. The Selective Service Act remained in force also for some time after the conclusion of WWII.

nominal, head of the seminary in its early years,[47] with the seminary dean providing the administrative and educational leadership. Its beginnings can be said to have been low-key and unpretentious, and the seminary has, over the years, not been maintained without a struggle, yet one would be remiss in not recognizing that the Lord's blessing has rested upon it.

Through the first half-century of the seminary's existence, the faculty has been composed in great part of those administrators and instructors who were called first of all and primarily to the seminary—though in most instances they have on occasion also taught courses in the college—and in lesser part by professors of the college faculty who were committed to teach primarily in that institution. The second man called in a full-time capacity to the seminary was the Rev. George O. Lillegard, who, together with N. A. Madson and S. C. Ylvisaker, was a graduate of Luther Seminary of the old Norwegian Synod. Prior to his coming to Mankato, he had been a missionary to China and a parish pastor in the synod. In the seminary he concentrated his efforts on courses of Biblical interpretation. On the seminary staff for ten years before physical disabilities dictated his retirement, his theological skill is exemplified in such writings as his monograph on the *Chinese Term Question*.[48] His pastoral strength can be noted, e.g., from his well-received book of sermons on the book of Genesis, entitled *From Eden to Egypt*.[49]

---

[47] Following Dr. Ylvisaker's brief years in this office, 1946-50, B. W. Teigen occupied the same for the years 1950-70, and his successor, R. M. Branstad, for the years 1970-76, at which point T. A. Aaberg was elected to the sole presidency of the seminary.

[48] *Editors' note*: George O. Lillegard, *The Chinese Term Question* (n.p.: n.p., 1929). Christian missionaries to China had long debated whether to translate the Hebrew Old Testament name of God (*elohim*) and the Greek New Testament term for "God" (*theos*) as *Shang-Di* (the name of a chief idol in China) or as *Shen* (a generic Chinese reference to any deity). The synod ratified Lillegard's endorsement of *Shen* by adopting a position statement at its 1936 convention, stating, in part, "We hold that the proper name of an idol [*Shang-Di*] cannot be used for God since Scripture prohibits such use," with reference to Exodus 23:13, Joshua 23:7, Isaiah 42:8, Hosea 2:16–17, and Zechariah 13:2. J. Herbert Larson and Juul B. Madson, *Built on the Rock* (Mankato, MN: Evangelical Lutheran Synod Book Company, 1992), 131–32.

[49] *Editors' note*: George O. Lillegard, *From Eden to Egypt: Genesis, the Book of Beginnings* (Milwaukee: Northwestern Publishing House, 1956). This series of sermons (which Lillegard had preached at Harvard St. Lutheran Church, Cambridge, Massachusetts) emphasized chiefly two themes: 1) the inerrancy of Scripture; and, 2) salvation by grace alone through faith alone in Christ alone.

The third full-time professor on the seminary faculty was the Reverend Milton H. Otto, who left the parish ministry in 1957 and taught in the fields of church history, pastoral theology, and dogmatics. After Dr. Norman Madson's retirement from his post as dean of the seminary in 1959 under the continuing stress of the problem of fellowship that plagued the Synodical Conference, the deanship was vested for a time in the office of the joint president of the college and seminary. But in 1968 Professor Otto was appointed dean of the seminary and served in that capacity until the office was finally eliminated at the time of the election of the first full-time president in 1976. Nevertheless, in recognition of Dean Otto's many years of faithful service, the Board of Regents bestowed on him the title of Dean Emeritus.

During these years, several other part-time instructors served on the seminary staff. Christopher U. Faye, who had once been a missionary to Madagascar but had spent most of his career as a librarian at the University of Illinois, came to Mankato in his retirement and did yeoman work in trying to bring order to the library. Pastor Joseph Petersen of St. Peter and Pastor Raymond Branstad of Minneapolis also taught courses for a brief time at the seminary. Pastor Julian Anderson joined the staff for several years before returning to the parish ministry. Pastor Juul Madson, after twenty-four years in the parish ministry, joined the faculty as professor in New Testament studies in January of 1970 and later was named dean of students and registrar, until retiring from full-time duty in 1991. Pastor Mark Harstad originally came on campus primarily to instruct at the seminary, but later found himself concentrating his teaching in the college department. The most recent full-time additions to the faculty have been Prof. Adolph Harstad in 1991 in the field of Old Testament studies and Prof. John A. Moldstad, Jr., in 1993 in the field of New Testament studies.

For several years in the last decade, Pastor Norman A. Madson reported on campus twice weekly to teach a course in homiletics, the art of preparing and preaching sermons. Special mention must be made of the many years of part-time instruction in Old Testament studies provided by the college's long-time resident Hebrew scholar, Rudolph Honsey. Other college faculty members who have taught courses in the seminary are Professors Erling Teigen, Glenn Reichwald, William Kessel, and Steven Reagles. The most recent addition to the staff has been Professor Thomas Kuster, who, as the incumbent of the endowed Chair of

Speech/English Communication, instructs the seminary students in communication skills and assists in homiletical critique.[50]

Significant Changes

Two events of considerable significance to the conduct of the seminary are closely associated in time. After the 1974 convention had resolved "that the office of President of Bethany Lutheran Seminary be administered by one man, and the office of President of Bethany Lutheran College be administered by another man,"[51] the Board of Regents in 1976 called the Reverend Pastor Theodore Aaberg of St. Peter, Minnesota, to be the first full-time president of Bethany Lutheran Theological Seminary. He was formally installed as the first sole president of this school on October 28 of that year.

The 1976 convention also adopted a recommendation from the Board of Regents to authorize a special thank offering for the cause of higher education, setting a goal of $600,000, two-fifths of which was to be allocated to the seminary. Pledges quickly exceeded the goal, and at the very next convention, ground was broken for the new seminary building just across the street from the college at 447 North Division Street. In his address at the ground breaking ceremonies, President Aaberg reiterated that this edifice would be used to promulgate the three-pronged watchword of the Lutheran Reformation: *Scripture Alone, Grace Alone, Faith Alone.*

The one-story brick and stone building that arose at this time became the first home-of-its-own enjoyed by this institution, a home that is now to be replaced by the new building which can be seen rising on a different site in the northeast quadrant of the Bethany property.[52] It was 1978 before formal dedication of that first building took place during the annual synodical convention. These two developments—the acquisition of its own institutional president and the erection of its own separate home—permitted Bethany Lutheran Theological Seminary more readily to gain an

---

[50] Eleanor Wilson, former member of the Bethany College Faculty, endowed this chair primarily in the interest of the college, but with the specification that "a portion of the chairholder's time be devoted to training seminary students in communications skills." *Seminary Catalog*, 22.

[51] *Synod Report* (1974), 83.

[52] The removal of the seminary to a nearby site permits Bethany College, by its purchase of the existing seminary building, to expand its facilities more advantageously.

Wilhelm Petersen was president of Bethany Lutheran Theological Seminary, 1980–1997.

individual institutional identity, and its students to live and learn in facilities and under conditions better suited to their needs and more favorable to fulfillment of the purpose of the institution.

When Professor Theodore Aaberg's increasingly failing health led him to resign from the presidency in 1979,[53] the Board of Regents appointed Prof. Glenn Reichwald of the college faculty as acting president for the 1979-80 school year. Before the start of the ensuing school year, the Board of Regents had successfully called Pastor Wilhelm W. Petersen, at that time pastor of Mt. Olive Lutheran Church in Mankato and president of the Evangelical Lutheran Synod, to direct the seminary program. After sixteen years of dedicated service to the institution, Dr. Petersen continues in the presidency at the end of the first half-century of the school's existence. He has, however, given notice to the Board of his intention to retire from that responsibility at the close of the next school year, at which time the institution should be gratefully and comfortably settled in its new quarters, where, by the grace of

---

[53] He had suffered for several years from sarcoidosis of the lungs, an illness that increasingly robbed him of a vital oxygen supply and finally brought about his death on January 8, 1980, at the age of fifty-four years.

God, it will continue the necessary and blessed task of preparing messengers of peace.[54]

The Messengers

At certain times in the history of the world, the Lord of the church sent messengers from heaven to make specific announcements or to divulge his plans to men. Despite the seeming advantage of employing these holy spiritual creatures for the work of the public ministry of the Gospel in the present New Testament era, we find that our Lord has other thoughts—thoughts superior to ours also in this matter. Paul understood and explained the Lord's choice thus: "We have this treasure in earthen vessels, that the excellency of the power may be of God and not of us" (2 Corinthians 4:7). Christ has commissioned the spreading of His Gospel to the flesh-and-blood members of His church, whom He has redeemed, justified, and sanctified from their fallen estate. To all of these he has granted the designation of "a chosen generation, a royal priesthood, a holy nation, His own special people, [who are to] proclaim the praises of Him who called [them] out of darkness into his marvelous light" (1 Peter 2:9). In other words, everyone who has been effectively called into the fellowship of Christ's kingdom is a priest before God and has the responsibility, as well as the privilege, of being a witness to the God who has saved him from sin, death and the devil. One cannot show forth the ultimate praise of God without in some way proclaiming the Gospel of salvation in Christ.

In his exposition of the fourth verse of Psalm 110, "You are a priest forever according to the order of Melchizedek," Martin Luther asserts that every Christian is a priest, having been reborn to that status in Baptism. Peter, in the citation a few lines above, endorses that claim. Luther understands that Christ is the only High Priest between God and mankind, but he states that even as we are called Christians after the Christ, so we are called priests after this one great High Priest.[55] Nevertheless Luther, in the company of other Lutheran reformers, as well as of the Lutheran confessions themselves, distinguishes between the ministry of the priesthood of all believers and the public ministry of the church.

---

54 *Editors' note*: See **Document 4.5** for a biography of Gaylin Schmeling, who in 1997 succeeded Wilhelm Petersen as president of the seminary.

55 Cf. Martin Luther, *Luther's Works*, vol. 13 (St. Louis, MO: Concordia Publishing House, 1956), 304ff.

The Public Ministry

The term *public* ministry is often misunderstood to mean merely that kind of ministry which is done in public, that is, out in the open or in the presence of many people. While much of the work of the public ministry may be done out in the open and before many people, that fact is not what makes it *public* ministry in the biblical and Lutheran sense of that term. What makes it public is that it is done by one who has been called by God through a Christian assembly to perform this office in their name—primarily *on* their behalf, rather than merely *in* their behalf.[56] A pastor who, *on behalf of the congregation* that called him, visits the sick patient in the privacy of a hospital room or of the person's own home in order to bring the comfort of the Gospel and Christ's absolution is also at such times functioning in the public ministry of the church. If a Christian friend visits that patient and likewise absolves the troubled but repentant individual, that friend is performing this function on the basis of his possession of the gift of the priesthood of believers and of the office of the keys. He is in such an instance not to be understood as being in the public ministry of the church.

So Luther found himself bound by Scripture to make a distinction "between the office or service of bishops, pastors, and preachers, and the general status of being a Christian." While he firmly believed that the office of the priesthood of believers is the common possession of all Christians, he went on to write that we deal with a different matter when we speak of those who have an office in the Christian Church such as minister, preacher, pastor, or curate. . . . For although we are all priests, this does not mean that all of us can preach, teach, and rule. Certain ones of the multitude must be selected and separated for such an office. . . . The preaching office is no more than a public service which happens to be conferred upon someone by the entire congregation, all the members of which are priests. . . .

Every Christian has and practices such priestly works. But above these activities is the communal office of public teaching.

---

[56] These two phrases, when employed in distinction from each other, have the following meanings: 1) *on behalf of* denotes *as the agent of, on the part of*; 2) *in behalf of* denotes *in the interest of, for the benefit of*.

It should be understood without special emphasis at this point that such ministry is always "in the stead and by the command of my Lord Jesus Christ." *LHy*, p. 16. Cf. John Dahle and Casper M. Johnshoy, *The Liturgical Service of the Lutheran Church* (Minneapolis: Augsburg Publishing House, 1922), 14: "By the authority of God, and of my holy office."

For this, pastors are necessary. This office cannot be attended to by all the members of a congregation. Neither is it fitting that each household do its own baptizing and celebrating of the Sacrament. Hence it is necessary to select and ordain those who can preach and teach, who study the Scriptures, and who are able to defend them. They deal with the Sacraments by the authority of the congregation, so that it is possible to know who is baptized and that everything is done in an orderly fashion. If everyone were to preach to his neighbor, or if they did things for one another without orderly procedure, it would take a long time indeed to establish a congregation. Such functions, however, do not pertain to the priesthood as such but belong to the public office which is performed in behalf of [sic] all those who are priests, that is, Christians.[57]

Qualifications

It is of those who are to hold the office of the *public ministry*, as well as of the preparation for that office, that we now speak when we consider the work of our theological seminary in this year of its golden anniversary. When the Apostle Paul writes to Timothy, his young co-worker in the public ministry, he states that "one who desires the office of a bishop desires a good work" (1 Timothy 3:1). Then he goes on to speak of the qualifications of such a public minister of the Gospel:

> A bishop then must be blameless, the husband of one wife, temperate, sober minded, of good behavior, hospitable, able to teach; not given to wine, not violent, not greedy for money, but gentle, not quarrelsome, not covetous; one who rules his own house well, having his children in submission with all reverence (for if a man does not know how to rule his own house, how will he take care of the church of God?); not a novice, lest being puffed up with pride he fall into the same condemnation as the devil. Moreover he must have a good testimony among those who are outside, lest he fall into reproach and the snare of the devil. (1 Timothy 3:2-7)

In a letter to Titus, whom the Apostle Paul calls "my true son in our common faith" (1:4), he both repeats some of the above listed qualifications and adds others when he directs Titus, in the

---

[57] Cf. *Luther's Works*, 13:329ff.

latter's appointment of additional elders, to search for such a man as is:

> blameless, the husband of one wife, having faithful children not accused of dissipation or insubordination. For [he goes on to say] a bishop must be blameless, as a steward of God, not self-willed, not quick-tempered, not given to wine, not violent, not greedy for money, but hospitable, a lover of what is good, sober-minded, just, holy, self-controlled, holding fast the faithful word as he has been taught, that he may be able, by sound doctrine, both to exhort and to convict those who contradict. (Titus 1:6-9)

These qualifications, with the possible exception of the aptitude to teach, on the one hand appear to be no more than is expected of any child of God. On the other hand, they are enough to trigger in one who aspires to this office the self-examination so strikingly expressed by Dietrich Vorwerk in his soul-searching poem entitled "A Parson's Sermon to Himself":

> A parson must be, first of all,
> Both very great and very small,
> A king's son in nobility,
> A servant in simplicity;
> A victor who has overcome
> Himself and brought his trophies home;
> One who with God has wrestled and
> Received a blessing at His hand;
> A fount of waters leaping high
> In plenitude of sanctity;
> A sinner living by the word
> Of pardon spoken by his Lord;
> His passions mastered, all intent
> To serve the weak and diffident;
> Not one to truckle to the great,
> He stoops to men of low estate;
> A learner still, but resolute
> To lead and guide where men dispute;
> A beggar in his nothingness,
> A herald scattering largesse;
> A man in battle, womanly
> Beside the beds of misery;
> In clarity of vision old,
> A child to trust and cling and hold;
> Aspiring high, he does not rise
> To slight the small, or to despise;

To grief no stranger, ever one
To give men's joy his benison,
Aloof from enviousness alone;
Clean in thought and true in word,
Peace is his love, but sloth's abhorred;
Foursquare he stands and solidly
—and he is not at all like me.[58]

Whoever, therefore, presents himself as a candidate for the study of theology with a view to entering the public ministry of the church ought to bring qualifications with him at entrance into his seminary training program. The seminary catalog, on the basis of the above cited pastoral passages, states that "the fundamental requirements for admission to the seminary are an unimpeachable Christian character and a heart-felt desire to enter the public ministry."[59] To seek to ensure that students do come with these desirable qualifications, seminaries generally require letters of recommendation from various sources attesting to the good character and perceived potential of the applicants.

Surely it is the desire of the staff at our seminary also to help the students cultivate these qualities more deeply while they are in residence, so that they will be examples to their eventual flocks, even as the staff will have opportunity during the years of study to observe to what extent these qualifications appear to be present in the men before them and to provide them necessary individual counsel also in these areas of their life which will greatly impact their ministry. Especially the admissions committee has great responsibility in seeking to screen out prospects who do not demonstrate the necessary qualifications for the ministry. Occasionally the administration has at some later point reluctantly had to dismiss a student from the program for failure to "measure up."

It is the qualification of aptitude for teaching (1 Timothy 3:2; 2 Timothy 2:2) that becomes an important focus for the preparation that takes place in a seminary program. The authors of *Shepherds under Christ* make clear what the goal is in this area:

---

[58] Dietrich Vorwerk, "A Parson's Sermon to Himself," trans. M. H. Franzmann *Clergy Bulletin*, Nov. 1952, 1. *Editors' note*: The antepenultimate line was boldfaced in Madson's sermon as printed in *Lutheran Synod Quarterly*, though not emphasized so in the *Clergy Bulletin*.

[59] *Bethany Lutheran Theological Seminary Catalog* (1995-98), 12.

This [mental endowment] involves the ability to learn, to remember, to use the imagination, to evaluate, to think logically; to present clearly. It also involves being able to communicate by commanding respect, maintaining discipline, speaking distinctly enough to be understood and loudly enough to be heard, and in general to fill the role of a leader. These gifts need to be cultivated and exercised through academic training and channeled by means of a thorough theoretical and practical theological training. The lack of the aptitude to teach disqualifies a man for the office of pastor, the loss of it likewise. ... Laying a sound foundation for the aptitude to teach is necessary because the pastor is to be "not a novice, lest being lifted up with pride, he fall into the condemnation of the devil" (1 Timothy 3:6).[60]

The Curriculum

Because the Evangelical Lutheran Synod has for the past fifty years had its own preparatory school for its messengers of peace, it is not inappropriate in review to ask in what that preparation has consisted. From the inception of the seminary it was understood that this institution would be geared to the preparation of individuals for the office of the public ministry, in particular to prepare men for work in the parish ministry and on the mission fields. As indicated in the earlier part of this essay, there is no single outward form or program by which the church has through the centuries prepared people for this office. An effective training program will be geared to the needs of the church, and those needs, as well as the basic means to fill those needs, are clearly set forth in the Holy Scriptures.

Man is by nature a fallen creature, suffering mortally from his self-inflicted wounds. His sin has separated him from his Creator God and has left him sorely in need of being restored to a harmonious relationship with that eternal Being from whom he has been so deeply alienated. That restoration is an impossible task for him to undertake, despite his often ill-advised attempts to seek it on his own. Fallen man will, in the end, be forced to acknowledge his utter dependence on the mercy of God.

He will not find a satisfactory solution to his problem except in our Lord Jesus Christ, the only Savior of the world, and in the

---

[60] Armin W. Schuetze and Irwin J. Habeck, *The Shepherd under Christ: A Textbook for Pastoral Theology* (Milwaukee: Northwestern Publishing House, 1981), 12.

eternal counsels of God, which are revealed only in the divine word which He has chosen to hand down to us through His holy prophets and apostles. It is therefore to be understood that any messenger training program is to focus on, gain its direction from, and derive its power from that Word of God. On this matter also we are in accord with Martin Luther, who was wont to say: *Die ganze Schrift treibt Christum!* (The entire Scripture urges Christ!) In an age when we are pressured to think that more and more matters extraneous to the Word of God are necessary for the preparation of the messengers of peace, it behooves us to beware of thereby drifting from our moorings.

That the Word of our Lord is the principal focus of the seminary's efforts to prepare messengers of peace is manifested in its curriculum. In the school catalog under "Program of Study" the opening words are those of the Apostle Paul written to Timothy: "Do your best to present yourself to God as one approved, a workman who does not need to be ashamed and who correctly handles the word of truth" (2 Timothy 2:15).[61] The reason for concern for the handling of this word of truth is the clear announcement through the same Apostle Paul that "faith comes from a message heard" (Romans 10:17), and in this case the message is that of the Gospel, which is "the power of God to salvation to everyone who believes" (Romans 1:16).

The catalog further states that "all instruction and training at Bethany Lutheran Theological Seminary is conducted in the light of the Gospel. The Holy Scriptures are regarded as the inspired and inerrant Word of God and the Lutheran Confessions as a correct exposition of the teachings of the Bible."[62] The curriculum is divided into four departments which coincide with the four major subdivisions of Christian theology.[63]

Biblical Theology

The first of these general categories is that of Biblical Theology. In this area of the curriculum there is direct study of the Bible in the Hebrew and Greek languages in which this collection of books was written by the appointed holy men of God as they were "borne along" by the Holy Spirit of God (2 Peter 1:21). For this reason one finds it readily understandable that one of the

---

[61] *Seminary Catalog*, 12.
[62] Ibid., 19.
[63] Ibid., 26ff.

academic requirements is "a good working knowledge of Greek and Hebrew."[64] Certain isagogical or introductory courses do precisely what those modifying words suggest, namely, introduce the student to the nature, content, and authorship of the books of both the Old and New Testament. In the exegetical courses there is in-depth study of selected books of the two testaments, such as Genesis, Psalms (especially the Messianic Psalms), and Isaiah in the Old Testament, and the Gospels, Romans, and Galatians in the New Testament.

A course in hermeneutics helps to prepare the students for the task of exegesis, for it instructs in the history, principles, and techniques of interpretation of the Scriptures, while the courses in exegesis put the hermeneutical principles to practice in mining the full and divinely intended meaning from the passages under study. Hermeneutics is thus defined as the art or science of interpretation, while exegesis is the actual practice of this art or science. The desired result of such labors is the arrival not at a "what it means to me" interpretation, but at the "Holy Spirit intended" meaning.

The work of the public ministry has been described as the task of teaching men to listen—to listen to the voice of their Good Shepherd.[65]

Three barriers to this kind of listening exist: the barriers of language, of history, and of the flesh. The barrier of language can be largely overcome by learning the biblical languages, for which task many helps are available. Not all people are in a position to learn the biblical languages, and it is not necessary that all do so. Nevertheless, "to be able, with a little effort, to hear the voice of the Good Shepherd more distinctly and more fully, and not make the effort? . . . [W]hat shall we call it but ingratitude to the God who has given us both the languages and the means of mastering them? The languages are not a burden; they are a gift and a privilege."[66]

For hurdling the barrier of time there is need to retrace our steps in history to listen to what the voice meant for God's people then and there. It is possible to locate stiles across the fence so that we can better see under what conditions this or that word was spoken. To know the context in which words are spoken is to have

---

[64] Ibid., 12.
[65] Cf. Martin A. Franzmann, in *Toward a More Excellent Ministry*, ed. Richard Rudolph Caemmerer and Alfred Ottomar Fuerbringer (St. Louis: Concordia Publishing House, 1964), 81ff.
[66] Ibid., 85.

a head start on understanding what they mean. This statement is not to be understood, however, as asserting that a total reconstruction or recall of history is necessary to an appreciation of the simple doctrinal truths of Holy Writ.

The final barrier is the most difficult to surmount, the barrier of our natural sinful flesh. No son of Adam wants to hear the voice of God, even as our fallen progenitor stated to a seeking God: "I heard your voice in the garden, and I was afraid" (Genesis 3:10). Nor *can* he of himself really hear it, as Paul forthrightly states: "The natural man does not receive the things of the Spirit of God, for they are foolishness to him; nor can he know them, because they are spiritually discerned" (1 Corinthians 3:14). We can teach men to overcome the barrier of language, we can teach them to overcome the barrier of history, but we cannot, in a strict sense, teach them to overcome the barrier of the flesh. Here only God himself by his saving grace and powerful word can make "willing people out of resisting and unwilling people."[67] And so it can rightly be said: "Unless our preacher and pastor, by the powerful grace of God, passes the barrier of the flesh, his skills in language and his knowledge of history are nothing and worse than nothing; *they feed his pride and inflate his ego.* But when he has learned to deny himself and follow the voice, then this skill and this knowledge are precious things indeed."[68]

Systematic Theology

The second category of curriculum studies is designated as Systematic Theology, in which the teachings of the Bible are arranged in a different scheme for study. Systematic Theology is essentially Biblical Theology and differs from it only in its approach and organization, for instead of studying the Scriptures book by book, it studies that divine Word doctrine by doctrine. This study serially answers the question: What does the Bible have to say about such matters as God, creation, angels, man, Scripture itself, Christ, redemption, conversion, justification, sanctification, the Means of Grace, the church, the public ministry, eternal election, and the last things?

A subdivision of Systematic Theology is titled Symbolics, a study of the symbols or confessional statements of various churches, principally the confessional writings contained in the

---

[67] Cf. FC SD II, 88 *et al.*
[68] Martin Franzmann, in *Toward a More Excellent Ministry*, 89.

Lutheran Book of Concord. These latter confessions, from the Three Ecumenical Creeds to the Formula of Concord, have arisen throughout the history of the New Testament church in response to some particular problem or need. It is still required among us that, for entrance into the public ministry of the Evangelical Lutheran Synod, one must subscribe to the Book of Concord, for these confessions are a correct exposition of the Word of God and define clearly for us what it means to be truly Lutheran.

Historical Theology

In Historical Theology the Christian Church in its life and teachings is studied from the standpoint of history. The seminary catalog declares that "a major purpose of Historical Theology is to reveal the gracious, always-present hand of the Triune God ruling over His church."[69] That study is often made according to various periods of history, such as that of the Apostolic and post-Apostolic church, of the church of the Middle Ages, of the church at the time of the Lutheran Reformation in Germany, of Lutheranism in the United States, and various subdivisions of any of these, especially the last mentioned. One may also find the individual course limited to the study of the history of missions in the church. To learn how the Lord has dealt with His church down through the centuries is to learn much about how He will deal with the church in the future.

Practical Theology

The final category of the curriculum has been termed Practical Theology, so called because it deals with the art of putting into practice, or applying, the teachings of Scripture to the members of the church in their real life situations. Because the *preaching* of the Gospel is at the heart of the practical life of the messenger of God, the study of Homiletics is vital to the curriculum. Throughout the seminary program, therefore, ample time is spent on the preparation and delivery of sermons,[70] the substance of which is largely furnished from the courses in dogmatics and exegesis. Courses in Pastoral Theology seek to prepare the budding messenger also for the day by day

---

[69] *Seminary Catalog*, 29.
[70] The terms "sermon" and "homily" are virtual synonyms, the former of Latin and the latter of Greek derivation.

performance of his holy office, both in respect to his relationship with his Chief Shepherd, and in his daily care of the flock entrusted to him.

The pastoral office necessarily involves the care of souls,[71] for which a review of the many situations that will confront a pastor, and the proper application of the Word of the Lord to the same, will greatly aid him who desires to be of significant help to his parishioners as he strives to keep them in the saving company of their Lord. And because the forms of worship and the liturgy, as well as the hymnody, of the church continue to have a strong influence on the life of God's people, examination of the historical development, as well as the importance, of liturgical forms finds a necessary and welcome niche in the realm of practical theology.

For three years academic studies in the above departments of theology are carried on in the environs of the seminary. In our training system, a fourth year of preparation is ordinarily added to the three academic school years.[72] This year is ideally spent working in a synod parish under the guidance of a supervising pastor. In effect this portion of the program would best be categorized as belonging to the department of Practical Theology, for here the student learns first-hand how to shoulder the many responsibilities of the parish pastor, while at the same time continuing his pursuit of deepening his biblical faith and knowledge and of enhancing his confessional understanding. At the conclusion of this final seminary year, he will, God willing, be approved by the constituted church authorities for entrance into the public ministry and recommended to the church as a candidate of theology.[73]

---

[71] The endearing terms *Seelsorger* and *Sjælesørger* (German and Norwegian terms, respectively, meaning "one who cares for souls") have never seemingly caught on in translation into the English language.

[72] In unusual cases, such as where older students are deemed by the seminary faculty to have had the equivalent of a vicar year (or internship) in their life and work in the church before attending the seminary—or even during their attendance—the fourth year may be waived.

[73] Present procedure calls for the seminary faculty to recommend the student to the Board of Regents for the Master of Theology degree and/or the degree of Candidate of Theology, and the Board of Regents to approve the recommendation.

> "What is the difference between the Law and the Gospel? The Law teaches us what we are to do and not to do; the Gospel teaches us what God has done, and still does, for our salvation. The Law shows us our sin and the anger of God; the Gospel shows us our Savior and the grace of God."
>
> An Explanation of Dr. Martin Luther's Small Catechism (Mankato, MN: Evangelical Lutheran Synod, 2001), 36.

All of this preparation of the seminary student takes place in order that he might be a messenger of peace. Though the holder of the office of the public ministry is to proclaim the whole counsel of God (Acts 20:28), which includes His revelation of both Law and Gospel, the proclamation of the former is to prepare the way for the rightful proclamation of the latter. Surely anyone who finds himself called into this office desires to be known as a minister of the Gospel or a messenger of peace, for it is finally the Gospel of peace alone which can bring comfort and strength to troubled souls.

Peace is of the very essence of the Gospel. Jesus Christ is Himself the Prince of Peace (Isaiah 9:6). This is not an earthly and temporal peace, but a spiritual and eternal peace. Our God is also the author of temporal peace, but He has not promised that that kind of peace will ever be ours in this world, nor is it always necessary to our true welfare. One speaks of peace in contrast to war. The war in question here is the result of man's spiritual rebellion against his Maker, which made him a candidate for eternal punishment. From his sinful side there was no prospect of gaining peace with the God whose will he had grossly violated. Man's rebellion consisted in his wanting to be like God in ways which were not permitted him. It was man who, yielding to Satan's temptation, started the war, the results of which he could not undo, for he was incapable on his own of reversing his steps. God alone can bring about that reversal, wherefore the prophet prays: "Turn us back to you, O Lord, and we shall be restored" (Lamentations 5:21).[74]

---

[74] For a convention essay by B. W. Teigen entitled "Peace-Temporal, Spiritual, Eternal" see *Synod Report* (1945), 30ff.

The great message of the Gospel is that God has established this peace with men through His Son. Paul states also that, after having gained this peace for mankind, Christ "came and preached peace to you who were afar off, and to those who were near" (Ephesians 2:17). And the same apostle, when writing to Christians in Rome, exults in the descriptive words with which we opened this presentation: "How beautiful are the feet of those who preach the Gospel of peace, who bring glad tidings of good things!" (Romans 10:15). Because our Lord Jesus Christ is the Preacher *par excellence*, His feet are, in the imagery of the prophet, more beautiful!

Document 4.5:

"Ask for the Old Paths": Sixtieth Anniversary Sermon on Jeremiah 6:16 (2006)

By Gaylin R. Schmeling

Gaylin R. Schmeling (1950–) *was born on September 27, 1950, at Litchfield, Minnesota. He grew up on the family farm near Hutchinson, Minnesota. In 1974 he enrolled at Bethany Lutheran Theological Seminary, Mankato, Minnesota, graduating in 1978 after vicaring at a five-point parish in northern Iowa. His first call was to a two-point parish, English of Cottonwood, Minnesota, and Zion of Tracy, Minnesota. In the spring of 1986, he was called to Holy Trinity Lutheran Church in Okauchee, Wisconsin (near Milwaukee), where he served until 1997 when he was called to be the president of Bethany Lutheran Theological Seminary. Since 1985 he has been a member of the Doctrine Committee of the Evangelical Lutheran Synod. He received his S.T.M. degree in the History of Dogma at Nashotah House Seminary, Nashotah, Wisconsin, in 1993. President Schmeling is the editor of the* Lutheran Synod Quarterly *and a contributor to a number of theological periodicals. He has written three books:* Baptism: My Adoption into God's Family *(Milwaukee: Northwestern Publishing House, 1999);* God's Gift to You: A Devotional Book on the Lord's Supper *(Milwaukee: Northwestern Publishing House, 2001); and,* Bread of Life from Heaven *(Mankato: Bethany Lutheran Theological Seminary Press, 2009). In 1973 he married Rebecca Christensen. Their marriage was*

blessed with two sons, Timothy and Samuel, both of whom are in the pastoral ministry.

Source: Lutheran Synod Quarterly 46, nos. 2-3 (June/Sept. 2006): 129-33.

Prayer

Dear Father in heaven, on this happy occasion we thank You for all the blessings that You have poured out on Bethany Lutheran Theological Seminary during the past sixty years, and especially for preserving our seminary in the old paths of Holy Scripture and the Lutheran Confessions. Through Your Spirit You have kept us in the doctrine of Scripture that centers in Your Son's atoning work for salvation. As You have blessed our seminary in the past, we pray that You continue to bless us in the future through our regular use of Your Holy Word and Blessed Sacraments. We ask it in Your Son's name. Amen.

Text

> Stand in the ways and see, and ask for the old paths, where the good way is, and walk in it; then you will find rest for your souls. (Jeremiah 6:16)

Introduction

Most people today are looking for new paths, new vacation routes to see something new and exciting. We are tired of the same old, same old. We want to see some new paths on our summer vacation to satisfy our curiosity, even when they result in dead ends or worse. But there is an old path that means more to me than all the new paths. It is the road outside of Hutchinson, Minnesota, that leads to my home farm and home church. My great-great-grandfather, my great-grandfather, my grandfather, and my father lived and worshiped there. These are wonderful old paths because they lead to home and family. No new path, regardless of how novel and exciting, would lead home.

On a much grander scale on this the sixtieth anniversary of Bethany Lutheran Theological Seminary, sixty years of God's grace and mercy, we want to *Ask for the old paths*. This is an important celebration for our seminary and our synod. We want to thank the Lord for all His blessings these past sixty years and we pray for His continued blessing in the future. Jeremiah says, *"Ask for the old paths."* We ask for the old paths because these paths are good and because here we find rest for our souls.

I. The Old Paths Are the Good Paths.

This text is probably more familiar to the members of the Evangelical Lutheran Synod than to the members of any other church body. In 1918 at the reorganization of the synod the Rev. Bjug Harstad encouraged the little group gathered at Lime Creek with these words. They were to remain on the old paths, the good paths where they would find rest for their souls. There are no other paths by which to find our true home in heaven and eternal salvation. Our synod and our seminary have remained on the old paths by preserving the faith of our fathers.

The source of this faith is the inspired inerrant Word of God. The Holy Scripture is the only source for doctrine, faith, and life. It is the doctrine of the inerrant Word that all the professors of this institution have taught and continue to teach. This is the doctrine that you, the Rev. Michael Smith, will teach as you are called and installed as professor in the seminary.[75] That life-giving Word we will diligently read, mark, learn and inwardly digest as the ancient collect directs.[76] The pastor and all his members for that matter are to meditate upon and contemplate the Word. That doesn't mean one quick reading and then off to the listserve on the Internet. No, we will contemplate the Word and inwardly digest it. Gerhard in his *Schola Pietatis* [*School of Piety*] says that the Christian will ruminate on the Word or roll it over in his mind as a cow chews on its cud. You have seen a cow resting in the pasture quietly chewing away. Thus you will take time to meditate and ruminate or chew on the Word.[77]

---

[75] *Editors' note*: Professor Michael K. Smith, who had been teaching Greek at Bethany Lutheran College, joined the seminary faculty in 2006. He previously had served as pastor of Lord of Life Lutheran Church in Holland, Michigan.

[76] *Editors' note*: The Collect for the Second Sunday of Advent in the *Book of Common Prayer* (1662) reads, in part: "Lord, . . . Grant that we in such wise hear [the Holy Scriptures], read, mark, and inwardly digest them."

[77] Johann Gerhard, *Schola Pietatis* (Jena: Georg Sengwald, 1653), 2:291-92.

We follow the old paths, the good paths, by a proper use of the Lutheran Confessions because they are a correct exposition of God's Word. We value the early church fathers: Irenaeus, Augustine, and Cyril.[78] We treasure the Reformation fathers: Luther, Chemnitz and Gerhard.[79] We will preserve that heritage of the Norwegian trio—Preus, Ottesen, and Koren[80]—and the important works of Dr. Walther.[81] In the same way, we will heed the exhortation quoted by the first president of the reorganized synod: "Stand in the ways and see, and ask for the old paths, where the good way is, and walk in it; then you will find rest for your souls" (Jeremiah 6:16). These are the paths that were followed by Dean Madson, Dean Otto, President Aaberg, President Reichwald, and President Petersen,[82] and, by the grace and mercy of our Lord, these are the paths that we continue to follow.

---

[78] *Editors' note*: The Lutheran Confessions frequently cited **St. Irenaeus of Lyons (ca. A.D. 200)**, **St. Augustine of Hippo (354-430)**, and **St. Cyril of Alexandria (376-444)** with favor. For example, Irenaeus correctly expressed the sacramental presence of Christ's body and blood in Holy Communion and rightly distinguished between Christ's divine and human natures (SD VIII, 14, 20, 22); Augustine was appreciated both for his strong judgment against original sin (Ap II, 22, 24) and for his clear exposition of God's gracious declaration that sinners are justified by faith for Christ's sake (Ap IV, 106); and, Cyril, like Irenaeus, clearly taught that Christ's body and blood are truly present in the Lord's Supper, not merely symbolized by bread and wine (Ap X, 3). The Lutheran confessors also looked to Cyril's example when discussing the closely related doctrine of the hypostatic union of Christ's divine and human natures (SD VII, 11, and VIII).

[79] *Editors' note*: **Martin Luther (1483–1546)**, **Martin Chemnitz (1522–1586)**, and **Johann Gerhard (1582–1637)** provided theological leadership for the founding century of the Lutheran Church. "If the second Martin [Chemnitz] had not come," so goes an aphorism dating back to the seventeenth century, "the first Martin [Luther] would not have stood." Similarly, Gerhard's systematic treatment of confessional Lutheran theology during the so-called Age of High Orthodoxy laid a foundation for sound theological studies enduring to the present age.

[80] *Editors' note*: **Herman Amberg Preus (1825–1894)** and **Jacob Aall Ottesen (1825–1904)** were two of the seven founding pastors of the Norwegian Synod (1853). **Ulrik Vilhelm Koren (1826–1910)** arrived in America three weeks later, becoming the first Norwegian pastor to serve west of the Mississippi River. Koren succeeded Preus as synod president in 1894.

[81] *Editors' note*: **C. F. W. Walther (1811–1887)** served as president of the Lutheran Church–Missouri Synod during its formative decades in the mid 1800s. Walther's *Proper Distinction between Law and Gospel* has long served as a chief homiletics text at Bethany Lutheran Theological Seminary.

[82] *Editors' note*: See **Document 4.4** for a discussion of these men's contributions to Bethany Lutheran Theological Seminary.

We are not to look for new paths, new and strange doctrines of man, that lead to destruction. These paths do not lead home to rest for the soul but to the gates of hell. All around us we see churches that have taken new directions and now they have nothing to offer but chaff and dust. Former brothers and sisters have taken new paths to the detriment of their faith. Concerning the pictures of the three founders of the Norwegian Synod—Preus, Ottesen, and Koren—that are displayed in the seminary atrium, Aaberg said that they are not merely for show but they remind us that the theology of these men is to be the theology of our seminary and synod. We will follow the old paths, the good paths.

II. Yet Why Will We Follow the Old Paths?

Why will we go the old ways? We will stand firm in the good old paths because here alone will we find rest for our souls in all the burdens and troubles of life. The new paths of this world provide no real peace and security in life even though great things are promised.

First and foremost, rest, peace, and security in life are sought in money and wealth. With enough money and wealth a person's every desire is to be satisfied and his every longing fulfilled. Enough horded wealth is to bring true, lasting happiness. Yet, can wealth really fulfill all these promises? The answer, my friends, is a definite no! In one natural disaster, as was seen in New Orleans last fall,[83] all our treasured possessions can so easily be destroyed. All the money we have stashed away for our old age is constantly dwindling as prices continue to rise. Then, of course, at the hour of death, as we stand before our Lord's judgment throne, a hundred-dollar or a million-dollar bank account won't make a particle of difference (Zechariah 1:18).

Also, true lasting security is sought in those around us, our friends and relatives. Yet, in times of crisis, friends have a tendency to fade away. Their help is, at best, weak because they too are made from dust. The Lord says, "Cursed is the man who trusts in man and makes flesh his strength" (Jeremiah 17:5). Finally, such peace and security cannot even be found in the strength of this body. No matter how beautiful or strong this physical frame may be, no matter how intelligent we may be, this

---

[83] *Editors' note*: Hurricane Katrina devastated New Orleans in August 2005, dislocating thousands of people from their homes and causing damage that took years to repair.

body can wither as the grass and return in a matter of days to the dust from which it was formed, as one of a variety of deadly diseases begins to grow within. The delusive paths of this world can never provide peace and purpose for this life and the hope of the life to come. The Law of God shows us our absolutely hopeless condition by nature.

Only in the old paths will we find rest for our souls, for our souls are never at rest until they are at rest in the Lord, as St. Augustine wrote.[84] There is hope even in our lost condition. Jesus became poor and lowly to raise us to His divine glory, eternal life in heaven (2 Corinthians 8:9). In the incarnation Christ took upon Himself our dying flesh so that, through unity with His divinity, He might conquer sin, death, and all our foes in that flesh and make us partakers in His divine nature as the sons of God with an eternal existence (Galatians 4:5; 2 Peter 1:4). He partook in our suffering, death, and hell so that we may partake in His glory, life, and heaven—a wonderful exchange (*der fröhliche Wechsel*). This wonderful treasure is brought to us through the means of grace and is received by a simple confident faith in the Savior that is worked through those same means of grace. This is the message that Professor Michael Smith will teach.

The means of grace are the greatest treasure there is because here Christ is present for us. Without Jesus, life has no meaning or purpose and our end is destruction. Without Him there will always be something missing in our life. There will be an emptiness within that will not be filled with wealth, power and prestige. Only Jesus can the heartfelt longing still. With Him as our Savior we have peace and purpose in this life and the blessed assurance of life beyond the grave. Regardless of our burden or problem He is with us strengthening us all the way through His Word and Sacraments, giving us the power to do all things through Him, the power to overcome and obtain the victory.

Our seminary has stood firm in the old paths and continues to do so because here alone will we find rest for our souls in all the burdens and troubles of life. Professor Smith, as you are being installed this evening you are committing yourself to making your stand on the old paths of the Holy Scriptures and the Lutheran Confessions. Then all your teaching will indeed be of benefit to your students and our entire church.

We thank the Lord for all the blessings that He has bestowed upon our seminary for these past sixty years. We are grateful that

---

[84] St. Augustine, *Confessions*, 1:1.

we have a faculty that is committed to the inspired, inerrant Scripture and the Lutheran Confessions. While other schools have turned to higher critical methods, church-growth methodology, and have imbibed postmodern thought, the Lord has preserved our seminary on the old paths. We are grateful that we have a student body that desires to grow in the knowledge of salvation and which is committed to inculcating those truths in their future calls. We have a beautiful building which more than meets the needs of the seminary. Our seminary is in the prayers and on the hearts of our ELS congregations. This is seen by the generous support given to the seminary. As the Lord has blessed us in the past, we know that He will continue to be with our seminary and bless it in the future.

As we look to the future we will strive to preserve the Word of God in its truth and purity in our seminary and we will strive to teach our students to be true shepherds under the Good Shepherd. They will be prepared to spread the Gospel of full forgiveness in Christ to the ends of the earth. The strength to go forward and do all things through Him—that strength He gives us in the life-giving Word and the Holy Sacraments. As we move forward, may our prayer be that of the sixteenth-century theologian and hymnist Nikolaus Selnecker:

> Lord Jesus Christ, with us abide,
> For round us falls the even-tide;
> Nor let Thy word, that heav'nly light,
> For us be ever veiled in night.
>
> In these last days of sore distress
> Grant us, dear Lord true steadfastness
> That pure we keep, till life is spent,
> Thy holy Word and Sacrament. (*ELH* 511:1–2)

SECTION 5:

A Christian Liberal Arts Education

Introduction

By Erling T. Teigen

Side by side with the general, the specific, and the Christian training goes the cultural, that indefinable something which adds richness, beauty, mellowness, refinement. The source and well spring of all true refinement is Christian faith, and no one is truly refined who does not own this faith. ... Christian education is therefore not true to itself if it does not include ... in its training ... some way [to] provide a mode of expression for this culture and appreciation of it in others.

S. C. Ylvisaker[1]

---

[1] S. C. Ylvisaker, *BLC Bulletin* (1941), as cited in Norman S. Holte, "Guide of Youth," in *Sigurd Christian Ylvisaker 1884-1959*, edited by Peter T. Harstad (Mankato, MN: Bethany Lutheran College, 1984), 113.

German Lutherans, primarily from the Wisconsin and Missouri Synods, founded Bethany Lutheran College in 1911 as a ladies' college. Those churches had a strong emphasis on educational institutions specifically aiming to train pastors and teachers for the church. The vision of the 1911 founders was primarily to train women in the arts needed in the home, which included the study of the fine arts and the humanities. They said in one piece of promotional material that they intended this school to become the Vassar of Midwestern Lutheranism.[2] In that aspiration, they indicated that they viewed themselves as aiming somewhat at a liberal arts education for women.

When, in 1927, the little Norwegian Synod purchased Bethany, it immediately refocused the college as a co-educational institution. The college would provide education for those who wished to prepare for the study of theology and would prepare teachers for the Christian day schools. But the mission would be more broadly aimed at the general education of the young men and women of the church.[3]

Nearly all of the founding fathers of Bethany had been trained at Luther College, Decorah, Iowa, whose founding and long-term president was Laur Larsen. Larsen described the educational vision of Luther College thus: "I thought that if a person had devoted his life to a study of Latin, Greek, Hebrew, French, Norwegian, theology, history, and other subjects, his intellectual vision might possibly escape extraordinary narrowness."[4] An "intellectual vision" enabling one to "escape extraordinary narrowness" would be a fit description of the general concept of the liberal arts.

The second president of Bethany, Sigurd Christian Ylvisaker, studied at Luther College under Larsen and others who shared his vision. When he became president of Bethany in 1930, Ylvisaker carried on that vision of education, and it found expression not only in the way that Ylvisaker presented the small, struggling school, but also in his successors, especially B. W. Teigen and Norman Holte (**Documents 5.1** and **5.2**). In the 1940s, the college, under the leadership of Ylvisaker and Paul Zimmerman,

---

[2] In "Prospectus" (*ca.* 1911), ELS Archives.
[3] Holte, "Guide of Youth," 102.
[4] Karen Larsen, *Laur. Larsen: Pioneer College President* (Northfield, MN: Norwegian-American Historical Association, 1936), 249.

The all-female student body of Bethany Lutheran College during the 1920s studied arts and humanities in preparation for service in the home and the church.

embarked on an experiment which, unfortunately, was not to see success. It was called the four-year junior college. It aimed somewhat at focusing on a university preparatory program like the European *gymnasium,* which schooled students from about the ages of sixteen through twenty in the broad, general education which was often denominated "liberal arts." Various external circumstances made it impossible to push the experiment through to completion. But it showed what the educational principles of the college and synod were.[5]

In 1969 the high school department of Bethany was closed, and the college then pursued accreditation with the North Central Association of Colleges and Secondary Schools. Until that time, the only accreditation the college had was through the University of Minnesota. In the course of its self-study preparatory to North Central accreditation, the faculty, administration, and regents struggled with the college's identity and reaffirmed its commitment to liberal education in various ways, especially in the format of its general education requirements. Frequently in the 1980s and 1990s, issues relating to the nature of liberal arts

---

5 Holte, "Guide of Youth," 115 ff.

education surfaced in discussions. When, in 1984, the college observed the centenary of the birth of S. C. Ylvisaker, the commemorative volume *Sigurd Christian Ylvisaker 1884-1959* published by the faculty again enunciated the college's focus on the liberal arts.

In the mid 1990s, under the leadership of President Marvin G. Meyer, the Board of Regents resolved that the time had come to transform Bethany into a baccalaureate institution. That decision, too, required some serious soul-searching: what sort of an institution would this be? The end result of the college's struggle with that question emerged in the fact that the first two majors to be established were Communications and Liberal Arts. From area concentrations within the latter, additional majors were to be developed.

As this process unfolded, the faculty had to rethink the nature of their disciplines in relation to baccalaureate education, an effort which resulted in 2001 with a document summarizing their "Common Understanding" (**Document 5.4**). Meanwhile, Bethany's faculty collaborated with professors from Martin Luther College and Wisconsin Lutheran College to hold the first triennial Lutheran College Conference in August 2000. Keynote speaker Rolf Wegenke cast a vision for continuing the Lutheran liberal arts tradition into the new century (**Document 5.3**).

One may read the documents included in this section looking for a precise, useful definition of "liberal arts," but will not really find one. The idea of the liberal arts has a long history. In the Middle Ages and later, seven areas of study have been singled out, grouped into two categories. The *trivium* consisted of grammar, logic, and rhetoric as foundational, first level studies. Then came the *quadrivium*: arithmetic, geometry, astronomy, and music. It has been suggested that the seven were established on the basis of Proverbs 9:1: "Wisdom has built her house, She has hewn out her seven pillars."[6] The Greek for "liberal arts" was *enkyklios paideia*—literally, "a rounded education," or a general knowledge. Plato described this education as suitable for the guardians of the ideal republic.[7] Aristotle labeled this education as *eleutherioi*—free, or befitting the free man.[8] Cicero, who equated being an

---

[6] Francis M. Crowley, *The Nature of the Liberal Arts* (n.p.: Bruce Publishing, 1946), 18n1. The application of this passage from Proverbs was made by Cassiodorus. Crowley cites R. A. B. Mynors, *Cassiodori Senatoris Institutiones* (Oxford: Clarendon Press, 1937), 39.

[7] Plato, *Republic*, Book VII.

[8] Aristotle, *Politics* VIII, 2, 1337b, 15.

educated person with being a good orator, was especially instrumental in formulating the liberal arts idea of education.[9] St. Augustine was the first to connect the ideal of the liberal arts to Christian education, especially in his emphasis on the study of literature as an important element in understanding Scripture.[10] Martin Luther, a product of the medieval education in the *trivium* and *quadrivium*, championed liberal arts education and especially extolled it in his two treatises on education[11] (**Document 5.5**).

The idea of a liberal arts education is not limited to post-secondary education. In the last decades, there have been a number of efforts to return elementary education to an approach based on teaching the liberal arts. In 2003, the Evangelical Lutheran Synod established a committee to investigate a new approach to establishing parochial schools. After a period of study, the Synod, in 2005, resolved to restructure the subcommittee on elementary schools.[12] The principles behind this restructuring are described in the final selection in this section (**Document 5.6**).

The emphasis that emerges from many Christian writers, and was felt as well by educators in the ELS, is an emphasis that we can say belongs to the First Article of the creed, as Luther confesses it in the Small Catechism: "I believe ... that [God] has given me my reason, and all my senses, and still preserves them." But that emphasis never stands in isolation from the Second and Third Articles: "that Jesus Christ is my Lord who has redeemed me a lost and condemned creature"; and, "that I cannot by my own reason or strength believe in Jesus Christ my Lord or come to him, but the Holy Ghost has called me by the Gospel" (SC II, 2,4,6).

---

[9] Crowley, *The Nature of the Liberal Arts*, 43 f.
[10] Crowley, *The Nature of the Liberal Arts*, 63 f.
[11] Martin Luther, "To the Councilmen of All Cities in Germany That They Establish and Maintain Christian Schools" (1524) in *Luther's Works*, ed. Helmut T. Lehmann (Philadelphia: Fortress Press, 1962), 45:339 ff; and, "A Sermon on Keeping Children in School" (1530) in *Luther's Works,* 46:207 ff.
[12] *Synod Report* (2005), 104 f.

DOCUMENT 5.1:

Sermon Preached (1977)
at the Fiftieth Anniversary of Bethany Lutheran College, and Thirtieth Anniversary of Bethany Lutheran Theological Seminary

By Bjarne W. Teigen

Bjarne Wollan Teigen (1909–2004) was born on July 21, 1909 in Landa, North Dakota. In 1930, he graduated from Concordia College, St. Paul, Minnesota, and in 1935 from Concordia Theological Seminary, St. Louis, Missouri. Teigen then was ordained and installed at Bethany Lutheran Church, Story City, Iowa.[13] He also served parishes in Minnesota and Illinois before accepting the positions of registrar and head of the English department at Bethany Lutheran College in 1945.[14] One year later, Teigen was installed at the newly formed Bethany Lutheran Theological Seminary, which shared the college's campus, and in 1950 he became the college and seminary President.[15] During Teigen's tenure as President, the college began the accreditation process, underwent expansion both physically and in terms of enrollment, and began hosting the annual Reformation

---

[13] "Bjarne Wollan Teigen: 1909-2004," *Lutheran Sentinel*, Aug. 2004, 19.
[14] J. Herbert Larson and Juul B. Madson, *Built on the Rock* (Mankato, MN: Evangelical Lutheran Synod Book Company, 1992), 119.
[15] Ibid., 119, 124, 224.

Lectures, which continue to this day.[16] Teigen retired from the presidency in 1970, but continued to teach at the seminary until 1983.[17] Even in retirement, he contributed to the synod's work by writing the I Believe series on the Lutheran Confessions and a book entitled The Lord's Supper in the Theology of Martin Chemnitz. Teigen died on July 11, 2004 at the age of 95.[18] [PG]

Source: Teigen, B[jarne] W. "Sermon Preached at 50th Anniversary of Bethany Lutheran College, and 30th Anniversary of Bethany Lutheran Theological Seminary, July 24, 1977." *Lutheran Synod Quarterly* 17, no. 5 (Fall 1977): 43–54.

Prayer

O Almighty and Everlasting God, . . .[19] we pray Thee, send Thy Holy Spirit, that we all may be firmly established in Thy Gospel. Grant us grace to present our lives a living sacrifice to Thee, that we may serve Thee and our fellowmen in pure, unfeigned love. For Jesus sake! Amen.

Text

But what things were gain to me, those I counted loss for Christ. Yea doubtless, and I count all things but loss for the excellency of the knowledge of Christ Jesus my Lord: for whom I have suffered the loss of all things, and do count them but dung, that I may win Christ, and be found in Him, not having mine own righteousness, which is of the law, but that which is through the faith of Christ, the righteousness which is of God by faith: That I may know Him, and the power of His resurrection, and the fellowship of His sufferings, being made comformable unto His death; If by any means I might attain unto the resurrection of the dead. (Philippians 3:7-11)

---

[16] Ibid., 121–22. The lectures began in 1965 under Teigen's leadership. "Teigen," 19.
[17] Larson and Madson, *Built on the Rock*, 212, 229.
[18] "Teigen," 19.
[19] *Editors' note:* The omitted words ("Thou who together as alumni and friends of Bethany;") apparently involved a typographical error. Possibly the intent was to acknowledge that God "has gathered us, alumni and friends of Bethany."

Fellow Redeemed—Alumni of Bethany Lutheran High School, Bethany Lutheran College, Bethany Lutheran Theological Seminary, Members of the Board of Regents, Members of the Faculty (past and present), Friends of Bethany: Grace be unto you and peace from God our Father and our Lord and Savior, Jesus Christ. Amen.

These three days have been days removed from the ordinary routine of all of us. What has brought us together from so many regions just at this time? It is, of course, the fiftieth and thirtieth anniversaries of our institution, and the celebration emphasizes that it is for the alumni. But with a little reflection, we can pinpoint more definite reasons than the general announcement which has caused the individual to return to his Alma Mater. Surely we must take note that it is a matter of nostalgia—the American effort to try to recapture the romantic past. The poet has said that distance lends enchantment to the view. And, no doubt, for many a romantic haze envelopes Bethany when viewed from a distance in time and place. Probably closely related to a general nostalgic feeling is the desire to walk where we once walked, see the rooms we once lived in, worked in, played in; yes, even tried a few escapades that brought us dangerously close to a frowning countenance of a forbidding dean or even before a judgmental faculty in solemn session assembled. Those who know and must work in these gray areas tell us that we human beings have a tendency to haunt the scenes of our former crimes.

But there must be more than this for the occasion that finds so many of us here. Friendship, we can say. There have been long-lasting friendships built here and built solidly on the first principles of friendship: love and esteem. Scripture tells us that "a friend loveth at all times" (Proverbs 17:9). And there are such friendships among us, and this weekend was a golden opportunity to renew and strengthen these bonds. And in many cases this friendship has deepened into something more: love and marriage. The book of Proverbs also says, "Whoso findeth a wife, findeth a good thing" (Proverbs 18:22). And surely it is not unscriptural to add the corollary, that she who finds a faithful and loving husband also finds a good thing.

Then, as you during these last three days have walked and looked around, you saw an enlarged campus of forty to fifty acres, several buildings added. The thought could not escape you that this complex belongs to someone. It does. In the eyes of the state of Minnesota, it is owned by a corporation. Through circumstances of membership by some of you in a congregation of the Evangelical

Lutheran Synod, you own this property. And it just could be that some of you have said, as the one in the parable, "I have bought a piece of ground, and I must needs go and see it" (Luke 14:16). Well, your eyes and sense of property values will tell you that what was purchased for $90,000 in 1927 (and those were years of inflation, too) is now worth considerably more. It might please you to know that one member of the owning corporation, your individual share, conservatively estimated, is $400 to $500. And there is nothing wrong with good stewardship in looking at what God has given you. That was not the problem of the man in the parable of the Great Supper.

But—dear friends, all of you—these reasons, even taken collectively together, can hardly account for your presence here during prime vacation time. There must be something greater, something more compelling, and I would pray and hope that it is the same as St. Paul's compelling motive for his life and actions. It is something else that you got, and I pray you still have, while you were here at Bethany: The Highest Wisdom.

Paul says, "But what things were gain to me, those I counted loss for Christ." To understand to what St. Paul refers when he mentions "things that were gain," we must briefly review his life, as he does in the verses preceding our text. Paul appeals to his remarkable history. He was born into a gifted family; he was a freeborn Roman citizen, whose forename and surname were recorded on one of the lists of the Roman tribes in that far-away, glittering capital of Rome. He was a pure-blooded Jew from the tribe of Benjamin—little Benjamin, the leading, loyal, and faithful tribe. At home he spoke common Aramaic; at school he learned Hebrew; and he handled excellently well Greek, the common universal language of the day. He entered a reputable theological seminary, founded by Hillel, and at Saul's time conducted by his grandson Gamaliel, a college or seminary president, we may say, highly esteemed even by the Roman Emperor Titus. Not only did Paul know Hebrew theology, but he was well versed in the Greek language and literature—the arts and the humanities, if you will. He knew the Stoic philosophy. He had more than a passing acquaintance with the great secular writers who are read even today—Pindar, Euripedes, Aristophanes. He quoted Greek authors in an off-hand way: Epimenides, Aratus, Menander. Today the vigor of Paul's writing, the beauty of his style—combined with his great intellectual gifts—are greatly admired both in sacred and profane circles. But he was not merely an egghead, an intellectual in an ivory tower, far removed from the hurly-burly of the day's business of getting a living in industry and commerce. He had learned a trade: tent making. This was a flourishing business, akin to our electronics and aviation industries. The Roman armies, always on the march over the then-known world, kept the tent makers of Asia fully employed.

Now all this tells us that Paul also had a well-rounded education. But before we move to the next part of our text, we must ask, are these things wrong in themselves? Is an education that provided such a background reprehensible in itself? Hardly. Paul, a few paragraphs farther in this short letter, gives this exhortation, "Finally brethren, whatsoever things are true, whatsoever things are honest, whatsoever things are just, whatsoever things are pure, whatsoever things are lovely, whatsoever things are of good report: if there be any virtue, if there be any praise, think on these things" (Philippians 4:8). Paul is saying that there are many things open to us in our lives. In 1 Corinthians 3:21 we have the great Magna Carta of Christian freedom, "All things are yours." All the adjectives that Paul piles up here in Philippians would indicate that he gives his blessings to what we would call culture, the humanities, the liberal arts, education, liberal education.

Dear friends, this has always been part of the educational philosophy of Bethany—high school, college, yes, the seminary as well. Dr. S. C. Ylvisaker, in the first volume of the *Bethany Bulletin* (June 1931),[20] spoke a definitive statement on the objectives of Bethany in his essay, "A Precious Heritage." In his opening statement he asserts that "an education is not a luxury but a necessity."

Later on we encapsulated this in our objectives, as you alumni know having read our catalogs. We have had the aim of helping students to "do independent critical thinking on their own ... to become more effective citizens by means of the study and appreciation of American and world cultural heritage, and the study of contemporary, social, economic and political life ... to acquire fundamental skills and understandings for achieving a satisfactory vocational adjustment."[21] Dear alumni and friends, we have done what we could to help you achieve a balanced roundness, in high school, in college, and in seminary. We must admit that our resources over the years have been modest, modest

---

[20] *Editors' note*: The source has not been located.
[21] *Editors' note*: Bethany Lutheran College, *Academic Catalog, 1957–1959*, 10.

in faculty, modest in financial resources and equipment over these fifty years. But the objective has always been to have broadly trained tent makers, homemakers, farmers, and businessmen who take their place in life as effective citizens. And it has been our hope that our pastors, too, would have been well trained, not only in the foreign languages, but also in the arts and sciences, so that they can take their place as pastors with sympathy and understanding for the work-a-day world of people going about their business.

This is something you have in common, an education patterned more or less after St. Paul's. Really, there was nothing wrong that the man in the parable of the Great Supper wanted to be a good steward of the property he had just purchased. His problem lay elsewhere. He had not learned to distinguish between the things of greater import and those of less. He hadn't learned to put first things first. He did not have his priorities straight. And that was disastrous. St. Paul hadn't at first learned to put these things in their proper perspective, and that is why Paul now says about all those attainments he personally had, "But what things were gain to me, those I counted loss for Christ." Here one must understand the big differentiation between values.

And since Paul doesn't want us to misunderstand him, he repeats himself and becomes even more emphatic, "Yea, doubtless, and I count all things but loss for the excellency of the knowledge of Christ Jesus my Lord: for whom I have suffered the loss of all things, and do count them but dung, that I may win Christ, and be found in Him, not having mine own righteousness which is of the law, but that which is through the faith of Christ, the righteousness which is of God by faith: That I may know Him, and the power of His resurrection, and the fellowship of His sufferings, being made comfortable unto His death; If by any means I might attain unto the resurrection of the dead."

What a burst of genuine eloquence—conclusive evidence of a careful university training in the art of rhetoric, but also an appeal that goes out to all, learned and unlearned. What depth of meaning in Paul's words! He is saying that in the final analysis there is a Higher Wisdom than the wisdom of the world. He asserts that when you come down to the very essence of our existence, there is only one knowledge worth knowing. The highest wisdom is to know Jesus Christ and what he has done for us: His righteousness which is perfect before God, and which satisfies the demands of God, and which covers the unrighteousness of our sinful existence.

Of this Christ Paul says, "For whom I suffered the loss of all things." Paul here uses what your teachers of rhetoric and literature would call a submerged metaphor, an implied picture which isn't expressly stated, but which undergirds the sentence and makes it concrete. The metaphor is from the life of seamen, who, when in danger of shipwreck near the rugged seacoast, throw everything overboard that the ship, being lightened, may carry the imperiled sailors safely into the harbor. It's a picture of desperation—they want to escape with their lives. So, Paul has one thing in mind: his final deliverance, his final eternal reunion with his God and Savior when everything else here in this world has been swept away.

A person who has become too closely attached to those things of this world, the gifts and graces of this life, which are not wrong in themselves, such a person may throw overboard with great regret some valuable item dear to his heart. Almost comic are some of the stories of what shipwrecked people have tried to save as the last thing nearest to their heart—a belt of gold, a favorite cat, a bit of clothing with some sentiment attached to it. But there is none of that feeling with Paul; no regretful separation from these great gifts and graces with which he was endowed and which had been developed in him through a sound education, "For whom I have suffered the loss of all things and do count them but dung, that I may win Christ." This is strong language that doesn't need any explication from the preacher.

And what is the one knowledge worth knowing—the highest wisdom—which can't be taken away from even the most desperate drowning man in the greatest of extremities? We are back to the central theme, "That I may know Christ and the power of His resurrection. That I may be found in Him, not having mine own righteousness which is of the law, but that which is through the faith of Christ, the righteousness which is of God by faith." In this four-hundreth anniversary of our Lutheran Formula of Concord, we think of how the authors of this remarkable confession formulated this central truth of Scripture, the truth by which the church stands or falls, "We believe, teach, and confess that our righteousness before God consists in this, that God forgives us our sins purely by His grace, without any preceding, present, or subsequent work, merit or worthiness, and reckons to us the righteousness of Christ's obedience on account of which righteousness we are accepted by God into grace and regarded as righteous" (Ep III, 4).

That is it, dear friends! That is the highest wisdom. That is why Dr. S. C. Ylvisaker in 1931 not only said that an education is not a luxury but a necessity, but he went on to ask, "But must we not go a step farther and say that a distinctly Christian education is not a luxury but a necessity?"[22] This was not because it would add one more skill or one more grace to one's equipment but because it was the one thing needful [Luke 10:42]. That is why our catalog says, as you will recall, in its objectives, that the chief objective is "to grow in grace and in the knowledge of our Lord and Savior Jesus Christ by means of His Gospel, the power of God unto salvation."[23] We have at Bethany recognized the need for an intelligent, well indoctrinated people of God, and we have tried to bring young men and women together that they might have opportunity to secure a deeper, a more mature understanding of their Christian faith before they enter into a world of shaken ideologies.

And, my dear friends, is not that the real reason that has brought you back here for this weekend? Pray God that it is! You learned some things at Bethany, and you've learned a lot more since that time. Pray that you haven't unlearned what the highest wisdom is.

Dr. Ylvisaker, sensitive to beauty, art, literature, which was revealed not only in his life but also in his writings, was not one to quote hymnody very often. He once told me that he regretted that he had never learned these hymns when he was young. But if one watched him at the services and the chapel talks, one noted what hymns made the hymnboard. One can learn a great deal about a pastor's literary preferences and his theological orientation by watching the hymnboard. And there was one hymn that often made the hymnboard when Dr. Ylvisaker was to speak. It was Wesley's excellent translation of the old Lutheran chorale, "Now I Have Found the Ground Wherein, Sure My Soul's Anchor May Remain." I can recall only one instance where he actually quoted a hymn stanza, and that was the third stanza of this hymn:

> O love, Thou bottomless abyss,
> My sins are swallowed up in Thee!
> Covered is my unrighteousness,
> Nor spot of guilt remains on me,
> While Jesus blood, through earth and skies,
> Mercy, free, boundless mercy! Cries. (*LHy* 478:3)

---

22 *Editors' note*: The source has not been located.
23 *Editors' note*: Bethany Lutheran College, *Academic Catalog, 1953–1955*, 8.

This is the thirtieth anniversary of our seminary, and one cannot forget another of our venerable fathers who was more intimately connected not only with the seminary but also with the College, Dean Norman A. Madson. Both President Ylvisaker and Dean Madson came out of the same background of a liberal arts education, but they had learned to take it in its proper perspective. Both stood solidly grounded in the Scriptures and the Gospel of Jesus Christ. They were not theologians who would be inclined to "seek for power, by doctrine fashioned to the varying hour."[24] But one need not have been in Dean Madson's services very long before he noted that one of his characteristics was quite different from President Ylvisaker's. He loved to quote religious poetry, and he did it with discrimination. And one need not have been around him very long to notice that one of his many favorites was the hymn based on Bethany's motto, "One Thing is Needful," and particularly this stanza:

> Jesus, in Thy cross are centered
> All the marvels of Thy grace;
> Thou, my Savior, once hast entered
> Through Thy blood the holy place;
> Thy sacrifice holy, there wrought my redemption;
> From Satan's dominion I now have exemption;
> The way is now free to the Father's high throne
> Where I may approach Him in Thy Name alone. (*LHy* 227:8)

There you have what Bethany has represented and continues to represent by the grace of God. It is more than nostalgia. It is more than a vague "spirit of Bethany" romantically constructed from a religious feeling. It is the body of doctrine grounded in the sacred Scriptures with Jesus Christ as the center.

When the tumult and the shouting dies off this weekend and you depart to your own, in some cases, far-flung homes, remember "the precious heritage," "the highest wisdom," the one knowledge worth knowing. Don't forget it. Pray for Bethany, that it may always retain it in its simple truth, as St. Paul did. And, as a former president, I would be remiss if I did not say: Support it with prayers, students, gifts, good words, kind sympathy, and understanding as far as God's truth will permit.

Above all, keep your priorities straight. But for God's sake, do it only because you have laid hold in your heart of the unfailing word of promise of Paul's inspired word. "That I may win Christ

---

[24] *Editors' note*: The source has not been located.

and be found in Him, not having mine own righteousness, which is of the law, but that which is through the faith of Christ, the righteousness which is of God by faith." Amen.

Glory be to the Father, and to the Son, and to the Holy Ghost: As it was in the beginning, is now, and ever shall be: world without end. Amen.

DOCUMENT 5.2:

A Christian Liberal Arts Education (1981)

By Norman S. Holte

Norman S. Holte (1918–) *was born January 7, 1918 in Eddy Township, Minnesota. The youngest of seven children, he attended a one-room public school, where enrollment peaked at fifty. Holte attended Bethany Lutheran College from 1940 to 1942, where he met his future wife, Violet Fevig, who had also attended Bethany during her high school years. After serving in a U.S. Navy shipyard in California, Norman returned to his home state to pursue a B.S. and M.A. at the University of Minnesota.*[25] *Holte joined the Bethany faculty at President Ylvisaker's invitation in 1945, teaching in the social sciences department. In 1978, he became the first lay president of Bethany Lutheran College. (The Synod had amended the college's bylaws in 1977 to allow for a layman to serve as president; during that time, Seminary President Theodore A. Aaberg was serving as acting president of the college, while none of the clergymen called by the*  *Regents would accept a permanent call to the presidency.) Holte retired in 1982, being succeeded by a second lay president, Marvin G. Meyer. Holte soon after served as a contributing editor for the commemorative volume entitled* Sigurd Christian Ylvisaker, 1884–1959 *(1984).*[26] *During*

---

[25] Personal interview, by Annie Williams, 21 Apr. 2010.
[26] J. Herbert Larson and Juul B. Madson, *Built on the Rock* (Mankato, MN: Evangelical Lutheran Synod Book Company, 1992), 212–13, 219; Peter T.

the 1990s, he served as the Synod Archivist and helped to establish the ELS Historical Society.[27] [RM]

Source: Holte, N. S. "A Christian Liberal Arts Education." *Synod Report* (1981): 62–n.p.

The liberal arts have a long tradition in the education of man, going back into the Roman and Greek period of history and, no doubt, even further. The Christians of the fourth and fifth centuries continued reluctantly to use the curriculum of the Romans, which consisted largely of the seven liberal arts: the *trivium*—grammar, rhetoric and logic; and the *quadrivium*—arithmetic, geometry, music and astronomy. The Christian writers of this period were well acquainted with the pagan literature of the Greeks and Romans. Some wished to ban the study of such literature, while others recommended their study. The trivium and quadrivium were largely adapted by the Christian church to serve its ends. In this process the liberal arts lost some of their vitality. This, the invasion of the "barbarians," plus constant warfare led to a decline in learning and education generally during the fifth through seventh centuries. Nevertheless, the liberal arts survived and, in some places, were studied with diligence and with greatly renewed interest and vitality during the Renaissance period.

This revival of the liberal arts, especially the study of the classics—the pagan literature of the Greeks and Romans—helped make the Reformation possible. The basic purpose of the liberal arts, the "cultivation of the mind," was restored. The study of Greek and Roman literature in the original languages brought a renewal of interest in grammar and in the accurate rendering of the meaning of the original texts. Luther and the Reformation certainly benefited from this revival of learning.

It is noteworthy that the Reformation had its birth in the universities and was led by a man whose education involved not only a study of the Scriptures and the church fathers but also of the liberal arts. We shall look later at his strong support for Christian liberal arts education.

During the Middle Ages the church was the institution largely

---

Harstad, ed., *Sigurd Christian Ylvisaker 1884-1959* (Mankato, MN: Bethany Lutheran College, 1984), x.
[27] Interview.

responsible for the discovery, preservation, and dispensation of knowledge. It may have performed this task poorly at times, but aside from the family, there was no other institution to perform this function. Thus Western civilization and Christianity became so intertwined that they were hardly distinguishable.

In America, the same close relationship continued between church and college. Harvard was established in 1636 largely as the result of a gift by the Rev. John Harvard "that tongues and arts might be taught and learning and piety maintained."[28]

Through the nineteenth century, American higher education remained dominated by church colleges. Historians Samuel E. Morison and Henry S. Commager described the pre-Civil War education of these small institutions as follows:

> Foreign visitors compared the institutions with Oxford, Cambridge and Göttingen, and laughed or sneered. But for an integrated education, one that cultivates manliness and makes gentlemen as well as scholars, one that disciplines the social affections and trains young men to faith in God, consideration for his fellow man, and respect for learning, America has never had the equal of her little hill-top colleges.[29]

In the twentieth century, higher education has become increasingly secularized. The percentage of college students attending private colleges has declined from 62% in 1900 to 21% in 1980. It is projected that by 2000 this will be further reduced to 15%—a smaller slice of a shrinking pie. Less than 5% of high school graduates who are members of a Protestant or Catholic congregation and who go on to a college or university choose to attend an institution of their denomination.[30] The establishment and growth of public colleges and universities had started before the Revolutionary War, but received tremendous impetus with the passage of the Morrill Act, 1862, the G.I. Bill after World War II, and, of course, the baby boom of the 1950s and 60s.

In addition to the growth of public institutions, many private institutions have become completely secularized, severing their church ties and serving only a secular purpose. Some retain their

---

[28] Ellwood P. Cubberly, *Public Education in The United States* (Cambridge, Mass: Houghton-Mifflin Co., 1919), 16.

[29] Samuel Eliot Morison and Henry Steele Commager, *The Growth of the American Republic*, vol. 1 (Oxford University Press, 1950), 514.

[30] Robert V. Schnabel, "Christian Education at the Crossroads," Part I, *The Cresset* 43, no. 8 (n.d.): n.p.

church connection in name only: their governing boards are chosen on the basis of the prestige and financial support they can offer the college; the faculties are chosen because of their academic credentials, loyalty to the church's confession is of secondary importance; and students represent a diversity of religious backgrounds. The religious beliefs of faculty and students are regarded as a private matter. No denomination or college has remained untouched by the unrelenting force of secular philosophies.[31]

We all know that the popularity of the liberal arts has declined. There has been increased emphasis on specialization in a specific discipline and on preparation for a career. It is important, in view of these developments, that we review the benefits of the education—a Christian, liberal arts education—that your synodical institution offers.

First, let us take a look at the college student of today. The following material is based on a number of studies done in the late 70s, the findings of which are summarized in *When Dreams and Heroes Died*, by Arthur Levine. He gives us a vivid portrait of the college freshman of the late 70s in comparison to the freshman of the 60s. He depicts the male students of the 60s as having long hair, a scraggly beard, carrying a Molotov cocktail in one hand, and clenching the other above his head. His counterpart of 1979 struck the same pose—his hair was carefully styled, he carried a diploma, and in the clenched fist was a wad of dollar bills. This, of course, is a caricature, but it conveys an important fact—the values held by college students have changed.[32]

Today's college student was born after the idealism of "Camelot" had been shattered in Dallas. The "Great Society" and "the war on poverty" were fading into the background, and the Vietnam War was brought into the family room just as he was beginning to be aware of the world beyond his immediate family. During his adolescence, he witnessed in his home the assassination of several national leaders and youth heroes. He saw cities burned by rioters, a national political convention disrupted by rioting college students, students killed by national guardsmen, a president and vice-president resigning from office in disgrace, and cabinet officers tried in the courts for crimes. These events have had a negative effect on today's students.

---

31 Robert V. Schnabel, "Christian Education at the Crossroads," n.p.
32 Arthur Levine, *When Dreams and Heroes Died* (San Francisco: Jossey-Bass, The Carnegie Foundation, 1981), 1.

In Bethany's early days as a ladies' college, sewing was part of the standard curriculum. The sewing tradition later took a new form, as students prepared costumes for theatrical performances.

They have had a greater impact on this generation than would have been the case in another decade. The very institutions that should have had a positive influence and that should have developed optimism and trust were waning: the family, the church, and the school. There is no need to give statistics on the increase in divorce and single parent families, inadequate discipline, assaults on teachers, rapes and attempted rapes, the decline in academic standards, grade inflation, homework cut in half, and declining test scores. "At worst, schools force youngsters to contend with the terrors of the adult world at an earlier age than many did in the past. At best, the decline in academic standards requires of the young people less commitment to school and provides more time for unplanned activities—frequently television—in less sheltered environments."[33] Pre-schoolers spend more time in front of the TV than any age group—from twenty to fifty-four hours a week. Television has largely displaced friend, babysitter, teacher and parent.

What do they watch? The college students of the 60s in their early years watched "Father Knows Best," "Leave it to Beaver," and

---

[33] Ibid., 16.

a number of spin-offs that portrayed an idealized family having normal everyday problems and solving them by democratic processes, always showing love and concern for each other. These were all gone by 1966. They were replaced by "All in the Family," which changed the course of television programming. "It brought a harsh reality to the TV world. ... Its chief character, Archie Bunker, was anything but bland ... he was uneducated, prejudiced, and blatantly outspoken. ..."[34] "All in the Family" launched a wave of new shows: "Maude," portraying liberal upper middle class suburban life; "Bridget love Bernie," about ethnic and religious intermarriage; "The Jeffersons," featuring social mobility and black racism; "One Day at a Time," showing divorced and single parent families—and so it goes, on and on—culminating in "Soap" and "Dallas." Violence has always been part of the TV diet, but "Gunsmoke" and "Wyatt Earp" deal with a romanticized past, while the "Streets of San Francisco" and "Kojak" deal with the present and could take place down the street.

To escape an inhospitable world, students, like much of the rest of the country, are turning inward. For many, the one remaining refuge is "me"; everyone is concerned primarily about himself. Levine describes it as a lifeboat mentality: "Each student is alone in a boat in a terrible storm, far from the nearest harbor. Each boat is beginning to take on water. There is but one alternative: each student must single-mindedly bail. Conditions are so bad that no one has time to care for others who may also be foundering."[35]

The shelves of bookstores further demonstrate our obsession with "me-ism" or the culture of narcissism. Titles such as "Looking out for Number One," "Winning Through Intimidation," "Getting Your Share," "Pulling Your Own Strings," "How You Can Profit from a Monetary Crisis," etc., testify to a ready market among college students and adults.

Levine describes trends in society as moving in one of two directions. There are periods of "community ascendancy" when society is perceived as moving toward the community ideal, individual ties with community are strengthened, emphasis is placed on duty to others, and responsibility is a major concern. In other periods, society moves toward "individual ascendancy." In such a time individual ties with community are weakened, the individual is dominant, and the emphasis is on "me." It is

---

[34] Ibid., 18.
[35] Ibid., 22.

hedonistic, emphasizing rights and taking rather than duty and responsibility.[36]

Today's college students have grown up in an unmistakable period of individual ascendancy. Levine's book goes on to describe how the values of today's college students have been affected: their main interest is in a career. They must have good grades and use almost any means to get them, in contrast to learning for the sake of acquiring knowledge. They must have fun, and alcohol has become the chief means of attaining this goal. Sex is not promiscuous, but casual—taken for granted and accepted. They are pessimistic about the future of the United States but optimistic about their own future. The "big me" is going to make it. The ship (Titanic) will sink, but I will lay my plans carefully to effect my own rescue.

It is a world where freedom of action seems pathetically limited and a time when situational ethics appears to make more sense than a philosophy of life. For nearly all college students (87%), life has dimensions that simply cannot be grasped rationally. To this Doonesbury offers the advice, "Go with the flow." A philosophy of life does not seem particularly necessary or even very helpful in such a world.[37]

The sources of these attitudes certainly go beyond television. They are complex and imbedded in the philosophies of life—secularism, materialism, and humanism—in which today's freshmen have been unwittingly indoctrinated during their twelve years of elementary and secondary education.

There has always been a great diversity of beliefs in America, but until recently there has been a general moral consensus. During the 50s and the 60s the nation was stronger, family oriented; there was general agreement about the undesirability of divorce, unmarried cohabitation, homosexuality, and other moral aberrations. Although there was constant and widespread violation of these norms, there was no inclination to defend the violations in theory. Family, church, school, and the mass media tended to accept and promote this moral consensus. In the past twenty years, a radical revolution has taken place. Our public schools and colleges, the media, and government agencies of all kinds profess—at best—a neutrality in regard to religion and moral standards. Often the traditional moral standards are openly attacked on the basis of the right of opposing standards to be heard

---

[36] Ibid., 25.
[37] Ibid., 113.

and promoted. Along with this is the promotion of the individual's right to fulfill every personal desire, regardless of the rights of others. "Me-ism" has become the dominating philosophy—or non-philosophy—of this decade.

On the basis of this portrait of the college student of 1980 and the growing secularism of education, let us take a look at the goals of a Christian liberal arts education.

The study of the liberal arts has been defined as the cultivation of the mind. When the intellect has been properly trained, it will display its power according to the ability of the individual:

> It will make itself felt in the good sense, sobriety of thought, reasonableness, candor, self-command, and steadiness of view which characterize it. In some it will have developed habits of business, power of influencing others, and sagacity. In others it will elicit the talent of philosophical speculation and lead the mind forward to eminence in this or that intellectual department. In all, it will be a faculty of entering with comparative ease into any subject of thought and taking up with aptitude any science or profession.
>
> ... The first step in intellectual training is to impress upon a boy's mind the idea of science, method, order, principle, and system; of rule and exception, of richness and harmony.[38]

Cardinal Newman, in *The Idea of a University*, urges that this training should begin with grammar and mathematics. Geography and the study of history, with emphasis on chronology and poetry, should follow. The student will develop

> a habit of method of starting from fixed points, of making his ground good as he goes, of distinguishing what he knows from what he does not know, and I conceive that he will be gradually initiated into the largest and truest philosophical views and will feel nothing but impatience and disgust at the random theories and imposing sophistries and dashing paradoxes, which carry away half-formed and superficial intellects.[39]

---

[38] Cardinal John Henry Newman, *The Idea of a University* (San Francisco: Rinehart Press, 1960), XLIII, XLIV.
[39] Ibid., XLV.

Norman Holte (seated) surveys the globe with Norman Madson, Jr. (second from the right) and other students at Bethany Lutheran College in 1951. Geography and history dovetail naturally with literature, philosophy, languages, and theology in a liberal arts education.

Such development of the student's intellect contributes to the student's career, to his service to society, and to his understanding of true doctrine.

The proponents of a liberal arts education also argue that the acquisition of knowledge for its own sake is a positive good. Seeking the truth in whatever field—theology, medicine, history— is a worthy objective. Knowledge is organized into disciplines— with its own limits or boundaries, its special methods of inquiry, and its specific content. It must be thus organized, if there is to be orderly research carried on to discover truth. Such advancement of truth, when based on a correct view of man and of the universe, will always be for the benefit of mankind. Such study also benefits the individual. It imposes upon him discipline in the application of his abilities and discipline in limiting his studies to meaningful, orderly subject matter. His intellect, through his senses and with the use of reason, will grasp knowledge and develop ideas. This is a sufficient goal in itself.[40]

Specialization is, of course, necessary for the furthering of research in a particular field and also for the advancement of individuals in their professions and careers. However, the purpose of such specialization is not to produce leaders, nor to produce good citizens. Its sole purpose is to prepare people for a job or for a profession. Luther, with his high regard for civic government as being divinely instituted, emphasizes the need for a broad liberal arts education for those who are capable of learning. He is very critical of the common people who are concerned only with the bodily wants of their children, "What a fearful and unchristian course they are pursuing, and what a great and murderous injury they are inflicting, in the service of Satan, upon society."[41]

In both "Luther's Letter to the Mayors and Aldermen of All the Cities of Germany On Behalf of Christian Education" and his "Sermon on the Duty of Sending Children to School," he again and again criticizes the German people for their lack of interest in learning, referring to them as brutes, blockheads, and dunces. He admires the education of ancient Rome, saying:

> They were masters not only of the choicest Latin and Greek, but also of the liberal arts, as they are called; and immediately after this scholastic training they entered the army or held a position under government. Thus they became intelligent, wise, and excellent men, skilled in every art and rich in experience, so that all bishops, priests and monks in Germany put together would not equal a Roman soldier. Consequently their country prospered.[42]

The welfare, safety, and power of a city, Luther believed, did not consist in its weapons and soldiers, but in "able, learned, wise, upright, cultivated citizens who can secure, preserve, and utilize every treasure and advantage." Although Luther saw a great need for the education of people entering the service of the government, he had a greater concern for the training of young people for the

---

[40] Ibid., 75-93.
[41] F. V. N. Painter, *Luther on Education* (St. Louis: Concordia Pubishing House, 1965), 218.
[42] Ibid., 181.

church. He regarded a faithful pastor as the "most precious treasure, no nobler thing on earth than a pious, faithful pastor or preacher."[43] For it is through this office and the Word that the kingdom of God is maintained in this world.

Luther therefore urges parents, the church, and the government, to provide education for their children. Of what should this education consist? First, a thorough study of the Scriptures and a study of Latin, Greek, Hebrew, and German. Without a knowledge of the original languages, the Gospel would disappear. Also, preaching would become "sluggish and weak, and the people finally become weary and fall away. But a knowledge of the languages renders it lively and strong, and faith finds itself constantly renewed through rich and varied instruction."[44] In addition, he recommends the study of literature of all kinds: history, music, and poetry. All these he regards as valuable in developing people of wisdom, even people pursuing a trade, "for it will benefit them in governing their household"; merchants, "for the merchant will not long remain a merchant if preaching and the administration of justice cease"; and physicians and jurists, for where would "they come from if the liberal arts were not taught."[45]

Good libraries Luther regarded as necessary to preserve all that has been written: the Scriptures—in the original languages and in Latin, German, and other languages; literature in many languages—both Christian and heathen; books treating all the arts and sciences; and, books on jurisprudence and medicine. History and chronicles should have a prominent place, for from the study of history students "learn to regulate their views and order their course of life in the fear of God, having become wise in judging what is to be sought and what avoided in this outward life and capable of advising and directing others."[46]

Luther recognized that lay people do not all trust educators and that they fear the exposure to heathen literature—

> But you say, "How if it turns out badly, so that my son becomes a heretic or a villain?" For, as people say, "education means perversion." Well you must run the risk; but your labor is not lost. God will consider your faithful service and will count it as successful. You must run the risk, as in other callings to which you wish to bring up your son. How was it

---

[43] Ibid., 224.
[44] Ibid., 192.
[45] Ibid., 262-263.
[46] Ibid., 197.

with Abraham, whose son Ishmael did badly; with Isaac and his son Esau; with Adam and his son Cain? Ought Abraham for that reason to have neglected his son Isaac, Isaac his son Jacob, and Adam his son Abel?[47]

Luther urges parents "without anxiety, then, let your son study, and if he should have to beg bread for a time, you give our God material out of which He can make a lord. It will remain true that your son and mine, that is to say, the children of the common people, will rule the world, both in spiritual and secular stations as the Psalm testifies" (Psalm 113).[48]

It is obvious from this that Luther regarded the liberal arts as valuable in themselves. The development of the mind to think logically—"the cultivation of the mind"—was a worthy endeavor and would contribute to the secular welfare of man, aiding him in governing his family, in his trade or profession, in his work as a merchant, or as a scholar, jurist, or any civic endeavor.

The cultivation of the mind, however, goes beyond the development of the intellect and the acquisition of knowledge and wisdom. It includes the appreciation of the beauties of nature, the ability to appreciate and enjoy beautiful art, music, and literature that man has produced with his God-given talents. But even more, it includes the development of the ability to create works of beauty that will further enhance and enrich society.

Try to view, for a moment, the rich heritage of western civilization that we have in our nation: the heritage of the Reformation, with its pure doctrine of the Gospel of Christ; the rich heritage of music, literature and art; the scientific development which is almost beyond our comprehension; our democratic system of government, of justice, and of care for the less fortunate; and our educational system. Our heritage of western civilization provides the basis for the way we live, work, and raise our families; the "right" way of doing things, the customs, traditions, and moral rules which govern our society. It forms a beautiful overarching structure for our society. Can you imagine, aside from Scripture, a more rewarding field of study? It is difficult to imagine that we can ignore the origin of all these benefits that we claim as ours and that we enjoy. Yet "me-ism" and existentialism consider only the present, looking at life and at civilization as though it were a novel with unnumbered pages that

---

[47] Ibid., 236.
[48] Ibid., 261.

can be arranged in any order the reader wishes.

There is order in the development of civilization, a divine order; and therefore we believe with Luther that Christian education, a knowledge of the Scriptures, must be a part of every aspect of education. Luther preferred that:

> Our youth be ignorant and dumb rather than that the universities and convents should remain as the only source of instruction open to them. For it is my earnest intention, prayer, and desire that these schools of Satan be either destroyed or changed into Christian schools.[49]

You have a Christian college in which the confessional position of our church is understood and taught, a place where young people can test the theological propositions that they have learned at home and in their congregations. The first two years of college are a particularly vulnerable time for young people. They are, perhaps, leaving home for the first time and are being forced to think more seriously about the choice of their life's work and of establishing their own home and family. They are confronted by a bewildering array of lifestyles and philosophies and are themselves searching for new ideas. They desperately need to be exposed to an education which teaches Jesus Christ as the way, the truth, and the life [John 14:6].

Bethany does this primarily through the religion courses. In December 1979, the Religion Division adopted a Statement of Purpose which was used as a guide to the study of the curriculum. The main points of the statement follow:

> 1. The purpose of the religion curriculum at Bethany Lutheran College is to enable the student to grow in grace and in the knowledge of the Lord and Savior Jesus Christ by means of His Gospel, the power of God unto salvation [Romans 1:16]; to assume a responsible Christian attitude toward the talents that God has given him and towards his obligation to develop and to use his talents for the glory of God and the welfare of his fellowmen. The curriculum seeks to do this through the study of various aspects of Christianity in an academic setting, realizing that this may be the finest opportunity for the student to examine his faith on a mature basis.
>
> 2. The proselytizing of others to membership in the

---

[49] Ibid., 175.

Evangelical Lutheran Synod is not the goal of the curriculum itself, nor a guiding principle in its development. The courses are taught academically, but also pastorally, and the college is committed to the Lutheran doctrine that the Word of God itself works faith and commitment under God's will. The college also follows the Lutheran principle that while reason does not judge matters revealed by God in His Word, growth in Christian knowledge implies the analytic and systematic study of Scripture.

3. The principle behind the curriculum of the Religion Division is Confessional Lutheran theology, which understands the historic, ecumenical creeds and the Lutheran Confessions to be the correct understanding of the Holy Scriptures and historic Christianity. These Scriptures are the inspired, inerrant Word of God. Because the Lutheran Church most highly values the Means of Grace, the Word and Sacraments, as the center of Christian life and worship are especially emphasized.

4. It is expected that through the study of religion in the classroom the student will become familiar with Scripture and the Confessions as well as other theological literature of the church, so that he can more effectively witness to the faith and function as a responsible and knowledgeable member of his church. It is also expected that he will become familiar with the methods and resources for good biblical study so that he can apply those resources to his private devotional life and his life in the Christian congregation.

5. The scope of the curriculum is noted under the two main headings of theology. It is understood, of course, that this terminology would not necessarily be a part of the course descriptions. They are used here, however, for the purpose of clearly delineating the intent and nature of the curriculum. These headings are: 1) Exegetical, the study of a single passage or book of the Bible, relating the unified testimony of Scripture to the particular passage; and 2) Doctrinal-Confessional, dealing with categories established by Scripture and the Confessions of the church and relating that testimony to the category or topic under consideration. To these main headings ought also be added 3) Historical and 4) Practical Theology. All of the courses, in whatever discipline of theology, are taught biblically and doctrinally.

Every student is required to take a course in religion each semester they are in attendance. The courses are so arranged that, although there is considerable choice in the selection of courses, the students all receive considerable emphasis on the doctrines of the Lutheran church and in-depth study of portions of Scripture. These four courses in religion form the core of each student's education at Bethany. From the students' study of religion flow certain basic Christian beliefs. Some of these are:

>That God created the earth and all living things and sustains it by His almighty power;

>That there is a natural order in creation. This natural order is divinely created and is a self-existing system of natural laws which are rational, and man, by use of his intellect, can learn about them and understand them. However, man is limited and can never have perfect knowledge;

>That man was created in the image of God, and that he fell from grace and is dead in trespasses and sin;

>That God in His love sent His Son, Jesus Christ, into the world to atone for our sins. This personal Savior suffered, died and rose from the dead, and on the basis of His merits, God has justified the world;

>That God gave us the means, His Word and Sacraments, through which He bestows His salvation on His elect.

These basic principles permeate the liberal arts at Bethany. No science can rule out the creation, man's origin, or his nature. No study of man, be it psychology, sociology, or economics, can disregard man's origin or his fallen state as a sinner. Neither can a course in government ignore the fact that all institutions of government are divinely instituted and that the powers of government are derived from natural law. No student of literature or philosophy can rightly interpret either Christian or heathen writer, for literature and philosophy almost always deal with the nature of man, his emotions and attitudes.

Thus the basic principles of Christianity—of confessional Lutheranism—provide a platform or a basis for all of the student's thinking and actions. All logical, analytical thought, as emphasized previously, must have a definite, fixed point from which to start. These Christian principles are that fixed point. These are the absolute truths, the fixed moral standards, the way of life that is pleasing to God. There is a worldview, a Christian philosophy, that is available to the college youth of the 1980s and for every generation. With such a basis for their education, they can say with Paul, "Whatsoever things are true, whatsoever things are honest, whatsoever things are just, whatsoever things are pure, whatsoever things are lovely, whatsoever things are of good report; if there be any virtue, and if there be any praise, think on these things" (Philippians 4:8). These Christian principles form the undergirding—the support—for the superstructure of Western civilization.

Stephen Vincent Benet, viewing the difficult depression years, the rise of dictators, and the loss of freedom, wrote of certain words that were dear to him: liberty, equality, fraternity, right, justice, and self-evident truths—

> I am merely saying—what if these words pass?
> What if they pass and are gone and are no more,
> Eviscerated, blotted out of the world?
> They were bought with a belief and passion, at great cost.
> They were bought with the bitter and anonymous blood
> Of farmers, teachers, shoemakers and fools
> Who broke the old rule and the pride of kings.
> It took a long time to buy these words.
> It took a long time to buy them, and much pain.

It took the blood—not of anonymous, faceless people—but of the Son of God to buy our salvation. Let us not permit this truth to pass away. "The good news of our justification before God in Christ is the chief doctrine and heart and essence of the Word of God. The forgiveness of sins by grace through faith in our Redeemer, Jesus Christ, is our mightiest incentive for educating eternity."[50] The primary goal of Bethany's entire program—the curriculum, chapel services, extra-curricular activities and dormitory living—must always be eternal life.

The Scriptures place responsibility for Christian education and preserving the truth directly on the parents. Psalm 78:5,6: "He established a testimony in Jacob, and appointed a law which he commanded our fathers, that they should make them known to their children: That the generation to come know them, even the children which should be born; who arise and declare them to their children," and also in Deuteronomy 32:7, "Ask thy father, and He will show thee; thy elders they will tell thee."

---

[50] Luther Vangen, "Educating for Eternity," *Synod Report* (1966), 23.

Luther takes this responsibility so seriously that he says, "In my judgment there is no other outward offense that in the sight of God so heavily burdens the world, and deserves such heavy chastisement, as the neglect to educate children." He goes on:

> In my youth this proverb was current in the schools: "It is no less a sin to neglect a pupil than to do violence to a woman." It was used to frighten teachers. But how much lighter is this wrong against a woman (which is a bodily sin and may be atoned for), than to neglect and dishonor immortal souls, when such a sin is not recognized and can never be atoned for? O eternal woe to the world! Children are born daily and grow up among us, and there are none, alas! who feel an interest in them.[51]

He goes on and applies Matthew 18:6–7 also to the convents and schools which "are nothing but destroyers of children": "But whoso offend one of these little ones which believe in Me, it were better for him that a millstone were hanged about his neck and that he were drowned in the depths of the sea. Woe unto the world because of offences, for it must needs be that offences come. But woe to that man by whom the offence cometh." Today cannot the same words be applied to our public educational institutions generally? And does not the responsibility of parents extend beyond confirmation to elementary, secondary, and college education? It surely must, and we must heed the words of the Great Commission, "teaching them to observe all things whatsoever I have commanded" [Matthew 28:20].

As stated previously, you do have a Christian college. You do have a committed faculty and staff that teaches students to know the Holy Scriptures, "which are able to make thee wise unto salvation through faith which is in Christ Jesus" (2 Timothy 3:15). The young people of our Synod should be here, at Bethany. The June 8, 1981 issue of *Time*, in an article on Christian schools, quotes a Pentecostal pastor as saying, "Can you imagine the children of Israel coming out of Egypt, camping in the desert, and the mothers packing lunches every day and sending their kids back to Egypt for school?"[52]

It will be a real challenge during the 1980s to provide education for both temporal and spiritual needs. The words of

---

[51] F. V. N. Painter, *Luther on Education*, 178.
[52] Rev. Charles Sustar, in Kenneth M. Pierce, "Education: A Case for Moral Absolutes," *Time*, 8 June 1981.

Paul to the Philippians apply to us also: "Those things which ye have both learned and received, and heard, and seen in me, do; and the God of peace shall be with you" (Philippians 4:9).

> O blest the parents who give heed
> Unto their children's foremost need,
> And weary not of care or cost:
> To them and heaven shall none be lost. (*LHy* 234:3)

DOCUMENT 5.3:

The Lutheran Liberal Arts College in the Twenty-first Century (2000)

By Rolf Wegenke

Rolf Wegenke (1948–) is president of the Wisconsin Association of Independent Colleges and Universities, the official organization of the twenty independent, nonprofit schools in the state. He has served as chair of the Board of Regents for Wisconsin Lutheran College in Milwaukee, Wisconsin, and was also awarded the Pro Gloria Dei Award for service to God and the world. Dr. Wegenke grew up in Montello, Wisconsin, received his bachelor's degree (Phi Beta Kappa) from the University of Wisconsin at Madison, and earned both an M.A. and Ph.D. from the University of Chicago. He also has been awarded doctorates (honoris causa) from Ripon College and Beloit College. He has actively promoted educational excellence, from kindergarten through college, through his positions on a variety of boards and councils, including service as co-chair of the Wisconsin "PK-16" Leadership Council. He and his wife are members at Wisconsin Lutheran Chapel and Student Center in Madison, where he has served on the Governing Board.53 [RM]

Source: Keynote address at the Lutheran College Conference, Bethany Lutheran College, Mankato, MN, Aug. 15, 2000; rpt., *Charis: A Journal of Lutheran Scholarship, Thought, and Opinion* 1, no. 1 (2001): 6-14.

---

53   Email interview with Rolf Wegenke, 25 March 2010.

I.

It is a high honor to be asked to speak at this historic joint conference involving the faculty of Bethany Lutheran College, Martin Luther College, and Wisconsin Lutheran College. I also want to acknowledge the seminary faculty as well.

I do a lot of public speaking. As a matter of fact, for our first date, I asked my wife to come hear me give a speech. Nevertheless, I find this a daunting audience because it is your calling to embody my topic, "The Lutheran Liberal Arts College in the Twenty-first Century."

Of course, my assigned topic is, in itself, daunting. It is daunting because it is broad. I could write volumes on the power and the problems of the liberal arts—and, indeed, many more qualified than I have done just that. Then, too, the history of the Wisconsin Evangelical Lutheran Synod and the Evangelical Lutheran Synod can be seen as one long exercise in definition of what it means to be Lutheran. As if these two dimensions were not sufficient in both their extent and their complexity, the call is to set them into the context of the twenty-first century!

On his death bed, Goethe is said to have called out, "More light!" As I considered the overwhelming nature of this topic, my first instinct was to cry out, "More time!" More time to prepare and more time to present. But, coming at the end of this conference, I recognized that your attention and your goodwill would not tolerate such an imposition. I also recognized that the organizers did not expect that I would say everything there is to say about "The Lutheran Liberal Arts College in the Twenty-first Century," but rather they expected (hoped?) that I would say something cogent and insightful.

As every teacher recognizes—and as every teacher wishes students would recognize—it is much harder (but also more useful) to be cogent and insightful than it is to be definitive or exhaustive (or, I might say, to be exhausting).

My next thought was to follow the lead of Dr. Martin Luther at the Marburg Colloquy, to cease debate and to write the words of Scripture on the table. Had I adopted this approach, these are the words I would have written: "Jesus Christ is the same yesterday, today, and forever" (Hebrews 13:8). Now, I know that writing on tabletops is not what you expected either. And, of course, Luther did a lot more than write on tables both before and after Marburg. And so shall I. This passage from Hebrews is a necessary, but not a sufficient, proposition for a paper on the Lutheran liberal arts college in the twenty-first century. It is necessary, that is to say, fundamental, that the Lutheran liberal arts college of the twenty-first century should not differ from the Lutheran liberal arts college of the twentieth century in its adherence to the Word, but I would argue that it is insufficient because no one assumes that the Lutheran liberal arts colleges in their twentieth century incarnations were all they could or should be. Were that the case, there would be no need for this conference or for me to have been assigned this topic. Also, as everyone on the front lines recognizes, the essentially conservative enterprise of preserving our Lutheran heritage cannot be accomplished without a radical transformation of the way in which we "do college."

My thesis, then, is that there is more to be done to make Lutheran liberal arts colleges all they can and should be, and that it will take strenuous effort to preserve Lutheran liberal arts colleges in the twenty-first century. We need to write on tables and on walls, on our hearts and on the hearts of our students, "Jesus Christ is the same yesterday, today, and forever."

II.

Were I in this distinguished audience, I would begin now to squirm in my seat. "Great, we had to come to Mankato in August to hear the self-evident."

Were I in this audience—and given my less charitable disposition—I also might begin to gather stones. "Great, we had to come to Mankato in August to be insulted! What does he mean (or who does he think he is) saying we need to do more to proclaim the Word?"

My response would be: As Christians, we cannot return too often to the source of every good and perfect gift (James 1:17); nor can we neglect the Biblical injunction to encourage one another (Hebrews 10:25).

That the presence of the Word is self-evident in the proposition, "The Lutheran Liberal Arts College in the Twenty-first Century," does not mean that the meaning of this proposition is either self-evident or broadly or deeply understood.

And, the fact that the faculty of all three institutions are all so faithful to the Word—and I personally know this to be true—does not mean that we cannot do better.

Honsey Hall, named in honor of Professor Emeritus Rudolph ("Rudy") E. Honsey, was dedicated during the June 2010 Synod Convention. It houses the departments of communication, humanities, social and behavioral sciences, and religion.

When I was in graduate school at the University of Chicago, I remember a semantically challenged fellow student pleading with a professor that he be exempt from critiquing a book because he "agreed with it." My critique—better, my challenge—to you as faculty, as servants of the Word, is to take radical action to make our Lutheran liberal arts colleges all they can and should be and to take these colleges which you will have transformed into the twenty-first century—better, into the "kingdom come." I extend this challenge not because I do not appreciate or because I do not think you appreciate the importance of the Word in your calling. Just the opposite, like the hapless Chicago student, I agree with you and appreciate you—better, I love you—and in love, we are to serve one another (Galatians 5:13). As St. Paul wrote to Timothy, "I remind you to fan into flame the gift of God" (2 Timothy 1:6).

III.

The radical action I propose is that you as faculty and that these colleges as institutions exponentially expand your focus on Christian scholarship.

I recognize that, as faculty, you have a three-fold calling: to be teachers, to be scholars, and to engage in service. By focusing my paper on scholarship and by challenging you to increase your focus in the same direction, I am not denigrating the other two; indeed, I would argue, but not here today, that revitalizing Christian scholarship will restore the proper balance among the three and lift up both teaching and service.

IV.

The God who created all things and who is everywhere present cannot be left out of our scholarship. God must be part of, be pervasive in—better—be Lord of our scholarship, for it to be Christian.

As Lutherans, we believe in the centrality of the theology of the cross. There is no question that the pivotal event in our personal history and in the history of the world is "Jesus Christ and Him crucified" (1 Corinthians 2:2).

But, there is more to God's revelation than the fact of our salvation. There is nothing more important than this fact, but there are more facts than these.

Those of us of a certain age remember an advertising slogan, "V-8—it's not just for breakfast anymore!" Let me offer a new slogan: "God—He is not now and never has been, just for church on Sunday mornings." The modern world has driven God from the public square.[54] Often, we Christians have been complicit in the denuding of the public square; all too willing to retreat; all to reticent to advance under the banner of the cross. The world of higher education is as much a part of the public square as are politics and government. The pretense of the sciences, arts, and letters is that they are as universal in their reach as is God himself. We cannot engage in scholarship that has any validity to its claim to be Christian unless the God who flatly stated "I AM ... the Truth ..." (John 14:6) is also there.

V.

Why am I calling for a renaissance in Christian scholarship? Because the decline of Christian scholarship in other colleges and

---

[54] Richard John Neuhaus, *The Naked Public Square* (Grand Rapids: W.B. Eerdmans Publishing Company, 1984).

universities can be directly linked to the decline in Christian teaching and in Christian service, and, indeed, in the decline of Christian mission and identity.

I commend to you two superb books on this topic: *The Soul of the American University: From Protestant Establishment to Established Nonbelief*[55] and *The Dying of the Light: The Disengagement of Colleges and Universities from Their Christian Churches*.[56] These two books document that the expulsion of God from the academy was not the result of militant atheists and ruthless secularizers storming the ivy-covered barricades. No, rather, the story is much less heroic. Faculty and administrators (deliberately and almost gleefully) traded their Christian heritage for the pottage of acceptance by their unbelieving colleagues. The Truth was not lost; it was thrown away with both hands. The recent history of much of Christian higher education parallels the modern development of sciences, arts, and letters. There has been a loss of nerve, which is really a loss of faith, in all fields of human endeavor. Wherein does this loss of faith consist? It is a loss of faith in the very existence of truth. If you could see my paper, you would see that I have not capitalized the word "truth" in this instance, although I did in all previous instances. What has been lost in all of modern academia is a belief that there is such a thing as truth. This loss of faith clearly has its intellectual antecedents in the loss of faith in the One who is the Truth (I used capitals here), but it is more pervasive. For millennia, thinking people—including those people who never heard of the God of Israel or of Jesus of Nazareth—searched for, claimed to have found, and, indeed, had found things that were true. In different ways, both Socrates and Einstein identified the truth. In the last century and a half, the term "truth" was reduced to "truth claims" and, then "truth claims" themselves were ruled unacceptable in sciences, arts, and letters.

A recent exchange in the *Chronicle of Higher Education* illustrates how pervasive this rejection of "truth claims" has become. Russell T. McCutcheon, associate professor of religious studies at Southwest Missouri State University, vehemently objected to an essay by Arthur Schwartz of the John Templeton

---

[55] George M. Marsden, *The Soul of the American University: From Protestant Establishment to Established Nonbelief* (New York: Oxford University Press, 1994).

[56] James Tunstead Burtchaell, *The Dying of the Light: The Disengagement of Colleges and Universities from Their Christian Churches* (Grand Rapids: W.B. Eerdmans Publishing Company, 1998).

Foundation regarding "character education." He strongly criticizes Schwartz's use of what he calls the

> rhetorically loaded terms "responsible," "mature," and "adult," ... [citing them as] the very reason that critics work to lay bare the unspoken politics that drive the discourse on principles, values, and character—whether politically liberal or conservative. In seeking to portray one set of *ad hoc* values as self-evident and beyond critique, writers on both sides of the political divide portray the world all too simply, as if we all have some built-in moral compass (call it a soul or human nature—same difference) which just happens to coincide with their group's interests.
>
> Not wanting to name their viewpoint too openly, writers often rely on empty terms that take on meaning only if their readers presuppose some undisclosed standard. In Schwartz's case, to deviate from this unknown standard renders one an irresponsible, immature child. What better way to characterize one's political enemies? Although he claims "character" is politically neutral, Schwartz's deft rhetoric of "responsibility" and "maturity" suggests that he knows otherwise.[57]

My quarrel with Professor McCutcheon is not that he opposes the use of "loaded" words to disguise the author's intent, nor do I carry any grief for Mr. Schwartz. Rather, it is his dismissal of the "built-in moral compass (call it a soul or human nature)...." What he is saying is that moral propositions and what used to be called natural laws are not true, do not exist. He rejects any presupposition that there are absolutes, any such things as standards, any such thing as the truth.

Contemporary culture and much of contemporary scholarship would say that a "truth claim," self-evidently, means, "What does it mean to me?" or, "What does it mean to you?" I am by no means dismissive of the psychic or emotional dimension of the truth. God, after all, is also the God of our emotions. However, to contradict Protagoras' dictum, "man is the measure of all things," I want to assert that God is the measure of all things, including scholarship. This assertion is itself radical not only in academia, but in all of contemporary culture. I recall hearing a broadcast interview with a woman at a shopping mall in Ohio where a gunman had just randomly murdered some shoppers. The

---

[57] Russell T. McCutcheon, "Letter," *The Chronicle of Higher Education*, 21 July 2000, B3.

woman said (as best as I can recollect), "Well, I don't know, but to me, it is wrong." The rejection of external and absolute standards is even more pervasive in academia because it has a longer history there and because, in large part, this "rejectionism" started in higher education.

Clearly, other Christians have addressed the issue of the nature of higher education. John Henry Cardinal Newman's *The Idea of the University*[58] and Jaroslav Pelikan's *The Idea of the University: A Reexamination*[59] speak to this topic, but in most cases, their presuppositions on the nature of truth are implicit. What I am proposing, then, is that the truth—capital and small letter *T*—needs to be made explicit in our Christian scholarship.

VI.

My task, then, is to be prescriptive, to provide a prescription for the rekindling of the light; or, to use St. Paul's language quoted earlier, "to fan into flame the gift of God." In essence, it all comes back to faith. "Out of the abundance of a man's heart he will speak" (Matthew 12:34). Again, I am not speaking primarily of saving faith. "Everyone who calls on the name of the Lord will be saved" (Romans 10:13). Saving faith is essential, but to fulfill the responsibilities of your calling as scholars in Lutheran liberal arts colleges, you must seek out the full counsel of God (Acts 20:27). God who is the Truth, who created everything, is, of necessity, part of your scholarship.

Many have said that Christian scholarship means nothing more and nothing less than the fact that I, the professor, am a redeemed child of God. As such, I follow the Scriptural dictum, "Whether you eat or drink or whatever you do, do it all for the glory of God" (1 Corinthians 10:31). Beyond this emphasis on the quality of our performance, this response could be read as an assertion that there is no difference in my scholarship (and, implicitly, in my teaching) in comparison to the scholarship found in any secular college or university, except that they are "better" or are reflective of a more highly-motivated effort. Another way to express it was summarized in two statements I have heard on the campuses of Christian colleges: "There is no such thing as

---

[58] John Henry Cardinal Newman, *The Idea of a University: Defined and Illustrated* (Washington, DC: Regenery Publishing, 1999).

[59] Jaroslav Pelikan, *The Idea of the University: A Reexamination* (New Haven: Yale University Press, 1992).

Christian physics, there is only good physics taught by a Christian." Or, "I open my class with prayer and there is daily chapel and Bible study here, but what we teach is the same." I would have to say that, if the quality of our performance or the coexistence of prayer and Bible study on the same plot of land is all there is to Christian higher education, we should close the doors of these colleges and support instead campus ministries at secular colleges and universities. The only rationale for the Lutheran liberal arts college is that what is taught in the classroom is based on the Truth, and that real truth, that complete truth, is based on the Word of God.

The denial that there is such a thing as Christian physics or sociology or linguistics or sculpting or biology is widespread. One Christian scholar has written, "It is a puzzling phenomenon that, among so many academics who are professing Christians, all but a tiny minority keep quiet about the intellectual implications of their faith."[60] It is the unraveling (or, better, knitting together) of the intellectual implications of our Christian faith within our respective disciplines that constitutes true Christian scholarship. This is not to say that there should not be opening prayer in classes or Chapel or separate Bible studies. They should all be there. But we should not privatize our faith. Remember, God is not just for Sunday morning.

There is a real and dangerous tendency, especially among Christian intellectuals, to reduce the revelation of God to a set of abstract propositions. This view identifies the rational with the spiritual and separates it from the material. Yet, our God created the heavens and the earth; the antichrist is the one who denies that Jesus Christ came in the flesh (1 John 4:3). We eat and drink the body and blood of Christ (1 Corinthians 11:27-29). At our resurrection, as Job said, in our flesh [we] shall see God (Job 19:26). "For in Him we live and move and have our being" (Acts 17:28). "For from Him and through Him and to Him are all things" (Romans 11:36).

"The modern solution is radically defective," my professors at the University of Chicago were fond of saying. Modern scholarship claims that only the material—that which can be touched and measured—is real, is factual. This leaves all the rest—love, beauty, morality, reason, religion—in a never-never land, neither true nor false because, in their view, they are not factual. This approach

---

[60] George M. Marsden, *The Outrageous Idea of Christian Scholarship* (New York: Oxford University Press, 1997), 6.

undermines and ultimately destroys scholarship—and particularly science—itself. If only the material is factual, then scientific predictions and theorems also fall to the ground (or, better, dissipate in ether), along with beauty and morality. In general, scholarship ignores the self-destructive implications of its methodology when it affects science, but applies it with vigor to moral and religious questions. Christian scholars fall into this trap when they over-intellectualize their faith, when they attempt to defend the Bible by saying it is not a science textbook. Of course, it is not a science textbook, but it is a book that can tell us the true meaning of science. Because modern scholarship has declared the immaterial to be unreal, it has told a big lie. A Christian college, then, is the last place on the earth where higher education is truly connected to the real world. Last week, at a conference in Colorado, I saw survey research which shows the general public believes that Christian education is not part of the "real world." They have missed the point. The Christian college is the only "real world" academic institution in this world.

The meaning of your call as scholars in Lutheran liberal arts colleges, then, is to engage in the kind of rigorous scholarship that reunites body, soul, and spirit; scholarship that reintroduces the Truth into all of the disciplines; that reconnects the material and the spiritual under their proper name: factual. There is no dichotomy of facts and values because, as the old spiritual says, "The Lord God made them all."[61]

Any basic compilation of the complete works of Aristotle contains both his *Physics* and his *Ethics*.[62] For millennia, scholarship did not brand the material factual and the immaterial nonfactual (and, hence, untrue). Your mission as Christian scholars, then (and you have all chosen to accept it), is to remedy the "radical defects of the modern solution" by restoring the ancient ways, the ways of the Truth. This is not easy. To be effective Christian scholars in Lutheran liberal arts colleges you must first be faithful to the One who has called you and second be scholars. There are precious few doing the kind of scholarship that I am talking about. You can not just regurgitate your notes from graduate school or keep up on the literature in the field. Remember, the bulk of modern scholarship is defective; it is

---

[61] Cecil F. Alexander, "All Things Bright and Beautiful," *Let All the People Praise You: A Song Book* (Milwaukee: Northwestern Publishing House, 1999).

[62] E.g., Aristotle, *The Basic Works of Aristotle,* ed. Richard McKeon (New York: Random House, 1941).

defective because it is incomplete, because the *God Who is There*[63] is not there at all.

VII.

I do not want to complain about the defects and failures of modern scholarship and just leave it at that. Too often Lutherans have given the impression that we interpret the Great Commission to be, "Go unto all the world and teach everyone where they got their doctrine wrong." Criticizing modern scholarship is necessary to make the case for Christian scholarship, but it still does not give us a clue on how to begin this great intellectual work.

One Christian scholar has written:

> Even mathematicians or technical scientists will be able to point out some faith-related considerations that have relevance to the **foundational questions** affecting the **frameworks** of their disciplines or the **applications** of their work. It simply does not follow that, because there is no special Christian view of photosynthesis, there is therefore not a Christian view of biology.[64]

The key points I take from this quotation are: one, "the foundational questions affecting the framework of their discipline," and two, "the applications of their work." Put another way, Christian scholarship must be Christian in its **foundational framework** and alert to the Christian **implications** of its work.

Again, this kind of scholarship is not easy, especially if it is well done. But, on the other hand, the Christian scholar's calling is the answer to every dissertator's dream. You are in a position to make "an original contribution to knowledge." Because of the radical defects of modernity, you, the Christian scholar, have unlimited intellectual—that is to say, scholarly—opportunity.

I want to be clear that I am talking about real scholarship here. It is necessary, but not sufficient, to do what I have done here today. It is not enough simply to assert that God is the Truth and that God is the Lord of the intellect. The comedienne Joan Rivers has told of trying to impress a date by placing an open Bible on the dining room table and writing "True!" in the margins.

---

[63] Francis A. Schaeffer, *The God Who is There* (Downers Grove: Inter-Varsity Press, 1968).
[64] Marsden, *The Outrageous Idea of Christian Scholarship*, 6 (emphasis added).

Proclamation is part of the task of the Church and of all Christians, including all Christian scholars, but proclamation is not the same as scholarship.

Including in your scholarship both your **fundamental framework** and an analysis of all the **implications** means that your work is harder and more complicated than that of secular scholars. To paraphrase the old adage, "Secular scholars work from sun to sun, but a Christian scholar's work is never done." Every monograph you write requires another chapter; every article another section; every lesson plan another theme.

Dr. David Whalen, an associate professor at Hillsdale College, has provided an example of this kind of scholarship. He wrote, "The best thing about biochemistry is not learning the mere procedural facility with say, acid-base titration, but entering into one's own nature and pondering the implications of our material being. The glory of economics [or business courses] has little to do with understanding multipliers or even scarcity, however useful these [concepts] may be, but rather [to explicate] what it means to be one who, in concert with his kind, moves among the myriad contingencies of material conditions and decisions."[65]

Or, take history. It has often been said that Christianity is a historic religion. Certainly, it has a long history; indeed, from eternity (Ephesians 3:9-11). Christianity also asserts that there are such things as historical facts, facts which are knowable and important. In 1 Corinthians 15 we read, "For what I received I passed on to you as the first importance: that Christ died for our sins according to the Scriptures, that He was buried, that He was raised on the third day, according to the Scriptures and that He appeared to Peter, and then to the twelve. After that, He appeared to more than 500 of the brothers at the same time. . . . And if Christ has not been raised, our preaching is useless and so is your faith" (1 Corinthians 15:3-6,14). In other words, if we find Christ's body fossilized in a grave in Israel, it is all over. History matters to the Truth, and the Truth is historical. Most recent histories of religion, on the other hand, talk of the "Jesus idea," while declaring it irrelevant whether or not Jesus ever existed. Contemporary history is historicist; that is, it denies that we can know facts, that facts matter, and that facts have implications; that is, that facts can be the basis of moral judgments.

---

[65] David M. Whalen, "A Student's Garden of Terrors," *Touchstone: A Journal of Ecumenical Orthodoxy*, 13, no. 4 (May 2000): n.p.

Bethany's Honsey Hall collects sunlight through windows on the upper level and reflects it down to the main level. An inscription beside the entrance expresses the spiritual significance of the architecture: "Your word is a lamp to my feet and a light to my path" (Psalm 119:105).

In letters, too, we have come a long way (downhill) from John Milton, who wrote *Paradise Lost* "to justify ways of God to man."[66] However, it is not just the content of literature that has lost its connection to the Truth, but also its form which seeks to disorient and to disturb, not to convey, the Truth.

Social sciences also have become enamored of methodology and description, leaving aside what are dismissively called "truth claims." For example, even among Christian social scientists you can find studies of the Sacraments that emphasize "smells and bells" or that measure personal preferences or opinions of those in the pews. Descriptions of the externals do not tell us whether a high view of the Sacraments is true. Nor do personal preferences of the opposition make a high view of the sacraments false. "Will their lack of faith nullify God's faithfulness? Not at all! Let God be true and every man a liar" (Romans 3:3-4; cp. 1 John 5:9-11).

Woodrow Wilson, before he became President of Princeton University and President of the United States, was a social scientist of some renown who recognized that the scholar's understanding of the nature of the world affected scholarship and its application. He wrote:

> Jefferson wrote of the "Laws of Nature"—and then by way of an afterthought—"and of Nature's God." And they constructed a government as they would have constructed an orrery [a mechanical model of the solar system]—to display the laws of nature. Politics in their thought was a variety of mechanics. The Constitution was founded on the law of gravitation. The government was to exist and [be] moved by virtue of the efficacy of checks and balances.
>
> The trouble with the theory is that government is not a machine, but a living thing. It falls, not under the theory of the universe, but under the theory of organic life. It is accountable to Darwin, not to Newton. It is modified by its environment, necessitated by its tasks, shaped to its functions by the sheer pressure of life.[67]

I am not saying that Wilson was right in elevating Darwin over Newton; indeed, a true understanding of the foundations of

---

66 John Milton, "Paradise Lost," *John Milton: Complete Poems and Major Prose*, ed. Merrit Y. Hughes (New York: Bobbs-Merrill Company, 1957), 212.
67 Woodrow Wilson, quoted in Larry P. Arnn, *Imprimis* 20, no. 6 (June 2000): 4.

government would come from the Word.⁶⁸ The Darwinian presupposition eradicates morality from the polity: politics becomes a matter of the survival of the fittest, while the so-called mechanistic system presupposes both original sin and the restraint of sinful impulses by checks and balances. Again, **fundamental framework** and **implications**.

I would be remiss if I did not distinguish the way in which we should integrate the truth (lower-case and capital *T*) into our scholarship. While we should make sure that our **fundamental framework** and our discussion of **the implications** of our scholarship are rooted in the Truth, we should not claim that all of the conclusions of our scholarship are therefore of the same status—are therefore true. It is possible, for example, for Christian scholars to be wrong in their conclusions about the relationship of hormones to muscle mass, or about whether an antiballistic missile system would enhance international security, without being wrong about who created life or about the blessings He bestows on peace. Faithfulness to the Word does not make all of our pronouncements *ex cathedra*.⁶⁹

VIII.

I want to say a word here about academic freedom. As I said before, the record of Christian colleges shows the faculty and administrators giving away their Christian heritage with both hands. In large part, this dreadful state of affairs came about because of a lack of nerve and because of the loss of faith, but often the *raison d'être* [purpose for existing] was academic freedom; it was argued that conforming scholarship to the Word of God was trumped (trampled?) by the pursuit of truth. Scripture was cited: "You will know the truth and the truth will make you free" (John 8:32). You see the omission here: the assumption is that Christianity is not, in its totality, true or that it is true only in churchly things, but not in sciences, arts, and letters. It all comes back to the loss of faith.

In reality, the truth does make you free. True Christian

---

68   Rolf Wegenke, "Christian Citizenship and Civic Responsibility," The Christian, the Church and the Government: A Symposium, Martin Luther College, New Ulm, MN, April 17, 1999.

69   This paragraph was added at the suggestion of Professor Thomas Kuster of Bethany. I am grateful for his insight. *Editors' note*: The phrase *ex cathedra* refers to the official pronouncements of doctrine that the Pontiff in Rome makes.

scholarship of the kind that puts God back into the center of all knowledge is liberating because it is valid; it is True. The one constant, valid thing is there.

In the great novel *Middlemarch,* the Rev. Casaubon was searching for the key to all mythologies.[70] We have that key which is powerful and effective because it is true. As I have said, there is the already-tired cliché that the Bible is not a science text. It is not. It is more than a science text. It is the key to the truth of the sciences. Using this key, you can write better (true) science texts. The key is like Archimedes' lever—with it we can move the world or, to use Scriptural terms, "I can do everything through Him who gives me strength" (Philippians 4:13).

There also are practical reasons for pursuing Christian scholarship as illustrated by my five-year old son, Erich. A few months ago, he said, "You know, Daddy, I have been thinking about the Big Bang. Do you suppose when God said, 'Let there be light,' there was a big bang, but, because there were no scientists around at the time, they didn't realize that God made the Big Bang?" I recount this story, not to endorse my son's cosmology, but rather to point out that, if you don't reconnect God to your disciplines, to your scholarship, someone else will do it, and there is a great chance something will go astray.

There are also spiritual reasons as well as practical reasons for emphasizing Christian scholarship. What you teach in your disciplines must be true. Not only must your data be verified and your citations be accurate, but, regardless of your subject matter, you must teach the One Who is the Truth. In Ezekiel we read:

> Prophesy against the prophets of Israel who are now prophesying. Say to those who prophesy out of their own imagination: hear the Word of the Lord! This is what the Sovereign Lord says: Woe to the foolish prophets who follow their own spirit and have seen nothing! . . . [T]heir visions are false and their divinations a lie. They say, "the Lord declares," when the Lord has not sent them. . . . Therefore, this is what the Sovereign Lord says: Because of your false words and lying visions, I am against you, declares the Sovereign Lord. (Ezekiel 13:2-8)

This is serious business. Scholarship which is purely human is a lie, is an offense against God. We must not think that if we fail

---

[70] George Eliot, *Middlemarch* (New York: American Publishers Corporation, 1897).

to reconnect our scholarship to the Truth, that we have nonetheless done something of value in teaching business statistics or astronomy or music; we must also not think that we will escape God's wrath.

Moreover, the Great Commission, "Go into all the world and preach the gospel to every creature" (Mark 16:15), applies to Christian academics as much as it does to other Christians. Martin Luther is lauded for translating the Bible into "the language of the people," an action of great scholarship and of great artistry, but, more important, an action which carried out the Great Commission.

The church—particularly our church, the Lutheran Church—has been slow to undertake similar mission work. We were slow to translate our liturgies from German and Scandinavian languages, just as we were slow to reach out to urban neighborhoods and to racial and ethnic minorities.

I would argue that we are similarly laggard in undertaking a new translation. The world is increasingly educated—knowledge is exploding, information is proliferating. However, a wealth of knowledge is no guarantee against a poverty of wisdom.

It is up to us, as Christian scholars, to translate the everlasting Truth into the new language of the New World. The New World is the world of the intellect. Mark Noll's *The Scandal of the Evangelical Mind*[71] documents a certain simplistic flabbiness in evangelical theology, but I would argue that it goes well beyond theology. I would argue that the Christian response to the life of the mind has frequently been one of bigotry, hostility, and neglect; that we have been dismissive of intellectual gifts and pursuits; that we have seen aspirations to scholarly life as "dangerous." Of course, it is dangerous; just as there was and still is the danger of losing one's life in foreign mission fields, there is danger of losing one's soul in this mission field. Jesus warns us not to expect our witnessing to be easy (Luke 9:62; Mark 10:30).

My exhortation today—whether you teach biochemistry or business or history or poetry or theology—is that you commit yourself to Christian scholarship. I am persuaded that a renewal of Christian scholarship will revitalize also your Christian teaching and your service.

Again, as teachers at a Lutheran liberal arts college, I would argue that you must engage in Christian scholarship which goes

---

[71] Mark Noll, *The Scandal of the Evangelical Mind* (Grand Rapids: W.B. Eerdmans Publishing Company, 1994).

beyond simple proclamation. You must do the hard intellectual work of uniting your **fundamental framework** with your disciplines and spelling out the full **implications** of the applications to your disciplines. You must bring reality—that is to say, the Truth, that is to say, God—back into sciences, arts, and letters. You must do this because to teach the same scholarship as taught on the secular campus or by your secular graduate schools on Christian campuses is to fail to teach the Truth and is to be derelict in your calling.

There is, of course, more to your teaching than your subject matter. The way in which you teach is to be patterned on Christ Himself. Your pupils are among those you are to love as you love yourself (Luke 10:27). Jesus was often called Teacher. And as a great (the greatest) Teacher, He can teach us about teaching. Certainly, He did not "dumb down" his lessons; Scripture is replete with things that are hard to understand (Luke 8:10; 2 Peter 3:16). At the same time, He used parables and demonstrations to drive home the truth of His message.

Such Christian scholarship will renew (I might say, sanctify) your teaching. It will also undergird the liberal arts.

A clear side effect of the knowledge explosion is that there is a loss of ability to communicate across disciplines, much less for them to enrich each other. This loss of the ability to communicate is a great tragedy. Not only are we diminished as individuals by not being able to understand areas outside of our specialty, but we also have a breakdown in community, which has other negative consequences for life on this planet.

Here Christian scholarship comes to the rescue of the liberal arts. We can restore communication and community by elucidating (in both senses of that word) the key to all knowledge, the God Who Is the Truth.

IX.

When I have discussed the topic of Christian scholarship in other venues, I have been told that it is too hard, that the opposition is too strong, that we do not have the critical mass of Christian academics necessary to bring it off, and (this is what I often think on sleepless nights) that I do not have the intellectual capacity to carry out this great task. Remember Moses, too, felt that he did not have the gifts to respond to God's call (Exodus 4:10-17). Elijah felt that he alone was left in Israel to do the work of the Lord (1 Kings 19:10,18).

Indeed, when I had finished the next to final draft of this paper, I stumbled upon George Marsden's book, *The Outrageous Idea of Christian Scholarship*. At first, I was troubled that so much of what I had written and thought for nearly twenty-five years was not original. Then, I realized the great comfort that we are not alone. And in this comfort, there is hope. Dr. Marsden has laid out a plan for Christian scholarship:

> Academic communities are invaluable and can sustain a depth of sophistication regarding the implications of faith and scholarship that is unattainable in diverse settings [i.e., the secular university]. Yet, while Protestants support educational institutions at every other level, they have almost nothing [yet] to offer at the highest levels of scholarship.
>
> An even simpler way to resist the trend toward secular academic conformity is to adopt faculty development programs that cultivate the Christian academic consciousness of faculty who are already seriously religious. Most church-related schools have many faculty who are personally pious but consider their religion a private affair and so do not relate it to their academic life. They have not been exposed to academic culture where discussions of faith and learning are high-level intellectual concerns.[72]

This is nothing less than a lesson plan for revitalizing Christian scholarship at the Christian college. And, note that it centers on faculty development. While Dr. Marsden hopes that Christian scholars at secular institutions can network to help each other with Christianizing their scholarship, you already have the network at your individual campuses and in this conference.

You never know what might happen when you ask someone like me to speak. I am going to stray into the next session and give my ten cents' worth on what should be done next. I think you could not go wrong in emphasizing, as one of your objectives, faculty development focused on Christian scholarship.

The God of all comfort strengthens us. St. Paul, who himself was lacking in certain gifts and who faced overwhelming opposition, declared, "I can do all things through Christ who strengthens me" (Philippians 4:13).

---

[72] Marsden, *The Outrageous Idea of Christian Scholarship*, 57, 102, 106 (emphasis added).

Our calling is not to fear but to go and to do. "For God did not give us a spirit of timidity, but a spirit of power, of love, and of self-discipline" (2 Timothy 1:7). I am confident that the Lutheran liberal arts college in the twenty-first century will be a great and mighty work of God because of Christian scholarship and Christian scholars like you. James Madison wrote regarding a university that "after all, the most effectual safeguard against heretical intrusions in the School . . . will be an Able & Orthodox Professor, whose course of instruction will be an example to his successors."[73] I know many of you. I am in awe of the Christian scholarship that has been done by the faculty at these colleges. But have we—will we—always succeed? No, we have failed; more than failed, we have sinned. And intellectual sins are particularly ugly. But remember, the success of our witness as Christian scholars does not depend on us. "Thanks be to God: He gives us the victory through our Lord Jesus Christ" (1 Corinthians 15:57).

---

[73] Arnn, *Imprimis*, 4.

Between the 1940s (above) and 2007 (below), enrollment increased substantially, the high school program was discontinued, a bachelaureate degree was added, and numerous other changes impacted the Bethany campus. Meanwhile, the Christian liberal arts ideal remained.

DOCUMENT 5.4:

The Liberal Arts: Our Common Understanding (2002)

By the Bethany Lutheran College Faculty

Source: *Bethany Lutheran College Faculty Handbook, 2006–2007*, Section 8. The statement was adopted by the Faculty in 2002.

During the 2000-2001 school year, Bethany faculty—individually and in their academic divisions—re-examined their conceptions of a "liberal arts education." Through discussion, lines of consensus emerged, best articulated not through lists of disciplines or courses, but rather a vision of a particular approach to teaching and learning which we term here "a liberal arts education." While differences in perception and emphasis remain, this consensus can guide us as we continue to define Bethany Lutheran College as it has been throughout its history—a Christian liberal arts institution.

A Liberal Arts Education Begins with Scriptural Illumination

Always understood and developed in Holy Scripture's light, a liberal arts education can provide students with a moral and intellectual compass directed toward the pursuit of truth, justice, and beauty. We consider a liberal arts education fundamental in achieving the college's basic mission, namely, to enable students to grow in the grace and knowledge of their Lord and Savior Jesus Christ by means of the Gospel [cf. **Document 3.7**].

A Liberal Arts Education Opens Access to Foundational Knowledge

We recognize the existence of a rich body of knowledge developed throughout the history of human endeavor, and consider a liberal arts education the doorway by which students gain access to it, providing them a common knowledge foundation, a cultural literacy which they can bring to bear in a Christian manner on their lives, vocations, and personal development.

A Liberal Arts Education Focuses on Fundamental Questions

A liberal arts education embodies perspectives that focus students on important, fundamental issues, not least among them the basic nature of human beings as spiritual, physical, rational, social, cultural, and ethical beings blessed as we confess in the Apostles' Creed.

A Liberal Arts Education Provides a Broad Perspective

Multidisciplinary by definition, a liberal arts approach encourages creative insights into the connections and mutual influences between various academic specialties, between culture and Christianity, between faith and learning, and between mind, body, and spirit, as each relates to the well being of individuals and their interaction with society and the physical world. Made culturally literate by a liberal arts education, students learn to view any question or issue, whether theoretical or practical, against its relevant historical, economic, aesthetic, and ethical background. Yet breadth of knowledge does not imply shallowness, since depth too is required as students develop a perception of reality conforming with Scripture and illumined by a comprehension of history, literature, science, and the arts.

Professor Rudolph Honsey, who served on the Bethany Lutheran College faculty from 1945 until 1994, exemplified the college's liberal arts ideal. His teaching repertoire included Hebrew, Norwegian, German, Humanities, Social Studies, and Religion; in each of these subjects, he showed pastoral concern for students' full development.

A Liberal Arts Education
Realizes Lofty Individual Characteristics

We expect their liberal arts education to endow students with a wide variety of desirable skills and motivations, so that, among other things, they are:

> active in life-long learning, with an engaged mind, and a "philosophical habit," inspired by a perpetual sense of wonderment.
>
> filled with a love of knowledge for its own sake—yet appreciating its usefulness, primarily in enabling them to become responsible and productive citizens of church and world, to live full Spirit-filled lives, and to pursue a fulfilling vocation.
>
> committed to universal intellectual standards of thought.
>
> creative in problem solving, as well as in expression.
>
> able to ask fundamental significant questions, in order to cultivate a perception of reality conforming to Scripture and

guided by comprehension of a broad spectrum of human knowledge.

skilled at thinking critically, at meta-thinking, and at communicating with clarity and power both orally and in writing.

zealous for what is true and good, Scripturally and ethically.

oriented to service of God and humankind.

liberated from prejudice and narrowness, and in touch with the resources that enable a full and satisfying life.

This understanding of our educational enterprise, then, is the background against which we believe all new and current programs, as well as individual courses, of the college should be developed. While a course oriented to professional preparation may appear in the curriculum from time to time, the programs in which these courses function should as a whole clearly reflect the principles of a liberal arts education reflected here. Moreover, we expect this vision to appear throughout the curriculum, not only in a "general education" component that, while important to a liberal arts education, is not by itself sufficient to provide one. This is our common understanding of a liberal arts education.

DOCUMENT 5.5:

Luther, Lutherans, and Liberal Arts Education (2005)

By Paul Lehninger

Paul Lehninger (1951–) is Professor of Theology at Wisconsin Lutheran College, where he also serves as chair of the School of Humanities and teaches dogmatics, worship, and New Testament. He previously served as pastor of The Lutheran Church of the Abiding Word, Somers, Wisconsin (1984–1990); Prince of Peace Lutheran Church, Yuma, Arizona (1979–1984), and Igreja Lutherana Brasileira da Consolação, Gravataí, Brazil (1978–1979). He received his B.A. from the University of Wisconsin (1973), his M.Div. from Wisconsin Lutheran Seminary (1978), and his doctoral degree from Marquette University (1999). His dissertation was entitled "Luther and Theosis: Deification in the Theology of Martin Luther." He  also attended Bethany Lutheran College for a year (1973–1974) as part of the Mequon Program. Dr. Lehninger serves as a consultant for Luther Digest *and an editor for* Logia.[74]

Source: Lehninger, Paul. "Luther, Lutherans, and Liberal Arts Education." 38th Annual Reformation Lectures, Bethany Lutheran College, Mankato, MN, 27–28 Oct. 2005. Rpt., *Lutheran Synod Quarterly* 46, no. 1 (March 2006): 44–67.

---

[74] Email from Paul Lehninger, 12 Apr. 2011.

The relationship between the Christian church and the secular academy has been by turns fruitful, challenging, and problematic since the earliest years of the Christian church. The question asked by Tertullian (*ca.* 160–*ca.* 230 A.D.), "What indeed has Athens to do with Jerusalem?" has been vexing Christian teachers from Tertullian's day until the present. At times, the answer has been that of Tertullian; in short, Athens has almost nothing to do with Jerusalem:

> When the apostle would restrain us, he expressly names philosophy as that which he would have us be on our guard against. Writing to the Colossians, he says, "See that no one beguile you through philosophy and vain deceit, after the tradition of men, and contrary to the wisdom of the Holy Ghost" [Colossians 2:8]. He had been at Athens, and had in his interviews (with philosophers) become acquainted with that human wisdom which pretends to know the truth, whilst it only corrupts it, and is itself divided into its own manifold heresies, by the variety of its mutually repugnant sects. What indeed has Athens to do with Jerusalem? What concord is there between the Academy and the Church? What between heretics and Christians? . . . Away with all attempts to produce a mottled Christianity of Stoic, Platonic, and dialectic composition! We want no curious disputation after possessing Christ Jesus, no inquisition after enjoying the gospel! With our faith, we desire no further belief. For this is our palmary faith, that there is nothing which we ought to believe besides.[75]

Many Christians today, who see the post-Enlightenment university as a bastion of rationalism and scientific method, with no room for the supernatural or the intervention of a God who reveals himself, would agree. On the other hand, some Christians long ago cozied up to the academy and today are so entangled in its embrace that they cannot distinguish between the Christian church and their own razed-and-rebuilt pseudo-Jerusalem.

But these are not the only two options. The Christian church has not always walled itself off against the intrusion of all extra-biblical learning, nor has it always surrendered to be occupied and ravished by marauding bands of Plotinian Neo-Platonists, Latin Averroists, Marxists, Freudians, and Neo-Darwinians. At times in her history, with the faith revealed by the Triune God in the Scriptures as her first principle, the church has sought further

---

[75] Tertullian, *Ante-Nicene Fathers*, 3:7.

understanding through a deep and detailed exploration of the world around her, and as a result enriched both the church and the academy. The contribution made by the Lutheran Church to this exploration has been valuable and is worth revisiting. . . .[76]

What emphases in Luther, then, contribute to an understanding of what should characterize a Lutheran liberal arts education?[77] The Lutheran principle of holding truths in tension, sometimes called the Lutheran principle of paradox, certainly applies. Faith and reason are not antithetical; although reason must always be subservient to faith, each plays its proper role, and each is indispensable. Languages and the arts are needed in order to read, understand, interpret, and proclaim the Scriptures, and faith must always direct the proper use of these arts. Since the Christian is *simul iustus et peccator*[78] (another tension), the question must always be asked whether reason is being applied properly to the study of the arts.

The Christian also lives, paradoxically, in two kingdoms. Here the Christian enjoys the best of both worlds. While using the arts for the benefit of the Church, the Christian does not have to "convert" or "Christianize" them, but can use them selectively and judiciously, even in their "unbaptized" state, recognizing the sacred and the secular "as two realms of a single reality, that is, God's creation."[79] Moreover, an education in the liberal arts is of benefit to both kingdoms. A state-supported education can provide valuable training for those who will serve in the church, and a church-sponsored education produces citizens equipped for service in the community and the nation.

A Lutheran liberal arts education will also take into account

---

[76] *Editors' note*: A section exploring Luther's own philosophy of education, as it related to his sixteenth-century German context, has been omitted.

[77] A study of references to the liberal arts in the Book of Concord would be a worthwhile topic for another paper. Similarly, a review of the educational reforms of other Reformation-era Lutherans would be beneficial, for example the significance of Melanchthon's *Evangelische Schulordnungen* (see Frederick Eby, *Early Protestant Educators* [New York: AMS, 1971], 180–87) and Johann Bugenhagen's *Braunschweigische Schulordnungen* (Eby, 193–206).

[78] *Editors' note*: This Latin phrase, meaning "at the same time, saint and sinner," refers to God's gracious declaration in Christ that we are justified despite our sin.

[79] Paul J. Dovre, "The Vocation of a Liberal Arts College Revisited," part of the web companion guide to *Our Calling in Education: A Lutheran Study*. http://www.elca.org/socialstatements/education/involved/dovre1.html.

Luther's affirmation of the goodness of God's creation.[80] The arts open a door to the entire created universe, which is waiting to be explored. Although the created order has been radically disfigured because of the effects of sin, God's goodness and beauty still shine through it. When reason, properly directed, undertakes this exploration of the created order, it begins a task that results in glorifying God.

Educators and students stand at the threshold of an adventure, and can undertake the educational enterprise with a spirit of optimism.

Luther is critical of those who reject formal education and pursue a trade for purely materialistic reasons.[81] But it is the motive, not the pursuit of a profession or trade, that he criticizes. Luther's understanding of the value of every honorable vocation must be central to a truly Lutheran liberal arts education.[82] Luther certainly honors the preaching office, the pastoral ministry, above all others. But because he recognizes the vital importance of education, the office of teaching runs a very close second. "If I could leave the preaching office and my other duties, or had to do so, there is no other office I would rather have than that of schoolmaster or teacher of boys; for I know that next to that of preaching, this is the best, greatest, and most useful office there is."[83] Although teacher training is often classified as a professional program and not part of a true liberal arts curriculum, a Lutheran college will certainly set as a priority training teachers for the church and for society at large. In addition, students who are training to be teachers will profit greatly from a thorough grounding in the liberal arts; later, this will be of incalculable benefit to their students, also.[84] The high value given to all vocations will be reflected in mutual respect among those teaching in various disciplines, in encouraging students to pursue excellence no matter what program they are studying, and in instilling in students an attitude of respect for people in all callings

---

[80] In addition to the references previously cited, see Luther's commentaries on Genesis and the Psalms.

[81] Martin Luther, "A Sermon on Keeping Children in School" (1530), in *Luther's Works*, vol. 46, ed. Helmut T. Lehmann (Philadelphia: Fortress Press, 1967), 207–58, at 216.

[82] See, for example, Gene Edward Veith, *God at Work: Your Christian Vocation in All of Life* (Wheaton, IL: Crossway Books, 2002), and Gustaf Wingren, *Luther on Vocation* (Eugene, OR: Wipf and Stock, 2004).

[83] Martin Luther, "A Sermon on Keeping Children in School," 253.

[84] Jaroslav Pelikan, *The Idea of the University: A Reexamination* (New Haven: Yale University Press, 1992), 176.

in life. After all, the liberal arts are not the exclusive possession of those who possess a specific kind of education and a particular degree. The created order is open to exploration and discovery by all people in all walks of life, and this exploration is beneficial to them no matter what their vocation(s) may be.

Luther's concern that education be made available to children for their formation as responsible citizens also raises the issue of community. A Lutheran approach to a liberal arts education will not regard education as a commodity or a bargaining chip for self-advancement, but as a means of greater service to one's neighbor. A liberal education too often liberates students from the personal attachments that nurtured them and turns them into learned cosmopolitans, citizens of the world. D. G. Hart expresses this concern:

> I am haunted by the potential narrowness of a liberal education, since it tempts us to look at students and ourselves as merely minds without bodies, that is, without reference to the families and communities in which we learned to talk, treat others politely, endure eccentric neighbors, root for football teams, and fall in love.[85]

Christians are little Christs who see Christ in their neighbor and use their talents, gifts, achievements, and possessions to serve others and to glorify God. A Lutheran liberal arts education will never neglect the church, the home, and the community for the sake of the career, the research project, and the salary schedule.

If Luther's recommendations are to be taken seriously, a Lutheran liberal arts college must affirm a commitment both to Lutheran identity—and confidence in that identity—and to the value of the liberal arts as first principles. It is well known that many denominationally affiliated colleges and universities in the United States gradually allowed their relationship to church bodies to erode, presumably in the interest of professionalism, higher scientific standards, and a European model of academic freedom, with the result that they ceased to be Christian in any real sense. As Mark Noll puts it,

> The religion of America's historic Christian colleges and universities has undergone slow evisceration over the course of the twentieth century because the piety in these institutions

---

[85] D. G. Hart, "Education and Alienation: What John Henry Newman Could Have Learned from Wendell Berry," *Touchstone* 18, no. 8 (2005): 35.

was intellectually shallow, their ecclesiology was self-destructively low-church, and their administrators all too often acted with craven short-sightedness.[86]

Roman Catholic and Lutheran colleges and universities were also affected by this crisis of identity.[87] Nor can commitment to the value of the liberal arts be taken for granted. The study of the traditional liberal arts is considered irrelevant, or even detrimental, to the pursuit of contemporary higher education, and those who choose to study the liberal arts have become a marginalized minority group. In addition, many colleges have taken a utilitarian turn that emphasizes a career-oriented practical course of study.[88]

In the face of these challenges, how can a college committed to both Lutheran identity and a curriculum that emphasizes the liberal arts respond? First, a curriculum that emphasizes the liberal arts is tailor-made to remedy the deficiencies of today's students and equip them with the tools they need to read, reason, and communicate effectively. As most educators have noted, many students today cannot adequately define a term, make proper distinctions, or present an argument in a satisfactory manner. They have difficulty making connections between concepts and between various disciplines. Study of the liberal arts trains students in habits of thinking and communicating that enable them to excel as they explore both the breadth and the depth of various academic disciplines. Herve de la Tour reminds us that in the past the classroom was not considered an assembly line that fitted students with the chunks of information they needed; rather, "The medieval classroom was viewed as a workshop where the students were apprentices learning to craft a work of the mind (e.g. composition in English). These tools, once acquired, enabled one to tackle any subject later on."[89]

---

[86] Mark A. Noll, "The Future of the Religious College: Looking Ahead by Looking Back," paper presented at the Conference on the Future of Religious Colleges, Program on Education Policy and Governance, Harvard, 2000, 2 (second of two pages numbered 1).

[87] See, for example, David M. O'Connell, "The Religious College: Dying Light or New Dawning?" paper presented at the Conference on the Future of Religious Colleges, The Kennedy School of Government at Harvard, 2000, 7, and Albert Anderson, "The Church and the Liberal Arts: An Immodest Engagement Proposal," *Dialog* 19 (1980): 111-16.

[88] Hart, 31.

[89] Herve de la Tour, "The Seven Liberal Arts," http://www.edocere.org/articles/7_liberal_arts.htm.

The contemporary secular university frequently is historically unprepared, and philosophically unwilling, to carry out this task. While some universities continue to rally around the post-Enlightenment standard of liberal, scientific, objectivist, progressive secularism, which has little use for religion as a component of the curriculum or of the conversation in general, this position began to be contested during the last third of the twentieth century. Sadly, it has been replaced by a model that, while more open to so-called spirituality, calls into doubt the ability of language to communicate propositional truth at all. For example, deconstructionist theory claims that language reflects much more the human person's perceptions of his or her experience than it does the reality of the world in which the person lives.[90] The ultimate purpose for which the tools of the liberal arts are employed as part of a Lutheran education is the understanding and effective communication of words—God's Word—but both modernism and postmodernism subvert this goal. Modernism's denial of the supernatural attempts to use scientific methodology to read behind the text and find the "real" truth, while the subjectivity of post-modernism leaves the text open to many interpretations and many truths, dependent on the perspective of the reader. The time is ripe for reformation at the college level.[91] Disciplined training in the liberal arts equips students to unmask both these errors and interpret texts, especially the Text, responsibly.

This is all the more urgent because "the faith . . . is embedded in language."[92] Not only the text of Scripture, but the ecumenical creeds, the Lutheran confessions, and the great chorales of the Lutheran church are written in language that *makes sense* and that communicates ultimate religious truth. Therefore, they call for readers and worshipers who, according to their capacity, are able to understand them. In the contemporary church, the area

---

[90] Noll, 7-8. See also the discussion of modernism and post-modernism in Paul Lehninger, "Playing the Discarded Image Card," *Logia* 13, no. 3 (2004): 11–12.

[91] "There is no work more worthy of pope or emperor than a thorough reformation of the universities, and there is nothing worse or more worthy of the devil than unreformed universities." Martin Luther, *Table Talk*, quoted in John S. Reist, "The Knife that Cuts Better than Another: Luther and Liberal Arts Education," *Perspectives in Religious Studies* 21, no. 2 (2004): 101. See also Angus Menuge, "Promoting Dialog in the Christian Academy," *Logia* 11, no. 2 (2002): 19-26, esp. 21–22.

[92] Robert Louis Wilken, "The Church's Way of Speaking," *First Things* no. 155 (2005): 29.

that perhaps suffers most from postmodern language malaise is that of worship. Take, for example, that all-time (since 1987) favorite praise song, "Shine, Jesus, Shine."[93] Jesus, the Father ("Fill this land with the Father's glory"), and the Spirit ("Blaze, Spirit, blaze!") are mentioned in the refrain—so far, Trinitarian theology. But then comes the vexing, "Flow, river, flow." The problem is not that the singer is unable to supply a meaning for the term "river"; e.g. the river of God's grace, the river of God's mercy, or perhaps the Word, the truth, the blood (all are mentioned in various stanzas). The problem is that different singers can supply different meanings, and therefore a hymn, which is used in corporate worship, will mean different things to different members of the body. The body is no longer united in praise. The uni-*verse* is shattered. The pieces don't fit. Moreover, because of the structure of the music and the lyrics, "the river" becomes a pesky candidate for a fourth member of the Trinity.

Some may argue that what goes on in chapel has little to do with affirming the importance of a Lutheran liberal arts curriculum, but "orthodoxy" can mean both "right doctrine" and "right praise": *lex orandi lex credendi est*[94] works both ways. As Alan G. Padgett writes, "First-class hymns are also first-class theology. The best liturgy has always been grounded in and expressed the best theology."[95] To expose students to illogical, disorganized, stream-of-consciousness chapel addresses that are not christocentric and that fail to distinguish between Law and Gospel, preceded and followed by vague, me-centered praise songs, all capped off with a rambling *ex corde* [from the heart] prayer and an "original" benediction, undermines whatever laudable efforts are being made in the classroom to encourage students to think and express themselves cogently about their Christian faith and the world they live in.[96] Alleged cultural

---

[93] Graham Kendrick, Make Way Music, 1987.

[94] *Editors' note*: This Latin phrase, meaning "the law of prayer is the law of faith," generally is attributed to Prosper of Acquitaine, a fifth-century follower of St. Augustine. His aim was that uniformity in liturgical prayers would promote uniformity in doctrine throughout Christendom.

[95] Alan G. Padgett, "Theology as Worship: The Place of Theology in a Postmodern University," in Tanner and Hall, *Ancient and Postmodern Christianity*, 243.

[96] One might add the increasing demands to omit a confession of sins from the service, or at least to eschew irksome phrases like "poor miserable sinner." Fr. George Rutler expertly connects this with a loss of awe and wonder: "Wonder becomes worship through humility, and through increased humility worship becomes conviction of disobedience. The reverse is also true: the refusal

relevance must not be allowed to trump a clear exposition and presentation of the truth. As Robert Louis Wilken writes:

> For too long Christianity has relinquished its role as teacher to society. Instead of inspiring the culture, it capitulates to the ethos of the world. The church must rediscover herself, learn to savor her speech, delight in telling her stories, and confidently pass on what she has received. Only then can she draw people away from the coarse and superficial culture surrounding us into the abundance of life in Christ. "Walk about Zion," sings the psalmist, "go round about her, number her towers, consider well her ramparts, go through her citadels; that you may tell the next generation that this is God, our God for ever and ever" [Psalm 48].[97]

Martin Luther certainly suffered from bouts of *Anfechtung*,[98] but overall he radiated a spirit of confidence. Some outside the Lutheran tradition encourage Lutherans to have the same confidence in their intellectual heritage:

> The Lutheran tradition possesses some of the most potent theological sources for sustaining the life of the mind that one could imagine. It encourages a dialogue between the Christian faith and the world of ideas, fosters intellectual humility, engenders a healthy suspicion of absolutes, and helps create a conversation in which all of the conversation partners are taken seriously.[99]

Lutherans need to recapture this spirit of confidence

---

to confess sin (and this includes the refusal to confess sin as Christ orders it to be done in the church) leads to a refusal to worship, and the refusal to worship leads to a loss of the sense of wonder. Any theorist who thought that the easing of penitential practices would encourage attendance at the Sacrifice of the Mass was sorely mistaken and should make haste to the closest retirement home for disappointed liturgists. And if any one thought a sense of wonder would be increased by turning worship into self-congratulation, he need only contemplate the glazed eyes staring at the song leader in the sanctuary as he yodels a limp pop ballad into the microphone. Empty confessionals empty churches, and empty churches empty the soul of holy awe." George Rutler, *The Seven Wonders of the World* (San Francisco: Ignatius, 1999), 111.

 97   Wilken, 31.
 98   *Editors' note*: This German word may be translated "trial," "affliction," or "temptation." For the multifaceted significance of *Anfechtung* in the writings of Luther, see David P. Scaer, "The Concept of *Anfechtung* in Luther's Thought," *Concordia Theological Quarterly* 47, no. 1 (1983): 15-30.
 99   Richard T. Hughes, quoted in Dovre, 8.

regarding the worth of their identity and of the Lutheran ethos, and of the critical role they play in the reformation of contemporary academic life.

This spirit must also be reflected in the confidence with which Lutheran education engages the world. The Lutheran ethos is infused with a spirit of freedom, not the *ersatz* contemporary notion of personal liberation from all external constraint, but a freedom born from the gospel message of forgiveness. Having been freed from sin, we are free to serve God and free—and eager—to investigate every corner of the universe, the drama of human history, the depths of the human mind, emotion, and will, and the revelation of God Himself. We can do so with the confidence of Luther and Augustine, that all truth is God's truth. Since the Lutheran spirit is dialectical and open, it is

> analogous to the wonder from which all understanding proceeds, and humanly akin to the academic freedom cherished by scholars. It complements the nature of wisdom: the capacity to be open without being indecisive; decisive, but not closed minded. And it encourages the spirit of engagement essential to the church and higher education alike, to come to terms with the legions of cultural spirits.[100]

This gives Lutheran Christian scholars confidence in carrying out their research. When confronted with two theories that appear to be equally valid within the parameters of their discipline, they are free to accept the theory that best harmonizes with the Christian faith—and then they are free to support that theory not based on faith claims, but on argumentation appropriate for their discipline. They can do so because they neither surrender human reason to a static fideism nor abandon the Christian faith to a hegemonic human wisdom, recognizing that "God's truth taxes the human reason highly; but it is not at the expense of human reason. Anyone who has thought so has been a menace in the annals of religion and a neophyte in the laboratories of science."[101]

Most importantly, a Lutheran Christian approach to a liberal arts education will emphasize that this world makes sense, the pieces fit, a deep meaning underlies all we study, because Christ is the grammar of the universe. All things were made "by Him and for Him . . . and in Him all things hold together" (Colossians 1:16-17). All things are reconciled to God through Him (v. 20), so not

---

[100] Anderson, 114.
[101] Rutler, 41.

only are the liberal arts tools we use to understand a world that makes sense, but when we use these tools, we can expect to find something good. With Christ at the center, we are equipped, and confident, to do theology and all academic work from the inside out (faith seeking reason), rather than from the outside in (reason as the critic of faith). "Wisdom's highest, noblest treasure, Jesus, lies concealed in Thee" (*TLH* 366:5). Therefore, the more we make skillful and Spirit-guided use of the tools of the liberal arts to study what Christ made, the more we discover about Christ; and the closer we grow to Christ in faith, the better equipped we will be to understand his creation. This perspective transforms our passage through the fallen world around us into a journey full of potential, an environment alive with reminders (*vestigia*) of the presence of God, a reflection of the full reality that will be heaven. This is an adventure worth setting out on! The unicorn got it right in the last of the *Chronicles of Narnia*: "I have come home at last! This is my real country! I belong here. This is the land I have been looking for all my life, though I never knew it till now. The reason why we loved the old Narnia is that it sometimes looked a little like this. . . . Come further up, come further in!"[102]

---

[102] C. S. Lewis, *The Last Battle* (New York: Collier, 1956), 171.

DOCUMENT 5.6:

Classical, Christian, Liberal Arts Education (2006)

By Lutheran Schools of America

Lutheran Schools of America (LSA) *was established by the 2005 Convention of the Evangelical Lutheran Synod in a response to a memorial submitted in 2003 by Redeemer Lutheran Church of Scottsdale, Arizona. Taking its cue from Proverbs 22:6—"Train a child in the way he should go and even when he is old he will not turn away from it."—the memorial urged the ELS to develop and implement a plan for expanding the number of Christian day schools among its congregations. More specifically, the synod's plan for LSA involved establishing two new schools per year, beginning in the fall of 2006 and continuing for the following fifty years. At its 2006 convention, the synod reorganized its Board for Education and Youth by establishing the Board for Parish Education and Youth and a separate Board for Lutheran Schools of America. The LSA Board has endeavored specifically to cultivate a "classical" approach to Christian education, centered around the liberal arts in service to the Christian faith.*[103] [RM]

Source: "Lutheran Schools of America," *www.lsaels.org* (accessed 26 Aug. 2006).

---

[103] *Synod Report* (2008), 111; *Synod Report* (2009), 88–93.

Defining "Christian Classical Education"[104]

A Narrow Definition. "Classical Education" is here more narrowly defined than those who simply incorporate ancient classical authors and readings in an educational enterprise. It is our desire to teach by the same educational principles and toward the same educational goals as the ancients, rather than in teaching the same literature as the ancients. We do not necessarily pursue the Classical materials—Homer and Plato or Caesar and Cicero. Instead, we necessarily pursue the Classical model of child development and the Classical method for teaching subjects. We call this the Applied Trivium.

Furthermore, as Christians our focus is yet narrower. Everything non-Christian is also anti-Christian because it fails to confess that Jesus Christ is Lord. There is no neutral ground. "He that is not with me is against me" (Matthew 12:30). We sift everything—including classical authors—through the critical screen of the Scriptures. As John Wycliffe wrote, "There is no subtlety in grammar, neither in logic nor in any other science that can be named but that it is found in a more excellent degree in the Scriptures."[105] Our focus in all cultures is upon what is redeemable in Christ. We choose to limit our meaning of Classical to include only what is of good form and lasting value (Classical) and which conforms to a Biblical standard within a Biblical worldview (Christian).

Trivium Terminology. Dorothy Sayers led the way in attempting to coin a terminology for the stages of learning. She suggested Poll-Parrot, Pert, and Poetic. Her terminology has never caught on. The three formal classical subjects of the Trivium are Grammar, Logic, and Rhetoric. Because Dorothy Sayers analogically applied these terms to the levels of learning development and subject development, those who have followed her application have, probably by default, simply applied these names to the levels of development. We suggest that the Biblical triad of Knowledge, Understanding, and Wisdom would serve

---

[104] *Editors' note*: The LSA website indicated that this section was "revised and adapted with the permission of Harvey & Laurie Bluedorn, www.triviumpursuit.com." The website also included the following "Suggested Reading List": "The Lost Tools of Learning," by Dorothy Sayers; *The Abolition of Man*, by C.S. Lewis; *Recovering the Lost Tools of Learning*, by Douglas Wilson; *The Case for Classical Christian Education*, by Douglas Wilson; *The Seven Laws of Teaching*, by John Gregory; *Repairing the Ruins*, edited by Douglas Wilson; and, *Classical Education*, by Gene Edward Veith, Jr. and Andrew Kern.

[105] *Editors' note*: The source has not been located.

better to describe the three levels of development. However, because others who have written on these subjects use the classical terms, we work with both terminologies.

The Trivium in a Capsule. Each child goes through three stages of development, and each subject has three levels of development. These three stages or levels correspond to the formal Trivium in the Classical sense—Grammar, Logic, and Rhetoric—and to the Biblical Trivium of Knowledge, Understanding, and Wisdom. We will describe the three stages from the point of view of the individual child's development, keeping in mind that this also applies to the development of each individual subject which is taught. Similarly, the development of each subject is not necessarily age-bound.

The Picture. Here is the picture. Man has three mental capacities:

1. One for gathering up information—Knowledge.
2. A second for arranging the information in a logical order—Understanding.
3. A third for putting this information and this ordering into practical use—Wisdom.

The Early Knowledge or Grammar Stage. These three capacities are mutually dependent upon each other, but there is, nevertheless, a logical and developmental order between them. All three capacities are developing in the child from before birth. The child is always learning facts, relating the facts to each other, and using these facts and relations in practical ways.

During the child's early years, while all three capacities are growing, the capacity for Knowledge experiences the greatest growth. At about age nine or ten, the developmental parts have reached such a state of maturity that the light bulb goes on and the capacity for Knowledge makes a growth spurt—a quantum leap—into an intensive period when capacity and ability for formal academic study of Knowledge-related materials is most profitable.

When the child is at this level, we teach him the skill of comprehension—to accurately receive information—to gather the facts. Knowledge is imparted through telling and demonstrating. It comes through the senses. We develop a vocabulary of facts and rules. At this level we do not need to separate subjects. We can combine 1) language with literature and fine arts; 2) mathematics with natural sciences; 3) history with geography and social studies.

Our goal is to develop competence in the tools of inquiry: reading, listening, writing, observing, and measuring.

The Understanding or Logic Stage. The intensive Knowledge period lasts about three years. When it is over, Knowledge, of course, continues to grow and develop. However, the capacity for Understanding—which has been developing all along—emerges as the frontrunner in this race. With a large foundation of Knowledge laid and the developmental parts of Understanding reaching a level of maturity, another light bulb goes on. The capacity for Understanding makes a growth spurt—a quantum leap—into an intensive period when a capacity and ability for formal academic study of Understanding-related materials is most profitable.

When the child is at this level, we teach him the skill of reasoning—to critically question, analyze, evaluate, to discern causes, motives, means, purposes, goals, and effects—to investigate the theory. Understanding is imparted through coaching, correcting, and drilling. We develop a vocabulary of relationships, order, and abstractions. Our teaching will become more sequential and systematic, separating the different branches of learning. Our goal is to develop competence in the tools of investigation: analyzing, comparing, contrasting.

The Wisdom or Rhetoric Stage. The intensive Understanding period lasts about three years and, of course, continues to grow and develop. However, the capacity for Wisdom—which has been developing all along—emerges as the front-runner in this race. When a large foundation of Knowledge and Understanding has been laid and the developmental parts of Wisdom reach a level of maturity, then a third light bulb goes on. The capacity for Wisdom makes a growth spurt—a quantum leap—into an intensive period when a capacity and ability for formal academic study of Wisdom-related materials is most profitable.

When the child is at this level, we teach him the skills of prudent judgment and effective expression, through communication and practical application. Wisdom is imparted through encouraging individual initiative and innovation, asking questions and leading discussions. We develop a vocabulary of philosophical ideas and values. We begin to recombine the knowledge and skills from separate disciplines. We seek the application of principles, values and goals. As with Knowledge and Understanding, the intensive Wisdom period lasts about three years. While Wisdom continues to grow and develop, all three capacities which have been developing all along emerge as a fully developed team of tools.

Why Do We Follow a Classical Model and Method? The best reason for choosing the classical way of schooling is primarily because this is the Biblical model written into reality. So what if the pagans borrowed it? We simply take it back and clean it up and put it to our own use. The classical way has been successful for millennia because it conforms to the created nature of things. It works well because it matches reality. If we ever learned anything, we learned it by the trivium method—whether we knew it or not.

Historical Perspective

In 1524, Martin Luther declared, "For the sake of the Church we must have and maintain Christian schools!"[106] Given the dramatic decline in the quality of public education today, this is a time for a call to action. It is a call to all who share in a desire to make a difference in the lives of the children of this generation and to positively impact tomorrow's society.

To God-fearing people, the case is clear. It's clear that the American culture has been gradually but certainly undergoing deep decay. The moral climate has declined to a level at which individual behavior is ruled by relativism rather than absolute values. "Ethical" behavior is no longer based upon a concern for the good of a neighbor, but rather upon what's best for "me." The role and importance of the family unit has been significantly minimized, even bringing into question the definition of a "family" or, for that matter, "marriage." National divorce rates fall only because the convenience of cohabitation without legal commitment has often replaced marriage as a lifestyle. Additional statistics consistent with these societal characteristics reveal years of marked decline in the church attendance and church-directed charitable giving of Americans.

The growth of secular humanism in our society has penetrated and significantly influenced the American public school system. Rather, it has become the rule to the point where even the symbols of religious values are forbidden. The mention of "God" in our national pledge has become a serious discussion topic. The impact of John Dewey's philosophy of education still resounds throughout public school classrooms. His influence has redefined "good, right, and beautiful" with only those things which can be scientifically proven and are consistent with human reason.

---

[106] *Editors' note*: Painter, *Luther on Education*, 133.

Today's educational leaders have placed man's will as the measure of good and rejected any sense of objective, absolute truth. With a citizenry in spiritual decline and our public schools advocating a secularized philosophy, the once strong fabric of America—home and school—can no longer be counted upon for the moral leadership required to strengthen and stabilize our society.

America's public schools are also troubled as revealed by the documented lowered test results attained by its students. Business leaders decry the inadequate preparation of those high school and college graduates seeking employment. School buildings, once considered safe and secure places of learning, greet students with metal detectors and are staffed by security guards both inside and outside of its hallways. The intellectual discipline and academic rigor which once typified America's public schools has been often minimized. While increasing numbers of parents have abdicated their guidance-in-learning role, teachers increasingly struggle to be inspirational and intellectually impactful. Finally, one must conclude that the root cause of educational failure may well be the underlying educational philosophy which disguises education as "modern and progressive."

LSA Case for Support

The historic tradition of the Lutheran church is that it has been proactive in attempting to strengthen the societal fabric. Lutheran congregations have given a firm faith witness to their community through the Christian education programs for their youth. It was in the mid 1500s when Dr. Martin Luther advocated the training of a productive citizenry in order to satisfy both the needs of the state as well as the church. Luther's position was that an education focusing upon the arts and sciences, and incorporated with theological education, would serve to prepare homemakers as well as physicians. Today that is the call of the Lutheran Schools of America being extended to Lutherans and non-Lutherans alike.

Since the early 1900s, the leaders of the Evangelical Lutheran Synod (ELS) have committed themselves and the Church to maintaining church-related schools. In 1919, one synodical forefather, the Reverend Bjug Harstad, declared his view of the importance of starting schools in these words: "Let [the starting and maintaining of Christian schools] be our chief concern and a life-and-death matter in all our life and work."[107]

Pastor Harstad's voice has been joined by countless other pastors and Christian parents who share his passion for Lutheran Christian education. Today nearly 20% of the 135 congregations of the ELS support a Christian school in a preschool setting and/or as a PreK-8 educational environment. Increasingly, these church-affiliated schools have become centers of outreach and service to the communities in which they serve. They are being sought out by parents outside of the related church who are actively seeking an alternative to the public education they have found to be less than what they believe to be best for their children.

In June of 2003, the Convention of the Evangelical Lutheran Synod demonstrated an unusual commitment to providing Christian education. A memorial presented by one of its member churches in Scottsdale, Arizona, offered the strongest possible urging of the Synod to consider a project challenging the moral decline and decreasing effectiveness of America's public schools. It was termed the "Lutheran Schools Initiative." Specifically, this memorial urged the Synod to undertake an effort to dramatically increase the number of church-related, Christian schools within the Synod. The proposed goal which was established is remarkable: to start at least twenty new schools in ten years for a period of fifty years.

The memorial was received by Synod delegates with a strong spiritual endorsement and a sense of awe at the magnitude of its stated goals. The synod's president, the Rev. John A. Moldstad, identified the project's great potential for spiritual and cultural good and created a committee to study the impact of the memorial. By June of 2005, the ELS resolved to extend this schools' initiative to an active project and approved its naming as the "Lutheran Schools of America." With the goal of starting two new schools a year, the members and leaders of the Evangelical Lutheran Synod have enthusiastically dedicated themselves to creating Christ-centered, excellence-focused, service-driven schools.

The Lutheran Schools of America is surely among the most aggressive and proactive programs in the history of the church. It is a resounding call which echoes in support of a return to the basics of classical education taught from a confessional Lutheran Christian-based ideology. Truly it merits the involvement, investment, and advocacy of Christians both in the ELS and

---

[107] *Editors' note*: Bjug Harstad, in *Synod Report* (1919), 21.

beyond for the sake of the church and for the strengthening of America. It is a new day of opportunity for people of integrity and leadership to strive together in weaving a refined cultural moral fabric.

Mission and Vision Statements

The Lutheran Schools of America (LSA) is a ministry support project of the Evangelical Lutheran Synod. It seeks to assist parents in nurturing the intellectual, social, physical, and spiritual growth of their children. At its essence, the mission of the Lutheran Schools of America is:

> to establish Christian, confessionally Lutheran, community-based schools which are characterized by academic excellence, high student achievement, and community service.

The strategic emphases of the Lutheran Schools of America project result in a creative and purposeful statement for its future existence. Through the structure and function of LSA schools, relationship-based Christian witness shall guide all school activities. The preeminent goal shall be sharing the Gospel and nurturing others toward a Spirit-led saving faith in Christ.

The Lutheran Schools of America will be known as Bible-centered schools of classical education where teachers and parents work together in leading students to demonstrate academic achievement, social involvement, Christian commitment, self-discipline, and service to their community.

SECTION 6:

Government Aid to Private Education

Introduction

By Paul Gunderson and Jeremy Costello

Congress shall make no law respecting an establishment of religion, or prohibiting the free exercise thereof.

First Amendment, U.S. Constitution

Christ's kingdom is spiritual, that is, it is the heart's knowledge of God, fear of God, faith in God, and the beginning of eternal righteousness and eternal life. At the same time, it permits us to make outward use of legitimate political ordinances of whatever nation in which we live.

Ap XVI, 2

Section 6: *Government Aid to Private Education* 337

Separating the institutions of church and state seems so rooted in the American tradition that to not have such a view is often considered foolishness. But as the Rev. Gerhardt Weseloh explained to ELS pastors in 1963, this notion of separation was not present in Europe prior to the settlement of the Americas, nor was it widespread during the colonial period in America. Indeed, an education system in harmony with this new idea of separation emerged only gradually, as the secular system to which Americans today are accustomed resulted from a slow process occurring throughout the nation's history.[1]

A major stimulus for this transformation to the modern secular school was a series of rulings by the twentieth-century Supreme Court that stretched separation ever further between church and state. However, as this section will demonstrate, not all of these decisions have been in opposition to private education.

In 1925, one of the century's first Supreme Court cases involving education, *Pierce v. Society of Sisters*, displayed a victory for parental choice in a child's education. The decision overruled a state law that had required all children to attend public schools. While recognizing a state's interest in requiring children's attendance at some school, the court also insisted that parents have the right to choose which school, public or private, their children would attend.[2] In 1947, the Supreme Court decided in the *Everson* case that a state law allowing reimbursement for students' transportation costs to a private school was constitutional. This case, however, also established a "wall between church and state," which would set the precedent for similar cases later in the century.[3] The next year the Supreme Court decided that a state law allowing students to receive religious education of their choice within the public school during school hours was unconstitutional.[4] This issue became cloudy again in 1952 when the Supreme Court declared constitutional a state law that allowed students to leave the public school for a time

---

[1] Gerhardt Weseloh, "The History of the Separation of Church and State, with Special Reference to Education in the Lutheran Church and in the United States," *Lutheran Synod Quarterly* 3, no. 4 (June 1963): 6–20.

[2] Mark G. Yudof, "Pierce v. Society of Sisters," *The Oxford Guide to United States Supreme Court Decisions*, ed. Kermit L. Hall (Oxford University Press, 1999); *Oxford Reference Online*, www.oxfordreference.com. See also Weseloh, "History of the Separation of Church and State," for an indication of how this and related cases were explained to ELS clergymen.

[3] *Everson v. Board of Education of Ewing Township*, 330 U.S. 1, 18 (1947).

[4] *Illinois ex rel. McCollum v. Board of Education*, 333 U.S. 203 (1948).

to receive religious education.⁵

The Supreme Court's hostility towards private education, as B. W. Teigen argued **(Document 6.5)**, was displayed in the 1971 *Lemon v. Kurtzman* case. The decision in this case set forth an opinion that there ought to be no "excessive entanglement" between government and religion. It declared unconstitutional two state laws that gave compensation to teachers of secular subjects in religious schools.⁶ Only a year later the Supreme Court, in *Wisconsin v. Yoder*, ruled unconstitutional a state law that required student attendance through high school. Members of the Amish community challenged this law on the grounds that it violated their right to free exercise of religion.⁷ In 1975, the Supreme Court ruled that a state-funded therapist working in a religious school results in an excessive entanglement of religious issues and therefore is unconstitutional.⁸

While some decisions of the Supreme Court seemed to reflect hostility towards religion, Teigen mentioned, when writing in both 1967 and 1975, a specific case that should be used to reveal an avenue of redress for private education (see **Documents 6.2** and **6.5**). The 1961 *Torcaso* case recognized secular humanism as a religion in itself to be placed alongside all of the other religions of the country.⁹ The schools of the country may adhere to strict separation of church and state on paper, but are they really just promoting secularism as a religion? If this be the case, do we as Christians have a duty to protect our children from this secular attack?

Staff members of Bethany Lutheran College, along with the seminary's dean, Milton Otto, advocated an active approach to correct the problem of government aid exclusively benefiting secularism **(Documents 6.1** and **6.3)**. During the 1960s they supported a group known as the Citizens for Educational Freedom, whose main platform advocated parental choice in education. An extension of this platform was the position that the tax dollar for education should follow each student, which would allow private schools to benefit from government aid. Was and is this still the proper solution to the wages of secularism in the public school?

---

5   *Zorach v. Clauson*, 343 U.S. 306 (1952).
6   *Lemon v. Kurtzman*, 403 U.S. 602 (1971).
7   *Wisconsin v. Yoder*, 406 U.S. 205 (1972).
8   "As Dr. Harold O. J. Brown Sees the Plight of Private Education," *Lutheran Synod Quarterly* 16, nos. 2-3 (1976): 77-78.
9   *Torcaso v. Watkins*, 367 U.S. 488 (1961).

While the decisions of the Supreme Court continually acknowledged the legality of providing federal aid to religious schools, Lutheran groups in the country were determining the propriety of accepting such aid for their Christian schools. In December of 1963, U.S. President Lyndon Johnson signed the Higher Education Facilities Act into law, which offered public funding to private institutions. That same year, the Wisconsin Evangelical Lutheran Synod adopted a statement declaring the acceptance of federal aid to be inappropriate. The synod stressed the importance for teaching its youth in a clearly Christian education and feared that by receiving governmental aid its schools "would thereby be yielding to the state the direction and control in the training of our children."[10]

During the following years, the Wisconsin Synod continued to examine the Scriptural basis for the resolution. The WELS convention of 1967 was presented with an updated document. This document looked towards St. Paul's words in 1 Corinthians 6:12, "All things are lawful unto me, but all things are not expedient: all things are lawful for me, but I will not be brought under the power of any." With this, the Wisconsin Synod found it proper to accept aid from the government insofar as the support did not impede the mission of the school, bring dependency upon federal aid, or hinder Christian stewardship.[11]

Meanwhile, the Evangelical Lutheran Synod also was deliberating the prospects of receiving federal financial aid for its Christian schools. The Bethany Lutheran College Board of Regents resolved in a May 1964 meeting to apply for governmental aid, noting that "by assisting only the secularized schools . . . [the state] imposes an unjust abridgment of religious liberty upon those parents who wish to make a choice regarding the education of their children."[12] The Board also expressed interest in discussing the matter with the Wisconsin Synod to develop a common understanding.

Another instance when church and state matters intermingled occurred during attempts of religious colleges to become accredited. During B. W. Teigen's tenure as president, Bethany moved towards accreditation by the Commission on

---

[10] "Statement Re Federal Aid to Church-Related Schools," *Lutheran Educator* 4, no. 1 (1963): 20.

[11] "Proclaim the Everlasting Gospel: Convention Reports," *Northwestern Lutheran*, 1 Oct. 1967, 311.

[12] Minutes of the Board of Regents of Bethany Lutheran College and Seminary, 11 and 12 May 1964, p. 4 (ELS Archives, Box S420, Folder S420A).

Colleges and Universities of the North Central Association of Colleges and Universities. Bethany had been accredited as a junior college through the University of Minnesota since 1937, but Teigen moved the school forward in seeking North Central accreditation. This began in 1967 with a Status Study identifying the college's goals and examining its standing in regard to finances, academics, faculty, and physical facilities. A visit by North Central on December 14-16, 1969, moved the process one step closer, but, as Teigen articulated in a letter to the Board of Regents regarding the visit, the routine had been long and tedious: "I don't know when we'll ever get closer to accreditation. I've been working on it for fifteen years, trying to plug every loophole, trying to gain every inch possible, but now we have come as far as we go. We're right down to the finish line."[13]

During a trip in early April 1970 to meet with North Central in Chicago, representatives of the college were informed that Bethany was granted status as Recognized Candidate for Accreditation. The next step was to conduct a more detailed Self Study of the college, which was completed in 1973. In December of the same year, another team from North Central visited the college. President Raymond M. Branstad, who had succeeded Teigen in 1970, and Dean Paul A. Helland visited a review committee in Chicago in March 1974, when Bethany received full accreditation. The review committee reported many strengths of the college, especially the college's "clear understanding of and commitment to its purpose[;] administration, regents, faculty, staff, and students clearly understand that the purpose of the College is to provide a two-year liberal arts education from a Christian and distinctively Lutheran perspective."[14]

It is quite a compliment that a secular institution recognized the college's spiritual mission so clearly. Meanwhile, both Otto and Teigen expressed confidence that ELS institutions could maintain such spiritual integrity even when receiving federal financial aid (**Documents 6.4** and **6.5**). As Bethany Lutheran College renewed its North Central accreditation in the coming decades—a prerequisite for maintaining federal financial aid—college leaders would rely, now with fewer questions and less discussion, upon the received wisdom of Otto and Teigen.

---

[13] B. W. Teigen to Board of Regents, 18 Dec. 1969, 2 (ELS Archives, "Accreditation" Folder B–A.3, Box #1).

[14] R. M. Branstad, "Bethany Accreditation," *Lutheran Sentinel,* 13 June 1974, 175.

DOCUMENT 6.1:

At the Crossroads in Private Education (1964)

By Bethany Lutheran College Staff Members

*The **Bethany Lutheran College staff of 1964** included Julian G. Anderson, Ella B. Anderson, Sophia T. Anderson, Luella Balcziak, Edna Busekist, Barry Coulter, Norman S. Holte, Carol F. Johnson, Iver C. Johnson, Thomas Kuster, Mildred C. Larson, Sigurd K. Lee, Dennis Natvig, James A. Nelson, Milton H. Otto, Glenn Reichwald, Dennis Soule, B. W. Teigen, Allan Unseth, Luther Wendland, Bruno Wilinski, and Jerry Wilske.*[15] *Most of these people served in more than one role on campus, whether by teaching diverse disciplines or by combining what by the century's end would become more specialized tasks of instruction, administration, and student services.*

Source: *Lutheran Synod Quarterly* 5, no. 2 (Dec. 1964): 6–10.

Many serious-minded people are these days giving considerable thought to the matter of private education in this country. They are thoroughly convinced that the future of the private independent church-school, with but few exceptions, is doomed to extinction within another generation. This should be of vital concern to us who have more than a mere academic interest in the survival of our Christian day schools. It should be our concern also from the standpoint of keeping our public school

---

[15]   *Fidelis* (1965); *Synod Report* (1965), 49.

Jerry Wilske, Calvin Johnson, Evelyn Schlomer, and Norman Holte, as pictured in the 1964 yearbook (Fidelis).

system from becoming one huge monolithic education machine which will tolerate no rival and, therefore, also no criticism of its aims, principles, and methods. The situation is so serious that unless we do something concrete, and soon, too, about finding a way to preserve our private schools, the relentless march towards their ultimate elimination will soon bring it to pass that we no longer have any private schools to worry about.

In that connection the Minnesota state convention of the Citizens for Educational Freedom (C.E.F.) in St. Paul on February 6[, 1964] brought out a number of things which we will do well to give some thought. A good example of what we have reference to can be found in the summaries here submitted of two of the thought-provoking addresses delivered at that convention.

One of these stirring addresses was given by the Rev. Donald Morrison of Detroit, Michigan. He is dean of a new liberal arts school (Michigan Lutheran College) of the Lutheran Church–Missouri Synod. Pastor Morrison stressed the need for hard work in getting a Bus Bill passed by the Minnesota state legislature. He recited similar efforts, and the eventual success, of the C.E.F. group in Michigan.

Using that as an introduction, Dr. Morrison went on to stress the rationale of a Bus Bill: that the health and safety of children is the concern, that the "primary effect" of a bill, which would include the transportation of parochial school children, would be

Milton Otto, Carol Johnson, Marvin Meyer, Orla Petersen, and Glen Reichwald, 1964.

the general welfare of the country. Parochial schools would be helped, he agreed, but that would be a secondary or indirect effect. Dr. Morrison called it "discrimination" to deny such aid and said that the purpose of the First Amendment, freedom of religion, would be served by passing such a Bus Bill. To those who object to giving "aid and comfort" to Catholic schools and other religious groups, he asked, pointedly, why they did not also object then to supporting the Christ-less religion preached in the state or public schools. By forcing more and more independent schools to close, the country will gradually "standardize its children" via the state schools. The child will become more and more a creature of the state.

The attention of his audience heightened when Dr. Morrison directed his remarks to the Catholic C.E.F. members present: he said they must realize the unfavorable reaction by many Americans in the past to statements by various popes about Catholic world domination. He appealed to the Catholics present to work to free the rest of C.E.F. and other Americans, as well, from those suspicions. In his conclusion, Dr. Morrison asked more Lutherans to get involved in C.E.F. "We have been slow to get involved in civic causes," he stated, "but that must be changed. We have no assurance that we'll always have religious liberty. We must work to preserve it—now."

The speech which undoubtedly made an even greater impact was the one given by Dr. Edwin H. Palmer of Grand Rapids,

Evelyn Daley and Allan Unseth, 1964.

Michigan. Dr. Palmer is an outspoken Calvinist affiliated with the Christian Reformed Church. Until about a year and a half ago he was dean of students at Westminster Theological Seminary in Philadelphia. He was and still is an ardent believer in the Church and state separation principle. But, after years of studying the matter, after an on-the-spot inspection of the "Freedom and Equity in Dutch Education," he is firmly convinced that there can and must be a more equitable distribution of the educational tax dollar, if private education is long to survive in this country and if it is to continue to be the force for good that it has been throughout its history in America.

The following are the major points of his well-received address delivered in St. Paul:

1. The Principle of Separation of Family and State. Education, too, is first of all an affair of the family. The State has an interest in this education, as it for example does in the practice of medicine, but it cannot take the matter wholly out of the hands of the parents. God gave the children to the parents and not to the state. The Bible commands the parents and not the state to train their children. The state has no biblical or natural right to demand that children be educated in state schools in a state way. Such a demand would be totalitarianism, the infringement by the state on the sovereign, educational rights of the parents. Fortunately, the United States Supreme Court firmly recognized this principle when, in the Oregon case of 1925, it stated that "the fundamental theory of liberty ... excludes any general power of the state to

Bruno Wilinski, Ella Anderson, Edna Busekist, Iver Johnson, and Thomas Kuster, 1964.

standardize its children by forcing them to accept instruction from public teachers only. The child is not the mere creature of the state; those who nurture him and direct his destiny have the right, coupled with the high duty, to recognize and prepare him for additional obligations."[16]

If this is a biblical principle, then the question may be asked: Has the state a right to enter into the parental field of education and set up as a norm for all children a type of education that by the interpretations of the Supreme Court must have a curriculum that is Bible-less, Christ-less, and God-less? Further, may the state then compel all parents either to send their children to these Bible-less schools, even if it is against their conscience, or to forfeit their school taxes and to pay a second time for an education according to their convictions?

2. Financial Justice. A striking example of financial injustice is to be found in St. Cloud, Minnesota, where the school population is evenly divided between the public and private or

---

[16] *Pierce v. Society of Sisters*, 268 U.S. 510, 535 (1925).

Karen Unseth and Claire Lieske, in 1964.

independent schools. The parents of the children attending the independent schools pay 100% of the costs for the support of that independent system and, in addition, 50% of the cost of maintaining the public school system which they for conscience reasons cannot use. In other words, one group pays 50% of the cost of the education of the youth; another pays 150%—*three times as much.* It is just as much in order to say, "If someone wants an education *without* God, let him pay for it."

3. Freedom of Choice. Legally parents may have the choice, but not actually, in the type of education they want for their children. There is little or no problem for the rich, but it is one for those of low or moderate incomes. There is no actual choice because of the financial equity involved. (Cf. #2)

4. Freedom of Conscience. It is often presupposed that the philosophy in state, or government, schools is neutral. But one cannot be neutral toward God. You are either for God or against him. This supposed "neutrality" on the part of government schools is actually a very subtle, powerful attack against God, for in their attempts to be neutral they ignore God—twenty-five hours a week the students are being taught to ignore God—and to ignore is to insult.

However, the philosophy of the government schools (public school system) is not neutral—it is definitely secularistic; and yet I am required to support this philosophy of life—secularism—to

Ken Biesterfeld, Erling Teigen, and Les Pfieffer, 1964.

which I am diametrically opposed. I do not have freedom of conscience in this matter. Rather, the government should take taxes from all, regardless of race, color, or creed (as it does) and give back to all, regardless of race, color, or creed. Then I will be able to use my tax dollar to send my children to a school where God's truth is taught, and my tax dollars will not be used to support secularist government schools.

5. Something for the Welfare of the Nation. The private or independent schools also perform a public function; they are training youth to be useful and knowledgeable citizens. If tax monies are given to independent schools because of this primary effect that they serve (as far as the state is concerned), such diversion of funds should no more be mixing church and state than the giving of federal funds to Catholic, Lutheran, or Presbyterian hospitals. The government does not consider it mixing church and state to have the 50% forgiveness feature on National Defense Loans apply to young people teaching in private or independent schools, because of their contribution to the welfare of the nation.

6. C.E.F. Is the Only Solution to the Problem Facing Us of Religion in the School. Rather than recognize one religion (Calvinism, or Lutheranism, or Romanism, for example) which would offend the other two groups, or the religion that is being taught by the public school system which offends all concerned Christians, it would be much better to recognize our pluralistic society and to take it from there. The C.E.F. slogan is: "Let the dollar follow the scholar!" Let the education tax monies come back to the family. Let the family spend the tax monies as they see fit. Let the family choose the school for their children. Let the dollar follow the scholar. This is the C.E.F. solution. The alternate solution is this: the government schools will continue to flourish, taking all the tax monies. The religion of the government schools—irreligion—will continue to be supported by all citizens. Independent schools will continue to decline.

7. The C.E.F. Program Will Encourage Pluralism. Our large universities are no longer free, despite all the claims for academic freedom in the same; the only school system which permits complete self-expression in matters of principle and philosophy is the independent school. The strength of America has been its pluralism: free self-expression in matters of principle and philosophy in independent schools. In the beginning years of this country all students went to such schools. But the picture has changed drastically. Around 1900 about 75% of college students went to independent schools. By 1950 it was about 50% in the independent schools, 50% in the state schools. Now in 1965 about 65% are in the state schools. (Dr. Palmer stated that in Michigan, 82% are in state schools; in Minnesota 74% are in the state colleges and universities.) The small, independent colleges are dying off—are being choked off—because of the tremendous tax support (which will get worse) given to state educational institutions. To quote Dr. Palmer, "the tragedy of America is that the small colleges are being squeezed out."

This is being offered our readers for their information and study. One may not agree with all that is reported here; at the same time one cannot escape the necessity of making a study in depth of the issues that especially Dr. Palmer has raised.—Ed.[17]

---

[17] *Editor's note*: Milton Otto served as editor of the *Lutheran Synod Quarterly* when this article was published.

DOCUMENT 6.2:

Separation of Church and State with Special Reference to Governmental Aid to Education (1967)

By Bjarne W. Teigen

*(For a biography of Bjarne W. Teigen, see **Document 5.1**.)*
Source: *Lutheran Synod Quarterly* 7, no. 3 (March 1967): 1–14.

What do we mean with the term, "Separation of Church and State," or as it is quite often stated today because it seems to be more precise and emphatic, "*Absolute S*eparation of Church and State"? I do not find the phrase in the Scriptures or in the Lutheran Confessions or in our United States Constitution. One wonders whether the term has become a *cliché* which covers a multitude of shades of meaning. Certainly, there is no question that some kind of "separation" is set forth in the Scriptures and the Confessions—and probably also in the Constitution—between the two powers or influences, namely, the secular and the spiritual. It is not always so clear how these two powers are to be separated in the practical day-to-day living of the Christian and the non-Christian.

Let us briefly look at some of the chief texts of Scripture which deal with the state and its relationship to the church. Romans 13:1-7 evidently sets forth the truth that civil government is a divine institution to which a Christian owes obedience and personal service.

Matthew 22:15-22 discusses the relationship between the two powers. For convenience' sake, let me summarize comments from two Lutheran commentators on this passage. First will be Dr. P. E. Kretzmann.[18] Verse 21 is the key verse, which Kretzmann translates as follows: "Caesar's give to Caesar; God's to God." Kretzmann declares that this is the "simple and most effective rule for keeping the distinction between church and state clearly defined . . . and should provide the necessary information on this vexed question for all times." (I wish it were as simple as it sounds to apply in all our relationships as Christian citizens.)

Dr. Kretzmann sets forth the following principles: God's people should, above all, give to God due honor and obedience. In things pertaining to the Word of God, we are obedient to God only. In merely temporal earthly things which cover money, possessions, body, and life, we will obey the government of the country in which we live.

Dr. Kretzmann then has long quotations from Luther with the following principles set forth: Jesus confirms the temporal sword because it is ordained and instituted by God (Romans 13:1). One dare not abuse the Government "unless it wants to take the Gospel from us or prohibit its preaching." The Lord condenses these two points (Caesar and God) very nicely and separates them from each other in one verse. So far Dr. Kretzmann.

Now I would like to bring a few summary statements from Dr. Johannes Ylvisaker's *The Gospels*.[19]

The Roman sovereignty was a matter of history and of historical truth. The political and subservient relation under the Emperor which must be acknowledged, and the obligations which follow and which must be observed, do not release them from the theocratic duties toward God. Here it is not "either/or," but "both/and." Augustine is quoted: "Give the money unto Caesar, thyself to God."

To continue summarizing Dr. Ylvisaker, the two domains must be kept separate and distinct. It is possible to be alive to our civic obligations and obey the civil magistrates, and simultaneously to be possessed of a heart that is acceptable to God

---

[18] Paul E. Kretzmann, *Popular Commentary of the Bible: The New Testament*, 2 vols. (St. Louis: Concordia Publishing House, 1921-1922).

[19] Johannes Ylvisaker, *The Gospels: A Synoptic Presentation of the Text of Matthew, Mark, Luke, and John, with Explanatory Notes* (1905; trans., Minneapolis: Fortress Press, 1932), 573.

President B. W. Teigen's penetrating discernment enabled him to become well-acquainted with the prevalent secular philosophies of the twentieth century while maintaining his roots in Christian orthodoxy.

so that it wills what God wills.

Jesus here also draws the line of demarcation between state and church. Each shall exist independently of the other but not mutually indifferent or impassive.[20]

The state and the church do not stand in a hostile relation each toward the other, but exist peacefully side by side. The church gives its children to the state, instructing them in a holy obedience to every magistrate. The state diverts with a protecting hand all outward perils from the communion of God's church. The church is the foster mother of the nations, teaching them even that which pertains to law and order, in civil affairs. The state, therefore, invests it with the crown of earthly blessings. So far Dr. Ylvisaker.

Another text which needs to be studied is Luke 12:13-21, especially since the Augsburg Confession makes reference to it (AC XXVIII). The chief verse here is: "Man, who made me judge or a divider over you?" (v. 14).

Kretzmann titles the section, "Warning Against Avarice." On verse 14, he says, "Jesus, due to the principle that spiritual and temporal affairs should be kept strictly asunder, immediately

---

[20] Cf. discussions in Ylvisaker, *The Gospels*, nos. 86 and 90.

shows that he was not in the least in sympathy with the man's object. He is neither a judge to decide the case on its merits, nor is he an arbiter to carry out any decision which he might be inclined to make."

Ylvisaker says that ecclesiastical and civil authority must not be confused. The Reformation came and demonstrated the necessity of keeping them apart.

> Not, to be sure, as if there were no bond of union, or that there were no inter-relation. *Civil authority must in many ways assist and serve the church, and the church shall sanctify and purge the body politic.* Yet there must always be a natural barrier between them so that the one may not interfere with, nor trespass upon the domain of the other. The one is concerned with bodies and physical things, the other with the souls and hearts of men.[21]

So far Dr. Ylvisaker.

It is hardly necessary to point out that Ylvisaker feels that there is some kind of interrelation between these two powers, and yet they must be kept apart. Civil authority must assist and serve the church, and the church should sanctify and purge the body politic.

Other passages which may be of significance here are John 18:36: Jesus' answer to Pilate, "My Kingdom is not of this world"; Philippians 3:20: "Our conversation (citizenship—AC XXVIII) is in heaven"; 2 Corinthians 10:4: "For the weapons for our warfare are not carnal, but mighty through God to the pulling down of strongholds."

Let us now look at the Lutheran Confessions. In general, the Lutheran Confessions' answer to the matter of separation of church and state is contained in Art. XVI (Of Civil Affairs) and Art. XXVIII (Of Ecclesiastical Power) in the Augsburg Confession, and Art. XVI of the Apology (Of Political Order).

Art. XVI (Of Civil Affairs) lays down five general principles:

1. Lawful civil ordinances are good works of God.

2. Those who forbid these civil offices to Christians are condemned.

3. They also condemn those who do not place evangelical perfection in the fear of God and in faith.

4. It (the Gospel) does not destroy the state or family.

---

[21] Ylvisaker, *The Gospels*, 469 (Teigen's italics).

5. Christians are bound to obey magistrates and laws save only when commanded to sin.

Then we come to Art. XXVIII, which really deals with ecclesiastical power. We are told that controversies have risen concerning the power of the bishops:

1. Some have awkwardly confounded the power of the church and the power of the sword. (Note the use of the word "power" throughout this section. It is strongly emphasized. We have the "power of the sword," *potestatas gladii*, and the "power of the keys," *potestatas clavium*.)
2. Our teachers are constrained to show the difference between the power of the church and the power of the sword and taught that both of them are to be held in reverence and honor.
3. The power of the keys (bishops) is the power or the commandment of God to preach the Gospel, whereby are granted eternal things [such] as eternal righteousness, the Holy Ghost,[and] eternal life.
4. Civil government deals with other things than does the Gospel. Civil rulers defend not minds, but bodies and bodily things.
5. Therefore, the power of the church and the civil power must not be confounded. Then comes the famous passage, "Let it (the church) not break into the office of another," etc.
6. After this manner our teachers discriminate between the duties of both these powers and command that both be honored and acknowledged as gifts and blessings of God.
7. If Bishops have any power of the sword, they do not have it by the commission of the Gospel, but by human law.

To sum up, then, the Lutheran answer to the meaning of the term separation of church and state is that *we should learn to separate the spiritual and the temporal power*: "Therefore, the power of the church and the civil power must not be confounded" (AC XXVIII, 12).

You will note that here it is clear that in the Lutheran Confessions' view, the Christian is viewed as using two powers, namely, the power of the keys and the power of the sword, and that he is under the influence of these two powers. Both really affect his entire life here on earth. But he has to learn the difference between these two powers and in what sphere they may be legitimately used. Both operate in the same community, but they must both respect each other. There is a real question whether each is dependent on each other.

How all this works out in every individual case is not always easy to determine. AC XVI says: "Christians are necessarily bound to obey their magistrates and laws, save only when commanded to sin, for then they ought to obey God rather than man (Acts 5:29)" (AC XVI, 6–7).

Suppose, for example, the state should command us to send our children to a school where false doctrine pervades all instruction, would this principle enunciated by the AC then come into play? Suppose, further, the state does not directly force us into such a situation but does it indirectly through compulsory school attendance laws, subsidization of only one system, and high taxes for all of us? I believe that we would not violate any divine law if we stand on our constitutional rights to have these inequities corrected. At least we would be in harmony with the Apology which insists that a "Christian can use with safety" legitimate civil ordinances (Ap XVI, 53).

To proceed a little further, it seems to be legitimate for the State to say that for the preservation of our country, our citizenry must be educated to a certain level. If the government, in its goal of achieving a well-educated citizenry, uses non-state educational agencies and reimburses these agencies for this service, it would not be wrong for a church-related agency to accept this aid. To put it another way, is it *per se* contrary to Scripture that government aid be given to independent schools and received by them? I believe that everyone has to work out for himself an answer to this question, put *in abstacto*. It is no use to go any farther in a discussion of this topic until one has formulated once and for all, on the basis of Scripture, a "yes" or a "no" answer to this question.

To continue, and assuming that the answer is that the acceptance of this aid is not *per se* contrary to Scripture, *other things being equal*, I believe a church school can accept this aid and be in harmony with these statements of the Confessions: "It is lawful, however, for Christians to use civil ordinances, just as they use the air, the light, food, drink" (Ap VII & VIII, 50). "Meanwhile, it [the distinction between the Kingdom of Christ and the political kingdom] permits us outwardly to use legitimate political ordinances of every nation in which we live, just as it permits us to use medicine or the art of building, food, drink, air" (Ap XVI, 54). "There are infinite discussions concerning contracts, in reference to which good consciences can never be satisfied unless they know the rule that it is lawful for a Christian to make use of civil ordinances and laws" (Ap XVI, 64).

The problems seem to lie in the fact that the government has a common concern in some activity in which the church also has a deep concern, the most evident of which is education. The church makes wise unto salvation through faith in Jesus Christ, and it leads its youth through the Gospel to live soberly and righteously, looking for the coming of our great God and Savior, Jesus Christ. The state wants us to live soberly and righteously so that its citizens may live a quiet and peaceable life. Hence, the state provides police, fire protection, and tax exemption to many institutions (including local churches), because they help the state in the state's purpose of having people live soberly and righteously. Now this seems to be extending financial aid to religion in a very real sense. The church could preach the Gospel without these aids, but it would be under a great handicap. Of course, as we have already noted, the church in cultivating the spiritual lives of its parishioners makes an important contribution to the state.

As far as the state is concerned with these activities of the church, its first concern is with the *secular effect*; namely to live a quiet and peaceable life. As far as the church is involved in these activities, its primary concern is with the *spiritual effect*, life and salvation, and the secular effect is secondary.

In actuality, it appears to me that we have always looked at these aspects of our daily lives in the two kingdoms in this way. There has always been a certain amount of overlapping. But what we have kept separate (or at least acknowledged that we ought to keep separate) is the *potestas clavium* and the *potestas gladii*. The Confessions reiterate again and again that Christian perfection consists "in dispositions of the heart, in great fear of God, in great faith, just as Abraham and Daniel, even in great wealth and exercising civil power, were no less perfect than any hermits" (Ap XVI, 61).

If you will go back to the quotation that I gave you from Dr. J. Ylvisaker, you will note that he indicated that there was *some kind of inter-relation between these two domains or powers*. Just how to nail down this relationship is not easy. It seems to me that what the Confessions ask us to do is to recognize that there is an inter-relationship, but we must also recognize that the one power which the Christian has to use to prepare people for the coming of the Great God and Savior, Jesus Christ, is the power which is "exercised only by teaching or preaching the Gospel and administering the sacraments, according to their calling, either to many or to individuals" (AC XXVIII, 8).

In view of the preceding discussion, one may well ask if there is not here an interdependence which is not accurately portrayed today by the term, "the absolute separation of Church and State" or the metaphor, "the wall between Church and State."

It is difficult to nail down Luther beyond these general considerations. Let me call attention to a few items from Luther. In 1524, Luther wrote "A Letter to the Mayors and Aldermen of all the Cities in Germany in behalf of Christian Schools." In this letter not only the teaching of the Gospel is stressed, but also the practical value of general education. Bomkamm calls our attention to the fact that in 1543, Luther directed his "fierce treatise" against the "lies" which he found among the Jews that they regarded themselves as the chosen people and still waited for the Messiah. Bomkamm says as a summary of this treatise, "If a government does not choose to provoke God's wrath, it must take steps against this open blasphemy." This sounds pretty strong, but it does seem to indicate that Luther felt that the state has some responsibilities for upholding the *moral law* as summarized in the Ten Commandments. Bomkamm summarizes Luther on this point by saying: "Self-evidently, it (the state) is obligated to proceed against atheism and blasphemy and to afford protection to divine worship, although it is not entitled to dictate it."[22] There seems to be some appeal here for government to maintain what the Confessions call "civil righteousness" and "righteousness of reason." Natural human reason, to some extent, understands the Decalogue, and this seems to be the basis from which the lawful pagan government is to draw its laws.

In the Smalcald Articles (the famous "Anti-Christ" section, SA II, IV, 11), Luther contrasts the government of the Turks and Tartars with the government of the Pope, and, on the basis of this comparison of the outward forms of government, the Turks come out better than does the Pope's external government, because the Turks allow for freedom of religious practice: "Even the Turks or the Tartars, great enemies of Christians as they are, do not do this (that is, will not permit Christians to be saved without his power), but they allow whoever wishes to believe in Christ, and take bodily tribute and obedience from Christians." Here Luther seems to indicate an affinity for religious freedom.

Without trying to unravel all the statements of Luther

---

[22] Heinrich Bornkamm, *Luther's World of Thought*, trans. Martin H. Bertram (St. Louis: Concordia Publishing House, 1958), 248.

regarding the so-called "Separation of Church and State" problem, it seems to me that if we would recognize that operating here is a principle which some modern political scientists call, "the primacy of the secular effects," we need not apologize for Luther. Certainly, we need not be uncomfortable when a noted contemporary legal authority says: "One of the strangest anomalies in the modern framework of church-state relations is the apparent willingness of those who protest even the smallest state recognition for aid to religion, to accept, without litigation, the massive government subsidy inherent in the various tax concessions to religious organizations."[23]

It seems to me that we should use our influence as citizens to call attention to and make use of this principle of the primacy of the secular effects. At the present time it will usually operate this way in our land: If the purpose and primary effect of a law are secular, the court will hold the law valid, even though, as a by-product, an incidental benefit accrues to religion. In 1961, the U.S. Supreme Court upheld Maryland's Sunday Closing Law against the contention that it violates separation of church and state (*McGowan*[24]). [The] *Schempp*, 1963 (Bible Reading in the Public Schools) [o]pinion sets forth the principle quite clearly: "The test may be stated as follows: What are the purpose and primary effect of the enactment? If either is the advancement or inhibition of religion, then the enactment exceeds the scope of legislative power as circumscribed by the Constitution. That is to say, that to withstand the strictures of the Establishment Clause, there must be a secular legislative purpose and a primary effect that neither advances nor inhibits religion."[25]

Keeping in mind this principle of the primacy of the secular effects as far as the state is concerned with the activities of the church, we possibly can, in our modern society, keep intact the right and duty of parents to educate their children and of the church to bring up its youth in the nurture and admonition of the Lord. But then we must use our constitutional rights much more vigorously than we have in recent years. The *Apology* very forcefully reminds us that "public redress, which is made through the Office of the Magistrate, is not advised against, but it is commanded, and it is a work of God according to Paul, Romans

---

[23] Dallin H. Oaks, ed., *The Wall between Church and State* (Chicago: University of Chicago Press, 1963), 9.
[24] Editors' note: *McGowan v. Maryland*, 366 U.S. 420 (1961).
[25] Editors' note: *Abington v. Schempp*, 374 U.S. 203, 220 (1963).

13:1. Now, the different kinds of public redress are legal decisions, capital punishment, wars, military service" (Ap XVI, 59–60).

In conclusion, I would like to point out that there are "certain legal decisions" that we ought to insist should be enforced. First the Oregon case (1925):

> The fundamental theory of liberty upon which all governments in this Union repose excludes any general power of state to standardize its children by forcing them to accept instruction from public teachers only. The child is not the mere creature of the state: those who nurture him and direct his destiny have the right, coupled with the high duty to recognize and prepare him for additional obligations.[26]

In 1961, the Supreme Court in the Torcaso case ruled that a man could not be denied a commission as a Notary Public because he refused to declare belief in God. The court held such a provision in the state Constitution violated the man's religious freedom. Yet he did not have a "religion" in the generally accepted understanding, but the court left no doubt whatever as to what it meant by "religions" founded on non-theistic beliefs. The court stated: "Among religions in this country which do not teach what would generally be considered a belief in the existence of God are Buddhism, Taoism, Ethical Culture, Secular Humanism, and others."[27]

Isn't it time that we recognize that the state school system has a definite religion, and that we ought to make use of public redress to obtain some kind of equality before the state? Is it not possible that through a superficial and thoughtless use of the term "separation of church and state," we have helped speed the day when in our country religious indifference is so well established that *all* religions are, in Gibbon's famous words: "to the people equally true, to the philosopher, equally false, and to the magistrate, equally useful"[28]?

---

[26] *Editors' note*: Pierce v. Society of Sisters, 268 U.S. 510, 535 (1925).
[27] *Editors' note*: Torcaso v. Watkins, 367 U.S. 488, 495n11 (1961).
[28] *Editors' note*: Edward Gibbon, *The Decline and Fall of the Roman Empire* (1776), vol. 1, chap. 2, pt. I.

DOCUMENT 6.3:

Aid to Private Education (1967)

By Milton H. Otto

*(For a biography of Milton H. Otto, see **Document 4.3**.)*
Source: *Lutheran Synod Quarterly* 7, no. 3 (March 1967): 36–41.

The lead article in this issue of the *Quarterly* [**Document 6.2**] constrains us to add a word about a certain group which seems to be taking a very sensible approach to the question of aid to private education. This group is known as the Citizens for Educational Freedom (C.E.F.), concerning which most people do not have very much accurate information; this is seen in the way the whole matter of aid to private education is discussed. While the average citizen gets excited about mixing church and state when discussing aid to private education, C.E.F. is concerned about the *children* on whom all educational legislation has its primary effect.

To correct some false impressions—C.E.F. is not advocating federal aid to education (nor, for that matter is this journal); it is only asking for equality if such aid is given. It furthermore is 100% for the separation of church and state—which means, as it wants no laws passed that would establish any kind of religion, neither does it want any laws enacted that would prohibit the free exercise of any citizen's religion. Neither is C.E.F. a Catholic organization; there are also Lutherans, Reformed, and

Pastor Milton Otto (right) sits with colleagues (from left to right) Arnold Kuster, Wilbert Werling, Luther Vangen, and Paul Anderson at a 1969 pastoral conference.

others interested in private education among its numbers.

It is the contention of Citizens for Educational Freedom that much legislation in our states discriminates against private education and makes it literally impossible for many parents to exercise their religion freely. Theoretically and legally, they have the choice of sending their children to any accredited school they wish, but financially such an assertion is meaningless.

To be more specific, because of the financial stringencies placed on them, parents, who for conscience reasons cannot approve of the secularistic, humanistic type of education offered in the public school, are in effect, by present tax laws, prohibited from giving their children a training they consider necessary, or are heavily penalized financially, if they do manage to do so—and this gets to be a form of tyranny. For example, the parents of 55,000 children in the Twin Cities are by law compelled to support the public school system in these cities, while they at the same time are penalized at least $25,000,000 annually in order to exercise their right to give their children a religious education (using the average cost per child in the Minnesota public school system). Could they not at least have the share of the educational dollar they contributed returned to them to use in the educational system of their choice? Furthermore, they—in educating these 55,000 young people—are rendering a public service, too: it is on behalf of others and it is for the public good.

For anyone to cry "that is mixing church and state" is most unfortunate, for that is not at all the point. The point is—does the parent have a real choice in the exercise of his religious convictions, as guaranteed him by the First Amendment to the Constitution? Once the general public sees that the very people, who can provide the moral backbone and supply the spiritual training the youth of our country so sorely needs, are being severely handicapped in that most commendable endeavor, the necessary changes in our present structure of public education should not be long in forthcoming. The fact that also other groups, for whom we might not have any sympathy, would benefit from channeling some of the educational dollar to the pupil who attends their private schools should never become the reason for our opposing any kind of aid to private education. To do so would mean using the law to prohibit others from exercising their religious choice, and that, too, is tyranny; it would be the same as cutting off our own nose to spite our face.

There is only so much money available for education, and if parents are already heavily taxed to support the public school system, which we grant we, for the sake of the general welfare of our country, need—they simply cannot be expected to start all over again to support another system. And that is why the second part of the First Amendment gets to be meaningless for many conscientious Christians—they are prevented, financially, from exercising their religion in the matter of educating their children. Besides that, there is the matter of building and supporting one monolithic structure, which if it were to be done in the business world, would soon be labeled a monopoly and a violation of Sherman anti-trust laws. In every sphere, except government itself, competition has proved to be the very life's blood of our nation. We ought think carefully about contributing to the creation of a servant which could turn around and become a cruel master.

There are other people, too, besides members of C.E.F., who are alarmed about the prevailing educational philosophy in America. Most recently the U. S. Chamber of Commerce issued a Task Force Report on Economic Growth and Opportunity, with particular attention given to the matter of Competition in Education. This report was the work of a large number of industrial leaders in this country. These people, who have a very great stake in our society, said:

> Either tuition grants or management contracts to private organizations would, of course, "destroy the public school system as we know it." When one thinks of the remarkable past achievements of public education in America, this may seem a foolish step. But we must not allow the memory of past achievements to blind us to present failures. Nor should we allow the rhetoric of public school men to obscure the issue. It is natural for public servants to complain about private competition, just as private business complains about public competition ... but if the terms of the competition are reasonable, there is every reason to suppose that it is healthy. Without it, both public and private enterprises have a way of ossifying. And if, as some fear, the public schools could not survive in open competition with private ones, then perhaps they *should* not survive.

Then the same group made this recommendation:

> Competition with existing public school systems offers a promising means of improving both public and private education. If all parents, at every income level, could choose between sending their children to approved private schools at public expense, both public and private education would improve as schools attempted to attract and hold pupils. Businessmen should press for the fullest possible consideration of proposals designed to enhance competition in education. Local, state, and federal governments should consider legislation which would enable communities to adopt programs establishing a public-private option for all children. Universities and educational associations should sponsor symposiums to explore the advantages, appropriate procedures, and possible pitfalls of establishing educational competition. (Pre-Publication Release[29])

Our purpose in speaking of these matters is simply this: we—by which we mean our own church people who are still convinced of the need of private education—ought to think through this matter of receiving any aid to private education very carefully before we in haste oppose it as unscriptural and un-American.

---

[29] *Editors' note*: The source has not been located.

Pastor Milton Otto served elderly residents of the Kasota home north of Mankato, Minnesota, 1958–1966. "The silver-haired head is a crown of glory, if it is found in the way of righteousness" (Proverbs 16:31).

DOCUMENT 6.4:

What Is Involved in the Private Education Struggle to Survive? (1975)

By Milton H. Otto

*(For a biography of Milton H. Otto, see **Document 4.3**.)*

Source: *Lutheran Synod Quarterly* 15, nos. 2-3 (Winter-Spring 1975): 1–10.

If private education was ten years ago wondering whether it would survive, it today may well ask whether it has reached the point when it should give thought to writing its last will and testament. As if that in itself were not a sad enough state of affairs, there are more than a few people only too ready to assist with writing that final testament.

Though the private school, especially the church-related school, made tremendous contributions to education even before our nation came into being two hundred years ago, and though it therefore deserves to be regarded as forming a very significant part in our national heritage, it is the "much later on the scene" public school which is looked upon as the ideal American system of education. As a result, the system which helped put this nation on its feet, which contributed much to its intellectual, moral, and spiritual well-being, and which is still able to provide such quality education at virtually no cost to those not in sympathy with its

Section 6: *Government Aid to Private Education*   365

offerings—this truly American institution is in effect being advised that if it can no longer make it on its own, it should "quietly fold its tent and steal away."[30] Is this to be private education's reward for all it contributed to the foundation and development of this country? For our country as a whole to assume such an attitude is tantamount to biting the hand that fed and nourished her through her difficult formative years and which still strives to supply that ingredient which our public education is in no position to supply, but which is more needed today than ever before; namely, an education that deals with the building and shaping of students' moral character.

What, then, is the problem with which private education has to grapple? The same one that faces public education—finances. Everyone knows how the cost of education in general has escalated at an alarming rate during the last decade. While the public school can just ask for more taxes, the private school has had to increase its tuition and fees to the point where, as one concerned commentator expressed it, only the affluent or very dedicated can afford it.

So what alternatives does private education have? To try to solve the problem by reducing the quality of the education it provides would be certain suicide. To raise its charges to its clients much more would likewise be inviting disaster. It is true there has been some governmental aid given, such as the tax credit provision in Minnesota, but that has been attacked by groups such as the Civil Liberties Union and, as a result, declared unconstitutional. The perennial argument is that any such aid would be a violation of the church-state separation clause of the First Amendment.

However, there is more to the problem than just the financial crisis. At the root of the problem are the contradictory philosophies involved. Private education clients are through their taxes compelled to support a system which we believe fundamentally indoctrinates a system of beliefs which the Supreme Court has labeled a "religion," namely, "Secular Humanism"![31] In other words, the so-called religious neutrality of public education is a myth. The center of its philosophy is man and his accomplishments, whereas the private school has God and His gracious

---

[30] *Editors' note*: The author likely was recalling Henry Wadsworth Longfellow, "The Day Is Gone" (*ca.* 1845): "And the night shall be filled with music / And the cares that infest the day / Shall fold their tents, like Arabs, / And as silently steal away."

[31] *Torcaso v. Watkins*, 367 U.S. 488 (1961).

disposition in Christ to sinful man as its philosophy.

But expecting the advocates of private education to foot the entire bill for their private education as well as paying a high tax to help support public education is an impossible burden. And that, we maintain, is also a violation of the First Amendment for the non-public school advocate, and a most flagrant one at that, because it amounts to prohibiting the free exercise of one's religion. When will the opponents of private education realize that this prohibition is unconstitutional?

Nor is that all. An organization like the Civil Liberties Union is constantly on guard to forestall any governmental aid accruing to the private school sector. Yet, just this spring, April 1975, the CLU brought suit against a municipality in Minnesota because said community had banned topless dancers at an entertainment center, on the grounds that the ban was a violation of personal freedom. It would then seem that at least some opponents of private education are ready to favor what can be destructive of morals but to oppose what is conducive to inculcating good moral character in children and young people through conscientious religious education. Is not this an ironic situation and, at the same time, a warning that unless some kind of relief is provided for private education, there soon will be only negative forces at work in the lives of our impressionable young people? It is bad enough now, when we hear of the alarming rate of increase in crime on the part of teenagers especially. If private education is not given a chance to provide a wholesome antidote, we may soon find ourselves in a veritable jungle as far as public morals is concerned.

Another example of the kind of opposition the Christian finds himself facing these days is a court decision that was made in Tennessee. Tennessee had a law which stated that books must give alternative views on the origin of things, the biblical view of creation as well as evolution. Groups like the Nashville chapter of Americans United for the Separation of Church and State took the matter to court on constitutional grounds. The Sixth U. S. Court of Appeals held that law to be unconstitutional in the spring of 1975.[32] Thus there is a law which does not even give people the option of hearing some kind of alternative to the usually accepted theory of evolution. We would not say the public school should be required to teach creation as an explanation for the source of what we have in this world, but it certainly could and even should be taught as a viable alternative. The next step could easily follow—that the state

---

[32] *Editors' note: Daniels v. Waters*, 515 F.2d 485 (1975).

require also all non-public schools to teach evolution as the scientific explanation for the origin of our world. There could also be a law requiring a humanistic approach in the teaching of social studies and other subjects. Let no one say it cannot happen in America when we see what is happening right now.

Still another indication that the inequity which obtains between private and public education is increasing is the recent Supreme Court decision (May 1975) relative to aid to children in nonpublic schools. This decision struck down a Pennsylvania law which provided for the loaning of instructional materials, such as magazines, films, and microscopes, to church-related private schools. In the same ruling, the Court also declared that it would be contrary to law if state-employed teachers provided specialized services, such as remedial reading or aid to retarded children, in such church-related schools.[33]

In reaction to this decision, columnist James J. Kilpatrick commented:

> In the Pennsylvania case, a majority of the Court flew off into great white clouds of conjecture in order to nullify the state's effort to aid in the education of all its children. The effect here is to align the Court positively against religion. By setting up imaginary evils, and then striking them fearlessly to earth, the Court professes to defend the Establishment Clause of the First Amendment. In the process, it ignores the Free Exercise Clause altogether. ... It may be—I suggest this with great caution as one who is wary of any amendment to the constitution—it may be that an amendment should be considered that would compel the Court and the several states to treat all children alike in terms of their education. Obviously, the Equal Protection Clause of the Fourteenth Amendment is not enough.[34]

People should give some thought to the implications of the court decision rendered on the refusal of the Amish in Wisconsin to send their children to the public school. In an opinion rendered by the Supreme Court in the so-called Yoder Case (1972), the Chief Justice said that the public school philosophy is hostile to the Amish way of life.[35] It is no less an authority than the Supreme

---

[33] *Editors' note*: *Meek v. Pittenger*, 421 U.S. 349 (1975). The court did, however, allow for private schools a limited borrowing of secular-content textbooks from public schools.
[34] *Mankato [Minnesota] Free Press*, 28 May 1975.
[35] *Editors' note*: *Wisconsin v. Yoder*, 406 U.S. 205 (1972).

Court which has made that judgment. Isn't that exactly what the proponents of church-related education have been saying all along, that public education undermines and is antagonistic to the Christian's beliefs and ideals? It would seem that the Amish, who follow the Scripture in a rather limited way, generally, have far deeper convictions in this particular matter than many who have been well indoctrinated in Scripture but who by their silence approve what, by the highest court in the land, has been called a "hostile" type of education.

It should, then, be evident that we must review our whole thinking in the matter of seeking some kind of relief from this "bondage" to which we through the years have become subjected. Worse, it amounts to a tyranny of conscience when a Christian parent, because of the limitation of his resources, is forced to expose his children to the philosophy of public education which is hostile to what he believes and what he wants his children to believe. What is so wrong about a Christian's appealing for some relief, such as having some of the money extracted from him in taxes for the support of public education (which, remember, is inimical to his Christian philosophy) returned to him so that he can give his children the kind of bringing up that will not contradict what he believes is most important to them and him, the salvation of their souls? It is rather interesting that the matter of channeling tax monies to church related schools is today accepted practice in practically every modern nation except the United States and Russia.

Christian parents and educators will do well to remember some of the things called to their attention by Francis Brown in the *National Review*. He maintained that the American state infringes on the academic freedom of churches which conduct schools, of teachers who have an educational philosophy other than the states', and of parents and students who wish to seek an education with a philosophy of their choice. He also made the observation that, "Powerful Protestant and secularist backing of the state public school system has thus far prevented the long-overdue assessment of the harm the American state has done to private schooling."[36] And what was his advice or judgment?

> They (the supporters of church-related education) must bring their case to the public and to both federal and state legislators instead of waiting about nervously for the next challenge from

---

[36] Francis Brown, n.t., *National Review* (12 March 1968), 235.

such enemies of academic freedom in this matter as the American Civil Liberties Union (ACLU), the American Humanist Association, the American Jewish Congress, the Horace Mann League, Protestants and Other Americans (POAU), and Madalyn Murray O'Hair, they must bring their own grievances to the courts. They must re-examine state constitutions and seek to remove therefrom all barriers to academic freedom. Finally, they must urge educational associations on all levels, and in particular the American Association of University Professors (AAUP), to take up the struggle for this aspect of academic freedom with the full force of their resources, energies, and powers.[37]

There has been some progress in this respect. At least twenty-three states supply bus transportation, wholly or in part, to children attending non-public schools. Ten states have laws making it possible to loan textbooks to private schools. (Two states actually outlawed textbook loans, which indicates how far people will go to keep private school children from getting even a small fraction of "equal treatment.") Altogether, thirty-one states provide aid to non-public schools in one or more of the following ways: transportation, books, or auxiliary services. That is a healthy sixty percent. That is but a pittance against what really is justly due private schools, which are also performing a public function by educating people who form part of the general citizenry of the land. At the same time, it indicates that there are a number of areas in privately financed education about which the leaders of the land are rightly concerned and to which they can lend some very helpful assistance.

Incidentally, it is sheer nonsense to argue that if the government, whether federal or state, directs a few dollars to church-sponsored education the church is immediately in possession of that much money for promoting its particular mission or religious educational program. When one keeps in mind that the State of Minnesota will at the end of the present biennium be giving state aid in the amount of $970 for every child in the elementary and secondary schools in the state, one begins to see how much education is costing today, and by the same token how much the private education sector is paying for the operation of its schools, *in addition* to supporting the public school program. It ought to be evident then that some form of relief is called for if the private school is to have any chance for survival—relief which can,

---

37 Ibid., 236.

without violation of church-state separation principles, be directed towards those functions of the non-public schools which are the same as those of the general public schools, similar to those listed above, plus others.

Almost ten years ago the U.S. Chamber of Commerce made this recommendation when its Task Force on Economic Growth and Opportunities reported:

> If all parents, at every income level, could choose between sending their children to public schools and sending their children to approved private schools at public expense, both public and private education would improve as schools attempted to attract and hold pupils. Businessmen should press for the fullest possible consideration of proposals designed to enhance competition in education. Local, state, and federal governments should consider legislation which would enable communities to adopt programs establishing a public-private option for all children. Universities and educational associations should sponsor symposiums to explore the advantages, appropriate procedures, and possible pitfalls of establishing educational competition. (Third Report, Pre-Publication Release[38])

It should also be evident that this is a matter over which concerned Christian parents should be doing some fervent praying. And what Christians pray for, they should automatically be working for, too. The same parents can consult like-minded parents or friends of private education to see what they, without compromising any Scriptural principles, can do to halt this "starving out" of private or church-related education. It is time for concerned supporters of church-related schools to take the initiative and strongly appeal for some badly needed relief—either in the form of some kind of tax credit or in the form of unrestricted vouchers with which they could secure some governmental aid for an amount that somewhat compensates them for the "public" function their church schools are performing. Our church people already accept, even sue for, tax exemption for their parsonages, which gets to be a form of governmental aid to religious institutions. A Christian should have the privilege of asking for equity in the field of education with the same right and same good conscience as the Apostle Paul could have when asking for equity and fairness in the area of civil rights

---

[38] *Editors' note*: The source has not been located.

for himself in his day. An objective study of his rights as a taxpaying and church-going citizen should lead one to see that there not only need be no conflict involved when accepting governmental aid for private education, but also that his religiously oriented education is morally, legally, and constitutionally entitled to a fair share of the monies raised for educational purposes.

To help our readers to understand the philosophy of present day education and to appreciate what we regard as a sane Scriptural view on governmental aid to church-related schools, we are presenting two articles on this matter, both of them penned by B. W. Teigen, president emeritus of Bethany Lutheran College, Mankato, Minnesota. The first is a reprint from the *Lutheran Synod Quarterly*[39] and the second [**Document 6.5**] an article prepared just recently. We are offering such material in the pages of this journal because it is our conviction that if the private education sector does not speak up and institute some counter moves, the day is not far off when we shall not only lose the tax benefits we do still enjoy (such as tax exemption for church property and deductions of church contributions), but with that even more of the kind of education which alone can benefit its recipients for time and eternity.

---

[39] B. W. Teigen, "The Philosophical and Religious Foundations of Modern Education," *Lutheran Synod Quarterly* 6, no. 2 (Dec. 1965): 1–43; rpt., *Lutheran Synod Quarterly* 15, nos. 2–3 (Winter-Spring 1975): 11–49.

DOCUMENT 6.5:

Some Thoughts on Governmental Aid to Educational Church-Related Institutions (1975)

By Bjarne W. Teigen

*(For a biography of Bjarne W. Teigen, see **Document 5.1**.)*

Source: *Lutheran Synod Quarterly* 15, nos. 2–3 (Winter-Spring 1975): 50–68.

The writings of the theologians[40] to which the Confessions refer are obviously the writings of Luther, and certainly the most important one would be his "Temporal Authority: To What Extent it Should Be Obeyed" (1523). For the modern-day student this is a complex piece of writing because one needs to understand the situation in which Luther found himself and also his doctrine of the church and his doctrine of the two powers: namely, of the Word of God and of the sword. Both of these powers belong to God. The one produces peace and joy in the Holy Ghost, and the other restrains the un-Christian and the wicked. Luther then goes on to say that the people who belong to the kingdom of God and are true believers really need no temporal law

---

[40] *Editors' note*: Several paragraphs in which Teigen recapitulates his earlier summary (see **Document 6.2**) of pertinent biblical and confessional passages have been omitted here for the sake of avoiding undue repetition.

or sword. Nevertheless, God ordained the "two governments" because one cannot rule the world by the Gospel, although it is certain that the Christian would not have need of the law or the sword. The Christian is not to use law and coercion, but when the cause of the neighbor or of the community is at stake he must fight against injustice with all the appropriate means that are available. Luther calls on the Christian to use the power of the sword to assist his neighbor who is being deprived of his rights. When one thinks about this, one sees that there are some tremendously important consequences here for the Christian.[41]

We should also keep in mind what Luther meant by the term "church"; namely, the communion of saints, the lambs who hear the voice of the Shepherd. Now the power of the keys is the only thing that can build the church, but to carry out the duty of using the keys we organize into external ecclesiastical groups or organizations. We are no longer *pure church* in the strict sense of the Word. As external ecclesiastical societies we are involved both in the use of the power of the keys and also in carrying out various secular functions. Whether we are congregations, day school societies, high school associations, or synods, we, in a certain sense, operate with both powers, because to preach the Gospel we also carry out certain secular functions, such as preparing for good citizenship, owning property, etc. Hence, Luther could, as is well known, urge the mayors on to set up Christian schools. In a certain sense he looked upon them as representing Christian societies who were wielding both swords. Luther recognizes the right of a government to provide for an educated citizenry for the preservation of the government. But Luther never believed that one could be forced into the true church of God by any power of the sword. Only the power of the keys could lead one into the kingdom of God. Luther was averse to the suppression of the Anabaptists, for example, by means of secular powers:

> Still it is not right and I truly grieve, that these miserable folk [the Anabaptists] should be so lamentably murdered, burned, and tormented to death. We should allow everyone to believe what he wills. If his faith be false, he will be sufficiently punished in eternal hell-fire. Why then should we martyr these people also in this world, if their error be in faith alone and they are not guilty of rebellion or opposition to the

---

[41] Martin Luther, "Temporal Authority: To What Extent It Shall Be Obeyed" (1523), *Luther's Works*, vol. 45, ed. J. J. Pelikan (Philadelphia: Fortress Press, 1962), 81-129, quoting 87, 89, 91.

government? Dear God, how quickly a person can become confused and fall into the trap of the devil: By the Scriptures and the Word of God, we ought to guard against and withstand him. By fire we accomplish little.[42]

One further point ought to be mentioned here: namely, that Luther recognizes that the family is the essential unit and that the parents are put over the children, whether they are Christians or not.

. . .[43] And more recently, Prof. Richard E. Morgan, in a book in the prestigious Macmillan series on "The Supreme Court in American Life," said: "It remains to note the perplexing fact that no one has yet convincingly distinguished for constitutional purposes a governmental subsidy from a tax exemption. And while we have seen a fascinating and hotly contested constitutional battle develop over the sorts of governmental subsidies allowable under the Establishment Clause, extensive tax exemptions for church and church-related institutions have been allowed throughout our history, and have gone virtually unchallenged until recent years."[44]

Now with regard to this overlapping in activities, the important thing for us to recognize is that there are two powers operating here. As far as the state is concerned with these activities of the church in the field of education, its first concern is with the *secular effect*; namely, that we have peace and order here. As far as the church is involved in these activities, its primary concern is with the *spiritual effect*, life and salvation; the secular effect is secondary. Without trying to unravel all the statements of Luther regarding the so-called "Separation of Church and State" problem, it seems to me that if we would recognize that operating here is a principle which some modern political scientists call "the primacy of the secular effects," we need not apologize for Luther. And we certainly need not be uncomfortable if the state, recognizing the secular effect which our spiritual work produces, reimburses us for it. The main thing is, of course, that we do not lose our freedom.

---

[42] Luther, "Concerning Rebaptism" (1528), *Luther's Works*, vol. 40, 225-262, at 230.

[43] *Editors' note*: Here Teigen repeated his earlier comments (see **Document 6.2**) regarding the question of whether it is *per se* wrong for a religiously oriented educational institution to accept government funds; he again repeated Dallin Oaks's comment that financial aid to religious groups already occurs in other forms, such as tax exemptions.

[44] *Editors' note*: Richard E. Morgan, ed., *The Supreme Court and Religion* (New York: Free Press, 1972), 103-4.

But eternal vigilance *is* the price of liberty. Hence we must ask ourselves whether education as such is the prerogative of the state. Are we letting the state preempt the child and its education? Do we not, according to Luther, owe it to our fellow-citizen that he retain his right to educate his children, since this is in accord with the divine law? It seems to me that we have already by default turned dependence and control over to the state, in a large measure, because of the fact that we were lulled into thinking that the state could be a neutral agent in education.

Another factor we must profoundly study is whether an educational system can be neutral, and whether or not the state educational system is not teaching the religion of secularism. In the December 1965 *Lutheran Synod Quarterly*, I investigated this problem in some depth in an article, "The Philosophic and Religious Foundations of Modern Education."[45] Suffice it to say here that as a summary I shall quote a letter by E. Earle Ellis, professor of Biblical studies at New Brunswick Theological Seminary, to *The Wall Street Journal*, December 8, 1970:

> They [who argue against state aid to parochial schools] assume that the public school is religiously neutral and that its exclusive claim upon the taxpayer's dollar poses, therefore, no questions of religious liberty. These assumptions, however, are patently false. Any education that rises above the level of the playpen has a religious dimension implicit within it, for it rests upon assumptions and addresses questions about man and the world that are intrinsically religious. This dimension is especially pronounced in such subjects as literature, history, and social studies, where, in the selection of texts and in the manner and context of presentation, a worldview is instilled, day in and day out, in the minds of the pupils. The myth of religious neutrality in public education represents a curious blindness to this fact.

I will not add more to this at the present time, although it is worthy of serious discussion, except to say that if anyone doubts the impact of an educational system on its students, simply consider the senior college at Fort Wayne and Seminex.[46]

---

[45] B. W. Teigen, "The Philosophic and Religious Foundations of Modern Education," *Lutheran Synod Quarterly* 6, no. 2 (Dec. 1965): 1–34.

[46] *Editors' note*: Seminex (Concordia Seminary in Exile) was formed in 1974, following the suspension of President John Tietjen from Concordia Seminary, St. Louis, by its Board of Control. The 1973 convention of the Lutheran Church–Missouri Synod had condemned the St. Louis faculty for teaching false

To help judge the present situation and to put this matter of governmental aid to private education in the proper perspective, let me give a little history. The first amendment says: "Congress shall make no law respecting an establishment of religion or prohibiting the free exercise thereof," etc., and then it goes on to the abridgment of freedom of speech, etc. This statement was something of a compromise, but one can probably get some idea of what the original framers of the Constitution had in mind when one looks at the original formulation of this amendment which was suggested by James Madison, who was in charge of preparing the Bill of Rights: "The civil rights of none shall be abridged on account of religious belief or worship, nor shall any national religion be established; nor shall the full and equal rights of conscience be abridged." I think that today we can say that nearly all the emphasis is on the establishment clause and hardly any emphasis on the freedom of religion clause, taking into account the full and equal rights of conscience. This is probably due to the 1947 Everson case, where Justice Black wrote the majority opinion and quoted from a private letter of Thomas Jefferson (who incidentally wasn't even at the Continental Congress when the Bill of Rights was adopted) which spoke of the "wall of separation."[47]

---

doctrine. Upon the suspension of Tietjen (January 20, 1974) the students and faculty observed a moratorium on classes. On February 20, 1974 a majority of students and faculty began holding classes off campus, at St. Louis University and Eden Seminary. Seminex was legally incorporated on June 21, 1974. On October 28, 1977 the name was changed to Christ Seminary—Seminex. It was now the seminary for the newly formed Association of Evangelical Lutheran Churches (AELC), which soon became a catalyst for the merger of the American Lutheran Church with the Lutheran Church in America. The three groups agreed, in 1982, to join as one, resulting in the establishment of the liberal Evangelical Lutheran Church in America (ELCA) in 1988. Meanwhile, the majority of the Seminex faculty relocated to the Lutheran School of Theology at Chicago. "Seminex—A Brief Historical Sketch," Lutheran School of Theology at Chicago, *www.lstc.edu/news/on_homepage/30_seminex/historical_sketch.htm*; "Rev. John Tietjen, Heart of Lutheran Unity and Controversy, Dies," ELCA News Service, 17 Feb. 2004, *archive.elca.org*.

[47] Editors' note: *Everson v. Board of Education of Ewing Township*, 330 U.S. 1 (1947). The comment concerning Jefferson appears to be confused. It was not the Continental Congress of the Revolutionary War era, but the new Congress under the U.S. Constitution, that submitted the Bill of Rights to the states for ratification. Jefferson had been a member of the Continental Congress when independence was declared in 1776. He was in France while the Constitutional Convention drafted the U.S. Constitution in 1787. When Congress adopted the Bill of Rights in 1789, Jefferson was serving as President Washington's Secretary of State. In any case, Jefferson supported the Bill of Rights (and in fact had been hesitant to support the Constitution when it lacked such guarantees). On the

Up to that time the Supreme Court had not dealt with this matter, except in 1899 when it said that it was constitutional for the District of Columbia and the Surgeon General of the U. S. to give funds to a Catholic hospital run by nuns in Washington with which they were going to construct a wing to house an isolation ward for contagious diseases. The court distinguished between the hospital as a corporation or an organizational form and the nuns who worked in it, recognizing that the hospital was performing a public service. It is true, however, that during the 1870s and 1880s the so-called Blaine Amendment was added to many state constitutions, as it was done here in Minnesota twenty years after the original constitution was adopted. This amendment forbade any tax money to go to religious schools.

In a practical way, Congress recognized that private schools render a public service by educating students and that the students were entitled to benefits that went to those attending non-public schools. For example, during the 1930s the NYA Legislation provided money for all colleges, and these monies were used by the Concordias, DMLC, Northwestern College,[48] and also here at Bethany, where a couple of our older pastors went along putting in a new sewer system, paid by the NYA funds.[49] In 1945, the first GI Bill was passed, which not only gave the returning veterans some money to pay their tuition, books, and living expenses, but also reimbursed the colleges directly for the expense sustained in

---

"church and state" question, he argued for greater separation than several of his contemporaries. Jefferson's own interpretation of the First Amendment as "building a wall of separation between church and state" appeared in his 1802 letter to the Danbury Baptist Association, when he, as President, refused their invitation to call for a national day of prayer. Not until *Everson* (1947) did the Supreme Court establish Jefferson's doctrine as case law. See Jefferson's letters to James Madison (20 Dec. 1787 and 15 March 1789) and to the Danbury Baptist Association (1 Jan. 1802), in Merrill D. Peterson, *The Political Writings of Thomas Jefferson* (n.p.: Thomas Jefferson Memorial Foundation, 1993), 82-84, 90-91, 145.

[48] *Editors' note*: The Lutheran Church–Missouri Synod operated a network of colleges named Concordia, offering specialized training for future teachers in the church; it is now known as the Concordia University system. Dr. Martin Luther College (New Ulm, Minnesota) served as the teacher-training school for the Wisconsin Evangelical Lutheran Synod, and Northwestern College (Watertown, Wisconsin) prepared men for pastoral studies at that synod's Wisconsin Lutheran Seminary. In 1995, those two colleges were amalgamated into Martin Luther College, New Ulm, for the training of pastors, teachers, and staff ministers.

[49] *Editors' note*: The reference is to the National Youth Administration, a New Deal agency that provided funds to high school and college students in exchange for work.

enrolling GIs. Here at Bethany, one of my first jobs assigned me by Dr. Ylvisaker, then president, was to work with our bookkeeper, Sophia Anderson, to cost-account the actual cost per credit hour for educating students here. This cost was determined and the government paid Bethany directly the difference between what the students paid and what the actual cost was. The only stipulation was that our figuring would be audited to see whether or not we had inflated the figures. I am sorry to report that at that time I was a novice as a registrar, and Miss Sophia Anderson was also somewhat new, and we were both conservative, with the result that our figures were "underflated," with the further result that Bethany should have picked up much more money than it did. At any rate, no outcry was raised regarding this system, although when the Korean GI Bill came into effect, this was done away with in the early 1950s, with the result that GIs went more to the public colleges than to the private colleges which had begun to raise their tuition to meet their expenses.

With the increasing inflation and the impact of Sputnik, Congress passed several laws to help higher education, notably the most important ones were the National Defense Education Act of 1958, the Higher Education Facilities Act of 1963, and the Higher Education Act of 1965. It was recognized by the Congress that private colleges were performing a public function and that in some way they ought to be reimbursed for helping take care of the tidal wave of students that was rolling into the colleges. And so certain limited grants were made to the colleges and also to the students who attended these private colleges. There were some restrictions. Notably, the Civil Rights Act of 1964 (P. L. 88–352) carried this statement in Title VI, Sec. 601: "No person in the United States shall, on the ground of race, color, or national origin, be excluded from participation in, be denied the benefits of, or be subjected to discrimination or activity receiving federal financial assistance." This clause became standard in the higher education acts and also in the Elementary and Secondary Education Act of 1965.

But Congress wanted to be very careful that there would be no control exerted by the Federal Government on the process of education at the colleges. Therefore, for example, the Higher Education Act of 1965, under Title VIII, Sec. 804, carried this statement:

> Nothing contained in this Act shall be construed to authorize any department, agency, officer, or employee of the United

States to exercise any direction, supervision, or control over the curriculum, program of instruction, administration, or personnel of any educational institution, or over the selection of library resources by any educational institution.

One would think that this would lay to rest the canard which still seems to circulate, that one cannot have a Bible in the library.

There has been, especially since the 1940s, a push to call on the government—not only to eliminate any aid to private organizations (schools particularly), even though they are rendering a public service to the country, which the nation otherwise would have to provide—but also to impose on private and religious organizations restrictions that may come into conflict with their conscience so that their full and equal rights of conscience are abridged. If one does a little investigating, one will quickly see that this drive has been spear-headed in the last thirty years by the POAU (now the AUFSCAS), the ACLU, the NEA, the AJC (American Jewish Congress).[50] One must give them credit that they have been most successful, especially in recent years, in promulgating the idea of the need for a single monolithic school system which inculcates the latest doctrines of the day under the umbrella of religious neutrality. The true nature of the beliefs of the hardcore POAU only came to light recently when they went on record for unlimited abortions.

A brief look at some recent Supreme Court decisions will indicate their success. The Cochran case (1930) held that it was not wrong to provide for free distribution of non-sectarian textbooks to private as well as public schools, on the basis that the students and not the schools were the beneficiaries. The Everson case (1947), while it promulgated the "wall" idea of Justice Black, okayed money for bus transportation also for private school children, since this was considered a legitimate public safety measure. The McCollum decision (1948) held it was unconstitutional when a school district allowed representatives of various religions to come to the public school premises during school hours for religious instruction. Zorach case (1952) saw the Court relaxing somewhat its more extreme absolute separation in favor of moderate "cooperative" separation by allowing released time from public school during the school hours to go to another place

---

[50] *Editors' note*: The other abbreviations refer to the Protestants and Other Americans United (which later merged with other groups to form Americans United for the Separation of Church and State, 1947), American Civil Liberties Union, and the National Education Association.

for instruction. In 1968 there seemed to be a change on the part of the Court in the Allen case, where the Court upheld the New York state law providing free textbooks for children in private as well as public schools as having a purpose that was essentially secular for the public welfare, and a primary effect that was secular rather than religious as far as the State was concerned, although there might incidentally be a benefit to private and religious schools. In 1970, in the Walz case, the Supreme Court also upheld as constitutional tax exemptions for religious institutions, including church-related schools, since this was thought to be a traditional and permissible form of encouragement to religion, showing a benevolent neutrality. One might now think that maybe POAU wasn't too successful, but in 1971 came the Lemon and DiCenso cases, where the Court declared unconstitutional public subsidies for the secular content of church-related education and also the payment of salaries of teachers of secular subjects in church-related schools. Here the fear of excessive entanglement was set forth. But in the Nyquist and Sloan cases in 1973, the Supreme Court went a very long way in satisfying the highest expectations of POAU. The Court declared that tuition grants and tuition reimbursements and tax credits for tuition paid in church-related schools were unconstitutional.[51]

The full sweep of these last decisions has probably not been grasped by many of us. For the time being I shall pass over the implications of the Lemon decision that implies that parents, or other groups, for that matter, are not to organize and enter into political activity, because this might induce political division concerning the funding of church-related education. It is a real question with constitutional lawyers whether or not the court is depriving citizens of one of the fundamental rights of speech, assembly, and petition—all thought to have been guaranteed by the First Amendment. Let me call your attention, however, only to the implication of the opinion that tax credits for tuition paid in church-related schools are unconstitutional. The difference between a tax credit and a tax deduction is not one of essence but

---

[51] Editors' note: *Cochran v. Louisiana State Board of Education*, 281 U.S. 370 (1930); *Everson v. Board of Education of Ewing Township*, 330 U.S. 1, 18 (1947); *Illinois ex rel. McCollum v. Board of Education*, 333 U.S. 203 (1948); *Zorach v. Clauson*, 343 U.S. 306 (1952); *Board of Education v. Allen*, 392 U.S. 236 (1968); *Walz v. Tax Comm'n of City of New York*, 397 U.S. 664 (1970); *Lemon v. Kurtzman*, 403 U.S. 602 (1971), a decision in which the appeal of *Earley et al. v. Dicenso et al.* was included; *Committee for Public Education v. Nyquist*, 413 U.S. 756 (1973); and, *Sloan v. Lemon*, 413 U.S. 825 (1973).

Robert Clark, on behalf of the Bethany Lutheran College Board of Regents, presented a gift of appreciation to Bjarne and Elna Teigen in the mid 1960s, which they used for a vacation in Europe.

merely one of degree; in a tax deduction one subtracts his gift to the church or school of his choice from his adjusted gross income, while in a tax credit he subtracts the deduction from his actual tax liability. Right now it boils down to this: that if you donate money to a school you may deduct this amount for income tax purposes, but if you pay tuition you cannot deduct it.

The state's real power lies in the power to tax. Right now that power to tax in the field of education is directed towards taxing for one educational philosophy, namely, Secular Humanism. To show you which way the wind is blowing, recently (1970) the state of Minnesota rescinded a part of its original constitution adopted in 1857 (Article IX, Sec. 1), which acknowledges that the state's power of taxation shall never be surrendered, or contracted away, but nevertheless insisted, no doubt so that the freedom of conscience to pursue one's religion would be protected, that cemeteries, hospitals, churches, schools, colleges, "and all seminaries of learning," etc., "shall be exempt from taxation." It is now left to the whim of whatever legislature that may be in session whether to tax or not to tax.

To round off this brief study, I should call attention to three Supreme Court decisions that conceivably could have some bearing on restoring the rights of parents to choose whatever education they want for their children without a penalty, but which really have not come into play in the school cases. In the first, the Torcaso case of 1961, the Court maintained that there "are religions based on a belief in the existence of God and religions founded on different beliefs." One of the latter religions which "do not teach a belief in the existence of God," said the Court, is "Secular Humanism," etc. Incidentally, the Court's definition of religion here is in harmony with the Book of Concord (LC I, 5-10).[52] In the Sherbert case (1963), the Supreme Court held that a woman who had become a Seventh Day Adventist was entitled to unemployment compensation benefits when she could not, for conscience' sake, take a job which necessitated working on Saturday. The Unemployment Security Commission had ruled that as Mrs. Sherbert refused to work on Saturday because of her religious beliefs, her employment was not "involuntary," and that therefore she could not collect unemployment pay. The Court said: "The ruling forces her to choose between following the precepts of her religion and forfeiting benefits, on the one hand, and abandoning one of the precepts of her religion in order to accept work, on the other hand. So, the government cannot force a citizen into that dilemma. It cannot force a citizen to make a choice between his religious beliefs and welfare benefits. So the Court declared further in the Sherbert case: "Governmental imposition of such a choice puts the same kind of burden upon the free exercise of religion as would a fine imposed against appellant for her Saturday worship." And the decision concluded with these words: "It is too late in the day to doubt that the liberties of religion and expression may be infringed by the denial or placing of conditions upon a benefit or a privilege."[53] And then there is the more recent Yoder case (1972) by which the Amish in Wisconsin were excused from the compulsory school attendance laws. The

---

[52] *Editors' note*: The reference is to Luther's discussion of the First Commandment in his *Large Catechism* (1529), where he states: "A god is that to which we look for all good and in which we find refuge in every time of need. To have a god is nothing else than to trust and believe him with our whole heart.... That to which your heart clings and entrusts itself is, I say, really your God." *The Book of Concord: The Confessions of the Evangelical Lutheran Church*, trans. and ed. Theodore G. Tappert (Philadelphia: Fortress Press, 1959), 365.

[53] *Editors' note*: Sherbert v. Verner, 374 U.S. 398, 404 (1963).

Chief Justice who wrote the majority opinion made three important points: 1) that religion is a large element in education; 2) that parents have prior rights; 3) that the public school philosophy is hostile to the Amish way of life.[54]

Now it seems to me that this emphasis on the freedom clause in the First Amendment ought to be applied in the governmental aid to education problem. There are people whose conscience tells them to send their children to a church-related institution for their education, but they can't afford it. What responsibilities do we have, as citizens who uphold the free exercise of religion clause, to help them in their struggle against this massive force of the public education monopoly arrayed against them? Shouldn't we use, as the Apology says, "with safety" legitimate civil ordinances, such as public redress, etc. (Ap XVI, 53)? Luther, as you know, in his brochure on "Temporal Authority: To What Extent It Should Be Obeyed," said that you may suffer injustice towards yourself as a true Christian but that you should "tolerate no injustice toward your neighbor. The Gospel does not forbid this; in fact, in other places it actually commands it."[55]

I recognize that the present situation in which we find ourselves is most complex and that there are dangers on every side. As I said, eternal vigilance is the price of liberty. Our Synod, during the past twelve or fifteen years, has been forced to look into these matters much more deeply than it had in previous decades. And the Synod has cautiously passed some resolutions to the effect that the matter of receiving governmental aid to its school is *per se* an *adiaphoron*, remembering that one must be very careful. WELS, too, rightly warns that all be alert to the dangers, but after studying a report from its Advisory Committee on Education, agreed with regard to governmental aid to education that this lay in the area of *adiaphora* and was not necessarily a confusion of church and state.[56] It is indeed true that this was something of a reversion of the 1963 statement they had adopted, but some of the WELS educators have done some studying, too, during these years. If I may be permitted an expression of opinion, I would say that it was unfortunate that this 1967 resolution was such an excellently well-kept synodical secret that a large number of people were not aware of it until the *Christian News* published a

---

54   Editors' note: *Wisconsin v. Yoder*, 406 U.S. 205 (1972).
55   Luther, "Temporal Authority," 96.
56   *Report of the Thirty-ninth Convention of the Wisconsin Evangelical Lutheran Synod* (1967), 186.

portion of a lengthy resolution of Pastor Koch and part of the Mt. Olive Lutheran Church of Colorado Springs, charging WELS with several points of false doctrine. Among the fifty or sixty "Whereases" there was one that charged WELS with refusing to heed the exhortations of the Lord when Wisconsin Lutheran High School of Milwaukee received some aid under the Elementary and Secondary Education Act of 1965. But there is no need to rehearse that here since the controversy was pretty well aired in the press.[57]

Among the sticky issues arising from this present controversy over governmental aid—and I'm thinking of the last Supreme Court decision—note that the tax credit was dismissed as unconstitutional.[58] The tax credit, of course, would go to the parents but, so the argumentation went, the parents were merely "conduits or channels" for government aid to church-related schools, and therefore it must be unconstitutional. This type of argument distorts the fundamental role of parents as responsible persons who exercise their freedom of choice over their children in what they consider their children's best interest. This is not only contrary to the scriptural point of view of parents as the fundamental institution of the family, but the Supreme Court has also recognized this institution (1925, the Oregon case[59]) and so has the United Nations' Declaration of Human Rights.[60] Parents have a right to direct the education of their children, and they are not merely, as someone has said, "the means but rather the cause."

Closely connected with such issues is one the Lutheran must directly face on the basis of the Confessions: "where commands of civil authority cannot be obeyed without sin, we must obey God rather than man (Acts 5: 29)" (AC XVI, 7). If, for example, the state should command us to send our children where false doctrine pervades all instruction, would this principle come into play? If the state does not directly force us into such a situation, but does it indirectly through compulsory school attendance laws, subsidization of only one system which teaches false doctrine, and high taxes for all of us, what then? Luther, in his tract to which I have already alluded, is quite clear about the limits of temporal authority when he says with regard to Acts 5:29: "Thereby he (i.e.

---

[57] *Editors' note*: The source has not been located.
[58] *Editors' note*: The reference is apparently to *Committee for Public Education v. Nyquist*, 413 U.S. 756 (1973).
[59] *Editors' note*: *Pierce v. Society of Sisters*, 268 U.S. 510 (1925).
[60] *Editors' note*: "Parents have a right to choose the kind of education that shall be given to their children," United Nations Universal Declaration of Human Rights (1948), art. 26, sec. 3.

St. Peter) clearly sets a limit to the temporal authority, for if we had to do everything that the temporal authority wanted there would have been no point in saying, 'We must obey God rather than man.'"[61] This particular tract was occasioned by the fact that on March 5, 1522 the Duke of Bavaris had forbidden all his subjects to read or discuss Luther's books. Duke George of Saxony had on February 10, 1522 issued a similar order to all his officials, and he had also proscribed Luther's German New Testament. So Luther says: "If your prince or temporal ruler commands you to side with the Pope, to believe thus and so, or to get rid of certain books, you should say, 'It is not fitting that Lucifer should sit at the side of God. . . . If you command me to believe or get rid of certain books, I will not obey; for then you are a tyrant and over-reach yourself, commanding where you have neither the right nor the authority.'" And so Luther boldly tells the people that they should not turn over to the officials a single page, "not even a letter, on pain of losing their salvation."[62] It seems to me that the situation Christians are facing today is closely parallel to that of Luther's time.

These last times are becoming dreadful. But I believe that we would not violate any divine law if we stand on our constitutional rights to have these inequities corrected. At least we would be in harmony with the Apology, which insists that "a Christian can use with safety" legitimate civil ordinances (Ap XVI, 53).

---

[61] Martin Luther, "Temporal Authority," 111.
[62] Ibid., 112.

SECTION 7:
Academic Freedom and Christian Integrity

Introduction

By Andrew Shoop

I have given them Your word and the world has hated them, for they are not of the world any more than I am of the world. My prayer is not that You take them out of the world but that You protect them from the evil one.

John 17:14-15

Just as religion and science are portrayed by some as combative fields, the relationship between individual expression and Christian ideals is often controversial. Rather than the two sides complementing and enabling the other, their relationship is mired with friction. Culture presses forward while Christianity applies the brakes. But is this really the case? When confronted with unorthodox expressions or ideas, how does a

Christian community determine their propriety? Institutions of the Evangelical Lutheran Synod have been confronted with this question and found that there is no hard and fast rule for a Christian appraisal of our dynamic culture. There are, however, valuable lessons to be learned. This introduction previews the articles that follow by highlighting a few interesting facets of this issue as it pertains to Bethany Lutheran College.

In the words of Dr. S. C. Ylvisaker, penned in 1933, the college was founded in order "to prepare the student at least to appreciate and love the beautiful and that which edifies and enriches life." Pastor George Orvick warmly recalled these words nearly sixty years later for the dedication of the S. C. Ylvisaker Fine Arts Center on September 16, 1990. Because of Ylvisaker's devotion to the school, it was thought proper to honor him with a lasting testament of his service. It is only fitting that his name graces this particular building, as Dr. Ylvisaker commented frequently on the importance of acknowledging the enriching power of the arts, the "indefinable something which adds richness, beauty, mellowness, and refinement." More important for this life than the appreciation of culture, as both Ylvisaker and Orvick pointed out, was a steadfast faith relying fully on the grace of Christ (**Document 7.2**).

The proper application of this faith would be questioned five years later in the Fine Arts Center when a provocative work of art—entitled "Prophesy"—temporarily housed on the campus created a stir among students and faculty. The piece, part of a regional art show, divided many observers over the bounds of freedom of expression. After President Marvin Meyer consulted with members of the Bethany faculty and staff, it was decided that the piece should be taken down. Meyer issued a formal response to the work (**Document 7.3**), explaining that to display the piece publicly on campus would compromise the college's mission. His response focused the issue on adherence to the institution's collective conscience, rooted in the Gospel message. The controversy produced a spirited debate over censorship and artistic freedom throughout the Bethany campus and the wider community, as indicated in the *Bethany Scroll* (**Document 7.4**). Some applauded the college for standing up for its beliefs in the face of opposition; others criticized how the school handled the situation. One newspaper editorial suggested that Bethany's actions mirrored the Spanish Inquisition and Joseph Stalin's political censorship.[1] In the end, the piece did make its way into the show—one local artist wore a t-shirt featuring a print of "Prophesy" to the show's opening night.[2]

Bethany Lutheran College was again visited by controversy in 2007 when Soulforce, an organization advocating the acceptance of homosexuality, informed the college that its volunteers would be demonstrating there that spring. The administration chose to prohibit the "equality riders" from holding forums on campus with the students because their message contradicted the Evangelical Lutheran Synod's position on homosexuality.[3] Members of the organization were eventually arrested for trespassing. In a booklet handed out to students prior to the protest, Chaplain Donald Moldstad commented on the Christian's response to homosexuality, pointing to the Savior's loving actions as an example to be emulated by His followers. According to Moldstad, true love in this case actually meant intolerance of the sinful actions of others (**Document 7.5**). Again, there were varied opinions within Bethany's walls over how the school responded to Soulforce's visit. Though many disagreed, others in the Mankato community supported the school's decision to forbid Soulforce from dialoging with students on campus grounds.[4] The underlying issues of the visit may resurface for the ELS in the future, so reflecting on Bethany's experience in this particular case may help the synod's members evaluate their own response to homosexual advocacy.

For the disciple of Christ, faith is the framework within which ideas are to be expressed and communicated. When Christian faith and freedom of expression find themselves at odds, one standard must trump the other. "All institutions will draw the line

---

[1] Sally Brasher, "Censorship Can Cause Avalanche," *Mankato Free Press*, April 6, 1995, 4.

[2] *Mankato Free Press*, 11 Apr. 1995, 13, 15.

[3] The synod adopted the following doctrinal statement in 2004: "We confess that Scripture condemns homosexuality and extra-marital relations (fornication and adultery) as sin. Nevertheless, when an individual caught up in such sins truly repents, the forgiveness of the Gospel is to be fully applied. We confess that the divine institution of marriage is to be heterosexual, in which, according to God's design, a man and a woman may enjoy a life-long companionship in mutual love. We teach on the basis of Holy Scripture that marriage is the only proper context for the expression of sexual intimacy and for the procreation of children. See Romans 1:26-27, 1 Corinthians 6:9, 18 and 7:2-9, John 4:17-18, 1 John 1:9, Genesis 1:27-28 and 2:18-24, and Matthew 19:4-6." *Synod Report* (2004): 82.

[4] See Soulforce Collection, ELS Archives.

somewhere," noted Bethany College President Marvin Meyer. "We have drawn the line on the basis of what is most near and dear to our Christian college—the Gospel message of Jesus Christ as the Savior from sin" (**Document 7.3**). However, as Dr. Thomas A. Kuster articulated, careful discernment should not lead to intellectual isolation or a removal from the study of God's creation. His children should "plunge into investigation . . . [of] the arts and sciences, not only as an excellent means of praising God by examining His works, but also in an effort to exercise a corrective influence on the cultures of the world." For Kuster, this kind of sound scholarship is absolutely vital in a Christian institution of higher education, and believers are to be leaders in the "wisdom of this world," not just individuals who glean little bits and pieces of secular knowledge. His article encourages educators to foster independent thinking among their students, with the instructor guiding the student to correct any erroneous conclusions (**Document 7.1**).

Combative moments between biblical values and culture, taken in the correct light, can be seen as opportunities for Christians to pursue the truth. The 1974 synod convention resolved to express it in this way:

> Paradoxically, it is the truly Lutheran academician's highest freedom to be bound and captive to Synod's scriptural and confessional commitments. He is liberated *from* the marshes of subjectivity and emotionalism and from the mazes of rationalistic, humanistic thought. He is liberated *for* thinking the Spirit's thoughts after Him and for bringing all his own thinking into subjection to the mind of Christ as revealed in the Scripture Word of Truth.[5]

In a thought conveyed by many in the Bethany community, the free discussion of ideas is pivotal throughout this process. The college recognizes this and encourages its professionals to solve their differences of views through consultation and mutual respect (**Document 7.6**). Arriving at a proper response to controversy can be admittedly difficult. However, everyone involved, and particularly students, have much to gain by looking at these issues with an inquisitive mind. As one teacher said amidst controversy, "This is one of the most teachable moments we've had in a long time" (**Document 7.4**). May the following articles be "teachable moments" for the reader.

---

[5] "Academic Freedom," *Lutheran Sentinel*, 10 Oct. 1974, 291, 304.

DOCUMENT 7.1:

The Importance of a Spirit of Inquiry in Christian Higher Education (1974)

By Thomas A. Kuster

Thomas A. Kuster (1939–) was born in Sarnia, Ontario, on November 17, 1939. Kuster graduated from Northwestern College in Watertown, Wisconsin, in 1961 and received his master's degree from Indiana University the next year. He taught at Bethany Lutheran College part-time and coached debate from 1962 to 1965 while attending Bethany Lutheran Theological Seminary in Mankato, Minnesota. After graduating, he served as an assistant pastor at Our Saviour's Lutheran Church in Madison, Wisconsin, alongside his father, Pastor Arnold Kuster. He married Judy Maginnis in 1967. During his time at Our Saviour's, Kuster also worked on his Ph.D. in Speech at the University of Wisconsin in Madison, receiving his doctorate in 1969. Faith Lutheran Church in Muskegon, Michigan, called Kuster in 1969, and he remained there until 1971 when he moved to New Ulm, Minnesota, to teach at Dr. Martin Luther  *College. In 1991, he began teaching at Bethany, where he continues to educate, emphasizing critical thinking among students. Dr. Kuster has been president of the League of Minnesota Human Rights Commissions and served on several governors' task forces on human rights. He was also the president of the National Parliamentary Debate Association. Within the Evangelical Lutheran Synod, Kuster edited the synod convention's annual tabloid report,* Convention Echo, *for twenty years, also serving on the Youth Board and the Publication Board for a number of years. He and his wife have raised nine children and have eleven grandchildren.* [AS]

Source: Lutheran Synod Quarterly 14, no. 4 (Summer 1974): 1–32.

"What has Athens to do with Jerusalem, the Academy with the church? . . . We have no need for curiosity since Jesus Christ, nor for inquiry since the Gospel."[6]

So said the third century church father, Tertullian, in a passage frequently cited by those who stress an apparent incompatibility between the "wisdom of this world" and the spiritual wisdom God has provided us in Scripture. This apparent incompatibility becomes so absolute for some that the rejection of intellectual pursuits becomes a positive Christian virtue, and "Christian scholarship" is disparaged as if the two terms cannot stand together.

Lesser strains of this anti-intellectual spirit find frequent voice in conservative Lutheran circles. Some, for example, express profound reservations concerning the practice in which faculty members in our Christian colleges receive advanced training and degrees in secular schools—as if fearful that the Christian cannot meet the world's knowledge on its own ground. Others, on a different tack, reflect the same anti-intellectual spirit when they attempt to define the values of Christian education entirely in affective terms—growth in love, a personal relationship with the Lord, commitment, fellowship—as if the Christian has no need to encounter the world's knowledge on its own ground. Such voices, dedicated and well-meaning as they are, would doubtless echo Tertullian's words approvingly. This paper intends instead to take issue with that church father on this point: there is, in fact, an important need for curiosity since Jesus Christ; and since the Gospel, inquiry is more necessary than ever.

In this paper, "inquiry" will be taken most often in its broad sense, synonymous with "scholarship." More specifically, scholarship is that kind of intellectual work that involves the

---

[6] Tertullian, *De Praescriptione Haereticorum*, 7. Trans. adapted from Alexander Roberts and James Donaldson, eds., *The Antenicene Fathers*, vol. 3 (Grand Rapids: Wm. B. Eerdmans, 1957), 246.

higher orders of independent or "critical" thinking[7]—i.e., thinking that does not stop with simple recall or even simple understanding of data, but soars beyond into analysis of thought structures, into synthesis of new structures, connections, and hypotheses, and finally into evaluation of thought structures against appropriate standards, and application of structures to new situations.[8] If a narrow definition is desired, perhaps none will serve better than that of Jerome Bruner, who describes inquiry as a "matter of rearranging or transforming evidence in such a way that one is enabled to go beyond the evidence so reassembled to new insights."[9] Viewing inquiry in this sense against a backdrop of the college classroom, one can generate this contrast: on the one hand, there will be knowledge acquired by a student's own search and question—by inquiry; on the other hand, there will be knowledge previously prepared by the professor and served up to students, cooked and garnished for their consumption. There is, of course, a place for both; the two even work in complementary fashion. But it will be the thesis of this paper that the former—knowledge gained by the student's own inquiry—should predominate in any school, including Christian schools.

The paper, then, will contain two major sections: the first and longer will defend the *necessity* of stimulating a spirit of inquiry in the Christian college student; the second will attempt to outline some *means* of doing so.

I. The Necessity of Stimulating a Spirit of Inquiry[10]

If the spirit of inquiry among us is at times pale and wan, or even if there is some inertia among those of us who are in charge of nourishing it to a healthy vitality, it might prove helpful first to re-examine the necessity of stimulating such a spirit in our college

---

[7] The Watson-Glasser Critical Thinking Appraisal defines critical thinking in terms of "attitudes of inquiry" and their accompanying skills. R. J. Starr, "Structured Oral Inquiry Improves Thinking," *American Biology Teachers* 34 (Oct. 1972): 408.

[8] Harold G. Cassidy, "Liberation and Limitations," in Boston College Centennial Colloquium, *The Knowledge Explosion: Liberation and Limitations*, ed. Francis Sweeney (New York: Farrar, Straus & Giroux, 1966), 183-84.

[9] *On Knowing: Essays for the Left Hand* (New York: Atheneum, 1970), 82-83.

[10] *Editors' note*: The original text included section divisions marked with I, II, A, B, C, etc., but without any subtitles; the editors have inserted subtitles to guide readers. The editors also have renumbered subsections I.B.i, ii, and iii as I.B.1, 2, and 3, respectively.

and seminary students. Such a discussion, it seems, falls under the purview of several of the stated purposes of our Christian institutions of learning. For example:

Bethany . . . aims to help students . . .

    2.   To assume a responsible Christian attitude towards the talents God has given them and towards their obligation to develop and use their talents for the glory of God and the welfare of their fellowmen.

    3.   To progress in the development of critical and creative thinking.

    4.   To develop and increase an appreciation of man's expression through the fine arts.

    5.   To become responsible citizens, aware of social realities through the study of our American and world cultural heritage, and our contemporary social, economic, and political society.

    6.   To acquire the ability to use written and oral English effectively.

    7.   To secure a foundation in mathematics and the sciences for a better understanding of the world in which we live.

    9.   To acquire the necessary skills for achieving a satisfactory vocational adjustment.[11]

---

[11]   *Bethany Lutheran College Catalog, 1971-73,* 8-9.

> *Whenever we* think,
> *we think for a* purpose,
> *within a* point of view,
> *based on* assumptions,
> *leading to* implications *and* consequences,
> *using* data, facts, *and* experiences,
> *to make* inferences *and* judgments,
> *based on* concepts *and* theories,
> *in attempting to* answer a question.
>
> Richard Paul and Linda Elder, *Miniature Guide to Critical Thinking Concepts and Tools*
> (Tomales, CA: Foundation for Critical Thinking, 2009), distributed for discussion by the Bethany Lutheran College Faculty Development Committee.

To fulfill such objectives effectively, our educational practice must be responsive to three factors. First, our practice must be true to the nature of reality, and how we know it. We neither live nor teach in a dream world of our own making, but rather in a world God has made, and in which He has placed us. This paper will argue that the nature of the world, and how we know it, necessitates inquiry. Second, our practice must be true to the demands of the educational task, particularly on the college level. This paper will argue that the nature of education necessitates inquiry. Third, our practice must be true to our Christian calling. This paper will argue that the task of the Christian necessitates inquiry. The final consideration in this section, lest the case for inquiry seem too strong, will be the limits of legitimate inquiry.

I.A. The Nature of Reality Necessitates Inquiry

First, consider the claim that the nature of reality and how we know it necessitates inquiry.

The present structure of "knowledge" in western culture is based on a philosophy of realism, a view basically compatible on this point with revelation, and first extensively formulated by Aristotle. In brief, this philosophy holds that "there is a reality out there," and with that reality the individual mind engages somehow, and so "knows" it. The picture of knowing so produced is one of an active mind rather than a passive one; reality and knowledge of it are not already in the mind,[12] but the mind must, in effect, go out and investigate reality, in order to learn it.[13] The basic process of knowing, then, is "research," in its broad sense. The purpose of the scholar, according to a view with a tradition extending back through the Middle Ages to Aristotle, is to develop the various disciplines by uncovering the rational structure of reality—to find out how things are, and why.[14]

Furthermore, the structure of that reality is so complex, and therefore so initially (and perhaps permanently) ambiguous, that it does not present itself for easy comprehension. To carry on the basic processes of knowing, then, must involve higher orders of thinking—analysis, synthesis, evaluation—those processes we have earlier defined as inquiry.

It would seem, then, that all knowledge, at least on a secular level, results from inquiry—either one's own, or someone else's.[15] The nature of reality, and of how we come to know it, permits no alternative. To advance the development of any discipline, as well as to understand fully its present development, requires an understanding of, and experience with, inquiry.[16]

I.B. The Nature of Education Necessitates Inquiry

Consider next that the nature of education necessitates inquiry. This necessity emerges in three specific areas: first, dealing effectively with the various disciplines requires inquiry; second, the process of effective learning requires inquiry; third, the activity of effective teaching requires experience with inquiry.

---

[12] As would be claimed by a philosophical idealist, for example. My purpose here is not to argue the validity of realism and its epistemology; there are of course many alternatives. But the fact is that the current structure of education is based on many of the premises of realism, and to function within that structure we must adopt those premises.
[13] A Christian knows that many aspects of reality lie beyond the power of his mind to search out and grasp by itself. Information about some of these is given us by revelation. A somewhat special relationship between revelation and inquiry is described in the third and fourth parts of this section, below.
[14] Calvin College Curriculum Study Committee, *Christian Liberal Arts Education* (Grand Rapids: Wm. B. Eerdmans, 1970), 8.
[15] Ibid., 48.
[16] A. C. Pugliese, "Meaning of Inquiry, Discovery, and Investigative Approaches to Science Teaching," *Science Teacher* 40 (January 1973): 26.

I.B.1. The Nature of Disciplines

The contents of any academic discipline involve three elements: a core of hard data or fact, a conceptual framework into which those data are fit, and a methodology by which conclusions of various kinds are reached.[17] Inquiry, as we have defined it, operates extensively within the third element, methodology. A full understanding of any discipline can come only from an appropriate consideration of all three elements.

Unfortunately, the third element, methodology, with its inevitable spirit of inquiry, is the one most often neglected in the classroom. Facts are easy to teach, concepts only a little harder. Methodology, however, is little understood and difficult and time-consuming to get into. As a result, the student learns to consider the discipline as merely a collection of things to memorize and never really gets the flavor of it, never feels its excitement—never, in short, fully understands it.

Prescription: a dose of methodology. To engage in the methodology of a discipline—to exercise inquiry within the limits a certain discipline imposes—turns the student from a mere memorizer into a practitioner (though of course an amateur one), and therefore one who is at least in a position to gain a full understanding of the discipline. Some fields do this routinely. On page 17 of the 1973-74 Dr. Martin Luther College Catalog, a picture bears this caption: "Embryonic scientists probe the mysteries of God's creation." If science labs make students into "embryonic scientists" who are engaged in the methodology of the discipline, then perhaps we should have other labs—or lab-type experiences—as well. The student of history should not learn just the facts and concepts of history; he should become an "embryonic historian" by writing some history himself, thereby learning, among other things, to be dissatisfied with the secondary and tertiary sources that characterize the footnotes of many a term paper. And what better goal for a Christian doctrine class than to produce "embryonic dogmaticians" who have gone beyond simply learning the pronouncements of the great dogmaticians (valuable as that is) to an ability to formulate, in view of some modern problems, a teaching of Scripture in fresh, clear, and faithful language. A full understanding of any discipline requires engagement with its methodology.

But if this is true, then inquiry becomes all the more

---

[17] Calvin Committee, *Christian Liberal Arts Education*, 52-53.

necessary because of the impingement of alternative views. Authorities within any discipline differ regarding details of methodology, as well as of conceptual frameworks. Conclusions, then, are likely to be biased according to the viewpoint of their author. Enlightenment historians, we are told, *set out* to prove that the Middle Ages were dark because of the influence of the church, and they adjusted their methodology accordingly. A Catholic historian of philosophy may set out to prove that after St. Thomas, all was regrettable decline. And a Freudian literary critic will try to show that the key to understanding a poem lies in the subconscious of author and reader. The proliferation of viewpoints resulting is certainly not to be deplored; indeed, the chief characteristic of college-level instruction is the investigation of viewpoints and their presuppositions. But the fact of proliferation underscores the necessity of inquiry; *it is simply not enough for a student to learn only his teacher's views*. Regarding details of subject matter, regarding evaluations of results as well as of presuppositions and of perspectives of mind out of which aspects of the subject matter develop, the student himself must learn to discern and to judge, without being dependent on the teacher's pronouncements. True, there is often a scriptural view which the teacher tries to present, but even here the teacher himself is often not fully apprised of all its implications—which Christian teacher has not gained new Christian insights into his subject, and has therefore taught new things year after year? The student must be free to go beyond what the teacher says. Even his examination of non-Christian views can have the effect of avoiding a deadening parochialism; by understanding better the various spiritual kingdoms of mankind, he can come to a fuller awareness of the significance of his own membership in the Kingdom of God.[18]

If effective dealing with any discipline, then, involves engagement with its methodology, as well as the ability to investigate alternative views, individual inquiry is clearly required.

---

[18] Ibid., 57-62.

The pastors of the Evangelical Lutheran Synod meet each fall for a theological conference, in addition to the June convention that lay delegates attend. Thomas Kuster stands third from the left in the back row of this gathering, hosted at Bethany Lutheran College in the 1960s.

I.B.2. Effective Learning

Mention "inquiry" to an up-to-date educator and he will immediately think of a particular teaching method currently in vogue in some quarters. This paper considers "inquiry" a far broader term than just the "inquiry method" (sometimes, with slight variations, termed the "discovery method"). Yet a glance at this somewhat controversial method will reveal enough evidence to suggest that the process of effective learning may well require inquiry.

Numerous studies launched to compare instruction by inquiry methods with more traditional expository methods claim to have demonstrated that learning is more effective when inquiry methods are used. For example:

- In a St. Cloud state experiment in consumer education on the high school level, Nappi found that a traditional treatment was less effective than an inquiry mode.[19]

- In a study of ninth grade biology teachers, Starr found that with many bright students, structured oral inquiry materials significantly improved students' critical thinking ability.[20]

- A study by Guthrie "of problem solving in cryptograms showed a marked advantage of the discovery method of instruction for transfer to a task involving new rules, suggesting that exploratory strategies relevant to such new learning may have been engendered by the discovery method of instruction."[21]

- In a study of fifth and sixth grade mathematics students, Worthen found that immediate recall was higher with expository instruction methods, but inquiry instruction resulted in better retention and transfer of concepts. The latter were judged a "more important practical outcome."[22]

In short, the studies suggest that while expository teaching is effective in direct and specific learning situations, inquiry makes for better and broader transfer of learning; learning by inquiry appears more effective from the standpoint of generalizability, applicability, and long-term retention. In addition, since the method is rich in reinforcement and intrinsic motivation value, some suggest that it may create a love of learning and a thirst for knowledge.[23]

This brief summary of research on a somewhat controversial topic is admittedly one-sided, but perhaps further illumination can be drawn from some theorizing on why inquiry seems to be an effective learning process.

- Jean Piaget conceives of a child's cognitive development as a process of successive disequilibria and equilibria. When a child meets a new situation, he gets "out of balance." To restore

---

[19] Andrew T. Nappi, "A Project to Create and Validate Curriculum Materials in Consumer Education for High School Students," ERIC ED 072-514.
[20] R. J. Starr, "Structured Oral Inquiry Improves Thinking," 408-9.
[21] Robert Gagne, *The Conditions of Learning* (New York: Holt, Rinehart, and Winston, 1965), 226.
[22] Blaine R. Worthen, "A Comparison of Discovery and Expository Sequencing in Elementary Mathematics Instruction," in Klaas Kramer, ed., *Problems in the Teaching of Elementary School Mathematics* (Boston: Allyn and Bacon, 1970), 107-20; Robert Gagne, *The Conditions of Learning*, 225.
[23] Robert Gagne, *The Conditions of Learning*, 229, 288; Lee S. Shulman, "Perspectives on the Psychology of Learning and the Teaching of Mathematics," in Klaas Kramer, ed., *Problems in the Teaching of Elementary School Mathematics*, 94-95.

cognitive balance he must modify his previous cognitive structure.[24] The similarity of this view to our earlier definition of inquiry ("a matter of rearranging and transforming evidence") suggests a close harmony between processes and general cognitive development. Inquiry may well be the "natural" way to learn, hence its effectiveness as an instructional method.

- Jerome Bruner notes four benefits accruing from learning by inquiry:

    1. *An increase in intellectual potency*—There are two "casts of mind" possible in students: "Episodic Empiricism" is characterized by gathering information bits as isolated units, without organizing them into larger structures; "Cumulative Constructionism" features persistence at maneuvers to connect information into larger structures. Inquiry learning encourages the development of the latter, resulting in an increase in intellectual potency.

    2. *A shift from extrinsic to intrinsic rewards*—By exercising the "competence motive" (an inborn need to deal with one's environment competently), inquiry learning reduces the effects of extrinsic rewards (e.g. satisfy teacher, satisfy parents, get grades, do just enough to get by) and strengthens intrinsic rewards (e.g. achievement and a love of learning).

    3. *Learning of the heuristics of discovering*—Inquiry learning develops by practice the ability to impose varying frameworks of discovery onto novel situations, thereby improving a student's skill at analysis and problem solving.

    4. *Aid to conserving memory*—When a student organizes complex material by embedding it into a cognitive structure he has *organized himself*, that material is more accessible to his memory. Many studies are said to support this observation.[25]

The studies and theorizing can be summed up as follows: if by "more effective" learning we mean that a student (1) understands what he learns, and so remembers and transfers it better, (2) learns strategies for discovering new principles on his own, and (3) develops an interest in what he has learned, as well as in learning

---

[24] Lee S. Shulman, "Perspectives on the Psychology of Learning," 87-88.
[25] Bruner, 83-96 [*Editors' note*: This source has not been identified.]; on point 1, also A. C. Pugliese, "Meaning of Inquiry," 26.

itself, then there might be good reason for concluding that the process of effective learning requires inquiry.[26]

I.B.3. Effective Teaching

If the foregoing two sections demonstrate that the nature of education necessitates inquiry, it becomes obvious that the activity of teaching, in which almost all church workers are engaged in some form or other, requires experience with inquiry. Anyone who teaches, after all, must continue to learn, and experience with inquiry is, in effect, learning to learn on one's own.[27] If someone who teaches depends perpetually on the knowledge he obtained in his own student days twenty, thirty, or more years ago, he puts himself hopelessly out of touch with the current state of knowledge, and finds himself at a loss even to evaluate, let along teach, the new approaches to disciplines, such as math and English, as they appear. We are tempted to suspect this reason for the lately reported "failures" of the new math in some quarters.

Further, if the adage holds true—despite methods courses—that "teachers teach as they were taught," and if as observed above effective learning (and so effective teaching) requires at least some concessions to inquiry, it follows that prospective teachers should be exposed to such methods in their training. Many of the new approaches to teaching science, mathematics, language, and social studies stress inquiry methods,[28] and often teachers unused to such methods are unable to make them work.[29]

In view of the current "knowledge explosion," where entire fields of knowledge are revised wholesale; in view of the rapid obsolescence of specific vocations, and the resulting necessity of frequent job-changing and retraining in our society today; and in view of the climate of questioning and changing values current today, any teachers our schools produce and the students they lead should be well trained and experienced in sound methods of inquiry. The nature of education requires it.

Consider, finally, that the task of the Christian necessitates

---

[26] Bert Y. Kersh, "Learning by Discovery: Instructional Strategies," in Klaas Kramer, ed., *Problems in the Teaching of Elementary School Mathematics*, 96.
[27] A. C. Pugliese, "Meaning of Inquiry," 25.
[28] R. J. Starr, "Structured Oral Inquiry Improves Thinking," 408.
[29] Robert Keith Hanson, "A Comparison of the Alternate Theories Formed by Students in the Classroom and Those Held by Student Teachers," Ph.D. diss., University of Illinois, ERIC ED 072-935.

inquiry. To enlist understanding of this point, let us entertain "the vision of Christian scholarship."

When God commanded Adam and Eve to have dominion over His creation [Genesis 1:28], He was doing far more than granting them the right to farm, hunt, and fish. He was giving man the right to build a culture, to develop arts and sciences—in effect, it was a "cultural mandate."[30] If this is so, then the Christian should not hesitate, but rather eagerly plunge into investigation and inquiry in the arts and sciences, not only as an excellent means of praising God by examining His works, but also in an effort to exercise a corrective influence on the cultures of the world. Men of the world, even after the fall into sin, continue to exercise the "cultural mandate," but no longer to thank and praise God; man's research purposes, as well as his results, were perverted by sin. Behaviorism in psychology, Marxist materialism in philosophy and political science, irrationalism in the arts and literature, as well as in contemporary lifestyles—all these represent fundamental distortions of the reality of God's creation.

But now, with redemption, it is once again possible for the Christian to fulfill God's cultural mandate properly—to put all things in subjection the right way. And with the perspective he has from Scripture, the Christian can work to eliminate the distortions introduced into the arts, sciences, and culture by the biased researches of the world. As one group of Christian curriculum developers put it:

> The Christian religion is not an irrational bias which we intend to hold onto at all costs, ignoring the facts. It is not an astigmatism which we resolve never to get corrected. On the contrary, it is the spectacles with which we are enabled to see the facts aright. But look at the facts we must.[31]

The product of good Christian scholarship, then, is a truer perspective on the reality of God's creation. And this claim can be readily advanced against the views of those, such as were cited above as this paper began, who would shrink in fear from matching the Christian viewpoint up against the world's and would instead draw the Christian's academic wagons into a circle. The intellectually gifted Christian's calling is not to withdraw into a spiritualized isolation, but to sally forth into the academic world

---

[30] Calvin Committee, *Christian Liberal Arts Education*, 63-64.
[31] Ibid., 57-61. The Committee lists seven effects of a Scriptural perspective on the various disciplines.

with sound scholarship infused with the Christian perspective.

Accordingly, we should deplore picturing the academic Christian as at best a scholarly gleaner, following along in the wake of the unbelieving researchers who work at the cutting edge of the discipline, picking up a straw here and a stalk there that he can fit into his Christian classroom. The image is, perhaps, all too real. Consider, instead, the following vision of Christian scholarly leadership: Christians ought to be producing *history*—not just parochial textbooks for our own elementary students, but history for the scholarly world at large, as well as for popular consumption. Christians ought to be providing the scholarly world with insights into *language* and *criticism*—where is the authentically Christian critic of the arts or of public affairs whose voice is heard today? Christians ought to be producing *art* and *music* in today's idiom, and Christians ought to be furnishing breakthroughs in science. Of course, one small faculty, or one small group of Christians cannot be responsible for all this. And there are, as we all know, more basic purposes for the church than to produce scholarship. And yet if a small faculty or a small group of Christians catches the vision of Christian scholarly leadership viewed here, would it not spread through students and beyond, producing in our own circles a generation of sound Christian scholars?

It would be a worthwhile goal.

But so far, this paper has discussed inquiry and scholarship almost entirely in connection with secular subjects. Do they have a place in a study of religion as well? Most certainly.

A historical survey will show that scholarship has played an important, if not crucial, role in Christianity. As God raised up judges to lead His people when needed in Old Testament pre-Kingdom days, it seems as though He has raised up scholars when needed in these days of the new covenant. The Apostle John's Gospel has been described as "not only a biography of unparalleled beauty and insight, [but] it is a work of scholarship in the broadest sense of the word—an attempt to relate the Gospel to its total cultural setting, both Hellenistic and Hebrew."[32]

The Pauline epistles, when fairly considered, reveal a breadth of knowledge unparalleled in that day. St. Augustine—so much admired by Luther—while impressed with the essential irrelevance of learning to salvation, yet applied his considerable powers of

---

[32] Elmore H. Harbison, *The Christian Scholar in the Age of the Reformation* (New York: Scribner, 1956), 3-4.

inquiry to produce "one of the most comprehensive and enduring attempts to understand the Christian faith that has ever been made."[33] And of course Luther's own powers of scholarship need no elaboration for this journal's readers.[34] Even today, the struggle for authentic Lutheranism draws heavily on the scholarship of its leaders.

To be sure, Christian scholars have always been aware of, and frequently have warned against, the dangers of being influenced by anti-Christian views. But their warnings were generally not directed against scholarship itself, but against its misuse. Even Tertullian, quoted at this paper's start, was not advocating intellectual withdrawal for the Christian, but (as the context of the quotation shows) rather was warning against a spirit of syncretism, of attempting to harmonize Christian and pagan views.[35] Gregory of Nazianzen, in the fourth century, is perhaps more representative when he said:

> As we have compounded healthful drugs from certain of the reptiles, so from secular literature we have received principles of inquiry and speculation, while we have rejected their idolatry, terror, and pit of destruction. Nay, even these have aided us in our religion, by our perception of the contrast between what is worse and what is better, and by gaining strength for our doctrine from the weaknesses of theirs.[36]

It is not from the church that the main attack on scholarship has come, but, at least in our day, from the secular educational establishment itself, where the obsession so often has been with the immediate, the "relevant" in its trivial sense, with "appreciation," "life adjustment," and "sensitivity."[37]

E. H. Harbison suggests a specific function scholarship can play in Christian thought. There are always times, he says, when a need arises to stand off from our beliefs and practices, to analyze

---

[33] Ibid., 17–18.
[34] Ibid., chapter on Luther, 103–35.
[35] Cf. Tertullian, *De Praescriptione Haereticorum*; also Frank P. Cassidy, "The Patristic Attitude toward Pagan Learning," ch. 5 in *Molders of the Medieval Mind: The Influence of the Church on the Medieval Schoolmen* (Port Washington, NY: Kennikat Press, 1944), 159–74.
[36] *Panegyric on St. Basil*, in *A Select Library of Nicene and post-Nicene Fathers*, ed. Philip Schaff and Henry Wace, 2d ser., vol. 7 (Grand Rapids: Wm. B. Eerdmans, n.d.), 398–99.
[37] Howard Mumford Jones, *Scholarship, Novelty, and Teaching: An Address* (Columbus: Ohio State University Press, 1968), 7.

and order them, to attempt better understanding of them in light of their origins, growth, and possible conflicts with other beliefs and practices. More specifically, he suggests the Christian scholar may have these legitimate motives:

1. *to purify religious tradition in a time of corruption*—Luther applied his powers of scholarship to this end, as do the apologists today in the current crisis in confessional Lutheranism.

2. *to bring faith into a more fruitful relationship with culture at a moment of crisis in secular history*—We are living now in times of severe cultural and moral crisis, which affect our people (our students, and people of the ELS in general) as well as others. Our culture is in desperate need of a meaningful injection of Christian insight, not to mention the balm of the Gospel in terms our culture can understand.

3. *to re-examine faith in light of some new discovery about the universe or man*—To cite an example: though the controversy over evolution has frequently generated more heat than light, the genuine scholarship into both science and Scriptures necessitated by that conflict has deepened our understanding of both.[38]

Working, then, with these legitimate motives, the Christian scholar can direct his inquiry into the Christian tradition itself (and especially, of course, the Scriptures), into the culture that forms the setting for Christian proclamation today, and into the intellectual casts of mind that characterize the state of popular as well as specialized knowledge. Each of these objects of legitimate inquiry should be held up before our students as direct personal challenges.

In the view of this writer, one of the biggest dangers the church faces today is the production of non-thinking Christians. Please don't misunderstand. This is not a suggestion that we train rationalists, but rather thinking people, who know not only what they believe, but why—and can explain it, even to someone who disagrees. The Christian whose understanding of his beliefs has not penetrated blind acceptance of some professor's pronouncement is a person who may be easily stumped, shaken in his faith, and misled. The Christian college teacher cannot condone or encourage, even in religion, a willingness to relegate analysis and inquiry entirely to any other mortal—be he an "expert," group of "experts," or even a synod. The Missouri Synod was characterized

---

[38] Elmore H. Harbison, *The Christian Scholar*, 4–5.

in the 1930s by an intense synod pride and loyalty that was the occasion for many to be led astray over the next four or more decades. People there—some of them friends and relatives of us all—just wouldn't believe "Synod" could do anything wrong, and so they wouldn't look into it, or even discuss it. These characteristics of synod pride and loyalty are observable in many young people in some of our circles today. And gratifying as it may be to know that the young people have confidence in us, it might well be more often frightening. We are, after all—as has been said—training disciples, not sheep. What we should want is campuses and congregations full of Bereans, who would not even accept just the word of the Apostle Paul, but "searched the Scriptures daily, whether those things were so" (Acts 17:11).

For these reasons, then, both in fulfilling a "vision of Christian scholarship" and in continuing the lengthy tradition of bringing the powers of scholarship to bear on Scripture and its surrounding culture, the task of the Christian requires inquiry.

C. The Limits of a Spirit of Inquiry

At this point, after a lengthy unmitigated defense of inquiry, a word begs to be said of its limits.

We should point out first that inquiry is not all there is in educational theory. The studies cited above supporting its effectiveness are not conclusive, and certainly inquiry is not the only method by which learning—even effective learning—can occur.[39] Furthermore, authorities agree that successful inquiry must be preceded by "preparation"—whatever that may involve.[40] It might well be that inquiry works effectively only with brighter students.[41] Considerations like these await the results of further research.

Of greater importance, however, are the limits of inquiry viewed from a spiritual perspective. There are, clearly, two kinds of inquiry: bad and good. Both can be illustrated from Scripture. Bad inquiry goes way back: the serpent asked Eve, "Yea, hath God said ... ?" (Genesis 3:1). On the other hand, Scripture abounds with examples of commendable inquiry. Nicodemus came to Jesus full of questions ("How can these things be?"), and the Lord reproves him, not for asking, but for not having inquired into them

---

[39] Robert Gagne, *The Conditions of Learning*, 58.
[40] Ibid., 226; Bruner, 82.
[41] R. J. Starr, "Structured Oral Inquiry Improves Thinking," 408-9.

before ("Art thou a master of Israel, and knowest not these things?") (John 3:9-10). The Bereans have already been cited as commended examples of those who inquire into the Scriptures. The calling of Nathanael provides an excellent example of a "thinking Christian," one who "transforms evidence for new insights" (cf. the definition of inquiry, above); from two pronouncements of Jesus he concludes, "Rabbi, thou art the Son of God." Jesus does not reprove him for his analysis, but merely suggests, in effect, to wait until *all* the data are in: "Because I said unto thee, I saw thee under the fig tree, believest thou? Thou shalt see greater things than these" (John 1:49–50).

And so inquiry itself is neither bad nor good, but the spirit behind it may be. Between the "bad inquiry" (of skepticism and doubt) and the "good inquiry" there is one essential difference: unbelief.

A student, then, does not need warnings against inquiry so much as understanding of it. To dismiss inquiry and scholarship wholesale is perverse. To dismiss whole disciplines, such as philosophy, anthropology, or psychology, and whole methodologies, such as the scientific method, is too simplistic. The student should be taught not to fear certain disciplines or certain methods, but rather to *discriminate among presuppositions, as well as conclusions, according to Scriptural parameters.* A total subjection of all intellectual processes to the truths of Scripture is the ultimate limit of inquiry. This subjection, in practice, has implications regarding conclusions reached through inquiry, as well as regarding attitudes entertained while engaging in it. When a conclusion is reached which contradicts Scripture, that conclusion is to be set aside as a product of fallen reason. Scripture is to be bowed to, on the grounds that human reason is limited by its nature as well as by sin, and revelation is the more reliable source. Furthermore, the inquirer's attitudes are guided by Scripture as well. In frequent warnings the Lord reminds us not to glory in our own "wisdom" (even as we do not glory in our ignorance), nor come to depend on it totally, but rather to use our scholarly talents—after the example of the apostles—in humility, for the furtherance of His kingdom.

Taught, trained, and exercised in principles like these, the Christian student can wholeheartedly agree that "pedagogical principles based on the Word of God demonstrate that all knowledge in all areas of human thought and endeavor is worthy of inquiry when viewed in the light of human sin and divine grace."[42] The student will engage in inquiry as an exercise of his faith, as a commitment to his calling in education and learning, and as an expression of his confidence in the truth of Scripture, which both sets his limits and permits him to search and inquire without fear of deception. For he knows that the reality described by Scripture, and the reality he searches, are the same reality.

II. The Means for Stimulating a Spirit of Inquiry

Having now found support in the realms of philosophy, education, and theology for the necessity of stimulating a spirit of inquiry in Christian students, we turn our attention to reviewing some means for doing so.

II.A. Teachers Can Model a Spirit of Inquiry

On the theory that imitation is an important key to learning, many feel that students will not get really excited about a subject unless the teacher is. Similarly, we cannot expect students to be stimulated to inquiry unless they perceive the faculty involved in it as well. Assuming an interest on the part of individual faculty members in scholarship, what can be done to encourage the pursuit of such work? There is doubtless considerable give-and-take of ideas on an informal level in any faculty. Could this perhaps be formalized to the extent that individual faculty members so inclined could meet in an informal group, regularly enough to provide continuity and perhaps the pressure of deadlines necessary to encourage progress? The goal of such a group would be to encourage individual research. Members would present papers intended for discussion, revision, *and eventual publication*—and publication not only in synodical outlets generally hungry for materials, but in the journals and at the conferences of the scholarly world at large. One need not read journals and attend conferences long before being convinced that any number of faculty members among us is fully capable of moving in those intellectual circles and substantially contributing to their quality.

---

42   *Dr. Martin Luther College Catalog, 1973-74,* 12.

> "The sabbatical program, a part of Bethany's broader faculty development program, exists to enhance the ability of the college to carry out its mission, to strengthen and enrich the faculty, and to foster excellence in general. All full-time personnel of the college who have faculty status are included in the program. ... A sabbatical leave shall consist of a one-semester leave with full pay, including all benefits. ... Suggested uses include: classroom work in one's academic field; studying educational methods; pursuing a new field; pursuing an advanced degree; research and writing; travel."
>
> Bethany Lutheran College,
> *Faculty Handbook, 2010–2011*, sec. 9.

And what administrative policies would encourage individual faculty members to write, to travel, to study? Every faculty has some policies that encourage and support faculty upgrading measurable by the attainment of advanced degrees. But after that, what policies encourage the pursuit of scholarship at the cutting edge of the disciplines? We know that congregations must sometimes be trained to know that when a pastor comes in off the road to "just read" he is not wasting his time, but enriching his power to minister. So perhaps supervising boards and commissions must continue to be reminded that a professor who may spend some months out of his classroom (or with a lightened teaching load) engaged in pure research is not just on vacation, but enriching the whole educational posture of the church.

II.B. Teachers Can Train Students for Inquiry

At last we turn to some suggested means for stimulating a spirit of inquiry directly among Christian students. Two important needs can be supplied: our students need an understanding of inquiry, and they need opportunity for inquiry.

It may not be wise to drop students, unused to an inquiry emphasis, into the deep end of the inquiry pool. Students who are accustomed to being given all the answers by their teachers often become quite uncomfortable, and even, in their own way, rebellious, when the teacher begins to give them all the questions instead. If inquiry is to become a major educational feature of a school, perhaps the matter deserves specific discussion in freshman orientation sessions. If entering students are not oriented toward inquiry, perhaps a phasing-in process should be planned either collectively or in individual courses.[43] Perhaps specific attention to the purposes, limits, and goals of inquiry should find its way into introductory courses in each discipline. The student needs to learn what thinking is. He needs to learn that the scholarship that impresses and influences him must be divorced from the personality of the one advocating it. He needs to learn what research is. A former colleague refused to honor most college term paper assignments with the term "research paper"; he called them "reference papers" instead, insisting quite rightly that the mere collation of a number of authorities' views on a subject is not research. Students need specific training to help them understand and undertake inquiry.

To exercise their understandings of inquiry, students will then need opportunities. Furnishing opportunities will involve, on the part of a faculty, providing facilities, room, outlets, and encouragement.

Inquiry, of course, requires facilities. Library facilities come first to mind; access to an adequate library is, of course, essential to scholarship. Beyond that, a school needs to tune in to the facilities available in the immediate, as well as the greater community around it. Most schools have long ago moved away from the notion that all learning is to occur in the on-campus classroom. But they need to explore systematically what the wider-community facilities for inquiry are, whether they be opportunities for observation or for hands-on in-service experience. The Reformation Lectures and Seminars at Bethany these past years are an excellent example of a school enriching its facilities for stimulating inquiry.

Along with a maximum exploitation of facilities, our students need room in which to inquire. That means the establishment of an intellectual atmosphere that permits questions to arise—any questions—and allows the students' minds to expand. Chief enemy

---

43 R. J. Folstrom, "Experimenting with the Inquiry Approach," *Music Educator's Journal* 59 (Nov. 1972): 36-37.

of such an atmosphere is the extremely autocratic teacher's role,[44] where, if a caricature is permitted, the teacher totally dominates all classroom plans and presentations; perhaps *some* feedback from students is occasionally permitted, but in it all the teacher is the expert, the manipulator, who supplies finally all the answers. In such an atmosphere the student is deemed working for the teacher (rather than, as is proper, the other way around); when a student works primarily to please the teacher, he learns to parrot, not inquire.

A more healthful classroom atmosphere might be one where teacher and student are considered to be engaging together in a discipline. The teacher, by virtue of his greater experience in the discipline, as well as his position, will be respected and important, but he will be an encouragement and guide to inquiry, rather than a barrier. The difference is subtle. It may not even mean, necessarily, that the teacher give up his major role in presenting material, or that the lecture method must be abandoned. Rather, the lectures will change in tone. Bruner distinguishes helpfully between two modes of presenting material for learning. In the "expository mode," all the decisions about content, style, pace, mood, etc., are in the hands of the speaker. He has worked through the material, considered all the options, made his decisions, and presents the material in the form of pre-digested conclusions. The student is just a listener, unaware of the decisions that had to be made or the internal options the speaker had to consider. He is not at all participating in what the linguists call the "speaker's decisions." In the "hypothetical mode," on the other hand, the speaker and student are in a more cooperative position. The teacher lets the student in on the "decision points." The student is made aware of the alternatives and options, and may consider and evaluate them. In short, the student is taking part in the formulation of materials, and at times even plays a principal role in it.[45] As a result, in the hypothetical mode responsibility for learning belongs more to the student; learning becomes a more personal matter, and is therefore hopefully more effective and more permanent.[46] Piaget furnishes food for thought when he suggests that every time we teach a student something, we deprive him of the opportunity, and pleasure, of learning it for

---

[44] Don Dinkmeyer and Rudolf Dreikurs, *Encouraging Children to Learn: The Encouragement Process* (Englewood Cliffs, NJ: Prentice-Hall, 1963), 117-25.
[45] Bruner, 85 ff.
[46] R. J. Folstrom, "Experimenting with the Inquiry Approach," 36.

himself.[47]

Syllabi and assignments can provide room for inquiry if they permit both teacher and student to engage in real problems concerning real knowledge—and all of the disciplines abound with such problems.[48] It is an artificial discipline that pretends that all the answers are in; students quickly detect artificiality and lose interest.

A number of specific classroom procedures are suggested as engendering inquiry—but recognize that students unused to inquiry may be made uncomfortable by some of these:

- Cultivate skills at leading discussions. Discussion is almost universally acclaimed as an effective teaching device, yet leading well requires specialized skills and experience.[49]
- Avoid dogmatism, where it is not in place, by cultivating expressions like...

    we do not know for sure...

    the evidence is not complete...

    there are two points of view about this...

    it is not certain why this happens...

    this is an unsolved problem...

    the evidence is contradictory on this...

    and so on.

- Use inductive approaches where appropriate. In simple form, this means being sure that the student has become aware of a concept before a name has been assigned to that concept.[50]
- Use "Socratic questioning," i.e., the teacher, by a series of questions, leads the student into a trap from which he must then

---

[47] Lee S. Shulman, "Perspectives on the Psychology of Learning," 90.
[48] A. C. Pugliese, "Meaning of Inquiry," 26.
[49] Don Dinkmeyer and Rudolf Dreikurs, *Encouraging Children to Learn*, 115.
[50] Bruner, 102; an example or application to slower students is found in R. Sposet and T. Asad, "Surgery in the Classroom: ETI Program," *English Journal* 62 (Feb. 1973): 278-80.

extricate himself.[51]

- Use "torpedoing," i.e., teach students something until they are sure they know it, then provide a whopping counter-example. Hopefully, students will resolve their discomfort by thinking it all through.[52]
- Give student a role in his own evaluation. Some theorists feel students learn through continuing cycles of *manipulation* followed by *representation*—i.e., they construct or do something, then stand back to size up what they have done and determine what should be done next. Permitting self-evaluation encourages this cycle.[53]

Along with facilities and room for inquiry, students might be encouraged by perceiving outlets for their findings. Products of student research should be used in class, and if someone's project has added substance to a professor's lecture notes for perpetual use, it should be made known. There might be room for a periodic publication of outstanding academic work by students; most teachers have had work handed in that was worthy of campus-wide or even wider distribution.

Finally, a word about general understanding and encouragement of students who show an inclination toward inquiry. Embryonic thinkers are easily discouraged by criticism, especially if it creates fears that their investigations are going to get them "in trouble." A faculty interested in encouraging inquiry will recognize that many students are beginners at this. They will draw rash and improper conclusions from inadequate evidence; they will be immature in their judgments regarding research methods; they are, in short, just learning—and learning, to a great extent, from their mistakes. Our attitude, as we guide and even correct them in their inquiry, should be one of calm and understanding, with "encouragement" being the watchword. This might become particularly difficult when we find students questioning the very principles we are trying to teach them in class. This writer too has felt the sense of threat that comes from such inquiry, particularly when it involves some of his favorite principles. But with effort a teacher can try instead to feel flattered that a student considers something he said to be important enough to merit the

---

[51] A. C. Pugliese, "Meaning of Inquiry," 27. Note that students will probably need preparation for this technique.
[52] Lee S. Shulman, "Perspectives on the Psychology of Learning," 87.
[53] Bruner, 101.

effort of, at times, elaborate investigation. He can be assisted in this feeling by the conviction that no bad outcome of such inquiry is possible. If the student's investigation is slip-shod, the teacher will have a chance to teach him something about sound inquiry. If through sound inquiry he finds the teacher was right, it is of course a good outcome. If through sound inquiry he finds the teacher was wrong, both should be glad of it, and teaching should be adjusted accordingly. If through sound inquiry he finds that a legitimate difference of opinion is possible, this too contributes to the scope of our knowledge. There can be no bad outcome, unless one or the other of them subverts the process by refusing to face the facts. For reasons like these, honest inquiry is, in all cases, to be encouraged.

Conclusion

When our Lord looked into the future on Maundy Thursday evening, He foresaw His disciples *in* the world, but not *of* it. In so doing, He was not suggesting a monastic withdrawal from the world—a kind of separateness, yes, but not isolation. On the contrary, He has "sent them into the world" (John 17: 14-19). As a result, He says, the world hates them. I submit that the world will not hate what it can safely ignore. But it *will* hate those who are making telling and significant encroachments on what it considers its own territory, and that holds true, among other places, in the realm of scholarship. The Christian suitably gifted might well consider it his calling to make such encroachments, for the realm of sound scholarship and inquiry is, after all, not properly the world's territory—it is God's territory. May we all strive to bring our scholarly voice, too, into conformity with the standard proposed by St. Paul: "sound speech that cannot be condemned; that he that is of the contrary part may be ashamed, having no evil thing to say of you" (Titus 2:8).

DOCUMENT 7.2:

Sermon for Dedication of the S. C. Ylvisaker Fine Arts Center (1990)

By George M. Orvick

George M. Orvick, Jr., (1929-) was born on January 9, 1929, near Hanlontown, Iowa. He graduated from Bethany Lutheran College, Mankato, Minnesota, in 1948, from Northwestern College, Watertown, Wisconsin, in 1950, and from Bethany Lutheran Theological Seminary, Mankato, Minnesota, in 1953. Following graduation, he was ordained and installed as pastor of Our Savior's Lutheran Church near Amherst Jct., Wisconsin.[54] One year later, in 1954, Orvick accepted a call to be pastor of Holy Cross Lutheran Church, Madison, Wisconsin. He served this parish for thirty-two years, during which time the congregation grew to be the largest in the synod. Meanwhile, Orvick served on the Board of Regents for Bethany Lutheran College and the Doctrine Committee for the synod. During 1970–1976 and again during 1980–1986, he served simultaneously as Holy Cross's pastor and the synod's president. That changed in 1986, when the office of synod president was made a full-time position.[55] Orvick was the first man ever to be elected to this full-time presidency and he was elected again in 1990.[56] Throughout his years as president Orvick was a member of

---

54 "Ordination," *Lutheran Sentinel*, July 1953, 204-5.
55 Gaylin Schmeling, "The President of Synod Retires," *Lutheran Sentinel*, June 2002, 5.
56 J. Herbert Larson and Juul B. Madson, *Built on the Rock* (Mankato, MN: Evangelical Lutheran Synod Book Company, 1992), 251.

delegations sent to overseas churches to strengthen ties with confessional Lutherans around the world.[57] These contacts were part of a process that culminated in the formation of the Confessional Evangelical Lutheran Conference in 1993.[58] Orvick retired from the presidency in 2002. He next served as curator of the Ottesen Museum, a museum of the synod's history, until his full retirement in 2010.   [PG]

Source: Lutheran Synod Quarterly 30, no. 4 (1990): 1–9.

> *Finally brethren, whatsoever things are true, whatsoever things are honest, whatsoever things are just, whatsoever things are pure, whatsoever things are lovely, whatsoever things are of good report, if there be any virtue, and if there be any praise, think on these things.*
>
> Philippians 4:8

Fellow Redeemed: Grace be unto you and peace from God our Father and from the Lord and Saviour Jesus Christ. Amen.

A dream has come true! A prayer has been answered! A fervent hope has been fulfilled! Bethany has at last a new center for the fine arts. A building that is entirely in keeping with the basic philosophy of the school. A facility that will be a blessing to students, faculty, and many others for years to come.

How did it come about that such an addition to our campus could be built? How did it happen that this school, which was taken over with such trembling hands by a little synod in 1927, could make such progress? We shall let someone else answer the question, namely the one for whom this art center is named. He writes:

What success may be recorded during these years is due solely

---

[57] Larson and Madson, *Built on the Rock*, 198–203.
[58] Gaylin Schmeling, "The President of Synod Retires," 5.

and alone to the guiding hand and the loving grace of Him who holds also the destiny of Bethany in his hand. You may point to feverish activity, loyal devotion, faithful service on the part of individuals or the general membership of our synod, to special friends within and without our synod, to faithful teachers and loyal students—neither these nor what they have done would have been there but for the blessing of the Lord of the church. . . . Today we gladly extend the hand to thank all these for their encouragement. But we shall not forget that these were all a part of that blessing that God sent from On High and an answer to the prayer of faith offered by many a friend of our school.[59]

In those beautiful words Dr. Ylvisaker, on the occasion of the twentieth anniversary of our school, points us in the right direction. It is to our gracious God that we lift up our hearts and voices in songs of praise and thanksgiving on this tremendous day.

As we now proceed to dedicate this building to the glory of the Triune God, Father, Son and Holy Ghost, our hearts and minds are flooded with thoughts and emotions. We cannot help but think of the labors of our forefathers as they struggled to keep Bethany going. We remember in particular Dr. S. C. Ylvisaker and his total devotion to this school. We think of the high and lofty goals that he had for the institution. We recall our own student days and the impression Bethany made upon our lives and values. Oh, yes, I am certain that such a day as this thrills the hearts of all who love Bethany.

But while we offer up praise and thanks to God for the blessings of the years past, let us turn our thoughts to the present and the future. Why do we have a fine arts center on our campus? What is the philosophy behind it? How shall we use it? What effect will it have upon the students? Let us bear all of these things in mind and on the basis of our text consider as our theme:

What Is at *the Center* of Our Fine Arts Center?

The words of our text are very fitting for this occasion. The Apostle Paul is giving directions to his beloved Philippians as to their life of sanctification. It is interesting to note that the Apostle wrote this letter while he was in a Roman prison. He could have been chained to a Roman guard and possibly even standing in water. And yet it is the most joyous epistle that he wrote, men-

---

59   *Editors' note*: The source has not been located.

The Sigurd Christian Ylvisaker Fine Arts Center houses the music, theatre, and studio art departments of Bethany Lutheran College.

tioning the word "joy" or "rejoice" some seventeen times. He was undoubtedly surrounded by those things which are base, filthy, obscene, irreverent, and blasphemous. How amazing, then, that in such confinement he would be thinking about these things which are true, honest, just, pure, and lovely. He encourages the Philippians to concentrate their hearts and minds on these things.

And is this not what Bethany seeks to accomplish? Yes, it was Dr. Ylvisaker who wrote way back in 1933, "Bethany seeks to prepare the student at least to appreciate and love the beautiful and that which edifies and enriches life."[60] Again in 1941 he describes Bethany as a school "where our young men and women are encouraged to study and appreciate what is noble and pure and beautiful, where they are exercised in habits of Christian culture, where they learn to express through the medium of song or other forms of art that which is beautiful and noble, and in general develop that sense of refinement which enriches our whole life."[61] It is almost as if he chose this text for us.

In accordance with our theme, then, what shall we list as number one of what is at the center of Fine Arts Center?

We can do nothing else but place as number one that which is the most beautiful, the most lovely, the most pure: namely, the

---

[60] *Editors' note*: The source has not been located.
[61] *BLC Bulletin*, Apr. 1941.

blessed Gospel of our Lord Jesus Christ. Is there anything more beautiful than that message that came into this sin-filled world, than the glad tidings of great joy that God in His mercy sent His Son to be our Savior? This is at the center of Bethany's whole existence with its motto, "ONE THING IS NEEDFUL" [Luke 10:42]. Can we build and dedicate a fine arts center which does not also have this as its purpose, aim, and goal: namely, to exalt the name of our dear Saviour? What is more noble, just, and pure than the message that we are so loved by God that He gave His best and dearest to rescue us from eternal death and destruction?

Or is there something in the heart of man that is by nature good and noble and lovely? Not as God sees it. Christ describes the natural human heart as being filled with sin and evil lusts. He doesn't talk about how good and noble it is by nature. No, he says, "Out of the heart proceed evil thoughts, murders, adulteries, thefts, and blasphemies" (Mark 7:21).

It is Christ that is pure and lovely. He took our place, assumed our wretchedness, and went to the cross to pay for our sins. In doing this He has made us also beautiful and lovely. Now His beauty covers our ugliness. His purity hides our impurity. Isn't that what the Bible says? "Though your sins be as scarlet they shall be as white as snow? Though they be red like crimson they shall be as wool" (Isaiah 1:18)? Do we not sing "Jesus Thy blood and righteousness, My beauty are, my glorious dress?" *(ELH 432:1)* Our Saviour invites us to this blessed Gospel and to find in Him salvation.

Yes, He *is at the center of our Fine Arts Center*! He is "fairer than the children of men!" [Psalm 45:2]. He is the "Rose of Sharon" [Song of Solomon 2:1]! He is the "Loveliest flower on Jesse's stem" [*ELH* 143:3]! He is the one of whom the disciples said, "We beheld His glory, the glory as of the only begotten of the Father" (John 1:14).

As we dedicate this lovely building, we are reminded that there is an indissoluble relationship that exists between religion and culture. One author, referring to the founding fathers of our country, states, "They understood that without religion, democracy lost its moral underpinnings, and culture devolved into license." And again he writes, "Politics is in the largest part an expression of culture and that at the heart of culture lie beliefs and practices that are religious in nature."[62] *Yes, without religion*

---

[62] *Editors' note*: "Putting First Things First," *First Things,* March 1990, n.p.

culture turns into license. Religion is at the heart and center of culture. And at Bethany, Christ is at the heart and center of our school and our fine arts building!

Some years ago a professor at Yale University carried out an interesting study. A minute analysis of three hundred prominent men who were born after 1450 was conducted. All possible information concerning these men was assembled and scrutinized. The purpose was to find out which of these men was the most highly cultured, which had the highest intelligence level. When all the research had been completed it was discovered that the German dramatist and poet, Wolfgang von Goethe, had received the highest possibly rating. What a remarkable man he was—in literature, arts, science, and law. His achievements were the most notable of his age. In intellectual stature he topped all of his fellows. If you visit the Goethe museum in Weimar, you can get a glimpse of his many talents.

And yet, by his own admission, he was a very unhappy man. Why? Because with all of his culture, he lacked faith in God. On a hill outside of Weimar a very impressive monolith has been erected on the spot where Goethe and his fellow philosophers used to meet for their discussions. It is quite inspiring until one realizes that one is standing in the middle of Buchenwald.

Goethe wrote his last letter on March 17, 1832. Here he states the hopeless philosophy, "The world is ruled by bewildered theories of bewildering operations." There is a painting of the closing moments of his life. It shows the dying poet half reclining in an old arm chair. His wife kneels sobbing at his side, but he doesn't see her. His eyes stare into space. Uncertainty and fear are on all his features. His hand is raised as if to ward off an invisible enemy and his lips are open to voice his last words, "*Mehr Licht,*" "more light."

Culture is not enough! *Without Him who is the light of the world, the most cultured walk in darkness. Christ is at the center of our Fine Arts Center!*

What Is at the Center of Our *Fine Arts* Center?

In the second place we would point to a strong desire on the part of our faculty and administration to do what our text tells us: namely, to direct young minds to focus on what is true, honest, just, pure, and lovely.

Permit me to quote again our sainted forefather whose name

graces this building:

> Side by side with the general, the specific, and the Christian training goes the cultural, the indefinable something which adds richness, beauty, mellowness, and refinement. The source and wellspring of all true refinement is Christian faith, and no one is truly refined who does not own this faith. Christian education is therefore not true to itself if it does not include in its training some way to provide a mode of expression for this culture and appreciation of it in others.[63]

There is so much in this world which is called by the name of art, which is not art at all, but obscenity. The works of Andres Serrano and Robert Mapplethorpe will not be displayed in our arts center. Even though in some places they are funded by the National Endowment for the Arts with taxpayers' money, they are so obscene that we blush to mention them. Likewise, the music of 2 Live Crew will not be featured in music appreciation class.[64]

In the midst of such obscenity and filth which washes like a tidal wave across our land, how essential it is that Bethany focus on what is true, honest, just, pure, and lovely.

There are three areas where we shall endeavor to direct young minds, as Dr. Ylvisaker put it, "to that indefinable something which adds richness, beauty, mellowness, and refinement." And our new fine arts center will greatly enhance our ability to do this.

The one area is that of art. What a beautiful world we live in! Consider the artistic beauty of all creation. Who can paint like our heavenly Father? Behold the colors of the glowing sunset, the blue sky, the stars in the heaven, the snow-capped peaks, the cattle upon a thousand hills.

Now this gracious God has also given wonderful gifts to many men and women throughout the ages to produce spectacular works of art. How enriching it is to study those works and to give

---

[63] *Editors' note*: The source has not been located.

[64] *Editors' note*: With NEA funding, Andres Serrano produced "Piss Christ," a work consisting of a crucifix submerged in the artist's own urine. The resulting public outcry led to debates in the U.S. Congress in 1989 over whether public funds should be appropriated for such controversial works. Congressional Record, Senate, 18 May 1989. Another artist, Robert Mapplethorpe, incited similar fury during the late 1980s when exhibiting photographs of homoerotic models. Grace Glueck, "Fallen Angel," rev. of *Mapplethorpe: A Biography*, by Patricia Morrisroe, *New York Times* 25 June 1995, n.p. Meanwhile, the "rap" music band 2 Live Crew released an album entitled *As Nasty as They Want to Be* (1989), featuring lyrics saturated in obscenity. Ethan Smith, "As Obscene as They Wanna Be?," *Entertainment Weekly*, 2 June 1995, n.p.

George Orvick (standing beside David Lillegard) addresses a pastoral conference in the 1970s.

our students the opportunity to try their own hand at creating what is pure and lovely!

Another area is that of verbal communication—speech and drama. What important works have been produced that set forth the meaning of life, the joys and sorrows of life, the humor that amuses us, the depth and feelings of the human soul! The Apostle Paul says, "Think on these things." Think upon the words of the Master Communicator. Think of Him of whom they said, "No man spake like this man" (John 7:46). Consider the Sermon on the Mount [Matthew 5–7], the Prodigal Son [Luke 15:11–32], the Good Samaritan [Luke 10:25–37], the Lost Sheep [Luke 15:3–7], and the House Built on the Rock [Matthew 7:24–29]. That is communication! Students at our Bethany will now have a better opportunity to learn to appreciate this area of culture.

The third area is that of music. It certainly wouldn't be a Bethany Fine Arts Center without the study and performance of music! In fact, we are told that Dr. Ylvisaker at one time thought of giving up the study of theology for that of music. He must have agreed with Luther that next to theology he considered music the highest gift. Now there is music that entertains and lightens the burden of life and thus drives away a gloomy spirit. But what kind of music takes first place? Why, that music that is inspired by Him of whom the angels sang and who sing around His throne in heaven. The greatest works that have endured through the centuries came from those who wanted to praise and glorify God. And so we want our young people to learn to appreciate and take part in the field of music, to enjoy God's gifts in this regard.

And so what do we desire to do with our new fine arts center? To do as the Apostle said, "to think on these things." And to do as Dr. Ylvisaker said, "to include in the training of young people some way to provide a mode of expression for this culture and appreciation of it in others."[65] *Thus we dedicate this Fine Arts Center to the glory of the Triune God.* Christ is at the center, accompanied by our strong desire to set before our students that which is true, honest, just, pure, and lovely.

Amen.

---

[65] *Editors' note*: The source has not been located.

DOCUMENT 7.3:

Bethany's Response to the Work "The Prophesy" by Joel Hansen (1995)

By Marvin G. Meyer

Dr. Marvin G. Meyer (1938–) *was born in Princeton, Minnesota, to R. Walter Meyer and Marvel (Wickter) Meyer on February 5, 1938. He was baptized at Our Savior's Lutheran Church in Santiago, Minnesota. He attended a Christian day school and then Luther High School in Chicago, Illinois, before beginning to study to be a veterinarian at Iowa State. When illness kept him from enrolling in the second semester at Iowa State, President Bjarne Teigen from Bethany Lutheran College in Mankato, Minnesota, convinced him to attend Bethany instead. Meyer went on to enroll in Bethany in 1957 and graduated two years later. Immediately after graduation, Meyer was hired by Bethany to teach math. After graduating from Mankato Teachers College, Meyer earned his Master of Arts degree in mathematics from Rutgers University. From 1967 to 1975, Meyer served Bethany as its athletic director and from 1975 to 1982, he served as the Dean of Students.*  *Then, in 1982, Meyer was elected to serve as president of Bethany Lutheran College. He stated that the goals of his administration were "to develop a strong financial base for the college; to develop a wider base from which to draw students; and to foster a stronger bond* between the college and the Synod."[66] *Upon his retirement on December 31, 2002, after twenty years as president, this is what Meyer had done. During his time as president he accomplished many things, including the construction of six new buildings and the establishment of Bethany as a baccalaureate institution.*[67] *Meyer retained the same beliefs at the end of his tenure as president as at the beginning. He believed "that a student needs to be challenged with the issues that a young adult will face in life, but that our true vocation is being a Christian and using our time on earth to glorify our Creator."*[68] *In 1960, Meyer was married to Patricia Saloman of Rochester, New York, with whom he had two children, Joel and Christa. He is now retired and living in Brainerd, Minnesota.* [AB]

Source: *Bethany [Lutheran College] Scroll*, May 1995, 5.

Bethany Lutheran College must exercise its rights as a Christian institution and must remove from display on campus the work entitled "Prophesy" by Joel Hansen. This decision has not been made in a vacuum, for I have sought advice from many on and off the campus of Bethany Lutheran College.

The purpose and mission of the institution is centered in the Gospel of Jesus Christ as the one and only Messiah. It is our determination that the work contradicts the heart and soul of our purpose and mission. Not only do we believe that it is important to give our students a broad education with exposure to different issues and teach them critical thought, but we equally believe that it is important to encourage our students to be men and women of conviction. All institutions will draw the line somewhere regarding what they will or will not allow to be displayed publicly on their campus.

We have drawn the line on the basis of what is most near and dear to our Christian college—the Gospel message of Jesus Christ as the Savior from sin. Our conscience is bound by this. This piece of art states that there will be a "New Messiah," which clearly contradicts our teachings and principles of Christ Alone, Grace Alone, Faith Alone, and Scripture Alone.

---

[66] "Marvin Meyer to Be President of Bethany," *Lutheran Sentinel*, Oct. 1982, 16.
[67] Matthew Thompson, "Bethany Lutheran President to Retire," *Lutheran Sentinel*, Sept. 2001, 10.
[68] Lance Schwartz, "Where the Lord Wills: The Presidency of Marvin G. Meyer," *Bethany Report*, Fall 2002, 13.

Marvin Meyer (pictured above, ca. 1958) served Bethany Lutheran College as a mathematics instructor, athletic director, dean of students, and, ultimately, as president. Meyer Hall (below) opened in 2002, featuring laboratory and teaching space for the Math-Science Division, as well as faculty offices and classrooms used by other departments.

DOCUMENT 7.4:

Religion and Censorship Make Art Show "A Teachable Moment" (1995)

By Ryan C. MacPherson and Rachel (Olson) Hermanson

Ryan C. MacPherson (1974–) served as co-editor of The Bethany Scroll *during his two years as a student at Bethany Lutheran College (1993-1995). For additional biographical information, see* **Document 1.8**.

Rachel Hermanson, née Olson (1975–), was born in Albert Lea, Minnesota, on September 16, 1975. Hermanson's formative years took place in her hometown, eventually graduating from Albert Lea High School in 1994. She enrolled at Bethany Lutheran College the same year, where she fostered a love for literature and art. She was able to combine these two pursuits in her co-authored article on a 1995 controversy in the Bethany Fine Arts Department. The article, featured in the Bethany Scroll, *was written after frequent conversations with members of the Bethany faculty. Hermanson graduated from Bethany in 1996 with an A.A. During her time on campus, she met future pastor Karl Hermanson, and the two were married in 1998. They have one child and currently reside in Oregon, Wisconsin, where Rachel works as a freelance writer.*

Source: *Bethany [Lutheran College] Scroll*, May 1995, 1, 4-5.

For the third straight year, Bethany's Ylvisaker Fine Arts Center (YFAC) hosted the Prairie Lakes Art Council's annual juried art show. The show is a regional event which allows artists from throughout the nine-county area to enter their artwork for judging in hopes of winning a cash or merit award. Unlike the previous two shows, this year's exhibit has been marked with controversy. After days of discussions, BLC President Marvin Meyer announced that one piece of art would not be displayed because "the work contradicts the heart and soul of our purpose and mission."

The controversial piece was a linoleum cut depicting a nude female child and bearing the words "The New Messiah Will Be a Girl." A halo floated above the toddler's head, and an angel and a fish were depicted by her side. Entitled "Prophesy," this work was produced by Mankato State University art student Joel Hansen, who said the composition was not religious-minded, but rather it reflected the hopes he had for his baby girl's success in life.

"Prophesy" was accepted among 153 other entries by Prairie Lakes on March 24. The entries were judged by St. Olaf College art professor Wendall Arneson on March 28 and the top sixty works were selected for display at Bethany Lutheran College during the month of April.

As Hansen's "Prophesy" was being prepared for hanging, students began to notice the piece and discuss it. Soon after, faculty members began expressing concern about hanging the piece.

The next day, BLC art professor Bill Bukowski brought "Prophesy" into his 9:00 a.m. art history class for an open discussion on the piece and its message. Of special consideration was its potential to offend visitors who might see it hanging at Bethany. Eighty prospective students would be on campus that weekend for pre-registration and numerous others would be attending the spring play.

Bukowski asked students whether the administration should permit it to be displayed on campus for the month-long show. Many expressed concern over the apparently unorthodox meaning of the linoleum cut, while others defended its right to hang and spoke against censoring the piece.

Later that day, Prof. Bukowski approached Pres. Meyer so that he could view the piece. Soon after, an administrative meeting was called. The question was raised if the artist could be asked to replace this piece with another one.

That night Prof. Bukowski talked to the judge, who said he would allow a switch to take place, but only with Hansen's consent. On Thursday, March 30, Bukowski spoke to Joel Hansen about the possibility of a switch, but Hansen declined.

The next day, Prairie Lakes Art Council members gathered at BLC to discuss the potential problem. Among the solutions discussed was the option of closing the show or moving it off the Bethany campus.

By Saturday, April 1, many of the winning entries had been hung on display in the YFAC gallery. Absent from the show was "Prophesy," which the administration discussed further in a meeting that afternoon. The decision to ban the piece was delayed by alternative proposals. Some advocated posting a disclaimer beside the piece. One faculty member even volunteered to stand beside it and explain the situation to anyone who might walk by and think that a Bethany student produced it.

On Monday, April 3, the *Mankato Free Press* ran a story on the front page of section two, together with a picture of the controversial artwork. The article discussed the possible censorship and reported that Pres. Meyer was expected to officially announce later that day whether "Prophesy" would be hung.

Pres. Meyer addressed the issue in a brief announcement after chapel by reading a prepared statement. Copies of the statement were made available to students and visitors in the YFAC lobby when the exhibit officially opened at 1 p.m.

"These issues are real issues," said Meyer before reading the statement. He described the tension "between our religious principles and what we have come to know, to believe regarding freedom of expression." Weighing Bethany's religious principles as more important than freedom of expression, Meyer decided that the piece should not be displayed.

"And maybe that tension has made this institution great because it makes us think about these foundational issues," he added before reading the statement.

Shortly after 1 p.m., Bethany's communications professor Dr. Thomas Kuster and drama director Pete Bloedel began discussing Pres. Meyer's decision in the YFAC lobby. Students and professors from Bethany and MSU gathered around to listen.

"Could the artist have said his message without that word [Messiah]?" asked Bloedel, who felt the Gospel account of Jesus clearing the money-changers from the temple was analogous to Meyer's decision to clear the YFAC of Hansen's "Prophesy."

"Bethany ties so closely to the church," Bloedel explained, adding that he himself was an artist and understood art, yet still felt the piece was inappropriate for Bethany's campus.

Kuster expressed concern over whether such censorship

really benefited the college, "Are we afraid of ideas? When we encounter an idea that we don't like, we should not make it shut up, but we should discuss it."

Kuster did, however, voice his support for Pres. Meyer. "I stand behind the president. I support him, but there is certainly enough freedom on this campus that we can discuss it. ... It's a teachable moment." And discussion is exactly what took place for the next fifty minutes as the crowd grew and students and professors—about thirty strong—from both Bethany and MSU voiced their opinions in the YFAC lobby.

One of Hansen's professors (who asked that her name be withheld) was present. She offered to explain the piece. "It's a wonderful story that the artist tells. ... What a wonderful gift a child is, and peace comes with a child."

As the artist had told the *Mankato Free Press* earlier, the message of his "Prophesy" was not religious at all. Rather, it symbolized his daughter and her potential success in life. He got the inspiration for the piece after watching her struggle to take her first steps. Hansen also told *Free Press* reporters that some may think he had a sacrilegious agenda: "I don't believe it's a [religious] proclamation, but it can be concocted as such."

In fact, his own art professor told the YFAC gathering that she did not understand the message at first, but she felt that "there is no religious imagery" in "Prophesy." She also explained that sometimes artists do not even understand their own work: "I have pieces that I've only now begun to understand why I did them, years later."

The professor showed respect for Bethany's decision, noting that BLC is a private institution and has the right to ban something which it finds offensive. She drew an analogy to certain policies that a state university like MSU follows to determine which works can be displayed in high-traffic areas, and which works should be confined to a secluded gallery with a disclaimer posted at the entrance. The question at MSU is not whether art is shown on campus, but where and to whom.

"There's no problem looking at this kind of art," agreed Pete Bloedel, "but displaying it outside of what is now being used as a chapel [the YFAC theater]" is of big concern, because "it is a high-traffic area" which is visible to "non-artists."

Some MSU students who knew the artist personally also joined the discussion, as did a few Bethany students.

After nearly an hour of opinion-exchanging, Dr. Kuster capsulized the controversy, "You can stand there and have that opinion, and you can stand there and have that opinion, except we can't stand in front of it [Hansen's "Prophesy"], because it's gone . . . . And that's the sad thing. Now we can't talk about it."

Yet everyone did see it, and everyone did talk about it. More people saw this single banned piece of artwork than those who saw the other items which remained on display in the YFAC last month. Tuesday's *Free Press* ran the image on its cover page, and MSU's *Reporter* did the same.

"Artist Joel Hansen's work was seen by tens of thousands more people than would have ever been possible within the narrow(minded) confines of Bethany," read a letter to the editor published in the April 7 *Free Press*. Seven days earlier Prof. Bukowski had predicted to his art history students: "I'm sure the artist [will be] so pleased that he has done something which gained so much notoriety."

Many feared that this notoriety would also mean bad press for Bethany. An editorial published in the *Free Press* two days after the banning, however, was regarded as "favorable" and "mild" by many Bethany administrators, including Pres. Meyer. The editorial placed blame not so much on Bethany, but more so on the art council because "its directors should have known that using a private college's facility could present such a problem."

Prof. [Erling] Teigen felt it was "fortuitous for us" that two strongly pro-Bethany articles appeared in the *Free Press* when the story broke. One of them previewed the inauguration of the Paul Ylvisaker Center, of which Teigen is the director. The other story featured Bethany athlete Dan Prehn who pitches for the baseball team.

"The *Free Press* did a great job," said Prof. Bukowski. "You could blame me or Prairie Lakes, but you cannot blame the artist and you cannot blame Bethany."

In some cases it was not a question of blame but of credit. Pres. Meyer's office received many calls praising the faith and courage behind his decision. "We're making a stand for something we believe," explained Dr. [William] Kessel.

Meyer was not the first to make such a stand for BLC. In his sermon at the YFAC's dedication in September 1990 [**Document 7.2**] synod president George Orvick made a similar declaration:

> There is so much in this world which is called by the name art, which is not art at all, but obscenity. The works of Andres Serrano and Robert Mapplethorpe will not be displayed in our arts center. Even though in some places they

are funded by the National Endowment for the Arts with taxpayers' money, they are so obscene that we blush to mention them. Likewise, the music of 2 Live Crew will not be featured in music appreciation class.

In the midst of such obscenity and filth which washes like a tidal wave across our land, how essential it is that Bethany focus on what is true, honest, just, pure, and lovely. [Philippians 4:8]

As a result of Bethany's religious convictions, Prairie Lakes is presently looking for a replacement site to exhibit some or all of next year's show. Meanwhile, Bethany administrators are drafting an art show policy which will make future exhibits run more smoothly. Pres. Meyer wants to ensure that any event hosted on campus reflects, or at least does not denounce, the Christian teachings upon which Bethany was founded.

As Prof. Teigen told his Lutheran church history class, "This is one of the most teachable moments we've had in a long time."

DOCUMENT 7.5:

How Would God Have Us Approach the Subject of Homosexuality? (2007)

By Donald Moldstad[69]

Donald Moldstad (1958–) has long had a passion for proclaiming the Gospel message to Christ's lambs. He was born in Mason City, Iowa, on September 10, 1958 to Rev. John A. Moldstad and his wife Gudrun (née Madson). Pastor John Moldstad was serving Richland Lutheran in nearby Thornton, Iowa. His family moved to Mankato, Minnesota, where Don attended Mt. Olive Lutheran Grade School. He graduated from Martin Luther Academy (New Ulm, Minnesota) in 1976. He received his A.A. degree from Bethany Lutheran College in 1978 and married Virginia Hassler in 1980. After receiving a B.F.A. from Mankato State University in 1984, he graduated from Bethany Lutheran Theological Seminary the following year. Moldstad served as an associate pastor from 1985 to 1987 at King of Grace Lutheran Church in Golden Valley, Minnesota. He was the pastor at Our Savior Lutheran Church in Naples, Florida, from 1987 until 1993,  when he returned to King of Grace, where he remained until 1995. He served at Mt. Olive Lutheran Church in Mankato from 1995 to 2005.

---

[69] *Editors' note*: As indicated in the pamphlet, contributing assistance came from the following members of the Bethany Lutheran College and Seminary faculties: Professors Michael Smith, Mark Harstad, Dr. William Kessel, and Dr. Ryan MacPherson.

Bethany Lutheran College extended a call to him in 2005. He continues to engage students there as the campus chaplain. Moldstad has been on the Evangelical Lutheran Synod Board for Parish Education and Youth since 1986, and he has two children. [AS]

Source: Moldstad, Donald. How Would God Have Us Approach the Subject of Homosexuality. Informational pamphlet. Bethany Lutheran College, 2007.

Introduction

"If you abide in My Word, you are My disciples indeed. And you shall know the truth, and the truth shall make you free" (John 8:31-32). With these words our Lord Jesus asserts that there is such a thing as Divine truth, that this truth is found in His Word, and the Christian demonstrates his/her discipleship by abiding in that Word. Christ's sheep know that the voice of the one who suffered hell for them, giving them the certainty of heaven, will never mislead them, even in matters of this life.

By contrast, this sinful world has no regard for the voice of Christ. The Christian is pressured by society to shape his/her thinking away from God's truth. Today many denominations have opted to cave-in to the "new morality" which pervades our culture. Those who desire to stand firm in the truth of Christ in Scripture are ridiculed, especially when it pertains to matters of sexuality and marriage. This pressure is not unique to our generation. St. Paul wrote to the Romans in the first century, "Do not be conformed to this world, but be transformed by the renewing of your mind, that you may prove what is that good and acceptable and perfect will of God" (Romans 12:2).

Only in very recent years has homosexuality become a central issue of contention in the Church. The gay-lesbian-bisexual-transgender community (GLBT) seeks to force Christian church bodies, institutions, and congregations into accepting and approving of what Scripture clearly describes as sinful behavior. Many GLBT organizations are determined to change the confession of the church by social, political and media pressure, labeling biblical teaching as "hate speech." By the inspiration of the Holy Spirit, St. Paul also predicted this, when he wrote to Timothy: "Preach the Word! Be ready in season and out of season. ... For the time will come when they will not endure sound doctrine, but according to their own desires, because they have itching ears, they will heap up for themselves teachers; and they

> *"We confess that Scripture condemns homosexuality and extra-marital relations (fornication and adultery) as sin. Nevertheless, when an individual caught up in such sins truly repents, the forgiveness of the Gospel is to be fully applied. We confess that the divine institution of marriage is to be heterosexual, in which, according to God's design, a man and a woman may enjoy a life-long companionship in mutual love. We teach on the basis of Holy Scripture that marriage is the only proper context for the expression of sexual intimacy and for the procreation of children. See Romans 1:26-27, 1 Corinthians 6:9, 18 and 7:2-9, John 4:17-18, 1 John 1:9, Genesis 1:27-28 and 2:18-24, and Matthew 19:4-6."*
>
> "ELS Reaffirms Position on Sanctity of Marriage," press release, www.evangelicallutheransynod.org, June 2004.

will turn their ears away from the truth, and be turned aside to fables" (2 Timothy 4:2-4)....[70]

How Should the Christian Respond?

Tolerance is often wrongly used as a synonym for love. When a behavior is sinful God does not command us to show love by tolerating it. In fact, intolerance can sometimes be a wonderful way to show Christian love. Jesus was extremely intolerant of the money-changers whom He drove from the Temple, while never ceasing to love them (Luke 19:45-46). We can certainly love and respect someone without accepting his immoral views or approving of his sinful behavior. There are also levels of toleration which God expects of us. Christians are called upon to love our neighbors, despite their sin. We can respect the homosexuals' rights and freedoms in our country, and seek to keep them safe

---

[70] *Editors' note*: Several paragraphs concerning biomedical investigations of the nature, causes, and ramifications of homosexual behavior have been omitted.

> *"Lord God, heavenly Father, we thank You, that by Your grace You have instituted holy matrimony, in which You keep us from unchastity and other offenses: We beseech You to send Your blessing upon every husband and wife, that they may not provoke each other to anger and strife, but live peaceably together in love and godliness, receive Your gracious help in all temptations, and raise their children in accordance with Your will. Grant that we all might walk before You in purity and holiness, put our trust in You, and lead such lives on earth, that in the world to come we may have everlasting life, through Your beloved Son, Jesus Christ, our Lord, who lives and reigns with You and the Holy Spirit, one true God, now and forever. Amen."*
>
> Veit Dietrich, Collect for the Second Sunday after Epiphany, in *ELH*, Collect #23, p. 150.

from those who may wish to harm them. Yet, believers must never condone behavior which God Himself has declared immoral.

When our Savior gently dealt with the woman caught in adultery, He demonstrated His divine love by forgiving her and restoring her. Yet, He never gave approval to her sin of adultery. Able to read her penitent heart, He instructed her to "go and sin no more" (John 8:11). He accepted her as a penitent sinner, but did not tolerate her sin. Christ has come to free us from our sins, not to give us freedom to sin. Holy Scripture likewise condemns verbal or physical abuse, as well as thoughts and expressions of self-righteousness or hatred. Sadly, some in Christendom have wrongly shown animosity toward gays and lesbians, and in so doing have brought shame to the Gospel of Christ. God exhorts us rather to "speak the truth in love" (Ephesians 4:15). The church must continue to take a stand against homosexuality. However, this must be done in the spirit of love and respect for the souls caught up in these sins, for whom Christ shed His innocent blood.

The Christian must always distinguish between godly judging and ungodly judging. Our Lord condemns any thoughts, words or actions by which we set ourselves up as better than others, or put others down in order to belittle them (Matthew 7:1-2). When considering the homosexual, may God spare us from ungodly judgmental thoughts of self-righteousness, which declare, "God, I thank you I am not like him" (Luke 18:9-14). As we seek to remove the speck of dust in our brother's eye, we must always do so having first removed the beam from our own eye (Luke 6:41-42).

Our Savior also commands us to properly judge all things contrary to His will, which would be harmful to ourselves or others. Godly judgment must be exercised to defend us and our fellowman from sin and evil. Such judging is even commanded of us in order to restore one to repentance and God's grace (1 Corinthians 5:1-5). True Christian love demands that pastors guide erring sheep back to the voice of the Good Shepherd, who has laid down His life for the sheep.

Today, as always, Christians are called upon to bring the wonderful message of Christ-crucified to the world. In so doing we must never compromise the truth of Scripture. If God's Law is diminished, then His Gospel is diminished. On the one hand, Christians must recommit themselves to being safe-havens where the penitent homosexual can find help and support to come away from this immoral behavior, without being treated like a second-class citizen. On the other hand, Christians must gently provide this help without tolerating the sin, or appearing to give it tacit approval. As with all matters of Christian faith, the God-pleasing approach is nothing more than the proper application of Law and Gospel.

Conclusion

In these challenging times, may God grant us strength of faith to confess His saving truth as we declare the marvels of His grace in Christ. He promises, "So shall My word be that goes forth from My mouth; it shall not return to Me void, but it shall accomplish what I please, and it shall prosper in the thing for which I sent it" (Isaiah 55:11).

May our prayer continue to be:

Lord, keep us steadfast in Thy Word;
Curb those who fain by craft and sword
Would wrest the Kingdom from Thy Son,
And set at naught all He hath done. (*ELH* 138:1)

DOCUMENT 7.6:

Position on Academic Freedom (2007)

By the Board of Regents of Bethany Lutheran College

Source: Office of the Vice President for Academic Affairs, Bethany Lutheran College.[71]

I. Fundamental Commitments and Procedures

Bethany Lutheran College, as a college of the Evangelical Lutheran Synod, accepts the Holy Scriptures as the inspired and inerrant word of God, and the sole authority for faith and life. The college is committed to the interpretation of Scripture found in the Lutheran confessional writings (Book of Concord). As such, all professionals in the service of Bethany Lutheran College (faculty, administrators, and others) are expected to uphold these Christian truths in the classroom and wherever else they function as representing the college.

As members of a learned profession and officers of an institution of higher education, professionals representing Bethany Lutheran College are entitled and encouraged to enjoy full freedom and autonomy in performing their classroom and campus duties, speaking and writing, conducting research,

---

[71] *Editors' note*: This position statement was approved by the Board of Regents of Bethany Lutheran College in November 2007 and distributed to the faculty in December 2007. The faculty had reviewed and contributed to earlier drafts in the preceding years.

pursuing publication, and fostering creativity, all under this commitment to the Scriptures and the confessions of the Lutheran Church.

The college recognizes there may be varied interpretations of some expressions and practices of its professionals regarding whether or not they conform to the college's confessional commitment. Professionals representing the college are expected to do their best to anticipate and recognize occasions where their work may be interpreted by others to be in conflict with the commitment, and to design plans in consultation with colleagues that will minimize negative responses or conflict as much as possible. Where differences of view emerge, they should not be resolved by unilateral intervention but rather through consultation, and if at all possible in a way that honors both the institutional confessional commitment and academic freedom.

II. In the Classroom

Professionals representing Bethany Lutheran College are entitled to freedom in the classroom as they discuss their subject. They should be careful not to introduce into their teaching controversial matter that has no relation to their subject. Each member of the faculty shall have scholastic and general control of his/her classes, including the grading of students, limited only by such regulations as are adopted by the faculty, or by the faculty member's division or department. Teachers should teach only in areas where they are academically qualified by formal study and/or experience, and should provide students opportunity to understand and experience the scholarship of the particular discipline in its commonly understood breadth and depth.

Students also should experience freedom of thought. Bethany Lutheran College values the student's freedom of learning and expression, and teachers should undertake to respect and guard these rights of the student. When expressing personal insights and perspectives, teachers should carefully identify them as such, in particular clearly distinguishing religious perspectives from political or ideological ones. Students should not be held responsible or made to feel that they might be responsible for reflecting a professor's political or ideological views.

David Munshenk teaches a chemistry lab at Bethany Lutheran College in 1965. Two chemistry professors at the college later served in the administration: President Dan Bruss (2003–) and Dean of the Faculty Eric Woller (2011–). Their predecessors also had taught in the science department: Marvin Meyer (mathematics) and Ronald Younge (biology).

III. In Research and Publication

Professionals representing Bethany Lutheran College have freedom in research and in publication of research results, subject to the adequate performance of their other academic duties. Published research should include due credit to the author's employing institution. Research for pecuniary return should be based upon an understanding with authorities of the institution.

Professionals representing Bethany Lutheran College are citizens, as well as members of a learned profession and officers of an educational institution. When they speak or write as citizens, they should be free from institutional censorship or discipline, but their special position in the community imposes special obligations. As scholars and officers of a Christian college, faculty and administrators of Bethany should maintain awareness that the public may judge their profession, and their institution, by the content and means of their various forms of communication. It is important that they make every effort to be accurate, exercise appropriate restraint, and show respect for the opinions of others, just as they can expect others to show appropriate respect for their opinion. When commenting on public issues, they should make every effort to indicate that they are not speaking for the institution.

IV. Application to New Teachers

During any probationary period, a teacher has the same academic freedom that all other members of the faculty have.

"The seal [of Bethany Lutheran College] is distinctive and most appropriate. The inscription 'Enos Estin Chreia' is Greek and means 'One Thing Is Needful,' the words of Christ spoken to Martha at the first Bethany [Luke 10:42]. The 'One Thing Needful' is the Gospel of the crucified Savior, expressed by the cross upon which the inscription is placed. For Bethany Lutheran College we thereby declare that there is no true education, even as there is no salvation, without the Gospel of Christ, Son of God and Savior of the world from sin. That Gospel is, and must remain, the heart and soul of every educational effort at our beloved institution. The cross is encircled by a star with twelve points, upon which are shown rays of light extending from the cross. As the twelve apostles were commissioned to be bearers of the light from the cross, so the goal of our training at Bethany must not be our own advancement, but the spread of the Gospel."

Commencement Bulletin, 13 May 2011, p. 10.

Scripture Index

Genesis
1-5: 67
1:27-28: 388, 435
1:28: 402
2:18-24: 388, 435
3:1: 406
3:10: 247
6-9: 223
8:21: 176
12:8: 223
41:42: 7

Exodus
1:8: 7
4:10-17: 309
32:31,33: 125

Numbers
11:23: 173

Deuteronomy
4:9: 143
6:4-5: 61
6:6: 61
6:6-7: 6, 12, 43, 65, 71, 88, 112, 121
11:18: 143
18:15: 224
30:9-10: 130
31:10-13: 24
32:47: 132
32:7: 289

Joshua
1:8-9: 122
4:21-24: 7
7:26: 7
8:29,32: 7
10:27: 7
22:26-27: 7
23:7: 235
24:26-27: 7

Judges
2:7: 7
4:10-12: 7
13:8: 72

1 Samuel
1:28: 72
2: 224
3:1: 10
15:22: 120

1 Kings
8:30,46,48,49-50: 8
18:17: 128
19:10,18: 310
19:18: 129

2 Kings
2: 224
6:16: 129

2 Chronicles
33:6,10: 7
34:14: 7
36:16: 8

Ezra
3:12: 8
9:13: 8

Job
39:13-18: 57
42:16: 30

Psalms
8:2: 84, 143
45:2: 419
51:5: 176
78:19: 5
78:2-7: 6
78:4: 3, 5, 7, 65
78:5: 35
78:5-6: 289
90:10: 96

90:15: 84
90:15,17: 85
110:3: 197, 137
119:9: 176
119:105: 67, 176, 304
127:3: 71

Proverbs
16:31: 363
22:6: 12, 328

Isaiah
1:18: 419
*9:6*250
16:28: 22
52:72: 22
54:13: 67, 84
55:11: 150, 437
66:2: 121

Jeremiah
6:14: 128
6:16: 10, 252-3, 255
7:25: 224
8:9: 89
9:23-24: 100
17:5: 256
17:9: 176
23:16: 224

Lamentations
5:21: 250

Ezekiel
13:2-8: 307

Amos
8:11: 10

Micah
3:5: 224-5

Zechariah
1:18: 256
13:2: 235

Malachi

3:10: 92
3:16: 126

Matthew
1:21: 8
5-7: 422
5:14: 172
6:33: 125, 178, 183-4
7:1-2: 437
7:11: 138
7:15: 183, 225
7:24-29: 422
7:9: 173
8:26: 173
12:30: 329
12:34: 299
13:24-30: 173
14:22-33: 134
16:26: 88, 93
18:2,5: 142
18:6-7: 290
19:4-6: 388, 435
22:15-22: 350
24:11: 225
25:21: 72
27:5: 128
28:19: 208
28:19-20: 11, 37, 65, 88, 103, 143, 181
28:20: 70, 103, 133, 290

Mark
7:21: 419
9:42: 125
10:30: 308
16:15: 129, 225, 308

Luke
1:39,55: 102
4:18: 121
6:13: 225
6:41-42: 437
7:34: 126
8:10: 309
9:62: 308
10:25-37: 422
10:27: 309

10:37: 128
10:41-42: 157
10:42: 24, 43, 84, 120, 176, 180, 191, 197-8, 271, 419, 441
11:1: 61
12:13-21: 351
14:16: 267
15:11-32: 422
15:3-7: 422
18:16: 88
18:9-14: 437
19:45-46: 435

John
1:14: 419
1:49-50: 407
2:18-22: 8
3:16: 114
4:17-18: 388, 435
4:24: 63
5:39: 171
7:46: 422
8:11: 436
8:31-32: 434
8:32: 306
13:15: 121
13:27: 128
14:16-20: 63
14:6: 178, 286, 296
15:13-14: 126
16:2: 128
16:23-24: 61
17:14-15: 386
17:14-19: 414
17:17: 132
18:36: 352
21:15: 26, 88, 103, 166
21:15-17: 57
21:5: 90

Acts
2:14-39: 8
4:13: 126
4:20: 143
5:29: 354, 384
6:7: 46
7:2-53: 8
17:11: 406
17:28: 300
19:9-10: 200
20:27: 299
20:28: 250
22:3: 225
28:30-31: 200

Romans
1:16: 245, 286
1:26-27: 388, 435
3:3-4: 305
8:38-39: 130
8:7: 65
10:13: 299
10:15: 222, 251
10:17: 245
11:36: 300
12:2: 65, 434
13: 58
13:1: 137, 350
13:1-7: 349
13:5: 85

1 Corinthians
2:2: 296
3-6,14: 303
3:11: 22
3:14: 247
3:21: 268
5:1-5: 437
6:12: 339
6:9,18: 388, 435
7:2-9: 388, 435
10:31: 299
11:27: 300
11:27-20: 300
11:27-29: 300
15: 303
15:14: 303
15:3-6,14: 303
15:57: 311

2 Corinthians
4:7: 239
5:15: 129

8:9: 257
10:4: 352
12:9: 85

Galatians
1:14: 225
1:17-18: 225
4:5: 257
5:13: 295
5:22-23: 61
5:25: 99

Ephesians
2:12: 16
2:17: 251
3:17,19: 104
3:9-11: 303
4:15: 436
4:17-18: 16
6:10,17: 105
6:3: 15
6:4: 6, 12, 43, 65, 76, 82, 88, 103, 112, 127, 166

Philippians
3:20: 85, 352
3:7-11: 265
4:13: 307, 310
4:8: 268, 289, 416, 432
4:9: 291

Colossians
1:16-17: 326
1:20: 326
2:8: 318

1 Timothy
2:4: 217
3:1: 217, 241
3:2: 243
3:2-7: 241
3:6: 244
4:15: 122
4:16: 218
4:5: 89
5:8: 43

2 Timothy
1:12: 129, 220
1:6: 295
1:7: 311
2:15: 245
2:2: 243
3:12,17: 107
3:15: 290
3:15-17: 99
3:16-17: 35, 89, 133
3:17: 167
4:2-4: 435

Titus
1:4: 241
1:6-9: 242
1:9: 218
2:8: 414

Hebrews
5:12,14: 104
10:25: 294
11:24-26: 85
12:11: 76
13:12-13: 85
13:14: 188
13:7: 83
13:8: 293

James
1:17: 294
4:8: 126

1 Peter
1:23: 176
1:5: 176
2:24-25: 220
2:25: 224
2:5: 223
2:9: 60, 168, 239

2 Peter
1:19: 29
1:21: 245
1:4: 257
2:1: 225
3:16: 309

3:17,18: 106
3:2: 224

1 John
1:9: 388, 435
2:1,2: 97
2:12,14: 96
2:15-16: 104
2:3,6: 99
3:1: 97
4:1: 217, 225
4:10: 63
4:3: 300
5:4-5: 104
5:9-11: 305

2 John
8,9: 106

Jude
3: 9, 83

Revelation
5:9: 153

Lutheran Confessions Index

Ausgburg Confession (AC)
XVI: 352
XXVIII: 352

Apology of the Augsburg Confession (Ap)
II, 22, 24: 255
IV, 106: 255
VII: 354
VIII, 50: 354
X, 3: 255
XVI, 2: 336
XVI, 53: 354, 383, 385
XVI, 54: 354
XVI, 59-60: 358
XVI, 61: 355
XVI, 64: 355

Smalcald Articles (SA)
II, IV, 11: 356

Small Catechism (SC)
Preface: 15, 38, 228
II: 132, 263
III: 34

Large Catechism (LC)
Introduction, 7-8: 33
Short Preface, 4: 14, 36
I, 5-10: 382
I, 133: 15
I, 141: 14, 66
I, 170: 71
I, 170-71: 54
I, 176-77: 55
V, 87: 13-14, 18

Epitome of the Formula of Concord (Ep)
Summary, 5: 33-4
III, 4: 270

Solid Declaration of the Formula of Concord (SD)
II, 88: 247
VII, 11: 255
VIII, 14,20,22: 255

General Index

2 Live Crew: 421, 432

A

Aaberg, Theodore A.: 9, 68-72, 75, 111, 131, 210, 212, 235, 237, 255-6, 274
AAUP *see* American Association of University Professors
ACLU *see* American Civil Liberties Union
AELC *see* Association of Evangelical Lutheran Churches
ALC *see* American Lutheran Church (ALC)
Amazon Jungle (Mission): 153
American Association of University Professors (AAUP): 369
American Civil Liberties Union (ACLU): 369, 379
American Lutheran Church (ALC): 178
Americans United for the Separation of Church and State: 366, 379
Amish: 338, 367-8, 382-3
Anabaptists: 373
Anderson, Christian: 213
Anderson, Ella B.: 195, 341, 345
Anderson, Julian G.: 236, 341
Anderson, Paul: 360
Anderson, Sophia: 378
Anderson, Sophia T.: 195, 341, 378
Anthony, Peter M.: 3, 157
Archimedes: 307
Aristophanes: 267
Aristotle: 262, 301, 394
Association of Evangelical Lutheran Churches (AELC): 376
Athens: 149, 318, 391

B

Bach, Johann Sebastian: 123, 129
Balcziak, Luella: 341
Barranquita (Peruvian Mission): 154-5
Baxter, Richard: 51
Bente, Gerhard Friedrich: 1, 31, 33, 35, 39
Bernthal, Albert C.: 190
Bethany Ladies College: 186, 193
Bethany Lutheran Church: 60, 264
Bethany Lutheran College (BLC): 42, 157-207, 209, 221-3, 232-4, 237, 264-6, 292-3, 338-41, 387-8, 415, 424-5, 427-31, 433-4, 438-41
academic catalog: 205-6, 268, 271, 393
accreditation *see* North Central Association of Colleges and Secondary Schools
administration: 431-2
art controversy: 387, 424, 427
Board of Regents: 158-9, 174, 180-1, 184, 186, 195, 205, 209, 233, 236-8, 249, 266, 339-40, 375, 438
campus: 107, 190, 312, 387, 429 (*see also* Honsey Hall, Meyer Hall, Ylvisaker Fine Arts Center)
chapel: 74, 195, 222

establishment of: 158, 196
faculty and staff: 205, 237, 274, 313, 341, 387, 390, 394, 409, 427
students: 192, 204, 429-30
teaching certificate program: 2, 107, 124, 135, 139-40
video broadcasting: 195
Bethany Lutheran High School: 11, 42, 174, 185, 221, 266
Bethany Lutheran Theological Seminary (BLTS): 3, 11, 42, 45, 64, 75, 208-57, 264-6, 390, 415, 433
Bethany Scroll: 195, 387, 425, 427
Bethany song: 198
Bethel Christian Day School: 185
Biesterfeld, Ken: 347
Blaine Amendment: 377
Blåkkan, Ingebrigt J.: 160-1
Blåkkan, Luther: 160
Blåkkan, Marie: 160
Bloedel, Peter: 429-30
Boehme, John: 107
Book of Concord: 1, 15, 209, 248, 319, 382, 438
Born, Silas V.: 139
Bourman, Abigail: 3, 200
Boy Scouts: 128, 182
Branstad, Raymond M.: 53, 58, 196, 210, 235-6, 340
Brown, Francis: 368
Bruner, Jerome: 392, 400, 406, 411-13
Bruss, Dan: 440
Buddhism: 202-3
Bukowski, William: 428, 431
Bunker, Archie: 279
Busekist, Edna: 341, 345
Buszin, P. T.: 16
Bye, Alice: 30

C

Calvin College Curriculum Study Committee: 395-6, 402
Calvinism: 17, 76, 219, 359
Caswell, Hollis I.: 109
Catholicism: 202, 343, 347
Chemnitz, Martin: 255, 265
Chinese Term Question: 235
Christ Seminary *see* Seminex
Christian Day Schools: 17-18, 68-75, 77-87, 91-4, 101-5, 111-13, 115-23, 127, 131-5, 137-8, 140-1, 145-7, 149-51, 155-6, 210
Christian Reformed Church: 344
Christian scholarship: 11, 295-6, 299-303, 306-11, 391, 402, 405
Citizens for Educational Freedom (CEF): 338, 342, 359-60
Classical Christian Education: 329-30, 332
Clearwater Lutheran Parish: 42
Concordia Church: 21
Concordia College: 39, 95, 190, 213, 264
Concordia Historical Institute: 2, 96
Concordia Lutheran Junior College: 190
Concordia Seminary: 39, 53, 77, 95-6, 111, 119, 174, 190, 214, 216, 229-31
Concordia Seminary in Exile *see* Seminex
Concordia Seminary in Springfield: 74
Concordia Teacher's College: 190
Concordia Triglotta: 1, 31, 39, 41
Concordia University

system: 39, 95, 190, 264, 377
Confessional Evangelical Lutheran Conference (CELC): 416
Coolidge, Calvin: 32
Costello, Jeremy: 4, 336
Coulter, Barry: 341
Crutcher, Anne: 101
Czech Republic (Mission): 70, 139-41, 144-5, 147

D

Dale, Pearl: 45
Dale, Rodger: 45, 50
Daley, Evelyn: 344
Damiano, Kyle: 4
Dewey, John: 332
Dietrich, Veit: 27, 436
Dietrichson, Johannes Wilhelm Christian: 5, 77-80, 83
Dr. Martin Luther College *see* Martin Luther College

E

Earp, Wyatt: 279
ELCA *see* Evangelical Lutheran Church of America
Elder, Linda: 394
ELS *see* Evangelical Lutheran Synod
Emery, Ardella: 60
English Lutheran Church: 216, 221
Evangelical Lutheran Church of America (ELCA): 202, 230, 376
Evangelical Lutheran Hymnary: 2, 11, 27, 119, 124, 258, 419, 436-7
Evangelical Lutheran Synod (ELS): 5-6, 9-10, 74-5, 83, 111, 158, 180, 192-4, 201-2, 212-14, 222-3, 230-2, 255-6, 333-5, 339-40
  Archives: 3, 10, 180, 182, 260, 275, 339-40, 388
  Board for Parish Education and Youth: 18, 111, 328, 390, 434
  clergymen: 10, 15, 17-18, 337
  conventions: 69, 71
  Doctrine Committee: 11, 252, 415
Evangelical Lutheran Synod Historical Society: 3-4, 64, 275
Evangelical Lutheran Synodical Conference: 75

F

Fairview Lutheran Church: 86
Faith Lutheran Church: 390
Faugstad, Adela May (Halverson): 124
Faye, Christopher U.: 195, 210, 236
Fevig, Violet: 274
First Amendment *see* United States Constitution, First Amendment
First American Lutheran Church: 221
Fremder, Alfred: 119-20, 234
Fremder, Emma: 119

G

Gaebelein, Frank E.: 55-6
Gerhard, Johann: 254-5
German Mass and Order of Service: 40
Germany: 37, 39, 57-8, 76, 164, 183, 230, 263, 283, 356
Gettysburg Address: 59
Goethe: 293, 420
Gospel: 16-17, 29-30, 65-6, 121,

218-19, 222, 239-41, 250-1, 271-2, 284-6, 352-3, 355-6, 387-9, 433-7, 441
Grace Lutheran Church: 42
Greek: 48, 57, 164, 200, 209, 225, 235, 246, 248, 260, 262, 267, 275, 283-4, 441
Gregory of Nazianzen: 404
Gullixson, George A.: 158
Gullixson, Walter A.: 2
Gunderson, Paul: 4, 336
Guttebo, L. S.: 213

H

Halverson, Adela May *see* Faugstad, Adela May (Halverson)
Haney, John D.: 48
Hansen, Emil: 213
Hansen, Joel: 424-5, 428, 430-1
Harms, Mrs.: 194
Harstad, Adolph M.: 214, 236
Harstad, Bjug: 79, 213-14, 254, 333-4
Harstad, Cheryl: 4
Harstad, Mark: 236
Harstad, Peter T.: 164, 259, 275
Hartwick, John: 230, 276
Harvard St. Lutheran Church: 235
Harvard University: 229, 276, 322
Haserot, Josephine: 39
Haustafel: 34
Hausvater Project: 64
Hebrew: 224, 235, 245
Heintz, Eileen: 4
Helland, Paul A.: 340
Hendricks, Howard: 49-51
Hermanson, Betsy: 4
Hermanson, Rachel (Olson): 427
Higher Education Act: 378

Higher Education Facilities Act: 339, 378
Hillsdale College: 303
Holte, Norman S.: 164, 195, 259-61, 274-5, 282, 341-2
Holy Cross Lutheran Church: 139, 415
Holy Scriptures: 1, 33, 35-6, 68, 89, 103, 107, 150, 176-7, 187, 193, 206, 244-5, 253-4, 435-6
Holy Trinity Lutheran Church: 252
Homer: 329
Homeschooling: 17-18, 62, 67
Honsey, Rudolph E.: 195, 236, 295, 315
Honsey Hall: 295, 304
Hoover, Herbert: 32
Hustavlen: 34

I

Immanuel Lutheran Church: 185
Ingebritson, Henry: 16, 213, 233
Ingebritson, Mrs.: 194
Israel: 5-8, 24, 35, 61, 67, 122, 224, 290, 297, 303, 307, 309, 407

J

Jecklin, Paul: 50
Jefferson, Thomas: 305, 376-7
Jensen, L. P.: 213
Johnson, Calvin: 342
Johnson, Carol F.: 341, 343
Johnson, Iver C.: 341, 345
Johnson, Lyndon: 339
Juve, Knut Aslaksen: 5
Juul, Ole: 82

K

Kaminsky, Philip: 4
Kasota Valley Lutheran Home: 30, 363
Kauzmann, Daniel: 34
Kennedy School of Government: 322
Kessel, William: 236, 431, 433
King of Grace Lutheran Church: 433
Kingo, Thomas: 119
Koehler, Edward W. A.: 99
Korean G.I. Bill: 378
Koren, Ulrik Vilhelm: 82, 193-4, 255-6
Kretzmann, Paul E.: 102, 350-1
Krikava, James: 143, 145-6
Kuster, Arnold: 360, 389-90, 430
Kuster, Thomas A.: 236, 306, 341, 345, 389-90, 398, 429-30

L

Larsen, Peter Lauritz ("Laur"): 77, 82-3, 231, 260
Larson, Mildred C.: 341
Latin: 31, 57, 209, 248, 260, 284
Law and Gospel: 65-6, 154, 215, 218-19, 250, 255, 324, 437
LCMS *see* Lutheran Church-Missouri Synod
Lee, Sigurd K.: 341
Leeson, Jane E.: 110
Lehninger, Paul: 317, 323
Levine, Arthur: 277
Lieske, Carol: 346
Lillegard, David: 422
Lillegard, George O.: 195, 210, 213, 235
Lillo, James: 50
Lime Creek Lutheran Church: 9, 212-13, 254
Lincoln, Abraham: 59
Little Norwegian Synod *see* Evangelical Lutheran Synod (ELS)
Longfellow, Henry Wadsworth: 365
Lord of Life Lutheran Church: 254
Lord's Prayer: 14, 33-4, 63
Louis Terry (Peruvian Mission): 154-5
LSA *see* Lutheran Schools of America
Luther, Martin: 13-15, 31-5, 37-8, 57-60, 65-9, 102, 151, 239-40, 283-6, 317, 319-21, 325-6, 356-7, 372-5, 382-5
Luther College: 21, 30, 74, 86, 138, 164, 234, 260
Luther High School: 199, 424
Luther Seminary: 21, 30, 74, 160, 214, 231, 234-5
Lutheran Church in America (LCA): 376
Lutheran Church-Missouri Synod (LCMS): 76-7, 92, 95-6, 183, 203, 213, 230-2, 255, 342, 375, 377, 405
Lutheran College Conference: 292
Lutheran Education Association: 165
Lutheran Elementary Schools *see* Christian Day Schools
Lutheran Hymnal: 2, 23, 110, 327
Lutheran Hymnary: 2, 180-1, 222, 240, 271-2, 291
Lutheran Institutional Ministry Association: 45
Lutheran Reformation: 7, 13-14, 57, 60, 194, 228, 237, 239, 275, 285, 323, 326, 352, 403

Lutheran Schools of America (LSA): 70, 328-9, 333-5
Lutheran Sentinel: 2-3, 9, 16-18, 20-1, 31, 60, 64, 86, 185-6, 189-90, 203-4, 214, 221, 415, 425
Lutheran Synod Quarterly: 9, 11, 75, 111, 210, 216, 243, 253, 265, 317, 337-8, 341, 348-9, 371-2, 375
Lutheran World Federation: 219
Luttman, Matthew: 141

M

Maanedstidende (Monthly Times): 79, 231
MacPherson, Ryan C.: 3, 5, 11, 13, 64, 204, 427, 433
Madison, James: 311, 376-7
Madson, Elsie: 221
Madson, Juul: 77, 164, 221, 227, 235-6
Madson, Mary: 74
Madson, Norman A., Jr.: 68, 282
Madson, Norman A., Sr.: 68, 70, 74-5, 160, 185, 195, 209-10, 221, 234-6, 243, 255, 272, 274
Madson, Paul G.: 3, 19, 36, 208, 212, 214
Mankato State University: 428-31
  Teachers College: 424
Mapplethorpe, Robert: 421, 431
Marsden, George M.: 297, 300, 302, 310
Martin Luther College: 139, 262, 293, 377, 390, 396, 408
Martin Luther High School: 139
Martin Luther School: 140, 145, 147-9, 152
Marxism: 318, 402
Marzolf, Dennis: 119
Mathesius: 31
Melanchthon, Philip: 228, 319
Mequon Program: 222-3, 317
Meyer, Carl S.: 2, 95-6, 98, 165, 231
Meyer, Marvel (Wickter): 424
Meyer, Marvin G.: 262, 274, 343, 387, 389, 424-6, 428-32, 440
Meyer, Walter: 424
Meyer Hall: 426
Michigan Lutheran College: 342
Milton, John: 305
Minnesota Valley Lutheran High School: 145-6
Moldstad, Christian: 86
Moldstad, Christian A.: 86-7
Moldstad, Donald: 185-6, 388, 433-4
Moldstad, John A., Jr.: 236, 334
Moldstad, John A., Sr.: 158, 185-7, 197, 433
Moldstad, John A., Sr., Sr.: 213
Moldstad, Joslyn: 16
Moldstad, Paul: 187
Morgan, Richard E.: 374
Morison, Samuel E.: 276
Morrison, Donald: 342-3
Moses: 6-7, 24, 43, 61, 85, 122, 125, 132, 218, 224, 309
Mt. Olive Lutheran Church (Colorado Springs): 384
Mt. Olive Lutheran Church and School (Mankato): 2, 42, 107, 124, 135, 153, 203, 238, 384, 433
Munshenk, David: 440

N

National Defense Education Act: 378
National Education Association: 379
National Endowment for the Arts: 379, 421, 432
National Parliamentary Debate Association: 390
National Youth Administration: 377
Natvig, Dennis: 341
Nebraska Association of Church Colleges: 191
Nelson, James A.: 341
Nerison, Effie: 194
Nesseth, G. P.: 213
Newman, Cardinal John Henry: 281, 299, 321
Noll, Mark: 308, 321-3
North Central Association of Colleges and Secondary Schools: 196, 198, 261, 340
Northwestern College: 42, 185, 221, 232, 377, 390, 415
Norway: 76, 160, 214
Norwegian: 34, 77, 160, 197, 231-2, 260, 315
Norwegian Lutheran Church in America: 9, 84, 230, 234
Norwegian Lutheran Church in Boston: 86
Norwegian summer school: 77
Norwegian Synod *see* Evangelical Lutheran Synod (ELS)

O

Olsen, Holden: 213
Olson, Rachel *see* Hermanson, Rachel (Olson)
Open Bible Lutheran Church: 45
Orvick, George M.: 4, 232, 387, 415-16, 422
Oslund, Ma: 195
Ottesen, Jacob Aall: 77, 83, 255-6
Ottesen Museum: 4, 416
Otto, Milton Henry: 210, 216, 236, 255, 338, 340-1, 343, 348, 359, 360, 364
Our Savior's Lutheran Church (Albert Lea): 21, 42
Our Savior's Lutheran Church (Chicago): 82
Our Savior's Lutheran Church (Princeton): 221
Our Savior's Lutheran Church (Madison): 390
Our Savior's Lutheran Church (Santiago): 424

P

Pacific Lutheran University: 214
Padgett, Alan G.: 324
Palmer, Edwin H.: 343-4, 348
Paul, Richard: 394
Pennsylvania Ministerium: 79
Peruvian Mission: 70, 140, 154
Petersen, C. N.: 213
Petersen, Joseph: 137-8
Petersen, Justin A.: 42
Petersen, Orla: 343
Petersen, Wilhelm Walther: 42-3, 210, 232, 238, 255
Pfieffer, Les: 347
Plato: 262, 318, 329
POAU *see* Protestants and Other Americans
Pope, Alexander: 28
Prairie Lakes Art Council:

427-9, 431-2
Preus, Herman Amberg: 36, 77, 80-3, 255-6
Preus, J. A. O.: 197
Preus, Robert: 201, 234
Protestants and Other Americans (POAU): 369, 379-80

Q

Quill, Carl Johan: 21, 23
Quill, Ingrid: 21
Quist, Allen: 11

R

Radichel, Denny: 135
Reagles, David: 4
Reagles, Steven L.: 158, 199-200, 236
Redeemer Lutheran Church: 328
Reformation *see* Lutheran Reformation
Reformation Lectures: 210, 264, 317, 410
Reichwald, Glenn: 210, 236, 238, 255, 341, 343
Roman Catholicism: 58, 120, 146, 202-3, 322, 347
Roman Empire: 267, 283, 350, 358, 417

S

Saturday school: 70, 109, 113-14
Saude and Jericho Lutheran Church: 72, 174, 216
Sayers, Dorothy: 329
Scarville Lutheran Church and School: 42, 71, 111
Schlomer, Evelyn: 342
Schmeling, Gaylin R.: 210, 239, 252, 415-16
Schmidt, F. A.: 231
Schultz, Terry: 153
Schwartz, Arthur: 297-8
Secondary Education Act: 378, 384
Secular Humanism: 332, 338, 358, 365, 381-2
Selective Service Act: 233-4
Seminex: 375-6
Serrano, Andres: 421, 431
Shoop, Andrew: 4, 386
Sieck, Louis J.: 226, 229
Škola Martina Luthera: 139, 144, 147
Smith, Michael K.: 254, 257, 433
Socrates: 297, 412
Solomon: 8, 101, 419
Soule, Dennis: 341
Soulforce: 388
Sparley, Steven: 151
Sputnik: 378
St. Augustine: 255, 257, 263, 324, 326, 350, 403
St. Basil: 404
St. Cyril: 255
St. Irenaeus of Lyons: 255
St. John's Evangelical Lutheran Church: 199
St. Mark's Lutheran Church: 86
St. Olaf Lutheran Church: 221
Stalin, Joseph: 387
Steffelova, Lenka *see* Wendland, Lenka (Steffelova)
Steger, Rev.: 213
Sunday school: 4, 17, 43, 51, 66, 70, 90, 109, 113-15, 121, 123, 133, 182, 215
Supreme Court: 55, 90, 337-9, 345, 357-8, 365, 367, 374, 377, 379-80, 382, 384
***Synod Report* (Evangelical Lutheran Synod)**: 11, 16,

19, 21, 31, 45, 53, 75, 81-2, 87, 96, 160-1, 209-10, 233-4, 328
Synodical Conference: 209, 232, 236

T

Tarapoto Bible Institute (Peruvian Mission): 155
Teigen, Bjarne Wollan: 11, 95-6, 182-3, 195, 210, 234-5, 250, 260, 264-5, 338-41, 349, 351-2, 371-2, 374-5, 381
Teigen, Elna: 381
Teigen, Erling T.: 50, 158, 164, 236, 259, 347, 431-2
Teigen, Torald: 50
Teisberg, Alice: 69
Teisberg, Clara: 69
Tertullian: 318, 391, 404
Thiensville Seminary: 221, 232
Thoen, T. J.: 213
Thoughts of Faith: 144
Tietjen, John: 375-6
Tjernagel, Helge Mathias: 72, 84, 233
Torgerson, A. J.: 213
Trivium terminology: 329-30; *see also* Classical Christian Education
Tweit, Bernt: 174
Tweit, Mabel: 174
Tweit, Milton Elmo: 158, 174-5

U

United States Constitution: 305, 336, 349, 357, 361, 367, 376
First Amendment: 336, 343, 357, 361, 365, 367, 374, 376-7, 383
United States Supreme Court: 344

Unseth, Allan: 341, 344
Unseth, Joseph B.: 15, 30-1
Unseth, Karen: 346

V

Vangen, Lois: 62, 186
Vangen, Luther: 62, 289, 360
Vietnam War: 277
Vorwerk, Dietrich: 242

W

Weber, Carl Maria von: 123
Wegenke, Rolf: 292, 306
WELS *see* Wisconsin Evangelical Lutheran Synod
Wendland, Lenka (Steffelova): 145-6
Wendland, Luther: 341
Werling, Wilbert: 360
Weseloh, Gerhardt: 337
Western Koshkonong Lutheran Church: 21, 69
Westminster Theological Seminary: 344
Wheaton Graduate School: 51
Wilhelm, Petersen: 42
Wilinski, Bruno: 341, 345
Williams, Annie: 4, 274
Willitz, Josiah: 4
Wilske, Jerry: 341-2
Wilson, Eleanor: 237
Wilson, Woodrow: 32, 305
Wisconsin Evangelical Lutheran Synod (WELS): 45, 64, 201, 223, 232, 293, 339, 377, 383-4
Wisconsin Lutheran Chapel: 292
Wisconsin Lutheran College: 146, 262, 292-3, 317
Wisconsin Lutheran High School: 384

Wisconsin Lutheran Seminary: 199, 221, 232, 317, 377
Woller, Eric: 440
Wycliffe, John: 329

Y

Yale University: 229, 420
YFAC *see* Ylvisaker Fine Arts Center
Ylvisaker, David: 187, 191
Ylvisaker, Johannes: 164, 350-1
Ylvisaker, Johnny: 192
Ylvisaker, Kristi: 164
Ylvisaker, Paul: 431
Ylvisaker, Sigurd Christian: 164, 166, 169, 260, 262, 271-2, 274, 350-2
Ylvisaker Fine Arts Center (YFAC): 387, 415, 417-20, 422-3, 427, 429-31
Ylvisaker Scholarship: 169
Younge, Ronald: 440

Z

Zager, Paul R.: 128
Zimmerman, Albert C.: 190
Zimmerman, Paul A.: 158, 190-2, 234, 260
Zion Lutheran Church: 22, 221, 252

Store Per: Norwegian-American "Paul Bunyan" of the Prairie

By Peter Tjernagel Harstad

Published in cooperation with the
Evangelical Lutheran Synod Historical Society

"I have read it with great interest. . . . Congratulations on a work well done."

Dr. Odd S. Lovoll
Historian of the Norwegian migration to America
Professor Emeritus of History, St. Olaf College

"Author Peter Harstad has certainly dealt with the subject in a delightful way and makes Store Per ["Strong Pete"] come alive for the readers. . . . *Store Per* makes a wonderful contribution to the story of our forefathers and their brave journey across the stormy Atlantic to make their home in [America]. The Lord made use of them to bring the pure Gospel to our area so that we might also benefit from the message of salvation by Grace Alone through Faith alone in our Savior Jesus Christ."

Rev. George M. Orvick
Past President, Evangelical Lutheran Synod

(See following page for ordering information.)

Order Form

Item	Price Ea.	Quantity	Subtotal
Telling the Next Generation	$23.95		
Store Per (see previous page)	$14.95		
Voting Membership* (includes subscription to *Oak Leaves*):			
Individual	$10.00/yr		
Husband-Wife	$15.00/yr		
Lifetime	$200.00		
Associate Membership* (includes subscription to *Oak Leaves*):			
Individual	$15/yr		
Institutional	$25/yr		
Student	$5/yr		
Total Payment Enclosed**:			

Voting membership is limited to communicants of congregations in doctrinal fellowship with the Evangelical Lutheran Synod.

**Shipping, handling and (when applicable) sales tax will be paid by the Evangelical Lutheran Synod Historical Society. Prices and terms of sale are current as of June 18, 2011.*

Name:	
Address:	
City, State, ZIP:	
Phone:	
Email (optional):	

Make Check Payable To:
Evangelical Lutheran Synod Historical Society
6 Browns Court
Mankato, MN 56001
www.els-history.org

www.ingramcontent.com/pod-product-compliance
Lightning Source LLC
Chambersburg PA
CBHW071233160426
43196CB00009B/1041